SNAPSHOTS

A Life Revisited

Frank Maraj

Trafford
PUBLISHING™

Order this book online at www.trafford.com/08-1049
or email orders@trafford.com

Most Trafford titles are also available at major online book retailers.

Co-authored by: Diana Maraj
Edited by: Diana Maraj
Cover Design by: Ron Hines & David McBride

Note for Librarians: A cataloguing record for this book is available from Library
and Archives Canada at www.collectionscanada.ca/amicus/index-e.html

Printed in Victoria, BC, Canada.

ISBN: 978-1-4251-8544-2

*We at Trafford believe that it is the responsibility of us all, as both individuals
and corporations, to make choices that are environmentally and socially sound.
You, in turn, are supporting this responsible conduct each time you purchase a
Trafford book, or make use of our publishing services. To find out how you are
helping, please visit www.trafford.com/responsiblepublishing.html*

*Our mission is to efficiently provide the world's finest, most comprehensive
book publishing service, enabling every author to experience success.
To find out how to publish your book, your way, and have it available
worldwide, visit us online at www.trafford.com/10510*

www.trafford.com

North America & international
toll-free: 1 888 232 4444 (USA & Canada)
phone: 250 383 6864 ♦ fax: 250 383 6804
email: info@trafford.com

The United Kingdom & Europe
phone: +44 (0)1865 487 395 ♦ local rate: 0845 230 9601
facsimile: +44 (0)1865 481 507 ♦ email: info.uk@trafford.com

10 9 8 7 6 5 4 3 2

DEDICATION

I knew why I wrote this manuscript. I wondered why I should publish it.
My wife, Diana, said simply, "For your children and grandchildren."
She is right.

With love, I dedicate this book to my three children,
Trevor, Lee-Anne, and Dee-Dee,
my grandchildren, Jayden and Jasmine,
and to the memory of Ma.

You are my inspiration.

ACKNOWLEDGEMENTS

Thank you, students of the Rainy River district (including my daughter's students at SCAP), for inspiring me, helping me, encouraging me, and giving me the courage to put my life's story into print.

Thanks to Jenn, one of my former students, for graciously accepting the onerous task of transcribing much of my handwriting into printed text.

Thanks to my colleagues, many of whom have "rescued" me with their technical expertise, endured my many tales and encouraged me to write them down.

To my friends here in the Rainy River district, and elsewhere, as well as those in Trinidad, I thank you for your abiding and valued support.

Special thanks to my daughter, Lee-Anne, who helped out with her special talents and valued expertise even though she insisted that it was a "daughter's duty." She does not know her own worth. I do.

This work would not have been complete without my family. Thank you ever so much Ma and Pa (departed), Clive (departed), Dolly, Boysie, Paula, Pinky, Kay, Basdaye, Suresh and Kalie. You may not know it, but each one of you, in your own, unique way, has enriched my life.

WITH GRATITUDE

Diana

Thank you, Diana, my loving wife of 37 years.

Your devotion to this work, a seemingly unending task,

has not gone unnoticed.

Thank you for editing, proofreading, revising, discussing, debating,

and toiling with me in this project.

Your clarity of expression—the way you were able to take my draft

and transform it—confirms what I have always known;

you are more than an editor—you are a writer.

Your dedication and spirit has enriched <u>our</u> work beyond measure.

Love,
Frank

PREFACE

After retiring from teaching in June, 2005, Frank kept in touch with many of his former students. The one question that was common to all was this: have you written that book yet, Mr. Maraj? This compilation of short events is his attempt to accommodate their requests. While writing the stories, he realized that he was doing it for another reason also. His three children and two grandchildren had not heard all the stories. It is for them also that he tried to recapture some of the major events in his life.

AUTHOR'S NOTE

Did everything in this work occur exactly as recorded? I have attempted to capture "life as it happened" in this work. I may have taken certain liberties and at times I might have unwittingly dramatized certain incidents to make the story interesting. Over the decades, I have told some of these stories from time to time and my wife tells me that each time a story is told, it changes; certain stories *may* have assumed a dimension of their own.

Not all the stories are in chronological order, yet I have attempted to give some logical order to the time of the occurrences. In some instances, fictitious names have been used.

At times I may have been strong and perhaps unduly critical. If I have, I ask for your understanding as I do not wish to disparage anyone, yet I wanted to capture a sense of the *reality* of what was transpiring.

Above all, I hope this project is a good read.

PART I

High School and the Early Years

1

MR. B'S TEST ON MACBETH

"BOODRAM! Sit down! Shut up and don't waste my time!" These are words that Mr. B, my *English* teacher, thundered when I was a third year high school student. I did not know it then, but those words changed me. His pronouncement seemed to lend credence to all previous and similar declarations. But, there was still some small part of my soul that rejected his implication that I was a waste of time. This declaration, while it paralyzed my body, it did not immobilize my soul. This moment that had stripped me of my dignity was the same moment that would become my inspiration and fuel my stubbornness to succeed.

What caused my teacher to make this declaration? What had I done? Surely, I must have done something! We were about to do a test on *Macbeth*. The test papers were passed out to the students. I read mine, and then I re-read the questions. I did not understand the language used to make up the questions for it was too sophisticated. It was almost impossible for students like me, poor Hindu students attending a Catholic high school, to understand. Language, and the correct use of it, plagued our kind! We came from a different background. Our parents and our grandparents spoke little English and what little English they did speak assumed a life of its own, a certain patois, bearing some feeble resemblance to the Queen's English. We struggled to understand formal English. Our neighbourhood belonged to the average poor family. Formal English was all but absent in our homes. We struggled from year to year to understand; English seemed so foreign a language. And yet, for all its complexities, I loved the English language, but, for a very long time, the English language was the dreaded Enemy.

Apparently, Mr. B, annoyed that I was the cause of an unnecessary distraction, determined that he must take immediate action. Accordingly, he proceeded to deliver the Queen's English in a style befitting royalty! He had a way of lecturing that could be deadly serious or humourously contemptuous. Students with an East-Indian background like me were often the target of his terrible onslaught of cutting words. I dreaded that ill-fated moment when any one of us was being corrected!

Today it was my turn.

"So, Mr. Boodram, you indeed have attracted my attention! In fact, you were *craving* my attention!" Laughter and smiles emanated from most of the class. "Now," he continued ever so slowly, but still commandingly, "you must have understood my instruction! After all, you are here at high school. Remember now, you *are* at a high school... Ah, Mr. Boodram, you do understand English." The class was quiet for a moment. Mr. B repeated his question and this time I knew that I was being baited. "Mr. Boodram, do you understand English?"

"Yes, Sir." I replied ever so feverishly.

"What was that? Pray tell! We cannot understand you, can we class?"

"Mr. Boodram, your comprehension is such that if I were to give you the answers, you would not be able to match them with their corresponding questions." My life's blood drained from my body and I felt my knees weaken.

"Oh, Lord," I thought, "please help me to remain standing."

Ripples of laughter followed this cutting slur. I became totally embarrassed. I began to lose my sense of balance and became confused. I could not understand what was happening to me.

Laughed at, scorned and ridiculed, I prayed that my teacher was finished. But, he was not. I was subject to his mercy and he had none.

He went in for the kill.

"Mr. Boodram, Mr. Boodram, I regret to inform you that the likes of you do not belong in the Queen's institution of higher learning! Convey to your father this sentiment: you wish to join him in his present endeavours perhaps as a labourer in the fields. At least, in that capacity, the promise of you being somewhat useful may be enhanced."

These concluding remarks were delivered with a smug, self-assured smile that invited laughter and ridicule from the rest of the class. My soul was once again drenched by this poison drawn from the well of ridicule of this insensitive teacher. He was not, however, finished with me yet.

"And Mr. Boodram, if you don't mind, why don't you simply sit down, shut up and stop wasting my time!"

I froze. I desperately wanted some kind of relief. My soul was damaged and I fought hard to hold back my tears. I needed to cry but I would not give them the satisfaction. They expected me to cry and I knew that if I did, I would become the target of boos; teased and humiliated until I crumbled. Whatever the attack, I tried to remain strong. No crying. I refused to let one single tear fall.

My teacher retreated to his desk, triumphantly. In his mind he had secured the kill of the day. One dumb student was taken down!

The walk home was long. I avoided everyone. I kept recalling Mr. B's sharp condemnation: "Sit down and shut up!" My body had complied. I did sit down. But my inner voice rose up in silent protest. I would not allow that voice to be silenced. All my life it had been that inner voice that vaulted me over the walls of crass rejection and allowed me to land on the surer ground of a struggling, but emerging confidence. It was then that I summoned an adage that was to become a familiar friend and a frequent visitor in my life: "I don't know that I am smart, but I know that I ain't that stupid." With these words I consoled myself against the hollow denunciation of my teacher. A life lesson stirred within me and I vowed: "Teacher you may take me down, but you won't keep me down. I will rise. I must." Every fibre of my spirit rose to strengthen my resolve to rise above my teacher's criticism. I would survive. It was in this state of renewal that I felt strengthened.

I wondered about the role of a teacher. Was not a teacher a teacher? Was compassion and understanding not part of the package? I pondered the nature of teaching and the role of the teacher and ventured to invent my own standards for this profession. Ironically, at that moment I had not the slightest clue that these quiet musings of a high school student would be summoned in the future when indeed I actually became a teacher myself.

2

TROUBLES IN COMPOSITION

M<small>Y TROUBLES</small> in Mr. B's class did not end. Another situation developed in my creative writing/composition class. I loved the creative part of the writing class. My mind could always think of different things to write about. What truly troubled me was the writing part of the assignment. My writing skills were limited as I was not proficient in either grammar or punctuation. My dread was understandable and was resurrected each time I was required to write a composition.

On this day, Mr. B announced that we had to write a composition.

Composition. Composition. Another composition. Fear would grip me and my mind would seize. I felt defeated before I had even begun. We had to write a story. Mr. B stood in front of our Form Three class. We were attentive. We knew the drill. No one, absolutely no one dared to be inattentive. Try and be inattentive, and Mr. B came down on you like an avalanche. In his arsenal of weaponry, two items were chosen. First he would choose the deadly poison of the stare. He would survey the offender from top to bottom. He would approach or withdraw. If you were the target you knew instinctively that he was engaging you. You were uncomfortable. You tried to get to the task but you could not concentrate. Mr. B was the master. He was in command. You were powerless. His stare was absolute.

When he spoke, he simply called your name. You immediately stood up. You managed to utter an awkward acknowledgment, "Mr. B." You then remained silent awaiting his next move.

It was in the midst of this kind of atmosphere that Mr. B gave us the topic: "Write four paragraphs on how you spent your weekend."

For most of the class, this was a kind of joy, perhaps even a comfort. Yes, it was easy enough. Many would tell of their adventures with their aunts and uncles and grandparents. We, East-Indians, what did we have to say? We were afraid to write anything. I wondered, "What did *I* have to write about?" Then I thought, "Why not describe the events of my weekend and hope that Mr. B approved my effort." Approval was sufficient. I did not dare dream of praise! Praise, that coveted idea was a stranger in my life although I witnessed it delivered so generously to so many of Mr. B's disciples.

And what did I do that particular weekend? What could I write about that would be acceptable? All day I became increasingly anxious. I could no longer concentrate. I absorbed very little of my other classes. The weight of that composition, that dreaded piece of writing, burdened me and I could not wait for the day to end. I was petrified. What was I going to write about? How did I generally spend my weekend? More importantly, did I want to share these experiences with my teacher? Certainly not! And yet, what was I to do?

Then I made a decision. I would write about what I actually did over the weekend. A part of me wanted to share with my teacher the kind of life I, and others like me, lived. My hope was that Mr. B, upon reading about my life, might see things differently. Perhaps he might even show a measure of understanding and compassion. If this happened, my desire to come to school and once again love the process of learning, could be resurrected.

I turned in my composition. A week later, I remember it was a Friday, our graded papers were returned. I was nervous, extremely nervous. My heart actually raced. Mr. B stood at his desk. He had a pen sitting sideways across his mouth. His eyes surveyed the class. He rose. We became quiet. The greater part of the class had a curiosity, a kind of glee, while they awaited their teacher's much anticipated performance. Mr. B was now stationed in front of his desk. He was holding the collection of papers in his hand. From the bundle, he extracted one paper. He read one paragraph. In that paragraph, the student shared his experiences. He recounted being with "Uncle This" and "Auntie That." They were on a yacht and all the nuances of family life on this yacht were captured. As I listened, I felt foreign. This student wrote about sailing, dining, and Mom and Dad, Auntie and Uncle: all at the table dining in fine fashion. He spoke of cutlery and teacups: items that were so strange and different in my world. It reminded me of life in the movies. Surely, this was another world, far removed from my reality. My world was modest and small. We had little cutlery; we ate with our hands. We had several teacups; but these were locked away safely for special guests. Everything in my world was simple and basic.

Then, Mr. B chose a second composition. He loved performing and the class was perfectly captured. The stage had been set. The expectation of the next reading was that it would be equal to or exceed the previous one in delighting the imaginations of the attentive listeners.

Mr. B launched his next performance with his usual approach. "I want to draw your attention, Class, to the writer, or should I say, what appears to be a writer. Now, mind you," he continued, "this writer has a vocabulary from which we all might learn." He paused, and at this point the mood of the class became expectant. The class knew instinctively that some unfortunate soul was about to be humiliated, and most were prepared to enjoy the show. Those of us from my community feared that it was one of us and were silently praying for personal exemption from certain humiliation. It did not matter, however, whose composition was selected. Each one of us would feel the pain of the unfortunate. I offered up my silent prayer. *Oh, Lord, not me, please, not today.* The question remained, whose essay was he about to read? My heart sank as Mr. B's gaze rested on me.

I wanted to die. I knew that Mr. B's missile of contempt was about to be launched at a most vulnerable target: me. I froze. Mr. B continued, "Class, as I was saying, we have a new writer, a certain kind of genius, even I was not able to comprehend this new style of writing." An onslaught of laughter ensued. Mr. B became the ringmaster and the students were now responding perfectly to his whip. "We have in our midst, and how fortunate we are Class, the likes of a creative writer that the world has not seen, up until now."

He paused. I perished. His stare was fixed on me.

"Mr. BOO-dram." (Now, please understand that my teacher took special delight in playing up the first syllable of my surname. He enunciated the beginning of my name with such evident pleasure, the sarcasm was impossible to miss. He was so successful in conveying his message of disdain, that most of the other students became eager disciples. They emulated his behaviour toward me on that occasion, and for a long time thereafter I was frequently greeted as BOO-dram.)

"BOO-dram, tell us, what do you mean by this paragraph?" His emerging laughter could not hide his scorn and contempt for me and my life as he continued his barrage of words. "What do you mean when you write: 'It was my turn to take care of the cows. I took them to the *bandane* so they could graze on the *tapir* grass.' Boodram. I need to inform you that I actually got out the dictionary. Now, surely, one would find your choice of words-*bandane* and *tapir* grass-listed somewhere in the dictionary." The classroom tempo was escalating. Laughter built upon laughter. All at my expense.

"Boodram," he continued, "since you are apparently a genius now, would you care to tell us what such words mean?" While I struggled to come up with some kind of explanation, he continued with his caustic sarcasm. "No doubt Boodram you are a writer. You belong to a group we have no knowledge of. *Tapir, bandane*. Do you have a dictionary perhaps? One of your own choice. Could you please show us these words?"

His slaughter was complete. His chosen animal was totally defeated in the arena of the classroom. I was rendered motionless and lifeless at the feet of the ringmaster, devoid of speech and incapable of thought. Whatever knowledge, intelligence or hope that I thought I possessed, were, in that moment, destroyed. A small voice within me knew that in order to go on with my existence, I must rescue one dying ember of my spirit. A spark had to be ignited, preserved, and nurtured deep inside the chamber of my soul. To not do so would be to invite certain death of the mind which to me would be complete and utter death.

"Boodram, you have nothing to say?"

I urged my soul, "Do not break down. Do not cry." I simply stood. Dehumanized. Demoralized.

Mr. B was relentless. "Mr. BOO-dram, would you be so kind as to write another composition for us and this time make it one that we can understand. And, if needed, would you please employ the standard dictionary that we all use?"

I managed to say, "Yes, Sir." I sat down in complete humiliation. Had the earth cracked open at that very moment, I would have volunteered to jump in.

When the class finally ended, a circus of students awaited me outside. A chorus of "BOO-dram" greeted me. Another wave of humiliation swept over me and again I was transported to the shores of scorn and ridicule.

I wanted to fight back. Desperately I wanted an expression of my own esteem, my very own self-respect. For now, I had to absorb these insults silently. To say something, anything, would lead to further conflict and I would be held responsible.

The teacher's sarcasm cut ever so deeply. The students' taunts crippled. From that kind of pain emerged a stubbornness born of sheer determination that emanated from the deepest part of my soul. It said simply, "Don't cry. If you cry in front of your hecklers, you lose." I would not cry. At least, not outwardly. No violence! But I felt it. I wished that I had super powers. I wished I could, with one fell swoop, silence my hecklers. That feeling of desiring physical power was so tempting, and yet, I let it diminish. Soon, that wish was replaced by a consuming will to appear stoic in the presence of my tormentors. I determined that I would not cry. I would be strong. In the midst of the circus of hecklers, I walked away. I was strong. Not one teardrop fell.

Finally, I was alone. I felt like crying. I wanted to cry. I needed to cry. Then, came a resolve. I would not cry. Save those tears for another day. I headed for home. I took the long way-- the solitary path. As I walked, a feeling of adequacy, a feeling that I was all right, enveloped me like a soft blanket.

3

MR. B'S HISTORY CLASS

R. B was not only my English teacher, he was also my History teacher. I dreaded him for reasons previously discussed. Yet, he was competent. He knew his subject material and delivered it well. It is true that we students feared him. Some more so than others. On the other hand, however, he unveiled History like he owned it. We were drawn to him, as he captured us with his vivid portrayal of historic events. It was obvious that he loved this subject.

One fateful day in the third year of my high school career, something happened which had a far reaching impact. Mr. B addressed us in his usual fashion. He stood poised in front of the class leaning slightly against his desk. His demeanour was dignified. His appearance was professional as always. Dark pants, white shirt and an eye-catching tie, set this teacher apart. The subject of the day was Martin Luther, the controversial monk from Germany during the fifteenth century. The course outlined the events of the British Empire from the 1400s to the 1600s generally. This particular teacher made the course interesting. There was, however, one slight problem.

The text for this course had to be purchased from the school which sold them at a profit. Because I came from a very poor family, I did not have the financial resources for this four dollar textbook. This amount was equal to almost one full week of my father's wages! I knew better than to approach my father for that kind of cash. I managed to have close to a quarter: a shilling to be exact. I travelled to the Capital, Port of Spain, by bus which was the cheapest form of transportation. From the Capital I walked to the edge of the city to a store that sold used

books. The books situated in the front section of the store were presentable, but too expensive for me. Furthermore, I could not find the particular text that I was seeking. A clerk approached and asked if he could
be of assistance. I explained my situation and my financial dilemma.
The clerk walked away and quickly returned holding a used textbook
in his hand. "Two dollars," he remarked. "Anything else?"

I was speechless. I wondered where in the world I would find two
dollars.

"Do you have a problem, man?" he inquired. Silence. "Talk to me,
man. What's the problem?" he insisted.

"I don't have that kind of money," I uttered hesitantly.

"Well, how much you have?"

"A shilling."

"A shilling?" Obviously he was shocked.

I was embarrassed.

"Sorry," I whispered and I began to walk away.

"Hey! Hold on! I think I can help you. Wait!"

I turned and again approached him. "There's a back room. Over
there," he pointed. "It is the repair section. We don't have the exact
book. But there is another text that covers the same course outline. Go
and find a copy. I will take your shilling."

My hopes were raised and I entered the back room. I searched frantically. Books of every description filled the room. Finally, I discovered
the History section. Soon, I actually found the text. One problem soon
became evident. The text was incomplete; various pages were missing.
I discovered that there were several other copies of the same text; each
one was missing different pages. I managed to make one complete copy
by combining various elements from each book. I was overjoyed. Yet, a
feeling of unease enveloped me. Deep down inside I had this feeling of
having done something wrong. Was I stealing?

I took the 'manufactured' text to the clerk. He perused my work-
manship and commented, "Smart move you made!" I relaxed, paid my
shilling, and returned home with my prize.

In preparation for History class, I borrowed a friend's copy of the assigned text and compared its headings to those of my own. They were
close. At school, I used my book, but I tried not to draw attention to it.
To disguise my deceit, I wrapped my text with plain brown paper. I
worried constantly that my teacher would uncover my deception. To
have a book that was different from the rest of the class would be a sin.
To have a text that was not only visually different but also contextu-

ally different because it was not written from the Catholic perspective, would be perceived as a rejection of all that the school stood for, and could result in 'excommunication.'

And believe it or not, excommunication was the very subject of that day's History class. I had come to class prepared. I had read my text and from my personal deliberations on Martin Luther, I came to ponder and understand his actions. Luther proposed that it was wrong to buy indulgences as atonement for sin. He questioned the actions of those who sold indulgences. Luther was adamant: one could not buy one's way into Heaven. This was the sentiment that filled my mind just prior to attending class.

Luther's ideas excited me. I felt a little bit smart, intelligent even. All my life, I had struggled to understand what I was being taught. Finally, a day of gladness, of hope; a day of emerging self-confidence had arrived. Such elation was hard to contain. I was somewhat fearful that a certain segment of my classmates would discover that I was actually understanding the work. Such a condition would not be tolerated. There was an unwritten commandment that a person such as me, an Indian and a Hindu, ranked lowest in the Catholic school hierarchy. For someone like me to lay claim, however short, to a meager moment of intelligence, would never be allowed. I would have been endlessly tormented. I entered the classroom with guarded happiness.

Mr. B began. "Today, class, I want you to understand that certain people are usurpers. They take what is not theirs to take. Consider Martin Luther. He deliberately undermined His Holiness with his Satanic views." I kept listening, fascinated. "How dare Martin Luther question the Pope!" he thundered. The room was silent. "He is nothing but a heretic and it was right that he was excommunicated." The class nodded in quiet acquiescence.

Suddenly, without my knowing, my right hand was raised. My brain had been wondering what a heretic was. My right hand responded automatically by going up. My hand did not belong to one of the usual classroom contributors. It did not belong to one of the class celebrities. No. It belonged to one of the class rejects. "Fool," I said to myself. "Take your hand down!" Too late! My body was frozen. My brain's message was undeliverable. Mr. B had me and my hand in complete focus. His stare was immobilizing. The class was very aware of the situation and was expectant. The students were not to be denied their moment of pleasure.

"Mr. Boodram," he announced. "Yes, Mr. Booo-dram," he repeated sarcastically. "Pray, tell us, we are all waiting. What is it that you desire?"

All eyes were now focused on me. "Sir, I... I... I...," I stammered.

Muffled laughter greeted my stammering.

"Mr. Booo-dram, please explain the nature of your untimely distraction."

From somewhere, I managed to summon up enough courage to speak. "Sir," I began, "Martin Luther, a heretic?" I had meant to ask what does the word 'heretic' mean. I sensed from Mr. B's passionate discourse that to be called a heretic was not a compliment.

Mr. B thought that I was disputing his assertion that Martin Luther was a heretic and he bellowed, "If I, your teacher, say that Martin Luther is a heretic, then Martin Luther is a heretic. Period!"

I must have looked incredulous because Mr. B continued his rant and hammered his vitriolic tirade directly at me. "What!" he thundered, "Are you, Boodram, a Hindu in our school, denying that Martin Luther is a heretic? Are you gone mad? Has your mind, whatever little mind you have, has it left you completely? Are you now, Booo-dram, mindless?"

Laughter, waves of laughter, filled the room. "But, Sir, all I was trying ..."

My feeble attempt at explaining was thwarted and again I was chastised. This time he used an expression that I had never heard before. "Impudent." This was followed by, "Get out. Now!"

"Sir..." was all that I could utter.

"Impertinent! Imbecile!" he snorted. "We want no heretics amongst us. Take this note to the principal."

I took the note. I did not even look at it. My world had collapsed. What had I done? I could not understand. I was dumbfounded. The principal's office was located some blocks away. The principal was the priest in charge, Father Fennessey. This priest was to play a pivotal role in my life.

It took a few minutes to get to Father Fennessey's. About one hundred yards away from his office was the girls' high school. During recess, the senior girls gathered around closer to the senior boys' class held at the building in which Father Fennessey resided. His office was completely visible to the girls. Anyone being reprimanded or belted by the principal was easily seen by the girls. Any such spectacle was cause for major gossip.

I arrived at Father Fennessey's only moments before recess. It was with the greatest of trepidation that I knocked nervously on his door. No answer. Should I knock again? I waited. Still no response. I knocked a second time. "One moment," Father acknowledged. The door opened. The bell rang. It was recess. I was on the threshold of the door. I panicked. I had to get inside before I was discovered. One more moment and all eyes, all the girls' eyes, would be on me, and the gossip that was sure to ensue, would be unrelenting. I stepped into the office without first being invited. Usually the offending student was required to remain on the threshold where he would receive his discipline—a belt on the hand. Such a scene delighted everyone, both boys and girls alike.

On the playground the boys looked at the girls while the girls pretended not to notice. All the while the girls were sneaking peaks at the boys themselves. All these antics were played out daily on the school grounds. I was never one to claim any attention. I was never one to be noticed. Imprinted on my mind, from my earliest memory, was the notion that I was ugly. Feelings of despair gnawed constantly in my soul. The best that I hoped for was that I would be presentable. Confidence in my appearance was a stranger. I was made to feel ugly so many times that it was hard to fight it. To be called stupid and a dunce repeatedly over the years by both my teachers and my peers, ate away at the very foundation of my psyche until one day, I stood up to myself and for myself and declared that perhaps I was no great looker, but I was not stupid. I did not know if I was smart, but I knew that I was not stupid. A sense of incompleteness, however, still consumed me. I did not feel on a par with my peers. The spirit of the Eternal Inferior Complex became my constant companion and would remain a part of my soul for what would seem an eternity.

And now, to be seen to be flogged by the principal during the recess break in front of everyone would have amounted to a public hanging. It would have brought with it such notoriety that I could not have survived. This explains my boldness in ushering myself uninvited into the office of the principal. As I entered, I closed the door behind me. I was so relieved. "Father," I began, I have a note."

Father read the note. "So, you are impudent, are you? Worse, you are also impertinent."

I nodded in embarrassment.

Father continued. "I would not have thought that you would commit such and offence." I kept my head down. "Well, let's get you your punishment."

His office was in disarray. It was under construction. Nothing was

where it should have been. Father actually stumbled over lumber trying to get to his desk. He opened the top drawer of the desk to get the
strap. He could not find it. I breathed a sigh of relief. I dared to hope
that, maybe today I would get a break.

Father looked at me and acknowledged, "I don't have my strap." He
smiled as he surveyed the room. "Ah," he said, "this will have to do."
From the ceiling he grabbed an electric cable cord. "Now, open your
right hand and extend it forward." He gave me six lashes with that
cable cord. The pain was severe. I breathed a sigh of relief when it was
over. "Now," he continued. "Extend your next hand." Another round
of six lashes followed. Excruciating pain enveloped my being. When
he was finished, Father looked directly into my eyes and repeated,
"Impertinent! I cannot believe it."

He then instructed me to go back to class.

I did.

Horror amidst horrors awaited me. I wished at that moment that
instead of heading back to class, I was in another place, another time,
another universe. To be born poor is one thing, to be rendered poorly
is quite another. I did not understand Father Fennessy's actions. I desperately wanted him to give me a chance. I needed him to understand
that there was a misunderstanding between my teacher and myself. I
looked up to this priest. (And, despite my treatment at his hands, I still
respect him to this very day.)

I entered class. All eyes stared. I sat down. I looked at my desk and
noticed immediately that my History text was missing. "Oh, my God,"
I thought. "What happened?" I looked up. There, in front of me stood
Mr. B holding my text. He had found it and had found me out. He
had captured me and was about to deliver me to the class much like a
Roman soldier would deliver a slave for public viewing.

"Mr. Boodram, here is your so called text. It was obviously written by a heretic for a heretic. Take it and yourself and leave for two
weeks."

This was one of the worst moments in my life. This was the moment
when I truly felt that the world had conspired against me. I needed desperately to find a way out of my humiliation; I needed to reclaim some
semblance of dignity.

Again, his venomous words seared my soul. "Boodram, go! As of
now, you are excommunicated from this class for two weeks. And, as
for your text, I have changed my mind." He held the offending work
high in the air and then tossed it unceremoniously into the garbage

can. Mr. B's pleasure was obvious.

I was devastated. I could not believe that Mr. B had actually thrown my history text into the garbage can with such obvious disdain. I felt compelled to rescue this precious book– a book that I had taken such pains to personally compile. Mr. B's cowardly and ignorant act doomed my precious text to an early grave. This book did not deserve to be treated that way by an arrogant imbecile who dared wear the title, "Teacher." My spirit soared in defence of my book and I wondered what I could do. At that moment, Mr. B ordered, "Now, go!"

"Yes, Sir," I acknowledged.

It was at this point that I managed to manufacture one final act of courageous defiance. Instead of leaving the class as I was instructed, I walked, head down, toward Mr. B. As I neared the garbage can, I reached in and retrieved my book. I cradled that precious book close to my chest and walked out with my head held high and my dignity reclaimed. My outcast friend and I were once again reunited. Something resembling a smile graced my face as I made my exit. This was as quiet an act of courage as I can remember.

I loved school. I hated school. I loved the idea of learning. I hated the torment to which I was regularly subjected. My intense desire to know things, to learn about ideas, was the instrument that propelled me forward despite the taunting and the ridicule. I desperately wanted Mr. B to regard me as an individual who wanted to learn. Mr. B possessed a knowledge that could inspire; yet, his deadly sarcasm quelled the modest aspirations of students like myself.

When my third year of school was concluded, Mr. B left and moved on.

It was during the fifth year of high school that we were required to write the dreaded Cambridge Exams in our various subject areas. These examinations were set in England according to British standards. Once written, they were returned to England for marking. I often wondered whether Mr. B would have been proud to note that of all the students from his former class that wrote the exam, I was one of the very few to earn a 'distinction' in History. It seemed an ironic twist that I who had once been 'excommunicated' from class should earn such a distinction. I struggled hard on my own to keep up whenever I was removed from class, and, when in class, I struggled even harder to find my voice. This mark of 'distinction' meant the world to me. Because of it, I dared to think that perhaps I was not that stupid after all.

My experiences with Mr. B in high school were as memorable as they were challenging. What had made me the person I was at high school is rooted in my early childhood. It was early childhood experiences that had molded me into the person that was somehow able not only to endure but also to surmount the challenge that everyday life presented.

4

MONEY GROWS ON TREES

ONEY WAS central to many events in our lives. One day when
I was in a junior grade, I approached my father. "Pa," I said
excitedly, "could I have a little change?"

My father's response was quick and simple. "Oh, Frankie, you want
some change? That's not a problem. Come. It easy to solve."

"Yeh, Pa, how so?" I inquired. I was so happy that Pa was being so
accommodating.

"Well, come with me. You see the mango tree there?"

"Ya."

"Well, Son," Pa continued, "money grows on trees."

"Really?" I asked in amazement.

"Yes, all you have to do is shake the branches until money falls
down."

"Really, Pa?" I asked incredulously.

"Now go shake the branch." Pa was serious. I took him at his word
and headed towards the mango tree. I selected a low branch on the
tree. I grabbed it and began to shake it. Nothing. I shook harder. Still
nothing. By then, Pa had disappeared. I tracked him down.

"Pa," I called.

"What's the matter, Frankie?" he returned.

"No money, Pa. I shook the branch like you said. No money fell."
I explained. My disappointment was obvious. I needed the money. I
wanted to buy some candy. My school mates had lots of candies. I had
none. They shared with each other, seldom with me. We Hindu students never had any candies. We often wondered why we never had
any candies. Deep down I think we knew intuitively that our parents

31

were not able to provide that luxury. We did not have many of the things that the regular Catholic students had. New clothes, new books, new toys, and new shoes were not in our repertoire of needs. None of that mattered. Today, the only thing that mattered was candy. Today I wanted candy. Today candy was important. I wanted to have candy to share with my friends. We needed to feel normal at school. Having candy to share with others was one way to feel normal. It was the focal point of our existence and it was my task to get the money to buy the candy.

It was in this state of dejection and failure that I again approached my father and informed him that no money had fallen from the tree. To my surprise, my father was very understanding. In a solemn and assuring voice he explained, "Frankie, you didn't shake the correct branch. And you've got to remember to shake it hard enough." Then he had another thought, "Yo too young to shake the tree hard. Maybe that's why no money came down."

Hearing those words made me twice as determined. "Pa show me the right branch, please," I begged.

"No, Frankie, if I did, the money would not fall down," he explained. "Now you have to choose the branch, and you have to shake the tree. If the tree feels yo grown up enough, it will give up its money."

"All right, Pa. I will show the tree that I am grown up."

"Good. Go to it," encouraged Pa.

I ran back to the tree with new resolve. "So," I addressed the tree, "you think that I am small and not grown up. Well, I am. Now, don't be mad at me because I am little. Be fair. If I shake hard enough, then give me my share. Okay, Tree?" My chat was finished. Now the serious business of choosing the right branch began. I checked out the tree. There were so many branches. Last time I chose a branch near the bottom of the tree. This time I decided to go higher. I climbed the tree and at about the eight foot mark, I chose a branch. I pulled down on that branch with all my strength until I had forced it nearly to the ground. I then descended the tree. From my vantage point on the ground I could pull on the branch with a greater force. Nothing happened. I wondered why. Perhaps I had again chosen the wrong branch. Soon I was back in the tree again. This time I went even higher. This time I was more selective about the branch. This new branch was bigger, smoother and stronger than the previous two. I made my way just past the half way mark of the branch and began bending it towards the ground. This time I could not let go of the branch for it would certainly spring back up and I would not be able to reach it from the ground. I decided that my best course of action would be to edge my way carefully to the end of the limb. Once there, I began to bend the branch at little at a time, and gradually, it started to give way. I held on to the tip of the branch and managed to lower myself to the ground all the while still grasping the ends. I was relieved to be safely on solid ground. I began to shake the branch slowly at first, but soon I was attacking with much vigour. I kept up the attack. "Come on, Tree," I enthused, "give me money. Give me money."

A moment later, there was a snapping sound at the point where the branch of the tree met the trunk. The snapping gave way to a splitting sound as the branch split in two. Then the unbelievable happened. Money began pouring down from the tree: coins, shillings and pennies. I grabbed the coins by the handful and stuffed them into every available pocket. I did not know how much money I had but I knew it was enough to fill all my pockets in both my shirt and my pants. The remainder, I bundled up in my handkerchief. I was elated. Pa *was* right. Money *did* grow on trees.

I allowed myself to delight in this dream while I headed back home to tell my father. I was so excited, I was beside myself. I remember saying, "Oh, God, Pa, thank you, thank you. You are right. Money does grow on trees. Look what it gave me." I showed him the coins.

Pa stood dazed and speechless. My mind went racing ahead to all the candy I could buy with the money. I ran away. What a feeling. I was the richest child in the world. There would be candy for me and candy for my friends for days to come. That delirious and luxurious feeling lasted, but only for one day.

The next day after school, my neighbour friend came over. He looked dejected. Utterly forlorn. "Raffi," I inquired, "what's wrong?"

"Boy, Frankie, somebody thief me money."

"What you mean, Raffi, thief your money?"

"Frankie, you know we all have our hiding spots for our money. I hid my money in your mango tree. I cut a slot in one of the branches and I put the coins in the slot. Look, the branch is on the ground and the slot is empty. They thiefed me money!"

Suddenly, I was sick. My stomach grew uncomfortable. I had already spent a lot of the money and I had even offered Raffi a treat.

Raffi looked at me. "Frankie, you not say anything. You know something, don't you?"

"Honestly, Raffi, I did not steal the money." I then went on to explain the whole situation.

Raffi was not placated in the least by the reasonableness of my explanation. "Gimmie all the rest of the money. And I want all the rest of
the candy too!" he added. Dutifully, I gave him everything.

"Frankie, you owe me," he said as he walked away.

For quite some months later I remained in Raffi's debt and under
his control. He generously exerted his right to extort justice whenever
and wherever he saw fit. Eventually, I paid off my debt. Perhaps several
times over.

5

MY DOLLAR BILL

THE INCIDENT with the mango tree taught me the value of money at a very early age. I came to understand that although I needed spending money, I was never to ask my parents for it; I was to earn it myself. I quickly learned how to get money, and my greatest source of income came from gathering up discarded empty pop bottles. I would then return them to local shops and stores for a modest refund. Often I would do chores for my neighbours, unasked, with the simple hope that they might offer me a penny. More often than not, they would offer me a simple, *Thank you,* or *God bless,* in lieu of payment. Then it dawned on me—they did not have any money to give away. All that they could freely give was their kind blessings. It was then that I decided to venture to "the other side of the tracks" where the rich people lived. Surely those people would be more disposed to being generous with their pennies, I reasoned. My high hopes were quickly dashed. So many times I was to be dismissed in a patronizing fashion. I felt out of place and secretly wondered where someone like myself, someone *willing* to work, someone *wanting* to work, would go to get a break in life. I wondered how I could create an opportunity to help myself.

I learned to stay the course. I learned to do whatever I had to do in order to earn those little rewards. I earned my way, penny by penny, performing millions of little chores. Eventually, the pennies became shillings and the shillings became a dollar. One whole dollar! I was the proud owner of a dollar bill. In my world, I was King. I did not reveal my wealth to anyone, not to my parents, not to anyone. Once again I dared to dream of luxuries. It did not matter that we had little to eat; I had money to buy candy.

Thinking about that dollar bill consumed my life. Knowing that I possessed such wealth transformed my physical and mental demeanour, and I walked with a light step and a confident air. I did, however, have one slight problem. I had no private place in which I could hide the dollar. We were nine children sharing a two bedroom home with our parents. Not one of us had the luxury of a private room; not even the luxury of a private space within a shared room. I possessed no chest of drawers to call my own. There were no secret spots in our house. Everything we had, we shared. One day, however, I did discover the perfect spot.

Our house was built on stilts, about two feet above the ground. The rough crossbeams on the underside of the house nestled on concrete bricks. Both the wooden beams and the concrete bricks were showing signs of wear. One day as I was sweeping the sand floor beneath the house I discovered a crevice in one corner of the house where the wooden beam settled on the concrete. It was the perfect hiding spot. I took my beloved dollar bill tenderly from my pocket and folded it again and again until it was almost unrecognizable as a dollar bill. I then placed it into the crevice. Once placed, it could not be seen; it was totally out of sight. I was relieved. My precious dollar had a safe home and only I knew of its whereabouts; only I knew of its very existence. That night I had the best feeling as I was going to bed. My mind raced; my thoughts were totally centered on that dollar bill and all the candies that I could buy with it. I was certain to be regarded as a prince among all my friends when I bought and generously shared some rare treats with them. Finally, I fell asleep.

Some time passed and eventually the moment came when I needed my dollar bill. I went happily to my secret hiding place, fully anticipating the joy of once again holding that precious dollar bill in my hands. I reached into the crevice. What I retrieved was not the same thing that I had deposited just days earlier. I was horrified. Instead of my carefully folded dollar bill, I pulled out the remains of a couple of dead cockroaches. I shuddered as the reality of my find filtered into my consciousness and my perfect world crumbled around me.

The roaches had feasted on my dollar bill and now they were dead. Did they die as a result of eating the money? I would never know for sure and furthermore, I did not care to know. All I knew for certain was that my treasure was gone, shredded by those unwelcome intruders. In my child's heart I reasoned that death was too easy for them. It was not sufficient punishment for what they had done to my world. Something in me died and I was at a loss to know what to do.

It was in this shattered and vulnerable state that my mind raced to thoughts of my mother and a sense of guilt and shame flooded my soul. Ma had always taught us to be righteous in all our actions. She often explained to us that keeping things secret was not right. She impressed upon us the idea that you do not keep things like money for ourselves. If we were to find money, the right and honourable thing to do would be to report the find to our mother. Ma would put such money to good use for the benefit of the whole family, not for just one individual person. She would probably purchase oil for the lamps or oil for cooking. In this way the money would be shared among the whole family and God would look favourably on the individual who provided such a blessing.

I began to question myself and my motives. *Was I being selfish in keeping the dollar bill all to myself? Was God punishing me for my sinful behaviour?* I pondered these questions for days and eventually I had my answer. I was not being punished for I had not committed any sin. I had not *found* the money; I had *earned* it. God was not unhappy with me. The fact that those roaches had found my secret cache was a product of my ignorance and not an overt act of punishment from God. I managed to move on.

6

THE BANANA TREE AND
THE TWO DOLLAR BILL

FROM MY experiences I came to understand two things: money did not grow on trees and money was indeed a valuable commodity. I truly understood the value of a coin. Having lost my dollar bill, I was more determined than ever to save every penny I could until I had two hundred. If I could collect two hundred pennies, I could exchange them for a blue two dollar bill. There was nothing that I would not do to earn a solitary penny. I scoured the neighbourhood for empty pop bottles and empty beer bottles. I volunteered in every way that I could to run errands and gradually the pennies began to mount up. Soon the elusive goal of reaching two hundred was within sight. It took me over a year to reach that target and soon I held in my hands the coveted blue bill. Once again the problem of where to keep the precious currency returned to plague me. I was not about to make the same mistake twice by hiding it under the house. Nor would I repeat Raffi's blunder by choosing to hide it in the branch of a mango tree.

One day Ma asked me to clean up around the banana trees at the back of our yard. There was a huge *chennet* tree that formed a border between our neighbour's yard and our yard. The boundary between the two properties was in dispute, hence the ownership of the *chennet* tree was also in dispute. Needless to say, I was not about to select such a contentious spot for my hiding place. As I went about performing my cleaning duties around one particular banana tree, I noticed a number of dead looking leaves hanging down from the tree. As I began stripping away at these leaves, the solution to my problem emerged. I discovered that the trunk of the banana tree was made up of several layers of soft tissue-like growth, much like the layers of an onion. I pulled out my homemade pocket knife.

As young children we rarely went anywhere without our trusty knives. We never knew just when we would be in need of one such instrument. The knives were never ever used to settle disputes; such a thought would never even have occurred to us as children. The idea of a weapon was an alien concept. Our knives were used to cut and peel our *liberated* fruits and vegetables, or, to fashion toys or play games. The idea that our knives could be dangerous never occurred to us; our knives had a utilitarian value only.

So, out came my knife, and with it I peeled back the dead leaves to reveal a green shiny layer underneath. It looked soft and juicy. I cut a small square out of the front layer. Then I cut a smaller square out of the second layer. To accomplish this successfully, demanded the precision and skill of an artist. After completing the task, I had an enormous feeling of accomplishment; I felt somewhat smart and grown up. I had indeed fashioned a most unusual hiding place for my prized bill. I decided to be proactive and went one step further by choosing to wrap up that two dollar bill in a series of layers of plastic wrap. Hopefully, this precaution would discourage any *critters* from eating it and also protect it from rot. Once the bill was safely wrapped and concealed within the core of the banana tree, I allowed myself to feel clever, even brilliant. Each cutting was returned precisely to its original place and after careful observation, I determined that everything looked very natural and normal. To ensure further that everything was hidden, I carefully layered some of the dead trimmings over the general area. All went well and I could not hide my feeling of self-satisfaction.

Who would have thought that the trunk of a banana tree housed a hiding spot for my much prized two dollar bill? I stepped back a little and as I surveyed the banana tree, I noticed that it boasted a luscious bunch of bananas that was almost ready for harvesting. "Thank you so much Banana Tree," I whispered. "You are my saviour."

For the next few days, life was normal. Then one day it rained heavily. Because our house bordered a ravine which collected the waters which ran down from the surrounding mountains, the ravine would often overflows its banks. On this particular day, when I returned home from school, I looked over at my banana tree as was my custom. It was a delicious luxury that I allowed myself every day. My heart delighted in the knowledge that I could retrieve my two dollars any time I wanted. Today, however, there was no banana tree. My heart raced.

"Ma, Ma," I yelled. "Where is the banana tree?"

"Which banana tree, Frankie?" she asked.

"The one that was over there!" I shouted impatiently while pointing.

"Oh, that one. I cut it down," was her casual response.

"But, Ma, if you cut it down, where is the banana tree?" I persisted.

"Stupid boy, Frankie, don't you see? When the rains came ah had a chance to get rid of the trunk. I was lucky it rained. I was able to throw the top half of the banana tree into the ravine where the flood waters would carry it away," she explained.

"But, Ma... that's not lucky. Why you had to cut it, Ma? It was a great tree. It was bearing bananas, Ma. Why? Why, Ma?" I entreated.

"Son, don't you know that when a banana tree has bananas, you got to cut it half away. Then the tree grows and produces again. If you cut the bunch of bananas and don't cut the top off, it won't bear again," she explained.

"Oh, no," I cried. "Not again." I was foiled. My precious two dollar bill was hidden in the part of the tree that had been tossed into the ravine. I was not, however, going to give up on my two dollar bill that easily. I changed out of my school uniform and put on my street clothes. I decided to follow the course of the ravine to see if I could discover if the trunk had become lodged anywhere along the bank. I inspected the ravine foot by foot. There was no sign of my tree anywhere. I soon came to the area where the ravine emptied into a huge pool of water some distance away from my home. It was rumoured that alligators had made their home in this pool. This effectively dashed any remaining hope that I carried of finding my money. I carefully surveyed the scene but I could not see any evidence of the banana tree anywhere. Exhausted, wet and devoid of all hope, I returned home to face the enquiring looks of my mother. Finally, I revealed to her the source of my devastation.

I tried hard to understand why yet again I had been denied my life's dream and labour. My parents had often said that God knows everything that we do and that He would take care of us. I looked up at the heavens and, at that moment, I wondered about God and the very nature of His existence.

"God," I wondered aloud. "Am I wrong to want a little money? Is it wrong if I am willing to earn it? Tell me, God. I sure need an answer." I received no answer.

7

BUTTER

USINGS ABOUT God and the nature of God would resurface from time to time. For now, I felt defeated. I wanted to share my story of loss with my mother but I did not.

I had always looked up to my mother. We all called her Ma, and Ma she would remain until the end of her days. Even her grandchildren called her Ma as she would not tolerate being addressed as Grandmother or Grandma. To her friends she was simply Miz B and to everyone else that she met, she was just Ma.

There was something about her, a haunting presence of constant sadness reflected itself in her dark brown eyes. Her form was diminutive and grew increasingly so as she entered her final years. Giving birth to so many babies, nine in all, combined with a life of constant physical labour, took its toll on her body. She was a woman of strong will and quiet determination. Although she was poor, poverty would never define her. Poverty was not an excuse to look poorly and she took pride in the fact that her children were always cleaned and groomed. She was a devoted mother to her children and her children, in later years, returned that devotion tenfold.

When we were young children we recognized something special about our mother. Her soul was quiet and gentle. This quiet, gentle soul however often managed to be quite the strict disciplinarian. One incident illustrates this quality very well.

One day Ma approached me and curtly instructed, "Frankie, go to the store and line up. They have butter, and we will have our portion of butter." Trinidad was still rationing items that were scarce and butter was a rare commodity. I was thrilled to go on that errand. Butter was such a rare treat in our household and Ma used butter to make her famous *roti*. *Roti* was a type of flat pizza-like bread that was made with white flour. Once prepared, the flat bread was rolled out into a circle and cooked over the heat from an open flame on a flat iron pan called a *tawa*. Once cooked, the top of the *roti* was covered with butter (when we could get it and when our family could afford it). Today was the day to get butter and I was the one entrusted with the task. I made my way to the shops and joined the long line of people waiting for their ration of butter. It did not bother me that I had to wait for what seemed like hours. I showed no impatience for I was already tasting the sweetness of the butter on my *roti*. Finally, it was my turn and I could hardly contain my delight. I stepped up to receive my portion, when the shopkeeper irritably announced, "No more butter! Everybody, go home!"

"Mr. Singh," I protested. Then I urged, "Could you scrape the barrel and give me the left over please?" I made this bold request with a sheepish but hopeful heart.

My entreaty was unceremoniously dismissed. "Frankie, you deaf? Go home!"

I persisted. "But, Mr. Singh," I tried pleadingly.

"Frankie," he thundered, "go away." Mr. Singh turned his back on me and walked away.

I left there with a heavy heart and started slowly homeward. The weight of the disappointment, combined with the length of the wait, and the knowledge that I alone had to carry the distressing news to my mother, manifested itself into sluggish feet barely able to make the short journey back home. I dreaded telling my mother. She would be so disappointed but she would try to hide from me the tears in her soft brown eyes. I could already imagine her quickly turning her head to wipe away the tears with her *orni*, the thin veil-like covering that gently graced her head. I simply did not know how I was ever going to face her and shatter her world with the distressing news that there was no butter.

I must not have been as overwhelmed as I thought because I heard a voice call to me from the home of one of my neighbours. This voice was entreating me to come and play marbles with a group of my friends. They said they were in trouble and they needed me to help them win. The game was already in full swing at the side of the road. Sweet Heaven! A game of marbles. I was being invited to play my favourite game. All else was forgotten. Pitching marbles was the one sport in which I excelled. In almost every other game—a cricket, soccer, police and thief, I was quite ordinary. But, when I played marbles, I was a champion. Everyone looked up to me and honoured me for my special skill. I rarely got to experience these feelings and I greedily devoured this fortunate opportunity. Time flew by as I was engrossed totally in the game. I never made it home and I never relayed the news of the butter shortage to my mother. All seemed well in my world of marbles.

My mother, on the other hand, was worried about me. A couple of hours had passed and I had not yet returned home from my errand. It was most unlike me not to return as soon as possible, for Ma considered me responsible and dependable. It was under these circumstances that she set out to look for me. I did not know that she found me.

Finally, the game ended. My team had won, naturally. I was championed as a hero by my peers. As I left the marble pitch and began the short walk home, all the pain and sadness that I had previously felt, once again permeated my soul as I remembered that I had to tell Ma that there was no butter.

Ma was waiting for me when I got home and I searched my heart for just the right words. Ma was standing near the corner of the room as I climbed the stairs to enter the home. Something was different about the way she approached me that afternoon. Her hands were not hanging loosely at her sides but rather, they were clasped together behind her back. Her usually relaxed face did not have a ready smile for me and she appeared somewhat agitated. "Frank, where yo went?" she demanded shortly.

"Ma, I went to the shop for butter and Mr. Singh said ..." I started but I did not get to finish.

Whack! A slap greeted one side of my face. This assault was accompanied by an even more hurtful accusation. "Liar!"

"Ma ..." I pleaded.

"Liar Frank. Never expected it from you."

"But, Ma ..." I tried again.

"Don't 'Ma, Ma' me, Frankie. Yo is a little liar!" She then grabbed me by my ear and led me to a corner of the room and instructed, "Kneel down." I did. "Stay there until I tell you to move," she ordered as she left the room.

I was shocked and hurt. My pride hurt more than my body. It mattered little that I had been hit. That hurt only my body. My soul had received the greater injury for I had been called a liar by my mother. I was given no opportunity to explain my side of the story. Even though my mother's anger was misplaced, I knew that in her heart she felt that she was justified. Because I knew in my heart that I was still her dutiful and obedient son, I would not disobey her and thus absorbed my punishment without complaint. My body would recover from the physical pain as it had so many times before but I wondered if the cut to my spirit would ever heal. Moreover, I questioned if I would ever be able to regain my former stature in my mother's eyes.

8

MR. ROBERTS' PINEAPPLE PATCH

LIFE WAS hard for us as children but like any child anywhere, we found time to play. Mostly, we played *police and tief* (thief). I was always the policeman. I loved the chase although I was not the fastest runner. I specialized in endurance and my target seldom escaped. However fast he would run through the cane fields, eventually he would run out of breath and I would find him bent over, gasping for breath, and crying for mercy. Often his cries were met with unsympathetic ears and I would lash him with my hand-fashioned police whip. After some rest, the chase resumed.

During the course of one such chase something different happened. As I was closing in on my friend, anticipating his capture, I heard a loud noise. This was followed by an agonized shriek. The sounds were close by. My mind raced happily ahead to the capture. I slowed down as I neared the area from which the sounds were coming. There, in the middle of the cane field, a few short yards from me, sprawled my friend. He, however, was not in the middle of a cane field. He was in the middle of a pineapple patch which was in the middle of a cane field. The patch was cleverly hidden. The sweet aroma of pineapples permeated the air. My friend could barely move. The rich cache of pineapples invited our intervention.

This secret field was owned by Mr. Roberts and it was widely acknowledged that he did not like children. Generosity towards us was an alien concept in his world. In our childish minds we rationalized that Mr. Roberts needed to suffer a consequence for his lack of heart and our game of cops and robbers was deferred temporarily. Other farmers in the region reacted quite reasonably to our boyish trespasses.

45

We once were caught enjoying a cucumber or two from one farmer's garden. The man sat us down and *offered* us a cucumber. He advised us to act responsibly in our ventures into other people's property. From him we learned to be reasonable in our thievery and to clean up after ourselves. His example guided us in all our future exploits. Whenever we were indulging our cravings in some poor farmer's crop, after feasting on the sugar cane, corn, or cucumber, we would carefully hide or even bury all evidence of our presence. We never removed too much. We took just enough to satisfy our hunger. We did not wish the farmer to feel hurt. We did not want anyone to even think that he had been robbed. In fact, we adopted the role as protector and guardian of the fields. This courtesy, however, was not to be extended to Mr. Roberts and his secret pineapple patch.

We whistled our secret call to announce our whereabouts to our comrades. Within minutes, everyone who was within earshot answered the call and joined us in Pineapple Heaven. That pineapple patch claimed our complete attention. Out came our homemade knives. We began our feast. We slit the pineapples, one after the other. We ate only the sweetest parts. As soon as we encountered a part that was less than perfect, we tossed the pineapple. We delighted in leaving visible evidence. We wanted Roberts to know that we had uncovered his secret.

Eventually Mr. Roberts did discover our intrusion into his hidden world and he wasted no time informing our small community about the invasion. I prayed that my parents would not ask me if I had any involvement in the affair. I would have to tell the truth. I simply could not lie.

The reason that I could not lie, is in itself, another story. Lying and such vices guaranteed with utmost certainty, a place for you in Hell. Oh, yes, we believed in Hell. All parents on our island ensured that each of their children knew about Hell. On one occasion, my mother gathered all her children into her bed to "talk." Outside, the raindrops were falling rhythmically on the galvanized roof. We were all cuddled snugly on the bed when Ma rose slightly to a sitting position and began to admonish us. "You children have to be good. Yo cannot hide or cheat or tell a lie. God knows everything. And, if you do bad things, yo have to pay. Yo see, yo children will have to go to Hell. God will send a messenger for yo. Yo will not know what form this messenger will take. He could be human or animal. This messenger will get yo and take all yo to Hell. There they will cut yo up in small pieces. And, if yo are really bad, yo go to Hell to be attacked by snakes, reptiles, and other hungry creatures and then yo are thrown in the burning fires of Hell, forever. Yo hear me?" She waited. No one could venture a response.

"I think," she continued, "that I hear a noise. Listen." There was a noise. A kind of whinny. We all moved closer to one another. Darkness surrounded us. Rain was now beating down on the galvanized roof. Then, we heard the noise. We rallied together and moved as one frightened mass closer to our mother. She warned, "Oh, there is a race horse outside. He has come to get someone. Has anyone been bad lately? Have you done anything wrong? Did you tell a lie?" Again her questions were met with silence. Everyone remained very still. I searched my memory hoping and praying that I had not committed any wrong. Her next words carried an even stronger image. "If you commit a sin, the horse wants your liver." I didn't really know what a liver was but I knew that it was something that was inside my body and I was certain that it was nothing that I wanted a horse to eat. Ma saw the horror on our faces and affirmed, "Yes, he eats your liver." Then she assured, "But, you are good children. The horse has gone away."

Years later I recalled the events of that day in my memory, and after consulting a few of my siblings on the matter, we all agreed that we had no collective memory of our eldest sister, Dolly, being among us as we hovered half frightened to death in Ma's room. Eventually we pieced together a plausible scenario. Ma and Dolly had conspired together. Dolly was the 'horse' outside the window. It was her job to provide sound effects at just the right time, thus making Ma's story plausible. It worked. We carried that image with us into our late teens. And, remarkably, we *were* all good children.

It was against this type of background that the Roberts' incident unfolded. As I expected, my father asked me in the presence of Mr. Roberts, if I had any part in the pineapple affair. I put my head down. I was embarrassed. Ma was more direct with her question. "Did you steal Mr. Roberts' pineapple?"

"No, Ma, I did not steal Mr. Roberts' pineapple."

Ma was so relieved. Her manner seemed to indicate that she considered the matter to be closed. I am sure that she reasoned, "Frankie said that he did not steal, therefore he did not steal." She reached out to hug me and just as she was about to whisk me away into the safety of the house and away from any further scrutiny, I was overwhelmed with the need to confess. I told the truth.

"Ma, I took the pineapple. I did not mean to steal."

Pa wanted to make certain that he had heard correctly. Before he hit me, he asked, "Did you have pineapple?"

"Yes."

The first slap seared my face and was immediately followed by a series of slaps and backhands. I was swollen and bleeding. Pa beat me until I could no longer stand. I fell to the ground completely broken. Pa turned to Mr. Roberts' and asked, "Satisfied, Mr. Roberts?"

Mr. Roberts nodded in affirmation.

To me, Pa announced, "And Frankie, that is but a sample of what is to come."

Yes, we had helped ourselves to Mr. Roberts' pineapples. Yes, we were guilty. But oh, how succulent, how utterly delicious those glorious pineapples were. Heaven could not be much sweeter than those pineapples. Would we ever do it again? Hmm...

9

MR. BOVIER

A S CHILDREN in Trinidad, our preoccupation with play became increasingly addictive with each passing day. The more we played, the more we loved to play; it was in our blood. We would do our requisite chores of course, but once our responsibilities were honoured, we assumed (rightly or wrongly) that the remainder of the day belonged exclusively to us, to fill as we saw fit, without fear of any adult interference.

We would remain outside for hours amusing ourselves with a host of innocent pastimes. Police and Thief, King of the Riverbank, Tarzan, Shoot 'em Up, cricket, soccer, cards, marbles and comic book sharing were a few of our activities. I don't ever recall a time when we were bored. There was always another game to play.

All these carefree days came to an abrupt end one summer holiday when my pa decided that I had too much spare time. He felt that my time could be better spent working at a job which would earn some money. Pa took me to a man named Mr. Bovier who owned a combination rum and grocery shop. Mr. Bovier agreed to hire me for a salary of $2.00 a week provided that I was productive. That $2.00 would go directly to Pa. Pa would then decide if I were deserving enough to receive some pocket change. As children, the money we earned could never be considered to be *our* money. It was understood implicitly that this money would be turned over to the head of the household and be used for the whole family.

Initially, Mr. Bovier brought me in to the grocery part of the shop and counselled me about my various duties. First, I was required to refill empty containers of butter, flour, sugar, salt and the like. Next, I was assigned the unsavoury task of filling the pork barrel. This presented a huge problem for me as a Hindu. Hindus were not only to abstain from eating pork but also to abstain from being near this meat which was a forbidden commodity in our religion. In addition, there was an extremely noxious smell coming from the pork barrel which caused my rather sensitive and weak stomach to become upset easily. I had to dip my hand in this barrel to procure some meat. This took tremendous courage both physically and emotionally. I felt that each time I reached into the barrel, I was betraying some fundamental principle of my Hindu religion. Nonetheless, I had to, and I did.

It wasn't long before Mr. Bovier decided that I was ready to assume more advanced duties. He began to teach me how to use the weigh scale to measure out specific quantities of goods. I was excited. Perhaps if I did a really good job I would not have to clean out the pork barrel any more.

Mr. Bovier demonstrated the technique of weighing: slide the ounce meter all the way across the bar to the very end at the 16 ounce mark; that measure was equal to one pound. To measure out more than a pound, I had to place the required pound weight on one side of the scale and the goods on the other side of the scale. When the two sides were balanced, I knew that I had the correct weight. Everything seemed simple enough.

I was very conscientious about my new duties. It was important to me to do everything as perfectly and as accurately as I could.

I remember the day when I went from doubting my measuring skills, to questioning the moral authority of adults. On that particular day I was eagerly weighing out five pounds of rice, one pound at a time. Each time I measured the pound, I noticed that Mr. Bovier had "accidentally" placed his index finger on the scale. He did this for each of the pound measures. My reasoning told me that the customer was being shorted a small measure each time this happened. I honestly thought that Mr. Bovier had become distracted and was not paying enough attention to what he was doing. I made preparations to re-weigh the order when I felt a cold chill run through my bones. I looked up and noted that Mr. Bovier's eyes were riveted on me. I felt the coldness in that stare and then he shook his fingers at me to indicate that I was not to proceed with the re-measuring.

I was confused. Did he actually "know" that he was shorting his customer? The only conclusion left for me to draw was that, yes, he knew. How many times had he done this before? My young heart was filled with the difficult understanding that Mr. Bovier, a respected business-man in Tunapuna, could actually cheat his customers. The very notion that an adult could be dishonest, had, up until that very moment, been inconceivable. Now, not only did I have to entertain the thought that such a thing was possible, unfortunately, I also had to believe it.

I remember trying to tell Pa the details about the scale incident with the hope that his adult understanding could give some meaningful explanation that would justify Mr. Bovier's actions. If this were to happen, it would serve to mitigate the seriousness of Mr. Bovier's deception. This is turn would begin to repair my vision of a collapsing morality in the adult world. This, however, did not happen. When I presented the particulars of the event, Pa became extremely annoyed with me and dismissed my inquiry altogether. In addition, Pa admonished me and advised me that I was to do exactly as Mr. Bovier requested and ask no questions. At that point, I suspended any further deliberations on the matter.

My tentative sojourn into the adult world was proving to be a great challenge to my youthful understanding and idealism. Nevertheless, I continued to work for Mr. Bovier; I was disillusioned but not irreparably shattered.

I worked long hours. I even worked weekends whenever I was needed. As time went on, it seemed like Mr. Bovier needed me all the time including Sundays. At the end of my first week I was given a modest salary. I handed over the complete salary to my father. Never for a moment did I entertain the thought that my salary belonged to me. This was a foreign concept. As children, we were taught that the money we earned was never to be considered to be *our* money. Rather, we sought to honour our father's position as head of the family by offering our full earnings to him. Pa, in turn, gifted a modest portion of the salary back for pocket change. That little bit of money always made me extremely happy; I soon forgave the long and tedious hours I had to labour to earn just that small bit of change.

Summer vacation was passing quickly. Soon I would be back in school (or so I thought). Near the end of the summer, a serious viral disease spread throughout the island and the schools did not reopen. The summer holiday was extended. I prayed that my father would allow me stop working and to enjoy the holiday like the other children on the island. Pa had other plans for me. He sent me back to Mr. Bovier to continue working for him. My heart was saddened; but I was obedient.

When Mr. Bovier invited me over to work in the other part of the store, the rum shop, I felt that I had been promoted. Mr. Bovier indicated that he was very pleased with the work that I had done for him in the grocery store and he wanted me to develop some new skills. Soon I was sweeping up the rum shop, emptying out the spit containers, and washing up the glasses. The work was far from glamourous but at least it took me away from the pork barrel.

The regular clerk at the rum shop took a bit of an interest in me and began to show me how to pour drinks for the customers. I enjoyed this task and over the next few days, I began preparing and serving drinks for the customers on a regular basis—always under the watchful eye of the clerk. Most people ordered "a shot" for which there was a precise measure so the job was really quite mechanical.

There came a day, however, when the regular attendant was absent. Mr. Bovier assumed his duties and I continued on in the role of enthusiastic assistant. This worked very well until Mr. Bovier was required upstairs on other business. He left me in charge. He assured me that if I needed him I could easily call out and he would come.

Once I was left alone in the shop, my imagination took wings. In my twelve year old mind, I now felt that I was the boss; I could make decisions. And, make decisions I did.

No sooner had my boss gone upstairs then my neighbour, Mr. Suni entered. I knew that Mr. Suni did not have a steady job. It seemed that the only times that he wasn't drinking were the times he was passed out in the middle of the street, drunk. Where he got the money to indulge his habit is not clear. His family was poor and his wife worked exceedingly hard to provide what little she could.

On this day when Mr. Suni walked in to the shop, it was obvious he had had quite a number of drinks already. He was inebriated but happy. When he saw me behind the counter he smiled at me and directed me to prepare him a drink.

"Now, Mr. Frankie, Mr. Boodram son. Pour me a drink from Vat 19 and gimmie a piece of lime."

I did as I was directed, collected the money and gave him the drink. Mr. Suni got up to leave, then thought better of the idea, and came straight back to me.

"Frankie, that was good! Gimmie another one."

It bothered me that Mr. Suni was wasting his family's money so foolishly. While his poor wife slaved at her crude roti stand, he drank. The more she worked, the more he drank.

I felt that this was wrong and, with the naivety singular to childhood, I believed that I could do something to help correct this situation. It was then that I decided to concoct an alcohol free drink for Mr. Suni. I reasoned that if I did not use any alcohol in the drink, and I still collected money for it, I could somehow save that money and return it to Mr. Suni's wife, Chachee. I justified not giving any money to Mr. Bovier for the drink for the same reason—there was no alcohol in it. Mr. Suni would be happy; Chachee would be elated. Mr. Bovier would be none the poorer and I would have accomplished a good deed. It seemed so simple.

I set about making the drink. I poured water, squeezed lime, added a bit of pepper sauce and finished it off with a touch of Trinidad's own esteemed Angostura Bitters. Once the drink was manufactured, I presented it to Mr. Suni.

"Mr. Suni, I made you a special drink. It's really good."

He handed me a shilling which I promptly placed on the counter so that I could give it to Chachee.

Mr. Suni downed the drink in one swallow. He did not flinch a single muscle.

"That was some drink, Frankie," was all he said before heading to the exit. He never made it to the door. He crashed to the floor.

I ran over to him. There was no sign of life in him at all. I thought that I had killed him. In my mind, I was already having visions of Hell opening its doors to receive me, for surely Heaven's gates would be closed to a sinner such as I. Desperately, I tried to revive him. Nothing worked. Suddenly, I remembered that Mr. Bovier was just upstairs. I ran upstairs, screaming.

"Mr. Bovier, Mr. Suni is dead. I killed Mr. Suni."

Mr. Bovier responded to my cries immediately and he rushed downstairs. Very calmly he ordered, "Frankie, get me a bucket of water."

I did not know how a bucket of water was going to get Mr. Suni to not be dead anymore, but I hastened to comply with the request.

Upon receiving the water, Mr. Bovier threw the contents of the bucket in Mr. Suni's face.

Mr. Suni sputtered, looked shocked, and somewhat annoyed when he saw Mr. Bovier and the empty bucket. Then, he saw me.

"Ah, Frankie, tell you what. That was the best god damn drink I ever had. Frankie, yo is a good man."

My fears of going to Hell for having killed Mr. Suni were put to rest.

10

MA AND PA

W<small>E WERE</small> a family of twelve: Ma and Pa, four boys and six girls. All twelve of us lived in a modest two bedroom wooden house. My father, the male head of the house, ruled supremely; even when—especially when—he was generously "re-freshed." As poor as Pa was, as far as I can remember, he always man-aged to have a drink when he wanted one. This propensity to drink did not however, distinguish him from any of the other males in our neighbourhood. While Pa obtained his refreshments with relative ease, he often had great difficulty providing sufficient food for his family. This placed a heavy burden on Ma as she struggled to take care of us. Ma always managed to find ingenious ways to provide for our needs. With the flour, rice and beans that Pa laboured to secure, Ma would add a tomato, or onion, or some other vegetable to create a visually appealing meal. Meat made rare appearances at our table. When meat was available, it would almost always be chicken. Ma could stretch that one chicken and make it last for two meals for our large family. There was no waste. Every part of that chicken was rationed precisely; even the liver, heart and gizzard were used.

It seemed such a special treat when Ma would call each of us and offer each one a small taste. Naturally we felt special—even first class. Ma was a generous and gentle soul and she never complained about having to work hard in her makeshift kitchen. The kitchen, about a foot lower than the rest of the house, was located at the back end of our home. Everything was basic but clean. The walls were constructed from mud and straw and the fireside /cooking area was on the floor. It was made up of rocks fitted in such a way that a pot could rest comfortably on them about ten inches from the base of the stones. There was an opening at the front of this make-shift stove. Ma would insert pieces of wood through this opening to fuel the fire. To ignite the wood, Ma used a match and an eighteen inch length of metal pipe which we called *pooknee*. She would blow gently through the pipe and eventually produce a flame. It is this image of Ma, crouched and intent, endlessly engaged in the task of cooking, that is captured in my memory.

Ma was modest and unpretentious. She wore a simple skirt and top. An *orni*, a light-weight length of cloth, was tucked into one side of her skirt at the waist, and then gently draped over her head and neatly tucked into the other side of her skirt again at the waist.

If Ma was not in the kitchen preparing meals for her family, she was outside consumed by the onerous task of doing the family laundry. This chore was accomplished by using large wooden or metal tubs and a corrugated washboard. The tubs stood on wooden planks in the back yard. And there Ma stooped, scrubbing the clothes against the ridges of the washboard, time and time again. When the washing process was complete, she began the task of hanging the clothes. A simple rope line, strung between two trees held the freshly washed articles. It was there on that makeshift line, that our clothes blew in the wind, rivaling one another for the sunlight. Those memories bring with them a special recognition of my mother– forever hardworking, but forever smiling. I wondered how anyone could ever disrespect this kind and loving soul. But I knew that someone had. That someone was Pa.

An incident involving crab perhaps best depicts Pa's callous disregard for Ma and her family.

Often, my father would come home from work irritable and agitated. One day stands out from the rest. This day happened to coincide with a time when my mother's parents (Nana and Nani) paid us a surprise visit.

When they came this day, they did not come empty-handed. They brought the family's favourite treat, crab. While my brothers and sisters were overjoyed to receive this gift, my mother was especially happy and relieved because it solved her problem of what to serve for dinner that evening. There was very little food in the pantry, and until her parents arrived, Ma had been stressing over how she would provide for her family. Ma wasted no time preparing the crab.

I, however, did not share the family's enthusiasm for this delicacy. I could not bear the cracking sound that escaped during the eating process, nor could I stomach the raucous sucking noises made when the meat was inhaled from the bones. Worse still was the fact that I had to contain my displeasure while being required to remain at the table and suffer in silence. I suffered while the choir of crab worshipers harmonized their vibrations in the collective ravaging of the principal feature of the feast, the crab.

Ma, noticing Pa's displeasure when he arrived home, tried to lighten his mood by announcing that she had prepared his favourite meal for him. My father, was not about to be coaxed out of his foul temper. He insisted that he had no "favourite" and attempted to walk up the two steps from the kitchen to the dining room. He failed. He ended up crumpled in a heap on the floor; the lower half of his body sprawled in the kitchen and the upper half spanned the steps into the dining area. Ma recognized immediately that her husband had once again overly indulged his penchant to drink and was now intoxicated.

Ma reached out to help Pa but he brushed her aside with the usual arsenal of invectives. This time he extended the range of vitriolic comments to include Ma's parents.

Ma quietly admonished him. "Why are you cussing my parents like that? They brought us supper. They brought us crab."

This comment, no matter how gently spoken, served only to increase Pa's agitation.

"Well, f*** the crab! And "f*** your parents too!"

And, in an instant, he reached up for the pot of crab.

Now, in my innocence, when I saw Pa reach for the crab, I assumed that he was most eager and impatient to begin eating.

I was mistaken.

Pa grabbed that pot and tossed the whole container through the open window onto the bare earth outside.

Without thinking, and driven perhaps by pure instinct, I grabbed an empty bowl from the table and bolted outside where the once delectable dinner now lay strewn on the ground.

Quickly, I set about rescuing what I could. I managed to recover enough for the family. The dinner was still warm. No one needed to be coaxed to the table.

Ma went into the kitchen to check on Pa.

"Oh, my gawd!" she yelled. "Come, help me!"

Recognizing an urgency in her voice, we all ran into the kitchen. What a sight! There was Pa, passed out in the middle of the kitchen floor clutching tightly to his empty bottle of rum.

We helped Ma get Pa out of the kitchen and in to bed. With him safely tucked away, everyone went back to enjoy the feast.

Perhaps because I played a role in the rescue, that crab eating session seemed somewhat less challenging to my sensibilities. Or, perhaps my brothers and sisters curtailed their individual appetites as some small measure of recognition for my role in salvaging their supper.

This effect, however, was limited to that one set of circumstances. Thereafter, whenever crab was served at our table, I was allowed to excuse myself so that all would be free to indulge their appetites.

That incident ended rather well. Events involving my father and alcohol were not always that innocuous. My father was not someone to be trifled with after he had been drinking. His inane disrespect for Ma continued.

I remember a time when Ma had gone to the cinema with my sisters to see a special movie. She had consulted with Pa before she went so he was perfectly aware of her plans. After returning home from the movies, Ma was radiant. It was rare to see Ma that happy. Something in Pa exploded and he upbraided Ma and accused her of going to the movies with another man! This was an utterly stupid accusation. To accuse Ma of all people, was simply unfathomable. I did entertain thoughts that my father was mad.

On more than one occasion, Ma suffered at the hand of Pa. On days when Pa was not getting enough work, he came home troubled and angry. On such days, he would have already befriended the bottle. It fed him its poison. Many a time, Master Poison lay beside Brother Rage. On this particular day, Pa came home and began the process of unharnessing the mule. Pa brushed the mule with steel combs, carelessly touching a sensitive spot– an old injury laid bare. The poor mule reacted violently and frantically kicked out in all directions. Pa was struck below the belt.

Perhaps his *precious privates* had been greeted.

Pa responded. He was determined to show this lowly animal who was the master. He staggered towards the cart and pulled a wooden piquet from its mooring. Pa proceeded to deliver an unending volley of blows to the soft hind flesh of the mule.

It was at this unfortunate moment that Ma appeared with her untimely and unwelcome questions.

"What are you doing to that poor animal?" she cried.

Pa, clearly agitated by what seemed to be a challenge, threatened, "Get inside, Woman. I am not in the mood for your interference."

Ma moved toward the house in compliance and began to climb the steps to the open gallery. Upon reaching the top step, she turned to Pa and hesitantly offered, "I have to buy groceries today and I don't have no money. Today is payday. Right?"

"Right!" he screamed back at her. Then he continued, "I will show you money– "

Pa then made his way up the steps and entered the living room. As usual, he had to establish his manly prowess. He looked around, and there, in the china cabinet, lay Ma's priceless set of china. It was used on rare occasions only and for very special guests. To Ma's horror, Pa grabbed the dishes and one by one he smashed them to the ground all the while swearing like a madman. One would have thought that such a violent act would have served to satisfy his manhood. Such was not the case. Pa's appetite was far from satiated. The dishes had been but an appetizer. He knew that Ma treasured something far beyond the dishes. Ma idolized a china teapot. This was kept on display on top of the china cabinet. Pa knew how much Ma cherished this. He reached up and grabbed the pot.

Ma, fearing what was about to happen, became distraught and pleaded, "Budricks! No! Please, don't..."

It was almost as though he took a particular delight in her torment and with an apish move, he held the pot high overhead and wildly declared, "Here, Woman, is my money!"

Once again Pa's uncontrollable rage reigned supreme and Ma's treasured pot was smashed beyond repair; itself a victim of my father's fury.

We were transfixed. We all stared at Pa in disbelief. A chorus of questioning voices banded together echoing similar concerns to the master of the house. To Pa, each voice must have seemed to be challenging not only his rationality but also his authority.

Pa, blinded by rage, reacted once again predictably, with violence. His voice thundered, "Now, I will teach all of you– every one of you– a lesson not to talk to me that way!"

He reached out and grabbed the nearest chair and threw it squarely at one of the smallest children. The chair splintered. A child fell to the ground and remained there, motionless. Blood began to pool about the helpless form.

Pa reclaimed a portion of the broken chair and moved in position to challenge the next nearest child. Ma dashed forward with one arm extended to envelop and protect the child. With her other arm she absorbed the blow intended for the small victim. Pa stumbled backward and grabbed another piece of the broken chair. The young ones rallied to Ma as she railed against the onslaught of the raging blows.

"Go ahead. Kill us all! Have your way!" screamed Ma in desperation.

So stood my mother, a mother amongst mothers, and took the blows that this deranged and blind father meted out.

And soon, this father, once steeped in poison and consumed in rage, standing defiant and uncontrollable, fell to the ground in utter exhaustion.

A disconcerting quiet descended. A new dawn of terror washed over us. The terrible vision would haunt my memory forever:

The cries of a mother
Shielding her children
Against a monstrous onslaught.
Defenseless.
Courageous.
Certainly my Ma stood
A Mother amongst Mothers!

I have often wondered what factors precipitated my father's occasional descent into madness. Was poverty the sole culprit? Pa never seemed to be able to earn enough to feed and clothe his large family. He tried, but far too often he relied for strength on his bosom companion, a bottle of cheap rum. I suspect that Pa's reliance on the bottle had more to do with these outbursts than the mere fact that we were poor.

Pa and the bottle were often inseparable. When life became too burdensome, Mr. Bottle—Mr. Poison– would come to Pa's aid and, unwittingly, my father would surrender his soul to the poison.

On one occasion when Pa was relatively sober I encountered a scene which shocked my soul and forever changed my perception of my world.

On this particular day, I awakened early and decided to surprise everyone by doing my chores before everyone arose. I headed out to clean up the yard. The sun was bright and warm; a beautiful day was unfolding.

The Prayer

Sunrise—A Beautiful Day Dawns
One half of the town is rising
The other half is already stirred.
Somewhere very close are grating sounds
Blasphemous and crude;
They are incarnate voices—
These can be heard miles away
And the Morning's Peace is broken—not merely shattered.
Nature's faithful voices withdraw
From these grating sounds
In the near distance their joint
Lament echoes in the early morn.

My father is up
He comes outside to the front
He carries a kind of urn
It is filled with water and fresh flowers
He is half dressed from the waist down
Both hands clasp the urn
He stands beside a sacred site
Faces the East—the Rising Sun
And chants ever so softly.
A lovely scene.

Then he raises the Urn above his head
And whispers aloud to the warming Sun,
"Lord Rama, oh, Lord Rama–
Greater God—Listen to me," he pleads.
"You gave me all these children,
So many
I cannot mind them;
I have no money for food.
I cannot get work enough to feed them.
So,
If you can take them from my hands—one by one–
I will find a way to bury them, one by one.
I promise."

"No! No!" was my silent scream.
Then he chanted,
"Omm Shanti, Shanti."
And poured out the watery contents of the Urn
Onto the sacredness of the bare Earth.
Then,
Father withdrew,
Hands beating rhythmically across his chest.

Mesmerized, I stood
Eyes raised to the Heavens
I pleaded–
"Lord—please let me live.
I know that I am but a child,
But please let Death turn away.
This is my prayer."

Alone what hope is there
Against the prayer of a Larger than Life Father!
Surely God does not favour the child over the parent
I reasoned.
A death-like silence stole over me as I realized that
I was going to die –
We children were all going to die.
Because
That was Pa's wish!

I felt so sad.
I wanted to live –

Is it not amazing that God
Does not always grant prayers?
And thank God for that.
He surely listens,
But reasons,
And decides.
And therefore,
God
Presides.

11

MY GRANDPARENTS

As a young child, I spent many memorable days with my grandparents who lived in the mountains. My grandmother, Nani, and my grandfather, Nana, had a young son, Kisson. The remarkable thing about Kisson, is that although technically he was my uncle, he was one year younger than I. Because Kisson was at least ten years younger than his nearest sibling, the only boy and the youngest child, my grandparents were always trying to entice one of the grandchildren to spend time with him in the country. On many occasions, I would be asked, and I was always willing and happy to visit my grandparents.

Life in the country was always an adventure and Uncle and I got along fabulously. I followed his lead and imitated his every move. There were no modern conveniences such as running water in their home. My grandmother collected rain water in a tank and that water was used judiciously for drinking and cooking only. About a quarter of a mile away there was a tiny stream which boasted fresh clean water. It was there that Uncle and I often bathed. On most days we accompanied Nana to work in the field where he cultivated various crops. Cocoa, coffee, bananas, oranges were among the crops planted. Nani always packed delicious lunches that were both generous and delicious. Uncle and I played amongst the trees on the fields, a freedom rarely felt in town. It was this carefree attitude that lured me to the country. Amidst these lighthearted moments were born flashes of sobering life lessons.

Uncle and I indulged in a carelessness that worried Nana. While walking to the field, we would often notice trees laden with fruit. Playfully, we would pick the ripe fruit. We especially liked the cocoa tree for it was not too tall, and when the branches were plentiful, they easily bent themselves. It was not difficult for us to reach those lovely cocoa shells– resplendent in marvelous hues of gold, orange, and crimson. Inside the ripened cocoa shell soft tissues surrounded the beans. These appeared sweet and luscious and seemed to invite our attention. We quite naturally picked many such cocoa. If the chosen fruit was not sweetened to our particular taste, we simply tossed it aside. We did this habitually until, one day we were corrected.

Uncle grabbed at a branch and lowered it. We wanted one particular cocoa that was located high on the branch. Without restraint or care, we pulled at the branch until it broke. We took the cocoa we had targeted, thoughtlessly ignoring the broken branch filled with many other cocoa.

Nana did not yell at us. He called us to come and sit. Usually Nana would tell us engaging stories about wild animals or stories about the dead that became the *undead*. We were starved for another such story.

Previously, Nana had recounted a story about a huge snake. According to our grandfather, this snake had the ability to imitate a log. After a long hike through the mountains, tired children would quite naturally want to sit and rest on what they thought was a log. If the child who sat upon that particular "log" was one who was not respectful to elders, then the consequences to that child would be fatal. Nana warned that the snake could sense the child's disrespect and would suddenly come alive and swallow the child. This story, and others like it, affected me greatly and I tried hard to be obedient.

We were expecting another fascinating story when Nana began to address us. Nana, however, engaged us in a story with a powerful life lesson.

Nana began, "Frankie, Kisson, you like cocoa very much."

"Yes," we affirmed.

"You get excited and break the branches..."

"Yes, but..."

"You know, you are not just damaging the trees when you do that. You are also damaging your own selves."

"But, how?" we wondered.

"Well, you are making 'Bad' for your own selves." Nana's somber tone caused an immediate quiet in us. Our carefree spirits faded and we listened attentively.

"You see, Frankie and Kisson," Grandfather explained, "after you die, you will return to Earth. The question is, will you come back as a human or will you come back as an animal?"

Both Kisson and I were in a state of quiet shock. Grandpa knew our minds only too well. We said nothing. He continued in this serious manner. He raised his hand and pointed directly at us. "Everyone dies, yes, and everyone has to face the Scales of Justice. God keeps two scales," Nana continued. "On one scale is placed everything that you do that is bad. Every goodness that you do is placed on the other scale. At death, the scales are tallied. If you have done more bad things than good things, you are returned to Earth to pay for the bad things you did. God knows and sees everything. If some of these things are really bad, then you will be sent back as an animal– an animal that has to work hard. And when you harm and damage things, well then you are adding this damage on yourself, you see, because God puts it all on the scale of the Bad."

We were silent. Something inexplicable was happening to us. We did not quite know it then but, our grown-up consciences were taking root.

"You understand now," Nana clarified, "the world was put here so we could use it and everything in it for a good. We are all connected. We are connected for the cause of goodness."

I am not sure how much of Nana's teachings I fully comprehended, but one thing I understood clearly—be good, think good.

As Uncle and I went about our regular activities we were very quiet and subdued. When late afternoon came, Nana gathered up everything and we began to make preparations for the trip back home to Nani. Nana reached into the sack on the back of the donkey and pulled out a gun. A moment later he fired a shot and a huge bird fell to the ground. It landed in a ditch that was encircled by jagged rocks. Nana carefully managed his way down the ditch to claim the bird. "Supper will be a treat tonight," he mused as he raised the bird in our direction. Then he added, "Kill only if you need to, for food, yes, not for fun. And remember, you are not to wound an animal and leave it to suffer. If you do, you will suffer too."

Nani was waiting for us when we arrived home and a pot of boiling hot water awaited the bird. As Nana had pointed out, we were in for a treat and that bird became a spicy gourmet feast. Visiting my grandparents certainly had its advantages. I indulged myself fully.

Good eating was not my grandparents' only indulgence. They also feasted on cigarettes. Nani was especially indulgent. She smoked endlessly. She did, however, point out the ills of smoking. The contradiction between her actions and her admonitions was not lost on us as children. But, still we strived to obey.

Each morning, Nani had a habit of throwing out her cigarette butts into the yard. One day, Uncle and I picked up one that was still burning. We carried it away from the house to a clearing behind the trees. The cigarette went out and Uncle and I took turns trying to relight it. We were frustrated with our attempts and we returned to the house feeling defeated and disappointed. Later on, we watched attentively as Nani took a smoke break outside on a little wooden bench. We memorized every movement she made. Between the two of us, we felt that we had mastered the smoking concept. Later that day, we asked Nani if we could go to the stream to bathe and to collect water for use in the kitchen. Nani consented.

We completely abandoned the idea of trying to smoke cigarette butts. Instead we adopted a bold plan. Since Nani kept a generous collection of cigarettes on hand to sell to her neighbours, Uncle and I decided to take a whole pack of fresh cigarettes for ourselves. We reasoned (wrongly) that she would not notice that one single pack was missing.

Together, Uncle and I headed for the stream, pails in hand. We reached the stream in record time and we quickly assumed our favourite spots near the water. I favoured the rock that edged the path from the road. From there I dangled my feet in the coolness of the stream. Uncle sat on a jagged rock directly opposite me. From his position, he had direct command of the path leading down to the stream. This was critical because we needed someone to be watchful once the cigarettes were brought out from their hiding place. Uncle passed me a cigarette. We had both matches and cigarettes.

Nani had made it look so easy. Put the cigarette into your mouth. Light a match and apply it to the end of the cigarette. This strategy did not seem to work for us. We must have emptied half a book of matches without having any success lighting a single cigarette. We did not inhale. We puffed out. Then, suddenly, I began to cough. I had inhaled inadvertently and had begun to smoke. I shared my discovery with Uncle. "Don't puff. Breathe in." Soon Uncle was coughing too. We were deliriously happy with our success and were shouting excitedly to one another. Suddenly, Uncle's face became statuesque. His mouth hung open and his eyes stared at an area behind me. Completely dumb, he raised his hand and pointed a finger in the direction of the path. Curious, I looked back. I was not prepared for what I saw.

There was Nani. She stood behind me with a white veil covering her head. The light colouring of her clothes and veil, combined against the scattering light that managed to filter through the trees, suggested a vision sprung from the heavens with the express purpose to right a wrong.

Her eyes pierced right through me. She spoke one single word and it cut me deeply. "Frankie."

I froze.

Nani walked away.

Kisson and I rushed after her. She walked faster. She said nothing.

Nani had cared for us and had provided for us. We had disappointed her greatly. We were ashamed.

Nani kept her distance. Her silence thundered. Our pleadings got us nowhere. Some days elapsed before Nani again spoke to us.

Thus ended my childhood flirtation with smoking.

12

SHOES

WHEN SHE was but fifteen, my mother was given in marriage to my father. The marriage was an arranged one, and my mother had no real voice in the matter. My father had been married previously but his wife died, leaving him alone to raise their only son, Clive who was just four years old.

It is my understanding that three years earlier, when Ma was barely twelve years old, she had been given in marriage to another young man from the village. She was sent to the other family to live and work as a daughter until such a time when she could assume the role of a wife. That twelve year old child could not fully comprehend her new station in life and became so visibly distressed and emotionally despondent that she was returned to her parents' home and the marriage was cancelled.

By the time she turned fifteen three years later, when the next offer of marriage was received, she was pronounced ready to be married. She entered into this second relationship understanding that there would be no option to go back home. This time the decision was irreversible. This too she also understood very clearly. She dared not shame her family twice in one lifetime. And so, at the still fragile age of fifteen, my mother stepped into the role of both wife and mother. By the time she was sixteen, Ma had her own first baby, a girl named Dolly.

Eighteen months later, another baby was born; this time it was a boy she named Boysie. Sixteen months later, I was born, her second son. Paula, Pinky, Kay, Basdaye, Kalie and finally, Suresh followed. There were two to three years between each of these children. Altogether, including Clive, we accounted for ten children.

Generally speaking, we were happy. Ma took great pride in caring for *all* her children. She took pains to ensure that we always had clean clothes to wear when we were out in public and that we were well-mannered. When we were very young children, we were accustomed to having very few amenities, and we were oblivious to the fact that we were lacking certain necessities.

Many would consider shoes a necessity. In our home they were a luxury. I went through four grades at school without ever having a pair to call my own.

One day my fourth grade teacher called me aside. There was a seriousness in her voice when she addressed me. There was a gentle earnestness in her tone. She did not want to embarrass me by making her request in front of the rest of the class. Her requirement was simple.

"Frankie, you have to wear shoes to school."

I assured my teacher that I would carry her message home to my mother that very day.

Upon arriving home, I went directly to my mother who was outside in the yard doing the laundry for we had no convenience of a washing machine in our home. In fact at that time we did not have even the small luxury of indoor plumbing. We had no taps indoors.

Water was brought daily from a public tap located on the street. My mother would bring water by the bucket to fill a wooden half barrel in which she first soaked and then scrubbed our clothes. From there, she would hang the clothes on an outside line to dry in the sun. These are the strongest images of Ma. Always working. Always struggling to provide for her family.

"Ma, Teacher says I must now wear shoes to school."

Ma ceased her scrubbing and simply said, "Okay, Son. I will try to see. Now you go on..." She turned her head away, quickly.

Was she crying? There was an emotion about her that I recognized as sadness. Upon reflection, I realized that my request must have caused her a great deal of pain and anxiety. She simply did not have the means to provide me with shoes. There was never enough money to provide for all our needs let alone extra money to secure a pair of shoes. The knowledge that she could not fully provide for her children must have weighed heavily on her heart. The simplicity of my request brought that reality painfully forward.

That very evening, however, my father approached me and there, in his hands, was a pair of shoes; they were worn-out adult shoes, but they were shoes.

"Frankie, wear these to school," he barked.

There was no discussion. No questions. The shoes were huge. I knew that I would be teased if I were to wear them. But, I had no choice in the matter. When your teacher says that you need shoes, and your father puts himself out to secure you a pair and commands you to wear them, you have but one option. You must wear the shoes.

The next day, just as I had predicted, I became the centre of attention. Again, I was to be set apart from the rest of my peers. It was not enough that I was a heathen and a Hindu attending a Catholic school, now I was a heathen and a Hindu in oversized shoes attending a Catholic school.

What a sight I must have been. "Flip flop, flip flop," went the shoes.

In the beginning, only mild amusement was expressed. But, as more people became aware of my condition, a chorus of abuse quickly escalated into a choir of ridicule. I felt like a trapped animal. I had no way out and I was forced to endure the merciless taunting until such a time as they grew tired of their own jokes.

I yearned for a way out. I yearned for a life less harsh. My mind wondered if there would ever come a day when the phrase "daily bread" indeed meant bread on a daily basis. I wondered if I would ever have a real table and real chairs to sit on. I wondered, moreover, if the concept of a life without cussing and swearing, a life without yelling and constant chaos could ever exist for me. Above all, I wondered if a world without "belts" could ever become a reality.

Could children ever truly find a safe haven: a place free from the harsh punishments and criticisms conferred on them daily by over stressed parents and overly critical peers. I claimed this idyllic picture for my soul. It became the driving force behind my need to escape this reality and create a new world. High school was the vehicle I needed to achieve that end. I simply had to make it. There was no other option.

13

MR. LATISSE

MY MIDDLE years at high school were marked by its own set of experiences. My early years, both at home and at school were marked by fear. My teachers were masters of this technique. My third grade teacher was a woman of massive size and she towered over her students. When she strode down the aisle she commanded attention. The ruler that she carried constantly ensured our obedience. That ruler was an integral part of her methodology when she began teaching us the times tables. As she walked around the classroom she would instruct us to repeat after her the facts of the times tables. At any given moment she would stop dead in her tracks and wage a surprise attack with her ruler on some unsuspecting desktop and demand an immediate answer to a times table fact from the unfortunate student who occupied the desk that had just come under siege. Her unpredictable antics often left us bereft of our senses. To demand an instant response to the thundering ruler seemed to me an unreasonable request, and many times I panicked and stuttered some unintelligible response. On such occasions the teacher would reach out with lightning speed, grasp me by the hand, and administer several lashes of the ruler across my knuckles. It was amazing how quickly one's knuckles grew under such circumstances.

That strap was an indispensable appendage for almost every teacher. I never would dream of going home to complain about my teacher's actions. To do so would have invited the wrath of my parents, especially my father's. This was a lesson I had learned very early in life.

Pa, had made this pronouncement repeatedly. "The teacher is right, always right-unless he draws blood." Put another way, any teacher can discipline any of Pa's children by any means. The teachers could slap, whip, strap, belt or otherwise hit any of the children and Pa would not object. They would have his support. The one exception was this—no teacher could administer such punishment if the end outcome of that punishment resulted in the drawing of one drop of blood.

One day, my brother Boysie, tested this edict and nearly got my father jailed.

My brother and I happened to be in the same grade even though we were a year apart in age. Mr. Latisse was the class teacher. He was so conservative, so proper. He lined the walls of his class with his famous slogans: Speech is Silver, Silence is Golden; Waste Not, Want Not; Cleanliness is next to Godliness. He had his own peculiar tendency to correct his students without a word of reproach. He would simply glare at the offending student and then direct the student's gaze to the particular saying that represented the remedy for the offence. He would then go to the blackboard and write a number on the board. That number, somewhere from one hundred to one thousand, represented the number of times the student had to write out the chosen phrase. If the student was caught talking, then that student would be required to write out: Speech is Silver, Silence is Golden. Mr. Latisse's class was well governed. He ran a tight ship and every student towed the line. Such a well-oiled ship had to be tested sooner or later and my brother and his friends were just the ones to do the testing. They did not care for Mr. Latisse and his methods. This captain and his ship were about to encounter a bit of a tempest.

Our classroom desks were built to house inkwells. One corner of each desk had a hole in it and in each hold was place a small container of ink. (Ball point pens were not yet widely available on the island.) Our pens had nibs which were dipped into the inkwells before being used to scribe on our papers. It is the inkwell that was to become the focal point of the next adventure in which my brother and his cronies played an integral part. These boys contrived a plan of which I was totally ignorant. They came to school early, exceptionally early for them. Finally, the morning routines began. The students entered the class and settled down awaiting the arrival of the teacher. Mr. Latisse arrived, dressed as always in an impeccable manner. That day he wore a white shirt, cream trousers and a maroon tie. Everything appeared normal.

Soon everyone became aware of a foul smell. We discovered that the distasteful odour was emanating from our very own desks. Indeed, it was coming from *our very own* inkwells. We soon discovered that these wells did not contain ink at all. What was the liquid in the well? Mr. Latisse knew and instantly he became agitated.

"Silence," he demanded. An uneasy quiet descended on the room. I was petrified. Mr. Latisse stared at my inkwell and thundered, "Who done it? Who put *pee* in the inkwells? I want to know!"

No answer was forthcoming. This increased his agitation. "Last chance, tell me," he ordered and then he began inspecting the faces of several students. Suddenly, he leaned towards me, his eyes blazing with fury and exclaimed, "Frankie, who done it!"

I was so frightened by his demeanor that I almost had an accident in my pants. I was exceedingly glad that I had no prior knowledge of the events. I was so afraid that I must have appeared guilty. "You know something, Frankie. If you don't tell me you are going to Hell. There you will burn. You want Hell, Frankie?" he threatened.

I managed a, "No, no, Sir."

He then singled out others without success. Soon, the usually cool, calculated and sophisticated Mr. Latisse was clearly exasperated. He had become a raging force.

"Line up!" he yelled. Fear gripped our hearts as Mr. Latisse grabbed his strap. At first, he brandished the strap with great energy and commanded, "Not a bloody whisper from any of you."

Each student felt his unusual strength as he claimed vengeance on our diminutive forms. I received his 'blessings' on my arms and hands. Others were not that lucky. Their behinds bore the sting of his punishment and they were unable to sit for days. We all endured our thrashings obediently and without so much as a whimper. We did, however, wonder who the culprits were. Never would I have thought that my brother, Boysie, was part of the conspiracy. But he was. Indeed, he was the ringleader.

On my way home from school that day I overheard my brother talking with his friends. They were evaluating the fairness of what had transpired that day in Mr. Latisse's class.

One reasoned, "He had no right to beat the class—the whole class."

Another lamented, "He not fair."

A third commented, "We can't tell our parents."

Then, came the unmistakable voice of my brother, "Tell you what fellas, we have to teach the teacher a lesson." His suggestion was met with a chorus of voices all in the affirmative. I was in shock. My own brother was plotting against a teacher.

I pondered on the day's events and wondered if I should tell my father. If I revealed what I knew Pa could easily misconstrue my intentions and think that I was merely trying to get my older brother into trouble. Since I was raised with the admonition to obey my elders (this included older brothers and sisters: and yes, even Boysie) I decided to do nothing.

Some time elapsed without incident. School life returned to normal. Mr. Latisse once again enjoyed a calm nature in his class. This, however, was short lived.

One day, my brother and his cohorts went to school early. Not one of them bore a look of suspicion. At the beginning of class, Mr. Latisse as usual was comfortably seated in his chair at his desk looking over some papers. The class was engaged in playful chatter when Mr. Latisse pronounced that class had officially started. He made an effort to rise from his chair in order to stand before the class with more authority.

He could not.

His chair was stuck to him both at the seat and the back. His consternation was exceeded only by his awkwardness. The glue that was used in this prank was not just normal glue. It was potent. It was locally made from the sap of our local trees. It was used to catch birds because the sap, called *lagley*, was extremely strong. Once a bird's foot stepped into the glue, the bird was securely fastened in place. So too, Mr. Latisse. The more he struggled, the worse his predicament became. The back of his pristine white shirt showed signs of being shredded. His trousers were damaged beyond repair.

Mr. Latisse's face turned purple first from embarrassment and then with rage. Once again, I was seized with fear for this time I had an additional anxiety. I did not definitively know that my brother, Boysie, was guilty, yet I sensed that he was involved. I was paralyzed by the fear that if Mr. Latisse were to ask me any questions, I would have to confess that I suspected that my brother shared some measure of complicity in the affair. Such an admission would be considered as an act of treason by my brother and his cohorts. One could only imagine the terrible punishment that would befall me after such and act.

I was spared.

One student was uncovered and he subsequently turned in the others. Boysie was among this famous group. Their bodies were duly sacrificed to the strap. I thought that this punishment would have been sufficient to tame the wild nature of my brother. I was wrong.

14

MR. CLOUT

BOYSIE'S REBELLIOUS nature surfaced once again the following year in the classroom of Mr. Clout, a man whose average frame contained an enormous temper.

Boysie did not embrace the academic life. He did very little work preferring to pursue the worldly life with a religious fervour. He loved friends. He especially loved friends who were equally indisposed to liking school. Boysie longed to be free of school and its shackles and regarded the act of going to school as a total waste of time. Teachers who lectured the class on the virtues of a good life, a life that could be obtained by staying in school and working hard, were easily dismissed by my brother. My brother doubted the teacher's ability to really know life. He usually concluded that he, himself, knew more about life than the teacher.

Mr. Clout and Boysie did not get along. Mr. Clout was intensely fond of humiliating his students. He was Mr. Right.

One day, Boysie accomplished little in class. When questioned by Mr. Clout about his lack of effort, Boysie responded in a surly manner and as a result, was strapped. Relations between the two became increasingly strained and soon escalated to a new level. Mr. Clout accused Boysie of some infraction. While Boysie may have been guilty in the past, this time he was innocent. Mr. Clout, believing himself to be right, whipped Boysie in a fit of rage. Boysie swore and left the classroom. Once outside the classroom, Boysie found a heap of rocks and stones which he began throwing angrily at the wall of the classroom. The wall was not a solid construction. It was covered in something much like chicken wire to act as ventilation for the classroom.

The rocks that Boysie threw at the wall were too large to penetrate the wire and therefore posed no real threat to us or the teacher. Mr. Clout however, felt attacked. He ducked instinctively each time a rock was thrown. He became infuriated. Boysie did not return to class that day. Further punishment would have to be deferred until the next day.

The following morning, after class was started, Mr. Clout summoned Boysie to the front of the class. He reached into his desk for his strap. It was missing. An awkward silence followed the movements of our teacher as he checked the other drawers.

A voice rang out from the back of the class. "Mr. Clout, I could get you a tambran whip!" The voice belonged to Godwin, Boysie's friend. Immediately, I became suspicious. Something was not quite right.

Mr. Clout regarded Godwin carefully then asked, "Can you get me a strong whip?"

"Yes, Sir," came the glad reply. He added, "And, I promise it won't break. It will be strong. You will be able to use it."

Clout was pleased. Excitedly, he dismissed Godwin and instructed him to get the whip for him right away. Godwin paused and made one final request. "Sir," he said, "I need a climber. I do not climb trees. I need someone to do that for me." Before anyone could respond, Godwin offered, "Boysie is a good climber. Send him with me. Sir, let him cut his own whip."

The irony of the situation gave Mr. Clout much pleasure and he ordered Boysie to go with Godwin and get a strong whip. Boysie appeared reluctant. "I ain't gonna get my own whip," he muttered under his breath.

"You will go!" thundered Mr. Clout as he approached Boysie menacingly.

None of this was making any sense to me. Godwin was our friend. How could he voluntarily assist in Boysie's whipping? Boysie was the type of person who would find a way to get even. I foresaw trouble, trouble between friends. I could not have foreseen, however, the kind of trouble that was about to unfold.

Godwin and Boysie returned. Boysie was in ill humour, muttering god knows what under his breath. Mr. Clout, hearing the utterance, challenged Boysie. "Did you just cuss in class, Boysie?"

"No bloody way," defended Boysie.

"You have quite an attitude, Mr. Boysie," baited Clout.

"Well, it's my attitude, not yours," defied Boysie.

Those words sealed Boysie's fate. There was no turning back now.

Stout accepted the whip from Godwin's outstretched hand. Godwin was smiling. I wondered how he could betray Boysie like that. Clout examined the whip, flexed it and found it satisfactory.

Boysie stood alone. He wore a look of pure misery.

"Boysie, put your hand out!" commanded a confident Clout. There was no movement, only silence. "Boysie, I said, 'Put your bloody hand out!" yelled an increasingly irate Clout.

Boysie moved his hand ever so slightly and slowly. It was not that Boysie was openly defiant; he was just not readily compliant. By now an agitated Clout grabbed Boysie's hand, stretched it out and admonished him to hold it there.

Clout had a firm grasp on the whip and prepared to deliver his first blow. By now, Boysie's hand was on the way down and it escaped the full power of the blow. The intended result had not been achieved. An obviously frustrated Clout forced Boysie's hand back in place with and order to keep it there. Boysie complied. Clout delivered a lash across the palm of Boysie's hand that would have made the bravest of us flinch. Boysie did not move a muscle. A hint of a smile played about his lips. Just as Clout was about to administer the next blow, Boysie challenged, "Mr. Clout, yo can do better that that, can't yo?"

Clout rose to the challenge. He raised the whip even higher in the air, and, pulling himself up to his full height, delivered such a cutting whip across Boysie's palm that the whole class gasped in horror. We were afraid for Boysie. Yet, Boysie appeared fearless. He came near to Mr. Clout and flashed him a grin. "Yo kidding me. Is that all yo got?"

Clout went berserk. He strapped Boysie continuously. Time after time he struck him. The punishment seemed endless. Suddenly there was a crack. The whip snapped. Its final blow penetrated Boysie's skin and a single drop of blood was shed.

Mr. Clout ceased his attack. I'll never forget that scene. Clout was visibly distraught. Boysie was eerily composed. Boysie approached Clout at his desk and hurled these parting words, "More to come. It ain't ended yet."

After school, I discovered Boysie and Godwin together. Neither boy could contain his excitement. An elated Godwin spoke, "You got him, Boysie. It worked better than we planned."

"What plan?" I asked, revealing myself.

Then came the unveiling of the plot. The boys had devised a scheme to ensure that Mr. Clout would lose his temper while punishing Boysie. Together they scored the *tambran* whip every six inches, virtually ensuring that it would break. They anticipated that Clout's rage would cause him to hit Boysie hard enough to leave scars and bloody marks on his skin. When the whip broke on Boysie's body, the cracks and splinters from the whip etched his skin and caused it to bleed. Boysie was ecstatic.

I soon came to discover the source of his ecstacy. Boysie knew that Pa maintained a belief that the teacher's right to discipline was supreme. Supreme that is, until such a time as blood was shed. Boysie knew that any teacher who caused a drop of blood to surface would have to answer to my father—Boodram style.

Previous to today's incident, Boysie had never been able to make a substantial case against any of his teachers after having suffered many indignities at their hands. Just once he wanted to have the upper hand. It made no difference to Boysie that most of the time his teachers were justified in their actions. It did not matter to Boysie that most of the time he was guilty. Today Boysie would be vindicated for the few times he had been punished when he was innocent. Today Boysie had physical evidence against his most hated teacher. Mr. Clout had drawn blood. Only Pa was entitled to draw blood from his children.

After arriving home from school, Boysie seemed subdued. It was unusual for him to stay home. Normally he would be out cruising with his friends, but today he was pacing out in the yard. It finally dawned on me that Boysie was waiting for Pa.

Pa arrived home a little later than usual that day. He looked exhausted; the mule looked even more exhausted. Pa began to unhitch the mule from his harness when he became distracted. It was Boysie. He was moaning, "Oh, God, me hand. Me hand, oh God." Pa looked over at Boysie but said nothing. He finished removing the harness from the mule and proceeded to comb the mule's hind section. The mule kicked back unexpectedly catching Pa in the leg. Pa became furious with the mule. It was at that moment that Boysie decided to go into high gear. "Oh, God, I bleeding! It paining!"

Pa approached Boysie. Boysie revealed, "He beat me, Pa. Oh, God, he beat me!"

"Who?"

"Mr. Clout."

Pa examined Boysie's hand and saw the bruises and marks on it. He also noted that there were blood stains on his hands.

Suddenly, everything became clear. A phrase that I had overheard earlier that day now made perfect sense. Godwin had cautioned Boysie,

"Don't forget to rub the nettle bush on good." A nettle bush is much like a thistle. When the nettles are rubbed on the body, it leaves blood-like welts on the surface of the skin.

From what I could tell, Boysie had been very liberal in the application of that nettle bush. When Pa saw the bloody, injured hand he asked, "Who done that?"

"Mr. Clout, my teacher," explained Boysie.

"Boysie, go inside the house."

"Pa?"

"I'll handle it."

Pa was angry. He had been kicked by a mule. That he could take care of immediately. He picked up a stick, approached the mule and delivered two fierce blows. The mule kicked back in pain. Pa began flailing the stick at the mule. This time the mule took his punishment in silence. Pa withdrew. He then entered the house for dinner. He did not speak throughout his meal. Later, he retired to bed but not before indulging heavily in some spirits.

The next morning I awoke and thought that the whole incident with Boysie had been concluded. I could not have been more mistaken.

Pa usually left for work around seven in the morning. It generally took him one and a half hours to travel the eight miles to Port of Spain with his mule and his cart. It was now after eight and Pa was still at home: brooding. Neither Boysie nor I ventured to speak to Pa and Pa showed no sign of wanting to speak to us. We left for school.

When we arrived at the school, classes had already begun but I could not keep my mind on my lessons. I was filled with a feeling of anxiety. I wondered why Pa had not gone to work. I looked at Boysie. He did not seem anxious. Quite the contrary, in fact, he seemed rather calm.

Our class was on the second floor. We were located in the middle section of that floor and we were always surrounded by the normal chatter and bustle associated with various school activities. A general buzz was considered normal and we were rarely distracted by activity. Suddenly, an uncharacteristic silence enveloped the school. It began at the front entrance and gradually made its way up to the second floor. My heart began to beat faster. Perhaps my heart knew intuitively what my head did not want to acknowledge. Not only was Pa in the building, he was approaching our class!

Pa loomed—shirtless, shoeless, toothless and unshaven. His long trousers were folded three-quarters up from his bare feet. I was beyond embarrassed. I was mortified. My father's disheveled presence was incongruous with the Catholic atmosphere of the school.

"Where is Teacher Clout?" he demanded.

There was a shocked silence. Mr. Clout, had momentarily stepped out of the room. Now, unaware of my father's presence, he had returned.

"Are you Mr. Clout?" Pa asked.

"I am," responded a somewhat nervous and subdued Mr. Clout.

Quickly, Pa moved toward him in order to block any attempt at retreat. Pa raised his right hand. Clutched in his hand was an iron picket about five feet long. "I'm going to teach you a lesson you will never forget you Son of a $#@&*. At that instant, another voice intervened.

The voice belonged to Teacher Hollace; he was the idol of the local townspeople. He was the first member of a poor family to become educated. The town loved and admired this young man for his accomplishment.

As Pa raised the iron we feared for Mr. Clout's life. He was certain to strike a deadly blow. Before the fateful blow could connect with the victim, Teacher Hollace grabbed at the iron in Pa's hand and quietly and earnestly pleaded with him.

"Oh, God, Mr. Boodram. He ain't worth it, Man. He ain't worth it."

Pa, still seething with rage, struggled to be understood. "Teacher Hollace, he drew blood. He shouldn't draw blood."

A desperate Teacher Hollace reasoned with Pa. "I'm sorry that happened. But what is going to happen to your children when you go to jail?"

Pa pointed threateningly to a very frightened Mr. Clout.

Then, Teacher Hollace took charge. "Mr. Boodram, please think of your family. I beg you."

Pa's hand neared Mr. Clout's face. We waited in shock.

Then Teacher Hollace called for Boysie. "Boysie, come here."

A confident and proud young Boysie advanced.

"Mr. Clout, you didn't mean to draw blood, did you?" urged a desperate Teacher Hollace.

"I am sorry, Mr. Boodram," a humbled Mr. Clout uttered.

"All right, Mr. Clout. You lucky Teacher Hollace is here. He save your neck. If you ever draw blood ... I warning you ..."

And, having said that, my father allowed himself to be led away by Teacher Hollace.

Once the two men were out the door, Boysie closed in on Mr. Clout and threatened, "Mr. Clout, you lucky you alive and in one piece. Touch me again and even Teacher Hollace won't be able to save you!" Boysie withdrew and walked away triumphantly.

Throughout the remainder of the day, Boysie bore the spirit of a champion and was treated like a movie star by his comrades. Teacher Clout had beaten him so many times. He had suffered ridicule and humiliation so many times. Today, he was the victor. Today he smiled.

This encounter between Mr. Clout and my father is indeed sad. Sometimes I can hardly believe that the incident really occurred. But, it did. A teacher carried punishment beyond reason. As a result, a protective and proud parent reacted irrationally. I am grateful, however to Teacher Hollace. He saved my father from a life in prison, not to mention that he also saved Mr. Clout's very life. Teacher Hollace did something even more. He gave me my first introduction to the power of civility in the person of a teacher. Civility in the classroom was virtually unknown in the school that I attended. Teachers such as Teacher Hollace were a rarity. The ability to instill fear in students was the common denominator uniting teachers. Fear was so prevalent in school that I could not conceive of one without the other. Fear and school were inextricably linked in my world.

15

MR. SERIES

SOON THE carefree years of childhood drew to a close. Thoughts of attending high school began to consume my mind. But, I knew that high school was for people with brains and intelligence. I did not dare dream that I could ever go to high school because I had been told that I was stupid so often that I had no option but to believe it myself. This reality, however, did not stop my mind from thinking about the possibility.

As I approached my senior years in elementary school, I acknowledged to myself, my secret desire. I wanted to go to high school. I told no one. This secret received some measure of nurture from Mr. Series who was both my principal and the teacher of arithmetic. It was through him that I had my first taste of success. If a student worked especially hard in Mr. Series' class, he would allow that student the rare privilege of tending to his private "kitchen garden." This garden was located in the far corner of the playground. I was selected to be a tender of that special garden. Mr. Series spent time with me. He gave me responsibility and encouragement. He never called me stupid. I felt safe with him. That empty spot at my very core that was waiting to receive some positive encouragement was finally being filled. He seemed so pleased with the effort I was making in the garden. Not a single weed was allowed to protrude above the earth during my vigil. Mr. Series went so far as to offer me a share of the produce. I did not witness him extend this offer to any other student. From this small act, I inferred that indeed, Mr. Series liked me. Thus I came to value Mr. Series. He changed the course of my life. He offered me guidance and a measure of respect. He gave me a taste of success that was inspiring. I never expected that Mr. Series would venture to visit me at my humble home.

One Saturday morning when I was outside playing on the street with my friends, we saw Mr. Series walking in our direction. We were surprised at this sight and we began to question one another as to "who done wrong" as teachers were not known to come home to visit unless someone had committed a serious offence. We all stared. Mr. Series was heading toward my yard. Surely he was not coming to my house. I thought he liked me and approved of me. My world shattered when he entered my yard. I wondered what I had done that was so wrong. He met with my mother. They spoke briefly and then Ma called my father to join them. I was terrified. Next, Ma called me.

I was in agony. I was almost too terrified to move. I made my way over to where the three of them stood and hung my head. I could not bear to look at Mr. Series.

Ma spoke. "Frankie, Mr. Series has something to tell you."

I looked up and prepared my face for the inevitable slap from my father.

Slapping time was near and at any moment I would receive that famous hand on my face. It did not matter if the slap was administered with the front or the back part of the hand. The sheer force of any such blow would temporarily rearrange and numb all the muscles in my face.

One may wonder why I was so certain that my father was going to punish me. My certainty was grounded in the knowledge that I had just recently been involved in some very unpleasant dialogue with our neighbour's son, Ramdeen. It seemed that Ramdeen could insult, curse, kick, or beat me because he knew that I could not respond or retaliate in a similar manner because of my father. Pa always admonished us not to participate in any kind of fight or any kind of argument that could lead to a fight. He maintained that it took two to fight. We were to remain strict pacifists. In the event that we did get involved in a fight, Pa would feel obligated to impose a generous whipping on us.

I knew that Ramdeen was aware of my father's strict policy and he continued to bait me knowing that ultimately I would get a beating, if not from him, then from my father.

Ramdeen did not like our family and often verbally insulted us. "Frankie," he insisted, "your brothers and sisters are no good. They stupid. All of you are stupid. And you ugly too. No matter what your sisters do to try to look good, they end up looking worse."

I was infuriated. My sisters were innocent. They did not deserve this blasphemy from this soulless individual.

My good friend Harry was close by and I could tell that he, too, was becoming angry and annoyed by Ramdeen's comments. Harry had two sisters whom I regarded as I did my own sisters. I would never hurt or insult them in any way. I was counting on Harry to remember this when I hatched my grand plan to counter Ramdeen's attacks.

By now, Ramdeen was flying high. He took a couple of steps toward me until he was right up in my face. He sensed my discomfort and my growing rage.

"And, Frankie, your mother and father, they are big time ugly. Your entire family, including you, are so ugly, they have enough ugliness to make up for our entire town." He placed his outstretched hand so that it covered my entire face and continued his rant. "Well, Frankie, that's how ugly you is. No hope for you. You know you are the ugliest of everyone."

I wanted to lash out against him. Yet, I knew that that was exactly what he was counting on, for then he could go home and tell his entire family that *I* was bullying *him*. Then his family would swoop to his rescue without questioning any of the facts. If I managed to survive their attack, I would surely be severely disabled by my father once he learned of my indiscretion. No, I knew I had to use a very different tactic on Ramdeen.

I put my plan into action. I turned to my good friend, Harry, and attempted to engage his attention. "Harry, listen up," I said as I winked my eye several times at him. "I have something to tell you. Yes, I've wanted to tell you this for the longest time."

"What you have in mind, Frankie?" responded Harry with sincere curiosity.

I winked at him again just to make sure he got it. Then, to make doubly sure, I nodded my head ever so slightly in the direction of Ramdeen. I was positive that between the wink and the nod, Harry would know that whatever comments that followed were to be directed at Ramdeen, not at Harry.

Confident, I continued.

"Harry, I never knew ugliness until I saw your sisters. They are so ugly that if a person never believed in Hell, one look at your sisters and anyone would have to believe that that kind of ugliness could only come from Hell."

"What?" stammered a confused Harry.

And, Ramdeen with his mouth wide open, was also visibly

unnerved.

I, however, completely oblivious to the real effect of my words, continued on in innocence. "And Harry, what definitely makes me believe there must be a Hell is the likes of your entire family. Your mother. Your father. Your sisters. Everyone. I do not know if Hell existed before, but when God saw your family it is certain that Hell was made. Your whole family is that ugly!"

Harry ran away, crying. I was shocked.

Ramdeen, however, understood my duplicity and quickly threatened, "Frankie, you think you smart. You going to pay big time."

This incident took place in the back of our yard. After everyone left, I remained trying to figure out exactly what had just happened and why Harry had run away.

Soon a strong voice urged me to come to the front of the house. It was my older brother, Clive. With him, on one side, were Harry and his dad and both of them looked exceedingly forlorn. On the other side were Ramdeen, his mother, and various members of their family. They were decidedly not forlorn. They came brandishing knives, sticks and a cutlass. I was certain that a bloody and brutal death awaited me.

I searched for my most innocent voice. "Yes, Clive?" I queried.

I could not understand why Harry and his dad were here. And why did his dad have such a disappointed look on his face? Surely Harry understood that all my remarks were intended for Ramdeen and his family.

Clive motioned for me to come closer. I obliged. "Frankie, did you tell Harry that his sisters are so ugly that they come from Hell?"

"Clive, please," I tried to reason.

"But he meant our family," angrily interjected Ramdeen's mother as she waved her machete. "I go kill you, Frankie!"

"Frankie," Clive yelled in desperation, "did you call Harry's family ugly from Hell?"

"Yes, but I..." I tried to explain.

Before I could finish, Clive had delivered a tremendous slap across the right side of my face. As I began to slip into an altered state of consciousness, I believe that I saw stars falling from the heavens. I faintly remember Harry's dad saying, "I thought Frankie was like family." Hearing the agony in his voice merely added an emotional dimension to the physical pain that I was already experiencing from Clive's slap. His slap had nearly rendered me unconscious. My face was twisted and distorted. Ma had to rub it with a special ointment for two weeks before it returned to some semblance of normalcy.

I did not see Harry or any member of his family for the next few days. The pain that I had caused them was unfathomable. When next I saw Harry, I managed to explain the whole situation to him. He received my explanation and once again we were friends.

In retrospect I have come to understand that my brother Clive had to have been pretty clever to quickly put together all the various elements of my unfortunate situation. By getting me to admit that I had wronged Harry's family, Clive spared me the wrath of Ramdeen's clan. I now consider myself very fortunate indeed to have survived the whole incident with just a slap.

Yes, I was regularly slapped by my brother and my parents and it is precisely this type of action I was anticipating when Mr. Series approached my parents in our back yard that Saturday afternoon. It was with great sadness and disappointment that I faced Mr. Series. I had dared to let myself feel that he had liked me. Now, here he was...

"Frank, I want to tell you something," he began.

"Yes, Mr. Series," I replied politely.

"Well, I just told your mother and father that you should go to high school."

"What?" I muttered.

"Frankie, I asked your parents to try and send you to high school. I believe that you will do well."

What a tremendous feeling of relief. Not only was I not going to get a slap, I also was receiving a compliment. What joy! Never had anyone in a position of responsibility ever shared such a sentiment about me. Immediately I felt that I was not that stupid. I still did not however, allow myself to think that I was smart. For now, it was enough of an affirmation to know that I was not stupid. Mr. Series had planted a seed. Thank God for a caring teacher.

16

THE ILLUSIVE DREAM

THAT VISIT by Mr. Series was the catalyst that ignited my desire to attend high school. I was more determined than ever to find a way. The obstacles, however, were huge. I do not recall any member of my family, past or present, having ever attended high school. My older brothers, Clive and Boysie, had both followed Pa into the workplace. My elder sister, Dolly, remained at home to help Ma with the household tasks and the rearing of the younger children. Such assistance was regularly anticipated and expected in families like mine who were barely managing to survive. I knew that my father expected me to get a job and be finished with school once I finished my elementary schooling. That knowledge plagued me every minute of every day.

A further hindrance to my dream was the fact that the government could accommodate only a fraction of all eligible students at its government sponsored schools. In order to reduce the number of possible applicants for an extremely limited number of free places, the government implemented a mandatory examination which would determine admission to the school. Only a designated number of students taking the test were deemed to have passed and thus be eligible for free secondary schooling. It seemed that so many children of rich or socially elevated parents were successful in these examinations and consequently only those children qualified to attend secondary schools. The rest were marked as failures and suffered feelings of inadequacy and inferiority. We assumed that the richer children were brighter and more intelligent. What we could not comprehend as children was the fact that the government could not provide free education to every child on the island. The inability of the government to provide for all students wishing to further their education inadvertently spawned a new industry. Those students who did not pass the government test but still wanted to attend school, had to be accommodated. Private schools began to spring up all over the island to accommodate those children whose parents wanted them to have further education and were willing to pay for it. The students who did not gain entrance to the government high school had a second chance. For a fee of sixteen to twenty dollars per semester, these children could attend high school. Most parents in my neighbourhood could not afford the expected five dollars per month. Economically disadvantaged parents who did send their children to private secondary schools did so with extreme sacrifice.

I was aware of all of these facts, so when illness prevented me from taking the government's Common Entrance Examination, I felt that my dream of attending high school had ended. To fail to take the test was the same as failing the test. My parents were extremely poor and could not afford to send me to a private school. My only hope had been to pass the government exam and gain free admittance to the government school. The day I failed to take the exam was the darkest day of my life. I felt as if my dream was dying. And, inside my soul, I was dying too.

17

THE WORLD OF MR. MORRIS

SOME DAYS later, as I was getting ready to go to school, Pa interrupted my preparations.

"Frankie, come with me. No school. No more."

I was dazed. It was in a state of shock that I followed him to a local mechanic shop. Pa spoke briefly to the owner, Mr. Morris.

After uttering these two curt sentences, "Frankie, learn well. Make something of yourself." He left.

My entire world became confused and distorted. Through my mental fog I heard Mr. Morris call me. Nervous and uncertain, I approached. He motioned for me to sit on an old tree stump at the side of the shop. My surroundings appeared greasy and old and uncomfortable. The smell of gas permeated everything and engine parts were strewn everywhere. It was a chaotic mess. Mr. Morris gave me but one instruction. "Frankie, you are to wash these things clean. Okay?" I looked around at the array of bolts, nuts, and bearings, and reluctantly assumed my duties. The hours went by slowly and the work was monotonous. I began to look around the garage. Pictures of naked women were pinned everywhere along the walls of the shop. More distressing to my young mind than the pictures were the conversations between Mr. Morris and his workers. They had adult conversations about women and their bodies. For the first time in my life I heard men openly exchange stories about their most intimate and private activities with women.

This talk shattered my world of innocence. I came from a home that still promoted the concept that babies were dropped into our lives by planes that flew overhead. Only a day or two earlier my mother had shown us the plane that had brought my youngest brother, Suresh, into the world. Every day thereafter we would watch the sky to see if we could discern which of the many planes flying overhead, was the one that had brought us our baby brother.

These were enchanting moments of our lives as children. Boys and girls played together on the street. When it rained, it was not uncommon for us to remove all our clothing, boys and girls together, and dash about in the rain. We did this without any sense of shame for we were innocent in the purest sense of the word. That innocence had now been thoughtlessly and thoroughly taken. I could not return to my former innocent state. A sense of confusion and helplessness consumed me and I busied myself washing and re-washing the various car parts. I laboured to occupy my mind; I was desperately trying to drown out this new and ugly reality. Mr. Morris even had a special post on which he etched a mark every time he managed to seduce a woman. Each mark on the post moved him higher up in the esteem of his men. The concept of manhood espoused by these labourers was clear; the greater the number of conquests, the greater the man.

By the time my day had ended, I was totally drained and disillusioned. I was devoid of feeling. I did not want to live. But, I did not want to die either. More than anything, perhaps, I was certain that I did not want to go back to work at the garage. I did not know how to convince Pa to change his mind about my working for Mr. Morris.

18

A VISIT TO FATHER FENNESSEY

M**Y FATHER'S** stubbornness was legendary and I was afraid to confront him. It was in this confused frame of mind that I began my lonely vigil from the garage to home. I could not go home directly for I had much to ponder. I wandered mindlessly throughout the neighbourhood eventually ending up at the railroad track that ran at the back of our property. I gathered loose pebbles from the tracks and tossed them aimlessly. Soon, a train rolled on past. Passengers, mostly high school students, disembarked. They were dressed in a variety of uniforms representing the colours of the various private schools that they attended. The majority of the students I recognized as being from St. Charles Boys' High School, right here in Tunapuna, my home town.

My imagination took over. I was now a high school student. I was dressed in that uniform. This image so totally consumed me that I was able to go home with a new sense of discovery and determination.

I arrived at home with my face beaming with new hope. Ma was hard at work in the yard scrubbing clothes on the outside washboard. She sensed my presence and turned to me, questioningly.

"Frankie?"

"Yeah, Ma?"

"How it went?"

"Not good, Ma. I need your help."

"What kind of help, Son?"

"Ma... Ma... please, please ask Pa to let me go to high school."

Silence. Ma was pensive, then sadly she warned, "If I ask yo fader to let you go he go kill you. He go kill me too."

"Ma, if I stay at that garage I dead anyway."

"Frankie, Son...," she began but I turned away before she could finish her thought. Every optimism had been dissolved. What was I to do now?

Night descended but sleep escaped me. Nothing had been resolved. I knew only too well that if I did not report to work at the garage, Pa would belt me without mercy. Ma knew this too. The next morning, Ma sought me out very early. She had made me my favourite breakfast of plantain and roti. I was unable to eat knowing that I had to go back to that garage. Ma was very apologetic and her heart was breaking as she said, "Frankie, I so sorry I cannot help you. You must go to work. I so sorry I can't send you to high school."

"Ma, it's not your fault. Don't worry."

My words were meant to comfort her but they brought no comfort to me. They left me angry and questioning. Whose fault is it that I am unable to go to high school?

As I made my way to the garage I looked up to the heavens. I don't know what I was expecting. God was obviously not going to come to my aid. He had far more important things to attend to.

I soon arrived at the garage. I stood motionless in front of it, unable to make myself enter the building. I was hesitant, unable to move. And then, a strange thing happened. It was as if the garage itself spoke to me.

"Don't come in," I heard it say. "You don't belong here."

The voice was very real to me. Whether it was just my overwrought subconscious speaking to me or whether it was divine intervention, I obeyed. I left immediately. I did not know where I was going. Only one thing was certain; I was no longer a worker at that garage. My soul could not survive another day in that environment. I walked away and headed towards the Eastern Main Road.

I soon found myself in the vicinity of St. Charles High School. The office of the principal was not too far away. Suddenly and without fully knowing, I found myself knocking on the door of the office.

I waited for a response.

Nothing.

I knocked again.

Still nothing.

My confidence began to dwindle and I was beginning to feel a bit stupid. I began to question myself.

"Why would the principal want to hear from the likes of me? Maybe this is a waste of time."

I was about to walk away, when I heard a voice call to me to come in.

Shocked by this invitation, I stood outside as if transfixed.

The door opened.

There was Father Fennessey. His green Irish eyes were unmistakable behind his thick round glasses. He looked me over and invited me in. I was unresponsive. He now extended his hand and motioned to me to enter. I felt encouraged.

Once I was inside, Father pulled out a chair and indicated for me to sit down. I did so, nervously.

"Can I help you?" Father asked.

I searched fruitlessly for the words to express my thoughts.

Father leaned in closer and asked, "Well, tell me your name. You can start there. Can't you?"

"My name is Frankie Boodram."

"Where are you from?"

"I live at 26 Back Street, Tunapuna."

"Then you live close to our high school, yes?"

"Yes, Father. That's why I came. I want to come to high school."

"That's good. Then come."

I was quiet. How do I explain my problem to him? I did not know what to say next. I felt ashamed.

Again, Father spoke.

"Frankie, you are so quiet, so troubled looking. Is there a problem? Can I help you?"

There was something so genuine in that Irish voice.

I ventured slowly, "Father, I have very little money. I want to come to high school."

It took a lot of courage to disclose even that little bit of information but Father listened thoughtfully and asked, "Frankie, do you have both of your parents?"

"Yes, Father, I do."

"Can they not pay the fees?"

"No."

"So, why do you want to go to high school? What are you doing now?

"My father pulled me out of school and he put me to work in a garage. He needs the money."

"But that is not such a bad idea. Learning mechanics is useful. Your pa's being practical. Would you reconsider and return to the garage?"

"Father, they teach little about mechanics. They talk... no, they cuss all the time. And so much is dirty talk. I will die there."

"Oh, goodness me! I think I understand. Tell me about your father and his work."

"Pa has a cart and a mule. He transports goods from Port of Spain to Tunapuna. He makes little money. Sometimes, he spends this money on drink." Shamed by this last disclosure, I bent my head.

"I think I understand your situation. Here is what I can do."

I raised my head slightly.

Father continued. "The fee for the term is $16.00. I will reduce it to $12.00. I expect to see you at high school. Okay?"

"Father, I will try." I was overwhelmed by his kindness.

Father then asked shyly, "Frankie, are you Catholic?"

"No, Father, I am a Hindu."

Father looked at me for a moment; his raised eyebrow indicated a measure of surprise. He seemed to have looked on me with favour only a moment ago. Had he really thought that I was Catholic? Was he now about to withdraw his offer of support? I grew nervous as the silence between us widened. Then he spoke.

"So, you are a Hindu. No problem. Most important is this. You have courage. You are a brave little Hindu. You are going to make it. I will pray that you find a way."

"Thank you, Father. Thank you so much."

I am forever in Father Fennessey's debt. His encouragement came at a critical moment in my life. A short while ago I was about to walk away. Had he not prevailed on me, had he not taken a moment to talk to me, I do not know what would have become of me. I thank God every day for Father Fennessey.

Encouraged and uplifted, I made my way back home. Ma was waiting.

"You did not go to work." It was more of a statement that a question.

I did not respond.

"Frankie, when your pa comes home he is going to..."

"I know, Ma."

"Frankie, where were you? What you do? Tell me."

"Ma, I went to the high school. I talked to Father Fennessey."

"What he say?"

"Ma," I began excitedly, "he is going to help. He is going to reduce the fees from $16.00 to $12.00 a term. He is expecting me to come."

"But, Frankie, things hard. We don't have money. I think...."

I did not let her finish. I was in a positive frame of mind. I did not want to think otherwise.

"Ma, I'll find a way."

"Frankie, I go help you, Son, no matter what you fader say."

At that moment, my mother and I became allies. It was wonderful to have her voice of support. I knew that she would do her best. I would worry about Pa later. Right now I had unfinished business.

19

I AM GOING TO HIGH SCHOOL

I WAS TOTALLY motivated. I needed to make some money. I needed $12.00. I grabbed a rake and a hoe and set off. I had to help myself.

I made my way to the richer neighbourhood where I presented myself to the first likely home. I rang the doorbell; a lady came out.

"What do you want?" the woman asked dismissively.

"I would like to weed your garden."

"Sorry, we already have a gardener."

Undeterred by this rebuff, I counseled myself not to give up and to keep on trying.

I knew that there was a restaurant close by. I decided that that would be my next target. I entered the restaurant and went directly to the man behind the counter.

"What do you want?" he asked.

"I want to work."

"What can you do?"

Encouraged by his question I now sought to impress him. "I can wash dishes. Chop up vegetables. I can sweep and clean up. I can pull weeds. I can do almost anything around the yard."

"Sorry, don't need help," was his curt response.

With that, he turned his attention to his customers.

Okay, another one down. I must try again. Soon I was outside the restaurant wending my way along a quiet residential street. I plodded down the street still daring to hope that somewhere someone would have work for me to do.

I looked up, and in the distance rose the shadow of the Monastic building on the northern range. Many referred to that site as *holy*. I paused a moment and concluded that this was perhaps the time to have a talk with God.

"Okay, God. Am I too small to talk to you? I hope not. Well, I have this problem. I need money to pay for school. I can't find work. So, I am turning to you. Will you help me?"

By now it was getting late. I reasoned that I should be heading home. But, I did not. I simply wandered and wondered. Then, I came upon this beautiful home. In front of the house stretched some wonderful fruit trees, some prized Julie mango trees. In between the gorgeous fruit trees were generous outcroppings of weeds. I was surprised. A residence such as this would never allow such negligence; this must be my lucky day. The gate was open and I entered the yard and walked up and knocked on the door. There was no answer. Undeterred by this lack of response, I set to work. I began pulling at the weeds. Suddenly there was a terrific bark followed by an intense shaking of the ground. A huge dog lunged at me and managed to rip a piece of my shorts. Not wanting to be the next part of the dog's meal, I ran outside the gate. Soon a large man approached and gained control of the animal. He beckoned to me to enter. I did so rather nervously. He observed that I had already started to pull the weeds and put them into neat piles.

"What's your name?" he asked.

"Frankie, Sir," I responded contritely.

"Well, Frankie, do you want to finish the job?"

"Oh, yes Sir, I do."

"Then go ahead."

The man disappeared quickly. Never was there a happier kid. I had a job. I had a real job. Excitement filled my heart and fresh adrenalin filled my veins. I made short work of those weeds.

When I was finished I looked around. I noticed that fruit lay rotting on the ground. I cleaned up everywhere. Soon the garden was tidy. Once more I knocked on the door. The man came out, inspected the grounds and seemed pleased with my work. He reached into his pocket and placed a shilling in my hands. A shilling was a most generous gift. I was thrilled. All I needed now was another forty-seven shillings.

I thanked the man for his generosity and looked longingly up at the mango tree and its abundant fruit. The man, sensing my unspoken desire, reached up and picked a sweet smelling Julie mango and placed it in my hand.

As I headed home savouring that fresh mango, I could not help but think that God was not so occupied that He did not have a moment to look after me. I treasured that thought.

I smiled as I made my way home.

That smile, however, was short-lived. Sobering reality awaited me. I knew that by now my father would be home and would be growing increasingly impatient with my absence. I imagined him pacing back and forth in the yard, belt in hand.

I entered the yard still carrying the companions of my labour, my rake and hoe.

My father was in the yard just as I had imagined, belt in hand.

"Frankie, come here now!" he commanded. His tone indicated that he would neither entertain any excuse nor engage in any negotiation. He was intent on giving me a belting.

Saying nothing, I walked boldly up to him and placed the shilling in his hand.

His look of surprise was obvious. He was taken completely off-guard. I capitalized on his confusion and walked away.

He did not yell at me to come back.

Soon I was inside the house, shaking. I saw Ma go out and talk to Pa. After they spoke, Pa went into the living room and called to me once more. Nervously, I entered the room. Pa was seated uncomfortably in his rocker, bent slightly forward, still holding his belt in his hands.

As I approached, he commanded, "Open your hand and stretch it out to me!"

Obediently, I complied.

Steeling myself for the customary belting, I was shocked to feel in my hand not the hot sting of the belt but rather the cool presence of the just forfeited shilling. I could not believe my luck. That action was nothing short of miraculous.

Then Pa spoke. "So, Frankie, you want to go to high school. Okay."

That was all he said. It was all I needed to hear. The colossal fear that had most recently gripped me dissipated. I was tremendously moved by my father's show of good will. That single gesture of returning to me that hard-earned shilling, spoke volumes about the inherent goodness of this loving father.

My world was good again. I now had the freedom from fear to pursue my dream to attend high school. All I needed was money.

Ma was ahead of me in her efforts to help in that regard. Ma negotiated to purchase a second cow on a weekly installment plan. Providing for two cows meant more work for everyone. The cows had to be fed and milked and their surroundings had to be cleaned daily. Having these two animals in our back yard was most challenging. At times, the stench from the cow droppings was most unpleasant. It was also difficult to obtain enough feed for the cows.

On one occasion, my father was apprehended by the police for stealing cane feed from government land for the cows. He was taken to jail and spent the night behind bars. While we were naturally horrified by his incarceration, we all understood the necessity of finding the cheapest means to provide for our cows. Poor families in Trinidad often found themselves caught in a tricky web of circumstance whereby they were forced to take what was not rightfully theirs simply to survive.

Such memories serve to remind me of my humble roots. I was one of the greater benefactors from the selling of the milk. Ma always endeavoured to put away some small amount toward my high school fees. I am forever mindful of all the sacrifices made by each member of my family, especially my mother. My family's sacrifices served to keep me grounded.

On those occasions when my peers would hurl thoughtless insults at me about the way I smelled, I absorbed the hurt without obvious retaliation but not without deep reflection. On such occasions I was always guided by the realization of the many sacrifices and acts of generosity that others made on my behalf. Ma went without any of life's amenities; she used whatever money and resources she had for the betterment of all her children. Pa, despite his many shortcomings, showed a generosity of spirit in allowing me to attend high school. I know that now. He could easily have demanded that I return to Mr. Morris' garage where I would have earned a small salary. This small salary would have been enough to make an appreciable difference in the family economics. Pa had to accept the difficult fact that his third eldest son would not be adding to the family income. He must have felt great disappointment. My not working placed an even greater strain on him. I am forever grateful for his sacrifice.

The beginning of the new term was at hand. I had some of the money necessary to pay for the school fees. I knew that as long as I had faith and strength that the rest would eventually come. My dream to go to high school was at long last, becoming a reality. Unbelievable! I could not be happier. Imagine me—stupid me—ugly me—about to place my feet on the threshold of a high school, St. Charles Boys' High School in Tunapuna.

PART II

The High School Years

20

HIGH SCHOOL: FINALLY

THAT LONG awaited day finally arrived. I was going to high school. I could not conceal my joy. After all the years of secretly yearning to be a part of high school life, after all the doubts, after all the challenges, after everything and despite everything, here I was deeply curious to begin. The first day saw me dressed in the customary school uniform—blue shirt, khaki shorts, and striped tie.   St. Charles Boys' High School was a modest older one-floor building that housed about six classrooms. Each classroom was close to the next separated only by rudimentary moveable wooden partitions. Often we would hear the spirited activities taking place in the other classes. We all adapted quite quickly to the expectations and routines of each teacher. It was understood immediately that homework—and homework from each teacher almost every day—was the norm. Therefore it was not uncommon to have several hours of homework each day. The more competent students accomplished their assignments with relative ease in a minimum amount of time. Those of us who were less confident in our competencies devoted many hours each night struggling: first to understand then to complete our homework.

My home environment was not conducive to the pursuit of quiet studies. Because there were too many family distractions, finding a quiet corner of the house to study was a major challenge. I therefore spent as much time at school as I was allowed in order to complete my studies. At other times I would hibernate in a secret place in a nearby farmer's field and pray that I would not be discovered. Discovery would surely invite taunting and humiliation.

On nights when I had no option but to study at home, finding appropriate lighting was a challenge. We could not afford the luxury of electricity; hence, we had to rely on the fickleness of kerosene lanterns. The light produced by lanterns was harsh, unreliable, and inconvenient. My eyes would often become irritated and watery, frequently blurring my vision.

These are the physical challenges that manifested themselves in my early days at high school. They were inconvenient but not insurmountable.

Soon, another type of challenge emerged. This one, because it involved circumstances largely out of my control, threatened to crush my enthusiasm for high school. The perplexing problem concerned my school fees. The original fee of sixteen dollars per semester had been reduced by four dollars to twelve dollars a semester. Even with this most generous reduction, I had managed to pay only half of the requisite twelve dollars. Father Fennessey, while accepting the six dollar partial payment, cautioned that I must pay the balance within the month or run the risk of being sent home. I wondered about the statement *'being sent home'*. *What did it mean?* I was about to find out.

I had been in high school for approximately one month. On the first Monday of the second month, Father Fennessey came to our school just as morning classes began. There was a sudden hush in the building; some students began filling out of the school. I had never seen this happen before and I thought it a most strange occurrence.
I attempted to ask, "Why are they leaving the building?" Before the words were out of my mouth, an announcement declared, "Attention students. Father will now address those of you who are delinquent in your fees."

Father was carrying a clipboard which recorded in alphabetical order, the names of students who had not yet fully paid their school fees. Delinquent students who now had the money to pay their fees lined up and approached Father. He took their payments and crossed off their names from his list. Noticeable relief registered on their faces as they returned to their classes.

Next began the process of calling the names of the still outstanding accounts. Father began by calling students with surnames starting with the letter *A*. It was about then that I understood the sudden exodus of the students at the beginning of class. Those who were familiar with the routine and knew what to expect, had already made their exit.

Father was now at the *B's*. I heard him call my name: "Boodram."

Paralyzed, I simply sat.

Father perused the class; then he saw me. Our eyes locked.

"Boodram, come here," he commanded.

Not knowing how to face him, I shrank from his gaze. I dropped my head into my hands and closed my eyes. I prayed that the embarrassment would end. I had no money to pay the fees. Furthermore, I had neither the strength to stand up to nor the courage to face the scorn of my peers, the pity of my teachers, or the disappointment of Father Fennessey.

The teacher stood by my desk and advised, "Boodram, follow me. You cannot keep Father waiting. It is rude."

"Yes, Sir" I mumbled.

"Grab all your books," he ordered. Wondering what was about to happen to me, I followed him sheepishly to Father. Everyone was watching.

"Boodram... sorry. Rules are rules. You cannot continue until all your fees are paid up!"

"I'm sorry, Father."

I walked out.

I was *being sent home.*

I was totally humiliated.

The knowledge that I could not return to school until I first paid my outstanding fees distressed me deeply.

I could not, however, blame Father Fennessey for this. I understood that the school had to have rules. Father was merely the instrument used to implement the rules. In time I also came to understand that this ritual, performed on the first Monday of each month, was as loathsome to him as it was to the students. As serious and as stern as he may have appeared on the surface, his eyes betrayed the sadness hidden within his heart.

On subsequent months, I, too, joined the legion of students attempting to avoid Father Fennessey's *eviction* Mondays.

21

Sammy

I WOULD HAVE had the required school fees on that first fateful Monday had it not been for a most unfortunate occurrence.

It was no secret that I needed money to attend school. The whole community knew that I was willing to do almost anything so that I could continue to go to high school. A farmer by the name of Sammy approached me with a proposal to work for him.

"Frankie, I hear yo looking for a job."

"Yes I am."

"Well, yo able to cut cane?"

"Try me."

"But yo small."

"Try me!" I urged.

"Well, it's important work; if I hire you, you must promise to finish the job."

"I will."

"All right, here's what yo do. Tomorrow I pick you up at six o'clock. Have a cutlass ready. Bring yo lunch." He hesitated before he spoke again, " Yo small and skinny. Yo sure about this?"

"Yes, of course I'll do it. I could really use the money for school. Thanks so much."

I had never really had much to do with Sammy before that day so I had no way of judging his character. I knew only that his daughter and my sister were friends. Based on this one fact, I felt that I could trust this man.

I was excited about the prospect of being able to earn enough money to pay the other half of my school fees all by myself.

I did not, however, have a great deal of experience cutting cane. On rare occasions I accompanied my father to the fields where he would cut cane for the farmers in exchange for the cane tops. Pa would then use these as feed for our two cows. This barter system worked well for Pa as he was able to cut back on some of the expenses associated with owning the two cows in exchange for his labour. Occasionally I had tried my hand at cutting cane when I was with Pa but my small size and limited strength restricted my effectiveness. Now, however, I had much to gain by completing the task I hoped that my determination and tenacious spirit, combined with my indomitable will would carry me through this trial. Of this I was single-minded. I went to bed confident and optimistic.

The next day I was up at dawn and sharpened my cutlass for the day's activities.

Sammy arrived at the appointed hour. I climbed into his cart and together we headed to his field. Upon seeing the size of the field, my heart became anxious. It was an extremely long and dense crop of cane. It had, however, been burned recently; hopefully this would have rid the field of the scorpions that liked to make their homes in amongst these crops.

We negotiated our terms and agreed on a sum of money. I had two days to complete the job. Sammy left me to begin my work and he headed for his regular day job.

With a steady hand, I grabbed each sugar cane in turn, and chopped it at its root; with a second slice, I removed the top of the plant. I soon fell into a steady rhythm; the minutes became hours and soon the day was waning. I stopped only for a few minutes to eat my bag lunch which consisted of a simple potato and vegetable roti. I had but one focus; I had to cut as much cane as was physically possible that first day. As the afternoon sun closed in around me, I stood back and surveyed my work. I smiled; I had cut more than half the field. I knew then that I could finish the rest of the job the next day. My heart was light as I made my way home that evening.

When I arrived home, Ma was there to greet me at the steps.

"Yo look so black, Frankie. Yo covered all over in soot."

"I know Ma. I got a lot done."

"You must be hungry. Go bathe. I'll have your supper ready."

Normally, I would have had to go to the tap located in the middle of our street and haul water to our outside shower. Today, even though I was completely exhausted, I was prepared to perform this one last task in order to feel clean and refreshed. As I was about to grab the bucket to bring the water, Ma motioned to me and said,

"Frankie, look inside the shower." Two full buckets of water awaited me. Anticipating my fatigue, Ma had prepared the water for me. This was my Ma.

I looked at her quietly and my heart filled with gratitude for her enduring faithfulness. I wonder if she knew then just how much I treasured her. Those precious moments, caused me to reflect on God. Where do such mothers come from, if not from the bosom of the Almighty?

While showering, I treated myself to a luxurious lathering with the soap. My whole body relaxed completely and after a quick supper, I fell into a deep and perfect sleep. When I awoke the next day, I hurried outside to begin my preparations once again. To my surprise, Pa was up and was waiting outside for me with my cutlass in his hand. He had already sharpened it; he handed it to me. That simple act meant the world to me; it was symbolic of his approval- his blessing. Ma handed me my lunch bag and I was off once again to the cane field.

The first half of the day went well. I was hungry but I chose to defer the pleasure of eating until I had made a good start to the work. By mid-afternoon, I was delighted with what I had been able to accomplish.

Suddenly, without warning, it began to rain. Such outbursts were common in the Caribbean and they often stopped as suddenly as they began. I decided that this would be a good time to have my lunch; I stopped my work. I picked up my now thoroughly drenched lunch bag and sought shelter under a cluster of cane trees. I settled down to enjoy the simple pleasure of eating. I opened the bag; even the inside was soaked. My roti was completely saturated with water. Not even my bottle of tea was spared; it too had been diluted by the heavy rains. I salvaged whatever I could however, and ate without complaint. At the bottom of the bag lay a single piece of chicken. This was a treat. I knew then that Ma understood some of the difficulty that I was going through to try to earn my own way. I truly felt appreciated. Rain or no rain, I enjoyed my lunch.

As quickly as it had begun, the rain stopped and the sun came out. I pursued the rest of the field with a vengeance. Some hours later, the job was finished. I was thrilled. I grabbed my cutlass and, imagining myself a grown-up, surveyed the field! I felt so proud; I did it! I cut the entire field by myself. Just as I sat down to revel in my accomplishment, Sammy arrived. He too expressed pleasure to see that I had indeed finished the job.

"Very good, Frankie. Yo done good."

I smiled; I was already anticipating the pleased look on Father Fennessy's face when I handed him the rest of the money for the school fees. It would be a double pleasure knowing that I had earned the money myself.

Then Sammy continued, "About yo money..." he hesitated. "I will have it for you on Saturday."

I bent my head to hide my look of disappointment.

"Oh, don't worry; I get paid on Saturday."

I managed to utter, "Okay," but my voice betrayed my disappointment.

Sammy appeared eager to be off. He never even thought to offer me a ride home in his cart. That should have been my first clue that things would not go well.

When I arrived home, Ma, sensing some disappointment in my manner, asked, "Everything okay?"

"Yes, Ma. Just tired."

"Yo sure, Frankie?"

It was then that I shared with her the wet lunch incident.

It seemed that Ma had anticipated the problem that the rain had caused because she had a wonderful supper waiting just for me. She made me feel like a prince. I truly felt special.

I could not tell her that Sammy had not yet paid me; I could not give voice to my real fear. I was anxious all week as I waited for Saturday to arrive.

Saturday came and went and Sammy did not make an appearance.

I began each day of the next week with the hope that surely this would be the day that Sammy would come and pay me. My hopes were never to be realized; Sammy never came.

I was forced to face the terrible reality—Sammy never was going to come. Upon deeper reflection I further concluded that it was most likely that Sammy never had any intention of paying me from the beginning.

On subsequent days, if by chance I spotted Sammy, he always offered up some lame excuse. I would have preferred it if he had not made any excuses for they were both an insult to my intelligence and a further smear on Sammy's own character.

I felt betrayed on two fronts. First, I had depended on the money he owed me in order to continue with my high school education, and second, as a young man on the threshold of adulthood, I was constantly in search of moral principles and precepts on which to model my life. When Sammy robbed me of my fair earnings, he also robbed me of the vision of an adult world that espoused the simple value of human decency.

Once again I was left with the impression that something was seriously amiss in the adult world. I could not fathom this type of deceit in the elders that I was taught to respect. I understood that children sometimes withheld or exaggerated the truth and made up ridiculous excuses. I knew that. That an adult would blatantly lie was simply unfathomable. That an adult would rob a student was inconceivable! A sense of betrayal, of disappointment, of sheer loss, consumed me, and for many days I was a dejected soul.

Sammy was known to my family; his daughter and my sister were friends. *Why would he rob me? Was he that poor?*

Needless to say, without that money, I was unable to pay the remaining school fees; and, when Father Fennessey evicted me from class that first Monday, more feelings of confusion and lost hope, crushed me. What lessons of life was I supposed to intuit from such an incident?

Feelings of hate stirred within me, but some force stronger than my own will would not allow the hatred to take root. As a result, I could not embrace, even for a short while, the pleasure of hating no matter how justifiable.

Why did I deny myself this pleasure? I do not know. I knew only that it was wrong to hate people. I could hate what Sammy had done to me but I must make an effort not hate Sammy.

I was struggling with so many confusing and conflicting emotions and the feeling of despair threatened to rule my life once more. Because of Sammy's deceit, once again the idea of actually getting through high school seemed a daunting task.

The game of cat and mouse with Father Fennessey continued throughout those first few months of high school. It was a struggle for me to raise enough money each month. I always knew when Father would be visiting the school. My name was always on the list, but I was nowhere to be found. I *stayed* away to avoid the humiliation of being *sent* away.

22

CHALLENGES

I MADE EVERY effort to keep up with my school work however, because the fear of being accused of being unprepared for class was almost as great a fear as the fear of being evicted from school. Each of my high school teachers expected his class assignments to take precedence over any other teacher's assignments. In any given day, it was not uncommon for students to have five or more hours of homework. Failure to complete homework assignments resulted in punishment. Punishment ranged from a simple detention to a serious strapping.

My math teacher possessed a humanity that set him apart from my other teachers. But, he too, was very demanding and insisted on a high degree of effort and dedication from his students. One Friday when we were studying algebra, I was unable to complete my assignment at school so I took the work home with me. One problem in particular fascinated me with its intricacies and complexities. Determined not to be defeated by the problem, I persevered into the evening hours, working under the flickering light of the inconstant kerosene lantern. This one problem took up the last two pages of my math notebook and still it remained unsolved. There was no more room in my notebook for any further calculations and I had no more paper at home.

I needed more paper. We had none at home. Knowing that our grocery stores wrapped up produce in large sheets of brown wrapping paper, I decided to go to the store and get a large sheet of the brown paper. I immediately folded the paper into four equal squares. I now had eight fresh sides of paper upon which to complete my assignment. I redoubled my efforts to solve the math problem. Once again, I soon became totally engrossed with the algebra and barely noticed that Pa had entered the room. He startled me when he spoke.

"Frankie," he called.

"Yes, Pa."

I was not thrilled to be distracted from my work, but I knew that I owed my father a respectful answer.

"Read this article for me. It is about the Boysie Singh trial."

The whole island was a buzz with talk about Boysie Singh. He was on trial for the murder of a very famous woman on the island. Every man in town had his own theory about who had committed the murder and why. The locals gathered on a bridge just outside of our little house to talk about the trial. Pa could not read sufficiently, so in order for him to participate in any discussion, he first had to have the details from the newspaper read to him. This was the reason he approached me. I, however, because of my own fervent preoccupation with completing my studies, was a bit insensitive in my reply. Given my own particular frame of mind, I thought that my response was reasonable.

I asked, "Pa, could you get one of the girls to read tonight? I have so much work to do."

My father did not share my perspective however, and to him, my response must have appeared most impertinent. I did not know it then, but my lack of sensitivity to his simple request was to have far reaching and long lasting consequences. An already tenuous relationship was to be altered forever.

My father took serious offence to my request to have someone else read to him. His massive body towered over my slight frame as he shot a barrage of curses in Hindi. His hands were outstretched and he was gesturing madly. I feared that he would strike me in his rage.

His ranting suddenly ceased, replaced by a cold calm. Coldly and deliberately he proclaimed, "Frankie, from this day on, never, never, ask me for a cent! Not one bloody cent!"

Fighting tears and fear I faced my father squarely and, matching his tone, phrase for phrase, I pronounced, "Pa, don't worry. From this day on, I will never ask or take from you one single penny. Not one penny."

No sooner had the words crossed my lips then I began to question the wisdom of my hasty proclamation. *What had I done? I had not meant to harm or disrespect my father.* Obviously, when viewed through his eyes, I was guilty of both offenses. We were caught in our own unfortunate web of words. Our irrational rants were to trap us for years in roles neither intended to adopt; each of us too proud to forgive or forget the words of the other.

War had been declared; a sizeable trench had been dug with Pa on one side and me on the other.

My math beckoned. It seemed to be saying, *"Pay attention to me. Think about your family problems later."*

I allowed myself to be drawn in by its allure and I directed my energy towards finding solutions to my algebra problem. All my efforts were spent in one singular occupation. The homework assigned by my other teachers was put aside because of my complete devotion to algebra. I accepted the consequences of that decision without complaint. My Latin teacher simply doubled my assignment while the others imposed various forms of discipline ranging from mild reprimands to substantial increases in the number of assignments.

Finally, it was time for math class. Even though I had not actually *solved* the problem, I knew that the amount of time and energy I had expended was impressive. As the teacher came around to each student's desk to inspect the assignment, my heart began to swell with pride and anticipation. I was certain that he would be sufficiently impressed with the quantity of my work. My face was shining, expectant with happiness.

He approached my desk and picked up my exercise book. He thumbed through the book until he reached the last two pages; after pausing momentarily at the last page, he then threw the book on the floor.

"Frankie Boodram, this simply will not do! I am disappointed!"

I stared up at him; my face was blank with amazement.

Someone picked up my book and handed it back to the teacher. Normally, the teacher, upon receiving the discarded work a second time, would again toss the unsatisfactory assignment, much to the delight of the class. As my exercise book was being presented to the teacher, the sheet of brown paper, which had been carefully folded into four squares, dropped out. Curious, my teacher unfolded all four squares to reveal the calculations filling all eight boxes. Surely he could see that this was indeed evidence of the Herculean effort I employed in order to solve the math problem. The teacher studied each of the eight squares in silence. The class remained hushed. Seemingly endless moments passed. Finally, the teacher looked as if he were about to speak. The atmosphere in the room was subdued and I dared hope that I was about to receive a compliment. I could hardly contain my excitement. I needed the vindication that a kind word of recognition would bring to my life.

"Frankie," he said, "you should have tried harder."

I was taken aback. This was not the response I had anticipated.

Yet, my book was spared a second tossing. This in itself was unusual and I was grateful. This uncharacteristic act was all the encouragement that I needed. The class remained in a state of calm. Did this mean that the students were feeling a measure of sympathy for me? I felt their unspoken support. That moment was incredible. A sense of quiet understanding—of empathy—pervaded the classroom and I was uplifted. I held on to that feeling with tenacity.

Twice in the past twenty-four hours I had been reduced and my spirit shattered. Now, unexpectedly, I was lifted and renewed. I clung to that feeling of renewal and allowed myself to be sustained by it for however long it lasted.

That day after school I chose to take the long way home. I walked along a street that led to the cemetery where a fresh grave was in the process of being dug. Although I was curious, I continued on towards home. I spent time roaming the empty fields that bordered the back of our house. Left alone with my thoughts, I realized that I would never be lonely as long as I had the ability to think and to reason. Knowing that I could be my own best friend gave me an inner peace. I nurtured that thought as I made my way home.

Once again the idea of actually completing high school seemed elusive. Now that my father and I were alienated my education remained solely my responsibility. I had to resolve my own financial difficulties. I alone had to find the necessary money to pay for my school fees. Although my mother was willing to share what little she had, my pride would not permit any such indulgence. The full reality of the impetuous declaration that I made to my father when I announced that I would neither ask for, nor accept, a single penny from him, confronted me now. Money—money—money. How was I to acquire enough of it to realize my dreams?

23

LOOKING FOR WORK

IN OUR neighborhood there were no fast food restaurants and there were very few jobs for young people. Because most small businesses employed members of their own family, finding employment in that sector seemed highly unlikely. I was feeling discouraged. Then I remembered that one of Pa's jobs was delivering films from Port of Spain to two of the local cinemas in Tunapuna: the Palladium and the Monarch. Since the management of both cinemas knew Pa, I felt that I might have a chance at a job as either a ticket seller or ticket collector. I felt that I could handle either position equally well.

I approached Mr. Seetaram at the Palladium theatre in Tunapuna regarding a job, and when he pointed out that I was too young, I noted that one of his sons, Chanka, was close to my age and he worked there. Mr. Seetaram seemed to take that into account. Somewhat encouraged by this, I bravely enquired if he would consider hiring me on a trial basis. He seemed to like this idea, and when he found out that I was actually working to put myself through school, he decided not to place me on a trial basis, but hired me right away.

When I visited the Monarch Cinema looking for work, events unfolded in a similar manner. Two brothers, Satrohan and Kamal Ojah, worked at the family theatre. Later, both these boys would become good friends of mine but I did not know either of them when I applied for work. After meeting with Satrohan about a job, I successfully persuaded him to let me try out for the job. My job search turned out much better than I had dared hope; I now had jobs working in both cinemas on a regular basis.

I developed a daily routine: at the end of my school day, I walked the mile to the theatres to begin my work. On weekdays, there were usually two shows: one at 4:30 and one at 7:30. I was a cashier at both theatres and sold tickets in an enclosed booth. This job ended around 5:30. If I went home then, I would have to rush supper and my homework in order to return to the cinema for the 7:30 shows. I decided that my time would be better utilized if I remained at the theatre and complete my homework. It was much easier to do my homework there under electric lighting than at home under the dim light of the lantern. I would get home around 9:30 p.m. Whatever homework I had that required a more focused effort was relegated to the weekend. My life assumed a most pleasant and predictable routine.

Occasionally I would stay to take in a movie after work. Sometimes when my father was acting up at home—quarreling and creating a ruckus—I would make a deliberate decision to stay at the theatre and watch a movie. The more that happened, the more movies I saw. The more movies I saw, the more I came to love movies.

Movies allowed me to see how other people in different parts of the world lived. I was fascinated by this experience. It was as though another world had been uncovered and soon I became completely enveloped in it. Movies offered me a sanctuary set apart from the everyday crass realities of life; movies transported me into another realm of existence. And, it was at the movies that I could begin to consider the various extremes of the human condition without any immediate threat to my own person. I soon became immersed in my new life.

As this time I was also striving to cultivate good friendships. Because I was one of the only boys from my neighbourhood attending high school, the other boys judged that I considered myself to be better than they were. This was far from the truth. I had to work to pay for my schooling, and consequently, I no longer had the luxury of time to spend with the friends from my street. But to them it seemed as though I was deliberately choosing to make myself a stranger.

While working at the cinemas I was gradually meeting other people and eventually I developed friendships with both Kamal Ojah and Chanka Seetaram who were themselves close friends. Soon I came to know and become friends with their other friends—Doc and Phillip in particular. Over time, a deep friendship grew amongst us all; this friendship provided me with a much needed distraction from the pain of my everyday home life.

At home Pa continued his daily rants. It was not uncommon for him to be a bit too *refreshed* even on a week day. Sometimes he lost complete control of his senses. On one occasion he decided that it was time for me to have a belting. Pa had arrived at this conclusion based on his own peculiar method of calculating my number of offences. Not every infraction was immediately disciplined. Pa would file these sins in his memory, and when it suited him, he would let me know how many I was guilty of by raising the appropriate number of fingers. Today appeared to be my day to be *disciplined*. I really was growing tired of this senselessness. After all, I was now attending high school and I was making every effort to be successful. I felt that Pa should appreciate the fact that I was maturing and trying to live a life that would make him proud. His insistence on continuing this ancient practice of beating me whenever it pleased him (which, more often than not, occurred when he was intoxicated) irritated me. *Why did Pa not talk reasonably and explain things calmly? Why did he have so many rules and edicts? Why did he always have the expectation that he would be obeyed instantly? Why did he constantly assume the role of dictator?* None of this seemed fair to me.

Midway through my critical musings about Pa, I realized that I should, at the very least, try to be more tolerant of him. I began to wonder what kind of life he had had growing up. I did not recall Pa telling us any stories about his childhood. It was then that I first came to consider that Pa must have had a difficult life. He, too, must have experienced his share of disillusions. How many disappointments were we children responsible for?

24

RIBBIERO

ONE DAY I bore personal witness to one blighted hope and through it I discerned another side of my Pa.

The incident occurred some time ago when Pa announced to the family that Mr. Ribbiero, his boss from Port of Spain, was to pay us a visit on Saturday. Not only was Mr. Ribiero Pa's boss, he was also a white man. These two facts combined, made the visit doubly important. The white boss was coming to our humble house! Ma was excited and nervous but she had a plan. She engaged all the children in the project. The cleaning began immediately. All the floors inside the house were thoroughly scrubbed; the yard outside was swept and broomed to perfection—it was important that all the brush strokes went in the same direction. All the dishes were taken out of the cupboards, cleaned until they sparkled, and then rearranged in neat piles on the shelves. Even the back yard received special attention.

In order to shield the eyes of our visitors from any unsightly visions, Pa instructed us to build a temporary wall in front of the cow pen in the back yard.

To further insulate our guests from experiencing the full range of odours that that we endured every day, Pa purchased special chemicals. It was his hope that these chemicals would contain the foul odours coming from the latrine which was also located in the back yard.

Our tiny garden at the front of our house was weeded and swept. The four concrete steps in front of the house were thoroughly scrubbed and a fresh coat of paint was applied to them.

Finally, it was Saturday. Everything was ready. Ma had risen early and was busy in the kitchen making preparations for our "guests."

She opened a special can of red salmon in honour of this singular occasion.

Pa told each of us where we were to be located and what we were to be doing when the expected visitors arrived. Each of us was given a specific designation. I had been instructed to remain outside on the driveway side of the house. Further, I was told to appear to be cleaning the outside of the house. Pa wanted to ensure that all of his children appeared respectful and industrious in front of his boss. Unknown to Pa, I gradually made my way towards the front; I was curious; I simply *had* to have a front row seat to see this god called Mr. Ribbiero.

Soon a highly polished, beautiful, black jeep pulled up outside. It was Mr. Ribbiero and his friend. Pa rushed to the front to open the door of the jeep and greet Mr. Ribbiero. Pa was positively glowing; he was so happy. I heard Pa invite Mr. Ribbiero and his companion to come inside. I did not hear Mr. Ribbiero's response, but, judging from the drastic change in my father's stance and demeanour, I surmised that the invitation had been declined. Mr. Ribbiero did not even step out of the jeep. He talked briefly to Pa and then handed him a document. Then they shook hands. Once again I heard Pa extend the invitation to come in for refreshments. Once again the invitation was declined. Having concluded his business, Mr. Ribbiero left. The vehicle seemed to vanish into thin air. The visit turned out to be no visit at all. Pa brooded; he was exceedingly disappointed. Ma was quiet; this too, was turning out to be a disappointment for her as well. We all felt terribly let down and defeated.

This incident helped me to understand my father a little better. I realized that this visit by Mr. Ribbiero carried a great deal of influence in our community. I came to understand the significance of a white man's visit to the home of an Indian labourer. Such a visit could immediately elevate one's status. It was a sign of validation to one's existence and importance within the quiet community. Knowing this helped to explain Pa's obvious disappointment. I did not understand however, how *Mr. Ribbiero* could not have understood the importance of his visit. *Why did he not take a moment to come inside and receive our hospitality? Had Pa been presumptuous in asking Mr. Ribbiero to come in? Did Pa attach too much importance to the visit?* All these questions puzzled me.

This incident, however, did not diminish our need to capture some kind of special status in society—some form of recognition or validation of our worth by others. We longed to have a family member about whom we could boast—someone who lived or studied abroad—some-

one whom we could call *auntie* or *uncle*, the way the non-Hindi community referred to their relatives. Somehow the terms *mausie* and *mausa*
which we used to refer to our relatives, carried with them a very real
stigma and made us targets for ridicule. To have an auntie or an uncle
seemed much more high class; these words carried with them a dis-
tinctly elevated status.

Such status could also be achieved by having one family member
employed in a *respectable* occupation. At that time in Trinidad, a respectable occupation would have been defined as any job other than
that of a common labourer or servant. These occupations, however
honest, were frowned upon and considered low class by some people
on the island—even though a great number of the people on the island
had those types of occupations.

Whenever someone from a "lower class" made an effort to advance
himself, he was often censured for "not knowing his place." It was a
common belief among islanders that no one was to appear to be better
than his origins. To do so would certainly invite instant disapproval
and ultimate rejection by the very ones one was attempting to impress,
even one's own family members.

25

NEIGHBOUR JOE

OUR LUCK as a family however, appeared to be about to change. Our very handsome older brother, Clive, was about to be married to a woman who came from a highly respected family on the island. I'm sure that my father regarded this marriage as promising. When one member of the family married well, everyone seemed to benefit. My brother Clive's exceeding good looks were sufficient in themselves to have merited him marrying well. When these looks were coupled with the fact that he was associated, albeit in a voluntary capacity, with the island's most prominent Hindu citizen, (Mr. Bhadase Sagan Maharaj) he was noticed by another very distinguished family who had ties to Bhadase. This family pursued Clive as a marriage choice for one of their own. When this happened our family was delighted with Clive's apparent good fortune. To further his cause, Clive's exceptionally disarming manner allowed him to claim the life of a prince in the very midst of our poverty. He was as handsome as he was charming. No one disliked Clive; he was adored by all who encountered him. The fact that he was getting married and was marrying well, brought supreme happiness to our family and indeed, to the whole community.

The one unfortunate blemish on all this happiness was the fact that Clive was currently unemployed. Because of this, Clive and his new bride, Bhougie, (which means "brother's wife" in Hindi) moved into our home. This put further strain on an already stressful situation for Pa. He had yet another mouth to feed. Because of this, Pa was most anxious for Clive to become employed.

The fact that he was unemployed and married did not seem to

bother Clive however, and he continued to live his princely life of socializing and partying in spite of the many protestations of both his new bride and our father.

This state was not endless however and one fateful day Clive's kingdom came crashing down around him. It began its downward descent on a day when Pa returned from work early in search of Clive. When Pa could not find Clive anywhere, Pa became agitated. This agitation further escalated to seething rage when Clive finally showed up accompanied by a friend neither liked nor approved of by Pa.

"Clive, where the **** were you! Ah had a job for you!" Evidently, Pa had approached someone in the telephone company in Port of Spain and had "secured" a job for Clive with the provision that Clive make it to the company within a certain prescribed time. That time had now expired and Pa was furious.

"Where were you!" demanded Pa.

"Pa, I went to the river. Me and my friend. . ."

Clive did not get a chance to finish his explanation. Pa had a huge stick in his hand which he hurled at Clive. The stick made contact with Clive's shoulder and in an instant Clive was on the ground writhing in pain. No sooner was Clive on the ground, when Pa jumped on top of him and pummeled him with his fists. Clive's efforts to block the blows were futile. Pa's attack was relentless. He was determined to teach Clive what it meant to be a man, to be an adult, to be responsible. Pa's verbal skills were lacking. The only way he could effectively communicate was with his fists.

Ma heard Clive's shouts for help and intervened on his behalf.

"Yo go kill him!" she cried.

Pa, unable to contain his violent rage, turned on Ma and struck out at her also. Remembering how many times she had sacrificed her body for our safety, I ran outside and threw myself between Ma and Pa. Pa was about to strike again when a male voice yelled out.

"Budrick. No!" The voice belonged to Neighbour Joe: one of the few people whom my father respected. Neighbour Joe moved in close to Pa, spoke a few quiet words to him, and then led him away from the scene of the conflict. Together they withdrew to the back yard. I truly believe that Neighbour Joe saved Clive's life that day. Pa seemed intent on teaching Clive a lesson that he would not soon forget. The whole scene was very dramatic. Clive's wife wailed over Clive's injured body and the rest of the household, in panic mode, cried hysterically.

Neighbour Joe left Pa in the back and approached the sobbing and wounded Clive.

"Clivey, what happened, Son?" He, too, was one of Clivey's many admirers and it hurt him to see Clive suffer.

"Neighbor Joe—oh God—me father beat me up so. Look what he did. I can't bend me arm."

"But, Clivey, why he do this? Yo provoke him?"

"No, Neighbor Joe. Yo know me situation. I am married and have no job. Every day ah trying to find one. No luck. So today, my friend Corsican, and me went to bathe in the river. I had to cool me worries! Y' understand, Neighbor Joe?" Clive sobbed.

"Clivey, Clivey, Clivey, my dear boy," Neighbor Joe consoled. "Yo a good boy. Yo did nothing wrong. Y' know, yer father getting old. An' he so concern for yer welfare. He losin' he senses. Don' worry, yo goin' do the right thing. Forgive him. He ol'. Yo'all young. Y' understand me Clive?"

"Yes, Neighbor Joe."

"Now, off y' go to the hospital and get yerself checked."

"I's okay, Neighbour Joe. I be all right."

Neighbour Joe reached out and put a coin in Clive's hand and said, "On yer way, Clive. Get a treat, Son!"

Clive accepted the coin gratefully and headed off to the hospital.

Pa was pacing back and forth as Neighbor Joe headed back to him. As soon as Pa saw him, he began to pour out his emotions. Neighbour Joe did not have to say anything.

"Joe, tell me what ah go do with me children? Dat Clivey is harden! He won' listen."

"Ah know, Budricks," responded Joe.

Pa continued. "Joe, this Clivey he married. I have to min' he and he wife. It hard. And, and, and, what is Clivey doing with he time? He gone river, skylarking with Corsican. I know dat dey up to no good. My God, Joe, what d' heck wrong with dose children? Dey don' care!" Pa stopped pacing and looked to Joe for his input. He did not have to wait. Joe was ready with his response.

"Budricks," Joe began, "Kids these days, stupid. Dey got no sense. No sense at all. Dey not like we." Pa seemed relieved at Joe's critical observation. "Ah tell you this, Budricks. Clivey will grow up. Forgive him, Budricks. He young an' he stupid. We ol' and we have to know better," urged Joe.

"I don' know." Pa fretted. Joe moved closer. He reached out and placed his hand on Pa's shoulder.

"Budricks, their generation different. Dey so ignorant. But Clivey, in time, he will change. Forgive he. Promise, yo'll gi' he another chance." He waited for Pa to respond.

"Okay," agreed Pa.

"Now go inside and eat somet'ing. Yo mus' be hungry and tired, Budricks. Go in an get somet'ing t'eat and den rest."

Pa heeded Neighbour Joe's instruction and we all heaved a sigh of relief. Another catastrophe was averted.

When Neighbour Joe was acting as intermediary, I must admit that at first I was taken aback and was confused somewhat by his apparent duplicity. First, he settled Clive down by taking his side, and then he calmed my father by taking his side too! How could he be on both sides at the same time?

Upon reflection, I gained a glimpse of Neighbor Joe's love and wisdom. He did nothing to exacerbate the situation; rather, he neutralized it by validating the pleas of both my father and Clive. Clive had received such vicious blows and humiliating insults from Pa that it would have been understandable for Clive to have harboured some hatred for him. And Pa, so humiliated by Clive's apparent unwillingness to accept his responsibilities as a married man, felt quite justified in "correcting" Clive.

Certainly, Neighbour Joe had diffused a very critical situation. From this act, I learned a most valuable lesson that was to remain with me for the rest of my life. Neighbor Joe espoused the principle of compromise and validation. By neutralizing anger, he also quelled any lingering hatred. I marveled at my wise neighbour.

I also gained some respect for my brother, Clive. He was a strong young man, but never once did he raise his hand against Pa; he absorbed every blow without retaliating. I came to respect Clive for his restraint in this situation.

26

A CASE FOR GLUTTONY

S HORTLY AFTER this incident, another situation arose that promised to bring a measure of delight to our family.

Deo, Clive's new brother-in-law, was returning home to Trinidad from Canada where he had been studying to become a doctor. We received word that he would be coming to pay us a visit and, understandably, we were quite excited. For the first time in our history, a "member" of our family who carried real social distinction, was coming to our home. In honour of this occasion, only the very best was good enough. Ma opened a can of real red salmon that she had been saving for such a singular occasion. She prepared enticing salmon sandwiches and instructed everyone not to touch a single morsel. Determined to be the perfect hostess, she took out her best china and set up her display on a tiny table in a small corner of our living room. As children, rarely were we allowed in that room; it was reserved for royalty or near royalty. Deo, because he was studying abroad, fell into the latter category. Ma then gave each of us our instructions. Under no circumstances were we to sit at that table; it was reserved strictly for our "guest."

The much anticipated moment of arrival came. A large white Chevrolet pulled up outside our home. Deo was sitting in the passenger side; a friend of his was the driver. When the car pulled up, Clive's wife, Bhougie, came outside to greet him. Ma stood behind her, waiting to do her part in welcoming him to our home.

Deo stepped out of the car, exchanged greetings with his sister, and then *left*. He gave no polite excuse; made no acknowledging gesture to anyone other than his sister; he simply left.

The rest of us looked on in stunned silence. Disappointment prevailed. I, however, was not entirely unhappy. My thoughts immediately flew to the appealing salmon sandwiches that Ma had so carefully prepared. They were still sitting on the delicate little table in the living room. I felt compelled to go in to the room for one last look. I did not know when next I would see such a display. The sandwiches were beckoning to me. One sandwich in particular seemed to be saying, "Frankie, you are special too—you are somebody. Eat me!"

I was convinced that I should indulge my appetite. This was a moment that may never again be duplicated; and that sandwich was truly irresistible. I reached out to it with a small measure of hesitation. My hand trembled slightly as I took a tiny portion. When I put it to my mouth, there was no turning back. It tasted better than any sandwich I had ever eaten before. I have no reasonable explanation for what happened next other than to say that I was totally bewitched by the salmon. I simply could not help myself. I ate every last morsel of every single sandwich on that china plate. To wash it down, I drank every drop of tea that was in the teapot.

Everything was so inviting. I truly felt special sitting there in the "forbidden" room, indulging my appetite. I did not linger, however, and once I was finished, I went outside and made myself busy in the yard.

Soon, I was to reap the consequences of my unrestrained gluttony.

I heard a scream. It came from my mother. Then, I heard her yell, "Who done this?"

Curious to discern the reason for the shouting, all the children, myself included, re-entered the house and stood by Ma in the living room. She was holding the empty platter. Again, she reiterated, "Who done this?"

No one came forward to acknowledge guilt. There was only awkward silence as Ma looked at each of us in turn hoping that our faces would betray our guilt. Before her eyes could reach mine, I stepped forward and admitted, "I did it Ma. I'm sorry. But I couldn't help it!"

If I had hoped to see the gentle side of my loving mother, I was sadly disappointed.

Grabbing me by the ear, she led me into the very corner of the room where the offence had been committed. "Yo little rascal. I'll deal with you! Kneel down!" she ordered.

I did.

"Now, lift your knees."

I obeyed.

Beneath my knees she placed a *grater*—an apparatus with rough edges used to grind the kernel of the corn into powder. It hurt, especially when I moved. Two hours later, Ma returned and released me from my punishment. As much as I hurt kneeling for hours on the harsh surface, I did not regret my act of indulgence. For that one single moment in my life I had been surrounded by extravagance and I loved every second of it. My punishment was small when measured against the grandeur of that experience.

When I went outside I could still see the hurt on everyone's face. Clive was especially disappointed that Deo did not come in to our home. Clive withdrew quietly to the back of the yard. Bhouige was sad. She felt the extra burden of guilt for it was her flesh and blood that was the cause of so much sadness. It truly pained her to see everyone in such a forlorn and wretched state.

I wondered if we had the right to be so disappointed. In fairness to Deo, I questioned whether or not he was fully aware that we were expecting an extended visit with us. In most occasions when someone from abroad comes home for a visit, it is tradition to make the rounds of the various relatives and family members. Perhaps Deo did not yet consider us to be close enough family to claim an extended stay. It may be that Deo had already made other plans. I may never know the answer, but the hurt and disappointment felt by all the members of my family was very real.

This incident serves chiefly to reveal how much my family longed for social recognition. Again it gave me further reason to try to understand my father and even when I was angry with him, I truly tried to see life from his perspective.

27

REFLECTIONS AND CHALLENGES TO FAITH

LATELY, I had become deeply contemplative and questioning; not just about my father, but also about life's circumstances in general. Because I was now attending high school, I had had occasion to witness the lives of other students. It came as quite a revelation to know that many of the other students had none of the worries to which I was subjected. They had their school fees paid; they were surrounded by loving and caring parents; parents who did not drink or curse; parents who were able to provide the finer things in life. I began to wonder why I had so many worries; why I had to be born into a poor Hindu family; why I had a father who spoke only with his fists. I confess that I coveted both the lives of my classmates and some of their possessions. I resented, however, the self-righteousness of some of those same students.

It was not uncommon for one or another of my good Catholic classmates to announce, with an air of haughty self-righteousness, that he knew God personally. These same students would loudly declare that my mother and my father, indeed, my whole family, were destined to spend eternity in hell. Of this they were certain. *What reasons could they possibly have for making such a pronouncement?* I wondered.

It seemed that we were being condemned to hell because we were Hindu. This made us worshippers of cows and thus of idols. We were called *idiots* and *heathens* and were often shunned by our Catholic adherents.

I never grew accustomed to their condemnations. Each year these insults stung with the freshness of the first piercing.

Over the years, a quiet rebellion grew within me. This year in particular, I had even more questions for I had been studying the Gospel of Mark and in particular the Sermon on the Mount.

The Sermon on the Mount held such significance for me. Through the Beatitudes, Jesus invited his followers to be generous and compassionate. Yet, here, at this Christian/Catholic school, where these very principles were being taught, there seemed to be a noticeable lack of compassion and a real paucity of generosity. Among some of the students there was no practical manifestation of the teachings of Christ. *How could someone be surrounded with Christian teachings and not have a Christian spirit?* I was completely baffled by the incredible self-righteousness that came from a soul that claimed to be Christian—a soul so far removed from the grace and civility that Jesus advocated both by word and by personal example! I was horrified by the shallowness and superiority of so many Catholics! (Forgive me if I seem to be disparaging all Catholics for the mistakes committed by only a few. That is not my intention.) What agony must Jesus endure whenever He witnesses one of His own condemning the faith of another! I wonder if God is tempted to disown such sanctimonious hypocrites. I wonder too, about my own journey of discovery. *Was I being a hypocrite? Were my views too strong?*

It was not only at school that the idea of the supremacy of the Christian faith reigned unchallenged. From time to time, Christians from other denominations would visit our homes offering pamphlets and other reading materials designed to convert us *heathens.* They would explain that our souls were in danger and that we needed to be *saved.* Ma always received these visitors and listened to their message with utmost respect and admiration but never converted. Her faith and beliefs were rooted in the faith into which she was born: Hinduism; a faith which she felt did not preclude her from taking all the best and kindest principles espoused by other faiths—be they Muslim or Christian—and absorbing them into her own. I believe that an element of my mother's spiritual nature is infused in my soul, for despite my quarrel with the self-righteous Catholics, I found the essential essence of Christianity as revealed in the teachings of Jesus Christ, permeating my spirit.

There were times when I became disillusioned with religion, or more precisely with God. In my struggles for simple survival and acceptance, I frequently asked God why He had made me so poor and why He had made me be born into a Hindu family when Hindus were so often despised. These questions never went away and the answers would take many years to unfold.

28

Explosions

MY REBELLIOUS nature was not restricted solely to school and religious concerns. As I matured, some of this rebellion spilled
over into my relationship with my father. While I felt that I
always tried to see life from his point of view, this task became increasingly difficult each time he threatened me with a belting.

The frequency of my father's irrational and explosive outbursts
embarrassed me and frightened my friends. Eventually, my friends
stopped wanting to come to my home because they never knew what
to expect from my father. But, fortunately this did not mean the end
of our friendship for they began to invite me to their homes. It was
through the vehicle of these friendships that I began to experience another type of living.

My new friends grew up in privileged homes. Unlike me and my
family who ate with our hands, their families used real knives and
forks at the table. When my friends first invited me to have a meal
with them at their homes, I was hesitant. I was overcome with feelings
of nervousness and awkwardness because of my lack of social skills.
Feeling inadequate, I returned home knowing that I needed help before I could again accept another invitation to dinner. Who better to go
to than my own father, I reasoned. Pa was a fully grown man; surely
he could teach me.

I waited for an appropriate moment to broach the subject. It came one
day when Pa was serving us breakfast at the table. He had just picked
up a ripe avocado, cut it into sections with a knife and proceeded to
peel back the skin. Once the stone was removed from the centre, Pa
placed the fleshy meat of the avocado into a bowl and mashed it into a

pulp with his bare hands. When the mashing was complete, Pa again used his hands to place a serving on my plate.

Since I had recently come from one of my friends' homes and had just witnessed the cultivated use of knives, forks and spoons, I thought that perhaps this might be a good time to introduce the topic to my father. Even though I had never seen him use a knife and fork, he might be very receptive and have some ideas of his own to help me attain some fundamentals regarding proper etiquette at the table.

I seem to recall asking Pa, "Pa, could you use a spoon to serve us, please?" I meant no offence with this remark, but Pa took personal exception, and before I knew that I had deeply offended him, I found myself the target of a large bottle of hot pepper sauce. Upon contact with my head, the lid flew off and the entire contents of the bottle spilled onto my face. The pain from the hot peppers was severe. I felt blinded because I could not open my eyes. Moreover, I dare not open my eyes. The burning was so intense I feared that it might prove a threat to my vision.

Suddenly I felt myself being picked up and hurled over the three foot high dining room wall. For a brief moment I experienced the sensation of flying. Literally, I was flying. I landed with a thud on the gravel driveway some distance from the dining room. Still covered in pepper sauce, I picked myself up and bolted blindly from the yard. A well-meaning neighbour intercepted me and dutifully returned me to my exasperated father who continued to exact his "pound of flesh" for my unfortunate comment.

Because of the frequency of these types of incidents, I felt forced to assume a somewhat rebellious nature at home. Pa was not aware of my new state of mind when once again he approached me to signal that I was due for another belting; I became the antithesis of the dutiful and respectful son that I had been raised to be. A powerful force came over me. My spirit, overwhelmed by the constancy of senseless beatings, and finding no solace anywhere, leapt over the chasm of fear that separated me from my father. I found myself walking toward him without fear. With both of my hands stretched out to him, I said,

"Go ahead, Pa. Beat me. Beat the daylights out of me. That's all you ever do; that's all you know how to do. Here I am; I am yours."

Dazed, Pa drew back.

I continued. "And I will tell you this, Pa! All you do is beat me. You never talk to me like a normal father. And you think that I am afraid of you? I'm not!"

My father was a large man and he towered over me; I had to look up at him when I was speaking. Until today, I had always been respectful of him in his presence. But, today was different; today some bold new freedom seized my soul and all fear was gone. I continued my protestations.

"Pa, you are always drunk and you always cuss! Well, the time has come for me to leave. We two can no longer live under the same roof." The mature boldness of this strong assertion must have shocked and startled him because he lost his balance and stumbled, falling into an armchair. He began to sob and covered his face with both of his hands.

What was I witnessing? Was this really my mighty father? Was he really crying? Was I the cause of all this? I had never seen my father cry! Never in a million years would I have thought that this giant of a father could be brought to tears. What had I done?

I did not know what to do next; I thought that I would try to talk to him the way I had always wanted him to talk to me. I began to reason with him.

"Pa, I know you work hard and you always do what you can for your family. But you cannot cuss and use foul language anymore. You have children in the house and girl children. So when you have a drink, you must sleep it off! You must not get on anymore, Pa. If you do, then I will leave."

I left Pa sitting alone in the living room. As I entered the bedroom and got into bed, I noticed that the entire house was quiet. Ma and the others had overheard the exchange. Suddenly, my body began to tremble and shake. *My God, what had come over me? Had I actually said that I would leave home if Pa misbehaved? Did I mean it?* Yes, I did. That knowledge scared me the most. The very real thought that I might have to leave home was frightening to a degree that I never thought possible. I wondered if Pa, out of sheer defiance, would *insist* that I now leave home.

I never had to face that possibility however, as Pa made no rash decision. He took time to reflect on the matter and I was ever so grateful.

A noticeable change came over Pa; he seemed less intimidating. In fact, he treated me very differently after our exchange. He never whipped me again. Furthermore, he began to defer matters of family discipline to me. The tables had turned, and I found myself assuming a role I did not always welcome. (Things had changed so much, in fact, that over the years, my sisters would threaten to tell on Pa to me if *he* did not behave in a way that met with *my* approval.)

Thereafter, Pa began favoring me; he especially favoured me over my brother Boysie. Boysie was the type of boy who did not like school. School held too much stress and Boysie much preferred the easy life. He always said he would like a *"real easy job"* in life, one like that held by the railway crossing guard in our community. The guard was responsible for closing and opening the gates that controlled the traffic. In Boysie's opinion, that guard possessed the perfect job. Because that job demanded little in the way of education, Boysie felt that it would be the perfect job for him.

As a boy, Boysie did not develop any real educational pursuits. He much preferred a life of *"liming"* with his friends. It always may have seemed to Boysie that he got twice the number of blows from Pa as I did. I may not have admitted it then but I can attest to it now; Boysie's perceptions were true. He did get twice the number as me.

It was shortly after my confrontation with Pa that he inadvertently paid me a compliment; this compliment got me into a lot of trouble with Boysie.

It happened at a time when Pa seemed to be particularly infuriated with Boysie's behaviour and conduct. Pa had repeatedly urged Boysie to make responsible choices. On this particular occasion Pa actually shouted, "Boysie, why can't you be more like Frank? Your brother is going to be somebody. You are a no good vagabond."

Pa will never know how that statement translated in Boysie's mind. Out of sheer exasperation, Pa was seeking for a way to reach Boysie. The unfortunate result was a furthering of the void between Boysie and me. Boysie turned on me and accused me of enjoying what Pa had said. He threatened to get even.

Boysie's threat troubled me deeply. I knew that he would not rest until he evened the score.

When we were younger, Boysie never failed to remind me that because he was older, I had to obey him. He knew that I was trapped by my desire to try to do the "right" thing. Sometimes this desire left me vulnerable by requiring me to sacrifice my own principles in order to show him the proper respect due to him as my elder. Boysie knew that he could hold my principles for ransom and get me to do whatever he wanted.

There was a time when we were both in elementary school. When we headed home for lunch, the rains started to come down hard. Boysie led the way to a neighbour's house where we sought shelter beneath the eaves. We were spared from the full force of the drenching rains. There was a section of the eave where the gutter was broken and the rain water flooded out in torrents. When Boysie notice this he headed straight for the downpour. He immersed himself fully in the flood of water and ordered me to do the same. Against my better judgment, I obeyed my older brother.

When we arrived home, Boysie took the lead in explaining to Ma how we had become trapped in the downpour. He even managed to squeeze out a tear or two for extra effect.

"Oh, gawd, Ma, the rain come down hard. It so hard, Ma. Frankie an' me we try not to get wet. We had no way out, Ma. We go get caught in the rain." To his credit, Boysie proved to be quite the thespian; he put on a convincing performance for Ma.

Following Boysie's production, Ma asked us to remove our wet clothes. Because she did not have a second school uniform for each of us ready, we had to stay home from school. Boysie smiled at me, and winked. That was when I knew that this had been his plan all along. He had scored a victory.

The next time it rained, Boysie tested his plan again. This time the plan did not work; Ma was prepared and she had an extra change of clothes for each of us. Boysie's scheme was foiled and we had to return to school.

Situations like these where I felt compelled to sacrifice one set of principles for another led me to wonder when I would get to determine what was right for me. *If Boysie decided to jump to his death and ordered me to do the same, must I obey?* I knew that the answer to that question was "No" but I did not know if I could apply the same reasoning to situations that did not involve a life or death scenario. *When was I required to obey someone older and when was I expected to exercise my own judgment?* I still had no real answer to my question.

Time passed and once again Pa found fault with something that Boysie had done. Pa and Boysie began to quarrel and I overheard Pa proclaim, "Boysie, you worthless. Ah hope your brother, Frankie, become a magistrate. And when he do, ah hope he lock you up in jail and t'row away de key!"

Boysie turned on his heel. I could feel his anger.

Later that evening, as I was leaving the house, Boysie confronted me on the steps. I was not prepared for the following assault. Boysie had a piece of wood in his hands, and before I could react, he struck me with a blow to my head. The pain from that blow was indescribable. I fell from the steps and blood pooled around me. Unfazed by the blood, and blinded by rage, Boysie dashed towards me frantically yelling, "So you goin' to be magistrate and lock me up for life. I show you a real magistrate, Frankie! An' you have to take my licks. Pa said so. You have to obey me. I older!"

He hit me with a stunning blow once again. My blood was everywhere. With every ounce of strength that I could muster I reached out, blocked the third blow, and jumped to my feet. I don't know from whence I found the strength but I managed to strike a blow of my own to Boysie's face. I think that he was more shocked than hurt and he reeled backwards. The fight was on. We continued to battle and our fighting moved out into the ravine where I held Boysie's head beneath me and I began smashing it against the hardness of the concrete ravine. I now had the upper hand and it was my turn to declare, "You may be older, but you are stupider! You ever touch me again and I will beat you Boysie. Don't you ever dare tell me what to do just because you are older!"

I was exhausted. I wasn't just battling my brother; I was battling generations of rules and edicts; rules that seemed (to me at least) to be both unfair and antiquated. For years I had been frustrated and consumed with efforts to conceal the frustration. Today all that pent up confusion and frustration came raging out and, when the battle was finally over, I felt free; I felt as if I had broken the chains of ignorance and stupidity and was finally set free to bask in the pure light.

Boysie said very little to me over the next few days. His silence caused me to reexamine the circumstances of our misunderstanding. For some time Boysie had been nursing a wounded soul; I felt that I had to acknowledge my responsibility for his suffering for previously, when I stood up to my brother I challenged his authority and his stature as the older male in the family. Our culture clearly defined the role of the older brother; every younger sibling must respect his position and yield to his wishes. Boysie did not just accept the role given to him by birth, he delighted in it. It allowed him to forge an identity for himself. He relished the extra importance such a role brought to his life. After this final battle it appeared that Boysie had been somewhat dethroned. This was received happily by many in the family. Boysie's world appeared to be crumbling.

In a sense, my world was unravelling also. Because my attack on Boysie had been so vicious and vengeful, I felt that I had failed to preserve that sense of civility and grace that I had long espoused. My own principles had been assaulted. I now truly regretted my role in the fight and detested myself for getting so carried away. I did not have sufficient time to heal from that situation for another disturbing battle awaited.

29

MALPIT

ON THE Saturday following the "misunderstanding" with my brother, my friend Kamal and I met at the grounds of the university which was just a couple of miles away. We decided to ride our bikes there. The ride was pleasant and safe and we thoroughly enjoyed the various sights we discovered along the way. When it was time to leave, Kamal gave me one of his most treasured books to read. I gladly accepted it and tucked it under my shirt for safekeeping. As we left the university, we each went our separate ways. I was almost home when a heard a voice yelling.

"Frankie, wait up!"

The voice was familiar. It was the voice of Malpit, the neighbourhood bully.

I stopped instantly.

"So, Frankie, yo t'ink yo better that we," Malpit continued.

I understood immediately from his tone that he was not asking a question. He was making a statement. Malpit had developed a reputation for attacking the defenseless and brutalizing the innocent. Other members of his family shared his predilection for violence.

Within moments, Malpit was at my side, grinning. His grin could not disguise his loathing and contempt for me.

As he moved in closer, he shouted, "So, yo goin' to high school!"

I noticed that he was wearing his famous white leather shoes made especially for him by the local shoemaker. The shoes were extremely strong and boasted a pointed toe. Up until that day I had only heard about the damage that he could inflict with those shoes; that day I bore personal witness.

"Maybe yo won't be goin' any more," he threatened as he shot a powerful kick into my groin.

I folded in pain. The first kick was followed by a second and then a third. Blood gushed from my mouth and nose. But, Malpit was not yet satisfied. He needed more.

As he approached my crumpled body, he bent over, picked me up and literally threw me against a neighbour's barbed wire fence.

Soon, members of Malpit's family joined him on the street. Their cheers and jeers encouraged him further.

My body was left hanging on the barbed wire and Kamal's book fell out from under my shirt. I was in extreme pain. My pain intensified when Malpit decided to hurl my own bicycle at me. While the bicycle caused me to suffer more, it also dislodged me from the fence and I fell to the ground covering the book with my body. I could barely think, I was in such pain. But, I had enough sense to know that I needed to protect my friend's book from Malpit. Darkness enveloped me. I passed out. This state lasted for only a moment. Coming out of the fog, I heard him say, "Be warned. I'm only getting started."

At that very moment, a volcanic force erupted within me and I jumped up and bolted. Because I was terrified that Malpit might go to my house and wait for me there, I ran in the opposite direction. No one followed. I stopped at a tap on the street and cleaned away some of the blood from my body.

Sometime later, I made my way home, haunted by the realization that I had just had an encounter with one of the residents of hell. I used to cling to this naïve belief that hell allowed its people out to roam the earth only at night. Malpit proved by his actions that the devil did indeed allow its citizens free reign over the earth during daylight hours too. I never felt completely safe.

The truly sad part of this, no, the truly ironic part, was that I could not tell anyone, especially my father, what had happened to me that afternoon. Because of his often and loudly announced belief that "it takes two to fight," I would automatically be in the wrong if ever I were to be in a fight, no matter what the circumstances.

There was, however, one further reason that prevented me from telling Pa. Malpit had drawn blood. If Pa knew this detail, he might have felt compelled to confront Malpit. Such a confrontation, given the nature of both my father and Malpit's family, would surely have ended in disaster. Malpit's family would be at his side immediately and would not hesitate for a moment to beat Pa. Such a beating would undoubtedly result in Pa being sent to the hospital.

For those reasons, rightly or wrongly, I absorbed the attack in complete silence.

The incident was over and I tried to dispel all memory of it from my mind. This, however, was not to be.

The following Monday at school was the customary day set aside to attend church. This happened once a week. The church was located right in the school compound and everyone was required to attend Mass. The non-Catholics were relegated to the benches at the back of the church. When services concluded, we were always the last ones to be dismissed and we often felt that we were on display. On many occasions some of the "Catholic" students made fun of us "non-Catholics." Sitting all together at the back, we were easy targets.

On this particular Monday, Father Fennessey preached his sermon on forgiveness. From the outset, Father placed his focus on the subject of hatred.

"Because you harbour hatred in your hearts," he began, "many of you are destined for Hell." Then he thundered, "If you hate, then prepare to go to Hell!"

His eyes surveyed the young audience assembled before him. Finally, they settled on me. I felt that Father was addressing his remarks to me alone. This thought was strengthened by his next admonition.

"And if one striketh thee on the one cheek, offer him the other also! So if someone hits you, you must forgive him!" *Was he speaking just to me? Did he know what had just transpired this past weekend? Did he know that I was entertaining very negative thoughts about Malpit?* Father's warning found its way directly into my soul and I shuddered. Up until that moment I had been enjoying the "idea" of wishing ill on the person who beat me up. This, at least allowed me a feeling of getting even in some small way. But, according to Father, I was not to allow myself even that one small luxury, for even having ill thoughts was sinful and would pave the way to hell. Father Fennessey insisted that forgiveness was the only way.

Such a warning could not have come too soon. This message, coming as it did right after the terrible event, did not allow me time to delight in any thoughts of hatred or ill-will toward my transgressor. By forcing me to think of forgiveness so soon, I felt that I had been denied even the small luxury of thinking vengeful thoughts. Indeed, it seemed as if the gods were conspiring with Father Fennessey in an effort to save me from myself. I did not want to be saved. I wanted to luxuriate in feeling hatred. I wanted hatred to consume me. I wanted to invite hatred to dwell in my soul for however short the time. I needed to feel the power of hate from the inside. I wanted desperately to hold on to the feeling of hate but the heavens were equally adamant that I should embrace forgiveness.

I was caught. Never before had I been placed in such a dilemma. Never before had I been so tested. Although in my heart I knew that it was wrong to hate, I thought that it was okay to hate for awhile. These words from Father had jolted my mind. He made me rethink my hatred for Malpit. While I wanted to relish the flavour of hatred, Father advocated the savouring of forgiveness. I was not yet ready to embrace this precept and I struggled to come to terms with it. To forgive my transgressor when my wounds were still so fresh was a challenge. I wondered why Father had to address this theme of forgiveness on this particular day. His sermon left my soul in turmoil.

As I was about to leave the church that morning, my eyes settled on a picture of Christ carrying the cross. Christ's pain was evident. I knew from the Scriptures that even as He was dying on the cross, He forgave His transgressors. At that moment, an incredible feeling stole over me—a swirling of unease of a soul in turmoil. Here I was, consumed with hatred for Malpit; there Jesus was, labouring in agony and about to die, yet still able to forgive. *How could I now choose to walk the path of hatred?*

I never fully resolved my conflicting emotions that day. I do know, however, that Father planted a seed that morning and this concept of forgiveness would continue to be a recurring theme in my life, constantly challenging me.

30

THE DREADED CAMBRIDGE EXAM

A S PAINFUL and unnerving as the events regarding my brother and my neighbour were, they allowed me an opportunity to grow. Following these incidents, both Pa and Boysie eased their aggression towards me and they left me alone for the most part. Furthermore, Pa indirectly handed over to me the mantle of responsibility regarding all family matters. I was expected to participate in discussions with my parents regarding any misbehaviour or perceived indiscretion of any family member. In matters of discipline both Ma and Pa deferred any ruling or judgment to me. All of this responsibility accrued to me when I was but a teenager. I know now that this unnatural reversal of responsibility caused great hardship on my siblings, but at the time I was aware only of how heavy a burden it placed on me. Indeed, in the eyes of the family, I was expected to conduct myself completely without fault or blemish. I was a teenager myself and desired to participate in the life of a teenager; this period of my life was suspended, and there were many times when I lamented that loss.

The cards were dealt. I perused the hand given to me; there was no ace. I resolved to create one for myself. I did not know how or when but I knew that at some point, my life would be better. That vision served to sustain me through the years of personal struggle that followed.

As I neared the end of my high school days, life had become a routine of school and work. I had managed to juggle my responsibilities and maintain a respectable degree of success in high school over the last four years. It was now the year 1959. It was a critical year for me as I had to write the dreaded "O" level Cambridge Exam.

This exam was demanding and many students failed in their first attempt. I invested a great deal of time, effort and preparation. The day of the exam finally arrived. All my thoughts were focused on this one event.

To further complicate my life, Pa chose that very morning to send me on an "important" errand. He must not have realized that I was about to write the Cambridge Exam that morning. I did not wish to argue with him, for to do so would disrupt my emotional preparedness. I felt that my best option was to run the errand quickly and get on with the exam. The shop to which Pa was sending me was located one mile away. I ran all the way there. When I arrived at the store, I explained to the shopkeeper what Pa needed. The man was not at all obliging. He berated my father for using me to do his dirty work. He informed me that my father had not been keeping up with his payments on his account and that he had greatly exceeded his debt limit. When I attempted to appeal on Pa's behalf, I, too, received a barrage of insults. I returned home empty-handed.

When I explained to Pa what had just transpired and why I did not get the required item, Pa too, started to yell, first at me, the bearer of the bad news, then at the shopkeeper.

It was getting late and the exam was about to begin. Pa wanted me to go elsewhere for the part. It was then that I explained to him about the exam. Amidst Pa's vehement protestations, I left.

The exam was not being conducted at my regular school which was just blocks away from my home; it was being held at an alternative site about a mile away. Even though I ran, I was still late and the exam had already started. I could feel my heart pounding as I entered the room; I felt awkward and out of place. Everything was so quiet; my mere presence seemed intrusive. I was escorted to my seat and given a reproving look by the invigilator. The reason for my tardiness was neither asked for nor given.

I took deep breaths to calm myself before I looked at the exam; it was an English exam and a major part of it was English composition. As I surveyed the various topics to write about, one in particular seemed to leap out at me. I read the topic as: "One Night Outdoors." Since I was already late starting the exam, I did not want to waste any more time agonizing over the other topics so I decided to settle on that one. Besides, a recent incident had occurred in our village which lent itself perfectly to the subject. Having a real live story to tell made the writing of the composition relatively easy.

The incident involved our young neighbour, Godwin, his brother, and a few of their friends. These boys had decided to go to Maracas for a day trip. The winding road to Maracus Beach was both difficult and dangerous to maneuver by car by the most seasoned of drivers. Young men, such as our young neighbours, were known to be both incautious and imprudent when traveling in groups. Later that day when news from the local radio station announced that there had been a fatal auto accident on the road to Maracus, everyone's thoughts turned immediately to Godwin and his friends.

At first, there were very few details regarding the incident. We knew only that a car containing several occupants, had skidded off the wet pavement, tumbled over a precipice and ended up at the bottom of the cliff. All occupants of the car were presumed dead. The newscast further explained that the recovery of the car and its occupants would be an extremely difficult, if not impossible, task. A description of the car came later. The description fit Godwin's car precisely; it was the same model, year and colour. The news that our friends had died spread rapidly throughout our community. Our whole town was in shock as the mourning process began.

Godwin's grandmother rushed to our home crying hysterically when she heard the news. Soon, other mothers assembled outside and added their voices to the growing throng of wailing women. Tears of agony flooded the streets.

The men began preparations to construct a large tent to host a wake for the boys. The town was wracked with grief. All commerce ceased as everyone struggled to come to terms with the tragedy.

The next evening, in the midst of all this drama and histrionics, Godwin and his friends arrived, completely safe and unscathed. Godwin's grandmother was sent reeling into another state of shock. Recovering somewhat, she sprang to his side, grabbed him and held him at arm's length, and delivered a resounding slap to his face. This was immediately followed by further hugs and kisses and a great reluctance to let him go. Joy replaced sorrow and the wake was supplanted by a celebration of life.

Later Godwin explained that he and the others had made it safely to Maracus and had ventured out on an exploration. They lost their way, however, and had to spend "one night outdoors." Because their car radio was not working, they were completely unaware that a real tragedy had occurred and that the whole community was in mourning.

When we first witnessed the boys' return, it was as if the dead had returned after spending "one night outdoors." This was the reason that I chose that topic for my composition.

After completing the exam, I was hopeful that I had written an acceptable story. As I was leaving the building however, I overheard a student tell his friend that he had aced the topic: "At Night Outdoors." I froze. *In my haste to make up for the lost time, had I misread the topic? Was it really "At Night Outdoors" and not "One Night Outdoors"?* That one word could change everything. My composition could be considered to be off topic. That one simple error would be enough to cost me my high school graduation. My hopes were shattered. To be successful at the Cambridge Exam, one must pass English. To fail the English component of the exam meant failing the entire exam no matter how well one performed in every other subject area. My current teachers could not be expected to intervene on my behalf because the exams were not marked by a local body. The exams were collected and forwarded to Cambridge University in England for evaluation there by an independent body of examiners. It was June and it would not be until late August when the results would be delivered to my school in Trinidad.

My future looked grim and I began to brood about the difficulty of having to repeat the year and all the exams. Because the course content in some of the subjects varied from year to year, I would have to master a whole new body of information if I were to fail. I questioned whether I had the emotional strength to overcome such an obstacle. I felt defeated.

31

SISTER DOROTHY AND MEG BATTOO

I DID NOT have the luxury of remaining depressed for an entire sum-mer however, as I needed to find work. A beloved nun, named Sister Dorothy, assisted me in this endeavour. She had come to know me over this past year. She was the French teacher at the girls' high school. When no one could be found to replace the French teacher at our boys' high school, Sister Dorothy agreed to teach us. Because her schedule did not allow her time to come to our school to teach us, we were re-quired to go to the girls' school for classes. The senior boys were to be accommodated in the same class with the senior girls. This was my introduction to a co-ed system of education. Many of the boys were ecstatic about this turn of fortune; I was mortified.

Sister Dorothy must have noticed how shy I was in the presence of the high school girls. I hardly spoke in class. Even though I had six sisters at home, I found it extremely difficult to relax in the now co-ed classroom. Sister Dorothy took an interest in me and worked hard to help me build up my confidence. As the weeks passed, I became less self-conscious and began to enjoy her class. Once exams were over, she wanted to know what I was planning to do with my time. I mentioned to her that I needed to work. It was then that she offered to help by writing a letter of recommendation to Mr. Meg Battoo, the owner of a prestigious car dealership just outside Port of Spain.

Following her recommendation, I contacted Mr. Battoo and sched-uled an interview for the next week.

I was nervous as I approached the magnificent building. The front office was filled with rich extravagance. Even the receptionist exuded

an air of superiority and confidence that was usually the exclusive re-
serve of the upper class. I felt intimidated from the moment I stepped
over the threshold.

I approached the secretary and explained that I was there to see
Mr. Battoo. She looked me over. I wondered, *Did I pass inspection? Was
I dressed appropriately?*

"Is Mr. Battoo expecting you?" she asked.

"Yes," I responded somewhat timidly.

"If I could have your name, please, Sir. I'll inform Mr. Battoo that
you have arrived." Her tone was professional, her diction was clear,
and her delivery was polished. This further increased my feeling of
intimidation.

"My name is Frankie Boodram," I uttered. My tone was muffled and
my delivery was awkward. I could not begin to match her standard.

"I'm sorry, Sir, I did not quite catch your last name?" she asked.

Feeling embarrassed, I could only manage a slightly stronger ver-
sion of the first utterance. "Boodram."

"Thank you, Mr. Boodram. I will inform Mr. Battoo. I will be right
back."

Left alone for a few minutes, I began to examine my surroundings.
Everywhere I looked I saw reminders of class distinction. Each person's
posture, language and attire indicated a social class much higher than
the one into which I was born.

The sound of footsteps brought me out of my distractions. The footsteps belonged to a very distinguished looking gentleman. It was Mr.
Battoo.

"You are Frankie Boodram?" he greeted.

"Yes."

"Follow me," he directed as he led me to his office. His office was impressive with its rich mahogany desk and leather couch. As he seated
himself in his leather high-backed chair, he motioned for me to sit on
the burgundy sofa.

I had a moment of hesitation before sitting on the luxurious furniture. I had never before been invited to actually sit on such fine furniture. I had only seen luxury like that in the movies. Trying not to reveal
my naïve reaction at being in the presence of such wealth, I composed
myself and sat down. I just felt heaven. If I appeared shy and awkward,
Mr. Battoo appeared not to notice.

Mr. Battoo pulled out a letter and began to read it, murmuring softly
to himself.

"Sonny," he said as he gazed at me, "you come well recommended. Sister Dorothy speaks most highly of you."

"Thank you, Sir."

"Well, based on her recommendation, I will give you a chance to work here."

Had I heard him correctly? Was he seriously offering me a job? There must be a heaven. Sister Dorothy is one of its angels temporarily on loan to Earth.

"Can you start Monday next?" he inquired.

Mr. Battoo exuded a natural air of command. He was decisive and forthright. I was completely impressed by his manner and style.

"Yes, Sir."

"Well, I will see you on Monday."

I thanked him and departed. I walked outside the building and checked the surroundings. I saw beautiful and impressive buildings and offices in that neighbourhood. The workers and clientele alike were all well-dressed. I looked at everything, smiled, and pinched myself. Was all this real? Would I really be working here amongst all this refined pleasantness? I considered myself to be most fortunate. I, who came from such a modest background, was now being engaged to work amid the elegance of city life. I could barely contain my exuberance.

32

DINING

As I left the car dealership, I started to pay attention to the signals that my body was trying to send me. I had been too excited to eat that morning because I was so preoccupied and anxious about the job interview. Now that the interview was over and I had the assurance of employment on Monday, I suddenly realized that I was starving. I noticed that there were a number of restaurants close by, but I was reluctant to venture into any of them. The reason was simple; although I was nearly nineteen years old, I still did not know how to eat with a knife and fork. I was not even sure that I knew how to hold a fork properly.

A couple of years ago, when I began making new friends at the cinema where I worked, I had asked my elder brother, Clive, to teach me how to use a knife and a fork. I felt that this was a skill that I needed to learn sooner or later.

The request seemed innocent and reasonable to me and Clive was the most likely person to ask because he was the one member of our family with style and charisma. I admired him greatly and will now admit to being slightly envious of his social skills. He was very comfortable in any and all situations. I approached my brother without any doubt about his ability or willingness to help me address my situation.

His response shocked me.

"Frankie, you think you white? You not! You Hindu. Remember that!"

How could I forget?

Forever I will remember the accusation hurled at me from the brother to whom I looked to for counsel. Forever I will remember the backhand which followed the accusation. I do not know which hurt me more, the verbal lash, or the physical slap.

To this very day, I have never understood Clive's objection to teaching me. Clive knew how to use a knife and fork. Why did he deny me my request?

I never let Clive's objection deter me from my quest, however. His refusal just made the task of learning more of a challenge. There was no one else in my entire family that I could ask.

I knew that between my two jobs at the cinemas and my new friends, the likelihood that I would be dining out was an increasing possibility. I resolved to find my own creative solution to my dilemma.

I remembered that my father had taken me to a restaurant in Port of Spain once. He had taken me to work with him that day and we were without our customary bag lunch. When it came time for lunch, Pa found this very clean and comfortable looking restaurant. Upon entering the restaurant, I noticed that the dining room was divided up into various small compartments; some of these were small rooms that had private doors.

Pa and I were escorted to one such private room. The waitress seated us at the table and took Pa's order. In a matter of minutes she returned bearing two plates of rice with red beans and vegetables. Then she handed each of us a spoon. Pa set his aside and ate his lunch with his fingers as was his custom. I used the spoon.

This restaurant was still in operation, and, after Clive's rebuke, it was the site I chose to begin my education in dining.

When I entered the restaurant, I was greeted by a most pleasant waitress. I told her that I wanted to order lunch and that I wanted to eat it in one of the private rooms at the back.

"You mean you want a room all to yourself?" she queried.

"Yes, please. Do you have space?"

"Well, we do have space, but you could be charged for two people. Every room has a minimum cover charge. You sure you want a room?"

I understood the stipulation and told her that I was prepared to accept the terms.

"Okay. Follow me."

As I followed her, she led me to a small room at the very back.

Once seated, she asked, "Now, what you want, Honey?" She had actually called me "Honey." I was encouraged by her friendliness.

"Miss, could I have some rice and beans?"

"Yes, but you should know that today we have rice and beans and chicken for the same price. Would you like that instead, Honey?" She had called me "Honey" again.

"Yes, please," I stuttered, slightly conscious of my awkwardness in this new element.

As she left to get the meal, I became lost in my own thoughts. I felt grown-up sitting in a restaurant, ordering a meal and paying for it by myself. I still had one problem, however; I still did not know how to eat with a knife and fork.

The waitress returned. She placed before me a huge plate filled with a large quantity of rice, beans and chicken. It seemed too generous a portion for me alone. I could hardly believe that it was all for me. I was impressed.

"Now, enjoy your lunch, Honey." she said so genuinely.

"I'll try."

She must have sensed a hesitation in my tone for she did not leave immediately. Instead, she paused and asked, "Will there be anything else?"

I looked at her and shyly asked, "Could you help me with something, please?"

"Help you with what, Honey?"

It took tremendous strength to get the next few words out, but I felt that I could trust her with my next request. I wanted her to teach me how to properly use the knife and fork. The fact that she was Negro and I was Indian could complicate the situation for in Trinidad, these two races had a history of negativity towards one another. By making this request, I was revealing my vulnerability. The waitress could easily seize the opportunity and use it to her advantage and humiliate me. Although I was risking my pride by asking her for help, I somehow felt that she was a person I could trust.

My heart was beating rapidly and before I lost what little courage remained, I blurted out, "Would you teach me to use the knife and fork, please?"

"Is that all?" she replied. "You wait here and I'll be right back."

Moments later, she returned carrying her own plate of food. She pulled up her chair right next to mine.

This wonderful woman sat with me and patiently taught me how to hold my knife and fork. Her manner was relaxed. Just when I was becoming comfortable, she was called away.

I was left with the impression that she had stolen those few moments just for me. I truly appreciated her effort and when she left, I practised my new skills. This was absolutely a defining moment in my life—for the first time I was using a knife and fork.

I felt a sense of accomplishment at this glorious achievement. I knew, however, that I owed my success to the compassionate soul of my gracious waitress. I was totally in her debt and utterly grateful for her generosity of spirit. Truly, she had captured my utmost admiration.

It is only now, as I look back at that incident that I recognize in her, a complete absence of pretension or censure. Her gracious act of forbearance in my time of distress won her a permanent place of honour in my heart. I will forever remember her caring act. It was executed with such civility that it represented to me a magic carpet which transported me into a heavenly realm of gratitude for all eternity. Words cannot adequately express my gratitude. Such is my admiration for this kind soul.

When I left that restaurant, I felt a little more grown up than when I had entered. Over the next few months, I returned to that restaurant a few more times. Each time I practised my new skills, and each time I grew in confidence. I was preparing for the future that I knew was awaiting me.

The future was here, now. This is the moment I had been preparing for all those months ago. It was time to put my skills and my confidence to the test. I was shy entering the restaurant, but I knew it was something that I had to do. Almost immediately I felt out of place. This was completely unlike the cozy little restaurant that my father had taken me to. Everything in this establishment was steeped in rich extravagance. I hesitated to commit myself to going any further. I was extremely tempted to withdraw and find another, more modest restaurant.

I knew at once that to do so would be to take the easy way out. This was a challenge, certainly. But I was not one to run away from a challenge and I would not allow myself to set a precedent that day. It was time for me to give myself a pep talk.

"Well, Frankie," I told myself. "This is what you have been striving to achieve. This is a new chapter in your life. Do you like what you see? Yes? Well then, let this mark a point of a new beginning for you. It is time to make fancy dining a part of your new life experiences now. You are important too! You deserve to enjoy a bit a luxury every now and then."

I listened to me.

The maitre d' escorted me to a table and handed me a menu. I surveyed the choices, and, since I did not eat pork or beef, chose a chicken lunch. The meal proved to be very satisfying indeed. But, most importantly, I felt very comfortable dining in the elegant surroundings. Again, I raised a silent thank you to my friend, the waitress. For a brief moment I was transported to a world where previously I would not have deigned to enter. That day I felt good, for I had taken an important step toward my future. The success met by that effort bolstered my confidence. All seemed well with my world.

33

FIRST DAYS AT BATTOO'S

MONDAY ARRIVED and I headed for work—my first official job—
at Meg Battoo's in Port of Spain. I dressed for work, caught
the bus into Port of Spain, and arrived early at the dealership.
I was excited and I could not wait to begin my new job at the front office (or so I thought).

I reported immediately to Mr. Battoo. He, in turn, phoned a Mr.
Robinson who came immediately and escorted me to my work area.
Although I was somewhat confused, I followed him, thinking that perhaps there was a secondary office located elsewhere. Mr. Robinson led
me right through the office to a huge set of doors. Mr. Robertson held
the door open and motioned for me to enter.

On the other side was a garage!

This was no ordinary garage; it was huge. There were various sta-
tions and each station boasted several workers. The initial disappointment I felt when I realized that I had not been assigned to the
front office was short lived; I was heartened to see that everyone who
worked at the garage appeared productive, enthusiastic and above all,
friendly.

At the far end of the garage adjacent to the street, was my assigned
area. Mr. Robinson introduced me to the garage manager, Mr. Otto,
and to the clerk whose job I was taking over. The clerk explained my
job duties to me. The job seemed simple and straightforward. When
a vehicle entered the garage, it was my job to raise the gate and allow
the car full access, provided that I had been given the go ahead signal
from Mr. Otto.

In time I learned that there were, however, certain clientele who were allowed immediate and automatic access. That list was extensive. Mr. Robinson gave me my first instructions regarding the list. Of course, Mr. Meg Battoo, himself, was at the top of the list. He had a number of different vehicles which had to be identified immediately so that the proper attention could be paid to them. As soon as Mr. Battoo entered the garage, someone would appear to park his car and attend directly to any need that may arise. If the car did not require any mechanical attention, it would be cleaned and shined until it sparkled. No directives were ever issued; this was always understood to be standard procedure. After Battoo, his wife and their many children followed a close second. Other members of his family, brothers, sisters, aunts, and uncles claimed immediate recognition also. Following these were certain close friends and colleagues who also expected immediate admittance. Mr. Robinson was my guiding star through the transition period. Because I was new to the job, occasionally I failed to recognize someone from the list. When this happened, the person would have to get out of the vehicle to identify himself/herself. This was considered to be a mark of disrespect on my part, and rarely did they fail to mention that fact to me. When they stepped out of their vehicles, they would look upon me with such great disdain and adopt an air of superiority, I sometimes wondered if their feet ever truly touched the ground. Their behaviour, insulting as it often was, required my polite acceptance. This was the one thing about my job that was troubling. Everything else was great.

The workers themselves were very open and welcoming. They worked hard and they enjoyed one another's company. As I began to feel settled and more at home in my job, I would visit the different groups of workers. Each group accepted me without hesitation and even invited me to take my breaks with them. I gladly accepted their invitations. From these workers I received an education; different from the one I received in high school. Unlike the workers at Mr. Morris' garage, these workers had wholesome conversations about the issues of the day or about philosophical concerns. It was always refreshing to speak with them.

Occasionally, Mr. Otto would allow me, under supervision of course, to write up the job descriptions of the repairs needed on some of the vehicles. Either Mr. Robinson or he would then deliver the work orders to the various departments. In time, I was permitted to both write up and deliver the work orders, especially when Mr. Otto was called away to attend to other business.

Sometimes when this happened, the workers would tease me in a friendly way by saying, "Frank, how does it feel to be the boss today?" or, "Frank, bring me an easy assignment, I'm having a bad day today." Whenever these comments were made, I never for one moment felt undermined or ridiculed. I always sensed their underlying respect and recognition for me as a person. Their easy acceptance and cordial manner actually made me feel somewhat important.

The days soon turned into weeks and time was flying by. I was growing into my own person at the garage; this in turn fostered confidence which allowed me the latitude to exercise some personal initiative.

One day a white man, dressed in Khaki shorts and sandals, approached my station and asked if he might speak to me. Of course I told him that he could. He reminded me so much of the overseers of Caroni Cane Plantations. They were the white bosses riding on horses, carrying whips and instilling fear among the poor who worked their plantations. I was accustomed to the often abrasive and condescending manner of the white men from the cane farm. This white man's mere colour already afforded him a large measure of respect if not fear. This man who approached me, however, proved to be both gracious and unassuming. He was the complete opposite of his plantation counterparts. He explained his situation.

"I am having a problem. My car is overheating and I don't have an appointment."

"Where is your car, Sir?"

"It is parked outside."

Imagine that. He parked his vehicle outside on the street. He had no air of superiority and no presumption of entitlement. He did not regard his white skin as a passport that conferred on him a special status. I was impressed.

"Sir, please bring your vehicle. I will get Mr. Robinson. We will see what we can do."

The moment he left, I went to find Mr. Robinson. After hearing my story, Mr. Robinson assured me that I had acted correctly. Mr. Robinson had very high praise for this white man.

"Frankie," he said, "you won't meet a nicer gentleman. He is humble and polite. And, he is very important. He is a professor. Everyone respects him."

Smoke was still billowing from the professor's jeep when he returned.

Mr. Robinson allowed me to write up the job card whilst he arranged to have the jeep fixed.

I was glad to write up the order for it gave me an opportunity to observe this gentleman as he gave details about his vehicle. I learned that he was Mr. Pitkin and that he was a professor at the University of the West Indies in Trinidad.

Mr. Pitkin apologized for his sudden intrusion and asked if he might be permitted to remain at the garage to await news about his vehicle. Of course I agreed to this request and immediately found him a chair to sit on while he waited. He expressed gratitude for that small act of consideration. While we waited for news about his jeep, we talked. In a very short time Mr. Robinson came and announced that the vehicle was repaired and ready to go. The professor was happy with the news and expressed surprise at the quickness of the work. He reached for his wallet.

Before Mr. Pitkin could take out any money, Mr. Robinson reached out his hand to stop him, boldly stating, "No charge, Professor; this one is on us."

Upon hearing that, I immediately wrote the words, "NO CHARGE" on the bill.

The professor was noticeably moved by this act of generosity and was momentarily stunned.

Mr. Robinson brought the jeep around and Mr. Pitkin still seemed unsure of how to respond to this kindness. I took the liberty of holding the driver's door open for him. He then extended his hand to each of us in turn and uttered an appreciative "thank you." Then he was gone.

After Mr. Pitkin left the garage I showed Mr. Robinson that I had written "NO CHARGE" on the bill. I knew that such actions were usually left up to the discretion of Mr. Robinson, himself. I hoped that he would understand why I did it and not think that I had been presumptuous in overstepping my authority.

My worries proved to be completely unfounded. Mr. Robinson simply stated, "You is a good man, Frankie and you learning fast."

That simple remark showed me that Mr. Robinson, like Mr. Pitkin, was a man to be respected. Both men commanded respect by their actions not by ordering it with their words.

Through the example of these two men I came to understand what real class meant. Yes, it was a division that separated society into two camps; but, the quality that determined class was not money or power or position; it was an inherent quality of civility and generosity of spirit—a quality that each of these men possessed.

Under the guardianship and guidance of Mr. Robinson, I found a haven of comfort at Battoo's garage.

34

"I AM MR. JOHNSON."

ONE DAY while I was working at my desk, I heard a loud screeching noise. A Mercedes Benz convertible entered the garage from the street. The car showed no indication that it was preparing to stop before it reached the gate, which was a good thirty feet from the entrance of the building. Stunned by the car's unconventional entrance, and mesmerized by its beauty, I did not open the gate. The driver, a wealthy black man, realized that the gate was not going to open automatically. He forcefully applied the brakes. The car came to a stop with the front windshield a mere hair's width from the gate. It was like a scene from a movie. All movement was suspended. In my mind I knew that something was wrong. I felt that *I* was wrong.

The driver got out of his car.

"I am so very sorry, Sir. So very sorry. Could you please ..." But, I did not have time to finish my apology.

"Shut your mouth!" he bellowed.

I withdrew in awkward silence while he inspected his windshield. I prayed that it was not damaged. I stole a glance; the windshield seemed all right, but the driver was not.

"Look at what almost happened to my car!" he shrieked. "You ignorant or something?" he clamored.

I felt so sorry for what had happened. I wished to apologize, but this irate and irrational man would not allow me to speak. He continued his tirade.

"I am *Mister* Johnson. The gate is *always* open for me. Are you stupid?" His disdainful glare made me feel worthless. "All you people are stupid. Give you a decent job, and you don't know what to do! Why don't you just go back to the gutter where you belong!"

I recognized that this attack was not the result of simple anger aris-
ing from an embarrassing situation; it was clearly rooted in discrimination and bigotry. All too often, I witnessed this prejudice in my own
neighbourhood. It was especially evident amongst the grown-ups during election time when Negroes and Indians clashed. I did not expect
it, however, from this well-dressed man. All 260 pounds of his mighty
frame showcased a magnificent beige suit. He closed in on my small,
shaking, 140 pound figure. His huge form was intimidating. I immediately felt that I was under siege. From somewhere deep within me,
an inner strength rose to my defense. Mr. Johnson then pointed at me
and threatened, "I will report you. I will make sure you are fired, you
little @#$%^!" The name he called me was most insulting. Something
in me snapped. (It was not that I was consumed with rage; it was more
that my injured soul demanded redress.) I gazed around for a moment,
searching for something, anything that would help me. Then I saw it
the perfect foil.

On the wall behind my desk hung a conspicuous frame. This frame
housed an inscription which was most appropriate for this moment. I
took a deep breath, faced Mr. Johnson, and declared unequivocally, "Sir,
may I invite you to read the sign above this desk?" I paused slightly,
noting that he was not responding. "Perhaps you are not in the right
frame of mind to read it for yourself. Let me read it for you." This giant
of a man was silent.

NO ONE, ABSOLUTELY NO ONE, IS PERMITTED BEYOND THESE
GATES UNLESS AUTHORIZED BY MANAGEMENT

"And you, Sir, were not authorized! Were you, Sir?"

Clearly, he was dumbfounded by my bold response.

My body was exploding with a host of memories—the sum total of
all previous put downs. My soul was crying for justice. I had been debased for being brown, for being young, for having bare feet, for tending cows, for being Hindu. The list of criticisms circled on and on in
my mind.

This man had assumed, like so many others before him, that because he had money and "position" he had a right to insult me. I knew
that I had to stand up for myself. To fail to do so would be to allow him

and others like him to treat me like a doormat, to walk all over me and leave their shameful presumptions to pollute and poison my soul.

He recovered from his momentary lapse, and became utterly exasperated.

"By the end of today—you will be out of here—you—you—I am going straight to Meg Battoo! I will teach you a lesson, Boy!"

I was mortified. The sudden strength and courage I had a few moments ago, now vanished. Images of disappointment flashed before my eyes. I could see Sister Dorothy's eyes fixed on me with regret and sadness! I was so perplexed. And what would I say to Mr. Battoo? He had been so kind to me in offering me this job. At that moment Mr. Robinson approached me.

"Frankie, man what got over you? You know if he goes to Mr. Battoo you're dead!" Others came and expressed similar sentiments. Clearly, no one wanted me to lose my job.

Shortly, we could see Mr. Battoo approaching the garage. Mr. Robinson sized up Battoo's famous gait and solemnly stated, "Oh, God. He has the firing walk!" Mr. Battoo could be seen from the far gate entering the garage. Everyone scurried to his station. Battoo was making his way directly to me. I felt small and diminished. I trembled, riddled with despair. Completely bereft of courage, I waited.

35

WONG'S WRONG

WHILE I waited, my mind drifted back to my childhood when I faced a similar agony. I was but eleven years old. Haunting memories of that long ago incident still plagued me.

My father had secured me a job at a warehouse in Port of Spain where he worked. Attached to the warehouse was a retail grocery shop and I was assigned work in both the shop and the warehouse. This particular Saturday I was instructed to clean up the premises. Once I was given a broom, I cleaned everywhere; not only the grounds of the retail shop, but also the floor of the warehouse.

Whilst I was sweeping, I noticed that the head shopkeeper, Mr. Wong, had thrown a warped tin of chocolate powder into the garbage bin; obviously, it had been discarded because it was damaged. I looked at that tin of chocolate and reasoned that the powder inside the can should still be good. I did not see the need to throw out the whole can when the damage was restricted to the outside. I knew further that my mother could never afford to purchase such a can; the cost would be prohibitive. I felt that my mother would be ecstatic to have such a treat. It was with these rationalizations that I reached into the garbage bin and picked up the discarded can of powder. I tucked it into my lunch bag for safekeeping.

Midway through the afternoon, a fellow worker came and announced, "Frankie, Mr. Ribbiero want to see you in the office. Now! Go!"

Well, since I had never really been in the front office, I was most curious to see it. It seemed that everyone who worked there had such nice jobs and I was happy to be included in their midst even if it was just for a brief moment. I wondered why Mr. Ribbiero wanted to see me. Perhaps he had seen all the hard work I was doing and wanted to say something encouraging. Maybe he was proud of me, and wanted to tell me so in person. I could already imagine him saying, "Frankie—keep up the good work." Such a comment would make me so proud. It would also make both my mother and my father proud. I walked into the office with a smile on my face ready to receive my compliments.

My smile quickly faded when I saw the serious look on the faces of Mr. Wong, Mr. Ribbiero, and my father. Before I could ask a single question, Mr. Wong shouted, "There is Frankie! He *tief* the can! I saw him. He put it in his lunch bag. You see—you no trust him. He big tief!"

Once the accusation was raised, Pa stepped forward, his hand already poised to deliver his famous slap.

"Frankie, you put this can in your lunch bag? Yes or No?"

"But, Pa -"

"No buts. Did you?"

"Yes, Pa."

"You see how yo shame me! How I go show my face round here with a tief for a son?"

Pa did not slap me, however. I guess he decided to set aside that action for the time being.

Now that I had been branded a thief in front of all these witnesses, Mr. Ribbiero surrendered me to Mr. Wong. Pa left the warehouse in utter disgust.

The zealous Mr. Wong was only too happy to administer his form of justice; he put me to sit on the very top of a stack of rice bags at the very back of the warehouse. He ordered me to stay there.

It was very hot and humid atop those bags and I used every plea I knew to try to get him to change the punishment site. He refused. After calling me, "a very bad boy," he left.

No one would speak to me. I wanted desperately to explain to someone, to *anyone* that I was not a thief. No one came. I remained on that sack of rice all afternoon.

When Mr. Wong came by later I was happy to see him. I hoped that perhaps he had had a change of heart.

"Frankie, promise me you be a good boy. You no steal no more. The boss knows you is a very bad boy. You bring shame on you fader. Promise, you no steal no more, and I beg Mr. Ribbiero forgive you. I give you your job back."

"But Mr. Wong, you know the truth. You know you threw away that can. It was in the garbage. I did not steal it!"

"You stupid boy, Frankie. I don't plead for you. Don't come back here. I want no *tief* here."

"Mr. Wong, please tell the truth. My father will believe you."

He rushed off, still yelling at me.

The day was coming to an end and I was still sitting atop the rice bags. I knew that my pa would soon be coming back for me.

I dreaded the trip back home. It would take more than an hour with the mule and cart. Pa would have the luxury of time to fully indulge his temper. God knows that he was as capable of extending a verbal lashing as a physical thrashing.

The sound of footsteps interrupted my thoughts.

It was Mr. Wong. He looked at me. Neither of us spoke. He reached up to retrieve his large lunch box. Someone called out to him. Distracted, he dropped his lunch box and the contents spilled out onto the floor.

I could hardly believe my eyes. Among the various items on the floor were two tins of chocolate! It did not take me long to realize that Mr. Wong had been pilfering goods from the warehouse.

I jumped down from the rice bags immediately.

Mr. Wong ordered me to go back up. I ignored him. He had no further authority over me. His credibility was forfeited the moment his theft was exposed. He no longer had any moral authority over me.

He tried to whisk the evidence back into his bag but it was too late. I had already grabbed them.

Mr. Wong then ordered me to give the cans back to him. I almost laughed in his face. How dare he presume to command me to do anything for him! Not only was he a thief but he was also a liar. He had sabotaged me in front of my father and his boss in order to curry favour with Mr. Ribbiero.

I became bold and challenged him.

"Who is the thief now, Mr. Wong? You are a big liar and a shameless thief. Why did you get me in trouble?"

He had no answers for me. Instead, he raised his hand to slap me. I ducked. And, before he could wrestle the cans from my grasp, I threw them away. I *happened* to throw them in the direction of Mr. Ribbiero's office with the chance that he just might be caught.

Mr. Wong slithered along the ground after the cans. It gave me great satisfaction to watch him all snake-like on the ground. He was finally revealing his true character.

Mr. Wong was fortunate in that he did not get caught. He grabbed the cans and scurried off to the store. I never saw him again that day.

When Pa finally returned for me, he yanked me by the arm and hurled me into the cart. Several of Pa's friends were outside. He had already told them of my disgrace. They offered him their condolences. In their eyes I had both shamed my father and disgraced my family.

Once we were out of view of these co-workers, Pa delivered a volley of slaps to my head and upper body. Each of these slaps was punctuated with the words *liar* and *thief*.

In silence I suffered those insults.

We traveled on without incident for a few moments, but I knew that Pa had not yet exhausted his anger. I could feel the intensity of his rage surging to the boiling point.

Then he delivered the most hurtful attack yet. Pa called me *stupid*. He began yelling this word to me over and over at the top of his voice.

My whole body recoiled at this word. I had suffered that insult so many times before but never from him. I wanted to scream back at him: *"Don't call me stupid! Not you, Pa, not you."*

If my own father could think that thought, then maybe it was true; maybe I truly was stupid. I could not bear to hear it. I wanted to shut my ears to his words.

I still said nothing.

More than anything I wanted Pa to know that I had not shamed him. I would rather die than knowingly shame him. I remember wanting to summon the Good Fairy to my aid. In my eleven year old mind, I still wanted to believe in magic. I wanted the Good Fairy to give me a magic potion that would allow me to enter my father's brain. Once there I felt that I would be able to erase disappointment, expel frustration and restore reason to this shattered man. I needed Pa to be rational and composed. I dared not attempt to speak to him when his mind was so troubled. I wanted to tell him that I was no thief; I was no liar; I was not stupid.

I could not find my voice however, and my defense remained unspoken and my innocence unproven.

What had I done that was so bad that it deserved such condemnation? I had simply salvaged a can of chocolate powder from the garbage. It was going to be thrown out anyway. *How could that be considered stealing?* I was actually rescuing the can. And, by giving it to Ma, I would be making her happy at the same time. Instead, I found myself heavy with the knowledge that I had brought shame to my family.

When we finally arrived home, I still had not said a word. I did not know what to say. I could not admit to something I did not do. And, I dared not tell Pa about Mr. Wong's deceit. I would never be believed.

My silence fuelled my father's rage. He demanded that I say that I was sorry. I could not, for I truly felt that I was guiltless.

Pa regarded my silence as rebellion and he vowed to beat the rebel out of me. I endured his blows until I felt that I was losing consciousness. I believe that I heard Ma yell, "God, you gone go kill him! Stop, before you kill him!"

Ma intervened and led me away from the madness. Pa made no effort to stop her. *Was he, too, relieved at this intervention?* Perhaps, but I'll never know for sure.

Ma took me inside and cried helplessly, anguished by the sight of my battered body.

"Frankie," she cried. "Why you fader call you tief?"

I had no answers for her. I had only questions—questions that could not be voiced. I wanted to know where this thing called decency resided; I wanted to know where fairness lived. In the courtroom of the adult world, I had been charged, tried and convicted without any opportunity for defense. *How could this be? Did I not matter at all in this world? When did I get to be heard?*

Through all this however, I did gain some insight into both myself and the adult world. I came to know that I was neither a thief nor a liar. I cannot say with certainty that I was innocent, but I can assert that I was not guilty. Thus, I was able to restore to myself a measure of respect. Even at this young age, I sensed the importance of having self-respect. Something told me that to lose respect for oneself would be to lose one's self.

I also learned not to place all my trust in the hands of the adults. Not all adults were worthy of trust. Mr. Wong proved to me that adults were capable of injuring the innocent. I felt helpless in their world.

36

A LESSON LEARNED

THAT FEELING of helplessness from so long ago, was not unlike the emotional torment that I was now feeling as I watched Mr. Battoo approach.

Then he was beside me, ordering, "Sonny, follow me!"

"Yes, Sir."

That had to be the longest walk of my life. Everyone knew that I was being lead to the office to be terminated. A look of concern and regret was stamped on their faces, and their eyes gave ample testimony to their feelings; they cared. I felt grateful that I was being spared the humiliation of a public firing.

As we walked toward Battoo's office, I found myself examining my predicament and resolved that I would accept my firing like a man. I also resolved that if I were to be fired I would discharge my mind about today's events. I may be fired but I resolved not to be silenced. Further, I decided that Mr. Battoo could not both fire me and then turn around and lecture me on my behaviour. It was one or the other. I would not accept both at the same time.

We entered his office.

"Showdown," I thought.

"Sonny, sit down."

I hesitated; I preferred to stand. If I were to sit on that soft couch, my posture would be compromised; I would lose the leverage that came with being in control of my own self.

"Sir, thank you, but I will remain standing."

"Sonny, please sit down. I have something to say to you." There was something disarming in his voice that made me listen to him. It did not sound dismissing or judgmental.

I sat down. Air made a swooshing sound as it escaped from the couch but I was not alarmed, only slightly embarrassed.

"Sonny, you were right!" he declared.

He looked at me and paused.

I was totally dumbfounded

Mr. Battoo turned away and looked upon the many awards that decorated his office.

With the skill and polish of an accomplished maestro, he asked, "Now, Sonny, what would happen to my business if you spoke that way to all my best paying customers?"

"Sir?" I queried. I did not understand.

"You see, Sonny, we depend on our customers, to come to us for repairs. We charge a fair price. They pay their bills. And that is how I pay your salary. Got the picture?"

I sure did.

"Now, Sonny, you think there will be any more incidents of this kind?"

"No, Sir."

"Now, that is excellent. You might want to proceed with your duties."

As I stood up to leave, I asked Mr. Battoo,

"Sir?"

"Yes, Sonny. What is it?"

"May I ask why the gentleman reacted so angrily? Who is he?"

Mr. Battoo obliged me with an answer.

"Sonny, he is a big time lawyer. And he wants everyone to know it. Everyone has to bow to him. Even I have to appear to bow to him. That's the price we pay for his patronage—and he pays good money!"

"Yes, Sir. Thank you, Sir!"

"Hold on, Sonny. Not so fast. You stood up to this man. And you did it with character. He is very angry because you challenged his power. You were upset too. Why was that? What exactly happened between you two? Did he do something to annoy you?"

I put my head down. I was searching for words to communicate my disgust towards the man who attacked my person and diminished my sense of self-worth.

Mr. Battoo, sensing my discomfort, offered, "Sonny, did you feel that he was racist?"

"Yes, Sir."

"Were you upset?"

"Yes."

"Now, Sonny, not every black man is racist. Even some of our own Indian people are racist. Now, we have a business to run and you have your duties awaiting you."

"Mr. Battoo, thank you, Sir."

I left Mr. Battoo's office. I was filled with admiration for this man. He accorded me complete dignity and I was humbled by his humanity. Mr. Battoo's authority was tempered with courtesy and understanding. He could have wielded his power and tossed me aside like yesterday's garbage. This he did not do.

I was so relieved that I had not been fired, I was delirious. I decided to capitalize on the moment and have some fun with my fellow workers.

I managed to look dejected and sad as I walked over to my desk. I opened a drawer pretending to examine my belongings.

"Frankie,—we sorry you get fired. You were doing so good," a saddened worker offered. Then, Mr. Robinson approached and said, "Frankie, I so sorry to see you go."

I could barely contain myself.

"Go where, Mr. Robinson? What made you think that I was going somewhere?"

"You got fired..."

"No!" I smiled. "I did not get fired."

I delighted for a moment, in their obvious confusion before I shared the details of the events that transpired between Mr. Battoo and me.

37

TWO SURPRISES

For the rest of July and right into August, I was extremely at peace at the garage. By late August the results of my June exams were in. Father Fennessey had our marks and I received word that we were to visit him to learn our results. I gathered my courage and went to see him at the school.

Remembering that I had made a terrible error in answering the main composition question on my English exam, I prepared for the worst. I knew that there was a very real possibility that I would fail English. I also knew that if I were to fail only the English component, I would still have to repeat all the exams in all the other subject areas the following year. I steeled my mind to accept the fact that I would have to attend high school for yet another year.

When I reached Father Fennessy's office, I knocked.

Father opened the door.

"Frankie Boodram," he uttered with a smile.

"Hello, Father. I came for my exam results," I said shyly.

Father produced the document containing my marks and stared at me for some time!

"How bad are they, Father?" I asked.

Then, without any warning, he responded, "How could an atheist like you get a *"distinction"* in Religious Studies?"

He glared at me trying to hide his smile.

"Father, did I pass?" Now I was becoming anxious.

"Barely, but surely. You passed!"

"I got a certificate, Father?" I asked incredulously.

"Here, take a look for yourself."

I could not believe my eyes. I had received a *RECONSIDERED* and this was stamped across my grade in English. Originally, I had received a failing mark, but then there had been a second consideration. The story I wrote about in the exam, although slightly off topic, must have been good enough to merit a *"Pass."* With only a pass in English, I was granted a third class certificate. At that moment the classification did not matter to me; what mattered most was the fact that I had passed the Cambridge Exam! I could hardly believe it. I was not stupid after all. I actually had a modicum of intelligence. I was both humbled and elated. As of that precise moment, I felt liberated. I was finally free from the ghosts of my past that wanted to keep me forever imprisoned in the house of the stupid.

That singular achievement completely redefined my spirit. I saw myself in a positive light for perhaps the first time in my adult life.

Father Fennessey was not finished with me yet. He had yet to deliver the strongest shock ever when he asked simply, "Frankie Boodram—do you want a job as a teacher?"

There was no cover letter, no interview. There was just the simple question. Did I want a job as a teacher?

The answer was equally simple.

"Yes, Father."

"Well, you start at the beginning of the semester. I will see you just before school begins."

And he was gone.

"My God," I reflected, *"what had just happened? Frankie Boodram—a teacher? Could this be real? Unheard of! Unimaginable! Was I sane?"* My mind was whirling and my feelings ran the gamut from complete happiness to utter bewilderment.

It was in that confused state that I began to make my way home. When I had almost reached home, a powerful urge overtook me. This force guided my path toward the place that had been my sanctuary since childhood. I made my way across the railroad tracks and entered the savannah. I must have been there a thousand times or more playing soccer or cricket. It was revitalizing to be there once again but I did not linger long for my favourite place was still beckoning.

The tree that had given me refuge from the heat of the sun and the pain of my life, welcomed me still. It seemed only fitting that I return to share my good news with one of the constants in my life. I climbed its outstretched branches one more time. I reclined into its strength. I felt peace. Reluctantly, I left this gentle repose and headed for home.

As I entered the yard, I saw Ma, sitting outside on the back steps—waiting. Was she waiting for me? She smiled a gentle smile and asked, "Well, Frankie—what's the news?"

I told her that I had passed the exam and that Father Fennessey had offered me a teaching job at the boys' school. She did not seem surprised. I asked her if she already knew.

She answered simply, "I had a feeling. I pray for you. God answer my prayers. You deserve this, Frankie." Then she touched my face and smiled.

I felt humbled by her simple affirmations. Her touch was like a blessing. "Ma, thank you for everything; I owe you so much." My heart was so full; these words could not begin to reveal the depth of my gratitude.

Ma received my words but immediately directed my attention to another course. "Frankie, you have someone else to thank. He go be proud of you."

Of course, Ma was referring to Pa, and as usual, she was right.

But, for a moment, the two of us remained on those steps in absolute stillness, soaking in that moment of perfection.

Everything else would have to wait until tomorrow. This moment was sacred. This was my moment with Ma.

The next day I informed Mr. Battoo of my new plans. He wished me well as I said goodbye. There was a sadness in me when I left that I could not completely explain. I had grown so much as a person under the expert tutelage of both Mr. Battoo and Mr. Robinson. I was leaving the safe and familiar garage to chart territory which was yet unknown.

My next visit was to Father Fennessey. He assigned me my courses. In looking back, I can only recall that the first class he assigned to me was a history class. I loved history and began preparing furiously for the first day.

The day finally came. Outwardly, I was dressed appropriately—navy blue dress pants, white shirt, navy tie. *But, was I prepared for what awaited me in the classroom? Did I have a clue as to what it was to be a teacher?* Up until the moment that Father offered me the job, I had never really considered becoming a teacher. It was such an honour to be asked.

Without any real formal training, and without any advanced education, I was about to enter a classroom as the teacher of third year high school boys. I was perhaps no more than two years older than most of the students. *Was this really happening? Was I about to teach my first class?*

PART III

New Challenges

38

MY FIRST DAY AS A TEACHER

IT WAS Monday. I was about to take my first walk to St. Charles Boys' School as a teacher and I was petrified.

Once the bell rang, a teacher would signal that it was time for the students to enter the school. The students preceded the teachers into the classrooms, took their seats and respectfully awaited their teacher's arrival. When the teacher entered the classroom, the students would automatically stand up and greet the teacher with a *good morning* or *good afternoon* as the case may be. This formality was seen as a sign of respect for the teacher and the students were required to remain standing until the teacher indicated otherwise.

It was now my turn to enter my first classroom *as a teacher.* My heart was pounding. My palms were sweating. The room was filled with thirty-five grade eleven students. Only one student stood up to acknowledge me.

I could feel the lack of respect in the room. I sensed the students' resentment towards me. In their eyes, I was but a young upstart; I was someone who only a few months ago, had been a simple student like themselves. *How dare I now presume to pass myself off as their teacher!*

I understood their point of view.

They did not attempt to hide their scorn.

He think he could teach us. He is a Hindu. What do he know? He come from the cow people.

These were but a few of the remarks made by my students on that very first day of my teaching career.

Their comments indicated that they questioned the legitimacy of my right to claim the title *teacher.* I understood their thinking. They saw me as a familiar person: one who came from a lower class. They saw me as one who had little to offer them; in their eyes, my position was laughable.

Their words were cruel and they cut me deeply: any more cuts to my psyche and I might have bled to death mentally.

I refused to reveal to them the depth of my pain.

My mind raced wildly as I walked to the front of the room. With great reluctance I realized that my carefully prepared lesson was completely unworkable under the present circumstance. The atmosphere in this classroom was like no other I had ever experienced. I felt unprepared: a timid gladiator at the mercy of a vengeful mob that was all too eager to pounce.

My mind searched frantically for a weapon that would counter the net of ridicule that was being hurled my way.

I reached the front, planted my feet squarely in the centre of the room and turned to face my detractors.

"Gentlemen!" I paused. I had their attention. I looked at the entire class. Well, if the truth is to be told, it only *looked* as if I was looking at the entire class. In reality, my eyes were raised slightly above their heads so that I would not be distracted by thirty-five pairs of eyes. I continued, my voice strong, my words calculated. "This course will examine the period of British history commencing with Henry VII and concluding with Charles II. Let me outline some key points and highlights of the era." I paused once more. The class was now quiet. "Gentlemen, it would be a good idea for you to record in your notebooks five or more key points pertaining to the course." I stopped. Notebooks came out; pens were at hand. "Gentlemen, let me introduce you to..."

There was a sudden interruption: a book had fallen off a desk.

My eyes searched out and found the culprit. There was no defiance in him: only an embarrassed awkwardness. He made an effort to retrieve the book. I motioned—*leave it alone*—he did. I resumed my discourse.

The students were listening and I began to highlight certain aspects of the course, drawing particular attention to the reign of Queen Elizabeth I. I revealed the fact that Elizabeth was the queen who, although never meant to be queen, survived and ruled longer than many of her predecessors. The students nodded at this achievement. The second bit of information that seemed to captivate them was my pronouncement that although Elizabeth never married during her long reign, there was ample evidence to suggest that she did not deny herself the fruits of a married woman.

I paused every so briefly after delivering this tasty morsel. A smile of enlightenment dawned on the face of one student. This was followed by a subtle ripple of laughter from another corner of the room. Knowing looks and small chatter were exchanged among the students.

This remark directed at Queen Elizabeth certainly claimed their interest. I now needed to redirect their attention to a more important point. I therefore announced: "It is said that Queen Elizabeth was among the most important monarchs who ever sat on the throne of England. Gentlemen, why was this so? As we examine the course, this will be a point of view that you will have to investigate. Your opinion is valued. You must be prepared to defend your position."

The students were listening. Was it because of the revelations regarding Elizabeth? Was it because of the manner of my delivery? I may never know. What did it matter? I had them. I was gaining a quiet confidence.

Even the fact that I tried my best to speak correct English seemed to work in my favour in that classroom.

When I sought to speak correctly in my youth, I was scorned and dubbed a *white man.* For this offence, I was regarded as an outcast, not only by my peers, but also by one of my own brothers.

In my early teens, whenever I sought to speak correctly, it was used against me and I suffered a lot of abuse because of it. In spite of that fact, I persevered. I felt that the use of our dialect, while it added a colourful flavour to the island, set us apart from the English and European elite and relegated us to a lower level in society. We were often dismissed as second class because our speech appeared second class. Thus, when I was nineteen, after years of concentrated effort, my speech was somewhat different as it assumed a style of its own and may have lacked Trinidad's colourful *patois.*

On that first day of class, however, all those years of derision and ridicule finally were bearing fruit: my delivery was a success. I felt the tension in the room relax. Soon the whole room was filled with laughter about something that I had said. The students were not laughing at me; they were laughing with me. They were laughing because of some historical trivia regarding a ruler in England so many thousands of miles away, so many years ago, that they found entertaining.

I knew then that I had them.

Some time later as I continued my discourse, the bell that signaled the end of class, rang. I stopped speaking. All thirty-five pairs of eyes looked at me. "Gentlemen, for tomorrow, I expect you to have read Chapter One of your text. Thank you."

All thirty-five young men stood up and in unison said, "Thank you, Mr. Boodram."

I was humbled. I had survived my first trial. I had entered the arena a frightened nineteen year old novice and emerged Mr. Boodram, the teacher.

What began as one of the most dreadful moments of my career became one of the most glorious experiences of my life. I felt totally engaged: fully alive.

39

THAT CERTAIN GROUP

CERTAIN HONOURS were attached to joining the staff at St. Charles Boys' School. The teachers, many of whom had been my former teachers, all insisted that I call them by their first names and to dispense with the title of *Mister*. I felt very uncomfortable with this request. I was still a teenager. I had just finished school a mere two months ago and it just did not feel right; it felt disrespectful; it did not sit well with my spirit.

Something that did sit well with me however, was being invited to join a group of three teachers on Fridays after school. The meetings began as simple gatherings of like minded individuals eager to share ideas, thoughts, and concerns about students and teaching in general. Soon they became a welcome ritual with the addition of sandwiches and beverages. Some of the group would add alcohol to their drinks. This, in turn enlivened the dialogue and soon the teachers were sharing more than mere professional conversations. When one teacher revealed that he was in love with a woman who did not return his affection, the others took that opportunity to break out in song. Their song of choice was most appropriately titled: *I Can't Stop Loving You*.

As time went on and as I came to know more about each teacher's personal life, I was amazed at the number of frailties they allowed to be revealed in my presence. I had always regarded my former teachers as near gods; they existed on a plane above that of us lowly humans. I had no idea that they were mortal and subject to the same pain and suffering that the rest of us endured. This was indeed a revelation.

Each Friday, at the end of class, one or another of these teachers would begin to pour drinks for everyone. I was always offered a drink

but I had always declined. I did not fully appreciate what effect my refusal had on the others until one of the more veteran teachers put this
question to me in a somewhat irritated and slightly indignant tone.

"Frankie, how come you won't have a drink with us? Is something
wrong with us?"

Sensing his frustration with me, I hastened to assure them that there
was nothing wrong with them. My refusal stemmed from something
personal within myself.

"Well, what is it? Tell us. We want to know."

They all had shared so much of themselves with me, I guess it was
only fitting that I reveal a little of myself to them.

"Well," I began, "you might think that I am stupid. I am not sure
that I fully understand the reason myself. It has something to do with
a promise that I made."

"All right, we are ready to hear the rest of it. Let's raise a glass to
Frank and his promise." With that cheer, they clanged glasses, downed
another shot, and turned their faces toward me expectantly.

The moment weighed heavily on me. I was not accustomed to sharing personal things about myself. I now felt compelled to share the
details of the promise. I began, hesitantly at first, but then decided to
hold nothing back. What kind of friendship could we have if we did
not know each other's truths? I started by telling them about my father
and his over indulgence with alcohol. I then revealed a little of the terrible toll it took on my mother and the rest of the family whenever his
mood escalated into a rage. I did not want to become like my father so
I made a vow to myself that I would not have an alcoholic drink until
I was twenty-one years old. When I asked them for their input regarding my decision, they regaled me with compliments and hailed me as
the wise one. I was not ostracized from their group for having made
this decision. They supported my choice and encouraged me to keep
my promise to myself. I was supremely happy to be a part of that staff.
There was no awkwardness with my decision, there was only understanding. And sometimes, to make me feel like I was actually having a
real drink, they would add a slice of lime to my soft drink.

40

DETENTION CLASS

TWO INCIDENTS from my early years teaching in Trinidad stand out in my mind. The first occurred during a detention class. Detentions were served after school, Monday to Thursday: never on Friday and the teachers took turns supervising.

On this particular day, it was my turn to supervise. I always tried to maintain a quiet and respectful atmosphere in the room. Suddenly a disturbing *roar* broke the silence. I did not let on that I knew who had created the distraction and asked for the guilty party to stand and reveal himself. The student rose on command. I asked him to remain standing while I searched my mind for an appropriate punishment.

"Stand on your desk!" I commanded.

The student looked at me blankly.

"Go on. Stand on your desk," I repeated.

Reluctantly, he complied.

"Now, Mr. Wilkins, roar like a lion!"

"Sir?" he questioned.

"Mr. Wilkins, you wanted our attention; you craved our attention; now you've got our attention. We want to recognize your regal domain. Go on, roar!"

He stood, completely abashed.

The class was hushed with expectancy.

I approached.

"Come down, Mr. Wilkins."

He stood down.

He had looked so frightened and embarrassed. Remembering how it felt to be so singled out, I wanted to ease his pain somewhat. "Mr.

Wilkins," I began, "I am sorry if I caused you embarrassment."

"Sir, I was the one who disrupted the class. I am sorry."

"Thank you. I appreciate your apology."

"Sir," Wilkins continued, "what is to be my punishment?"

"Wilkins, you have paid your dues...in full. You made a mistake. I trust that it will not happen again. You are a good student."

"Thank you, Sir. It will not happen again. And, Sir...remember that first day you came to our History class?"

"Yes, I remember."

"No one but me stood up."

"How could I forget?"

Wilkins continued. "I just want you to know that all the students regretted doing that to you, Sir. We apologize, Mr. Boodram."

Unsolicited, tears welled up in my eyes. I could barely speak. "Mr. Wilkins," I managed. "You honour me. Thank you."

I reached out to him and placed my hand on his shoulder and whispered, "Now, go to your seat."

As he sat, he smiled, signaling that all was well between us.

The incident was concluded. I acted simply in my capacity as a teacher. I had dealt with a disruptive incident. It was not until much later that it dawned on me that this disruptive student was also white. It was only then that I truly appreciated and respected Mr. Wilkins' attitude and knew that in turn, I had gained his trust and respect.

41

HARRY

THE SECOND event also happened early on in my teaching career and involved my long time boyhood friend and neighbour, Harry Narine.

Because I was a year older than Harry, I graduated a year before him and was now in the most unusual position of being one of his teachers.

It never dawned on me that my being Harry's teacher could create problems for either one of us. We were friends before I became his teacher and we would continue to be friends thereafter.

One day, Harry and I decided to go to a movie in Port of Spain. We checked our collective resources. Between us we had enough money for the movies. Just as we were about to leave for the cinema, Harry expressed some hesitation. When I asked him what the problem was, Harry explained that he had a great deal of homework to do: homework from me in particular.

My focus was on the movies. I really wanted company that night so I told Harry, "Forget the stupid homework; you can do it some other time."

Pleased, but somewhat surprised by my answer, Harry shelved his homework and we were off to the movies.

When we arrived at the theatre, we discovered that that night an Errol Flynn double feature was playing. He was our absolute favourite and we were not disappointed with his performance. It was nearly midnight when the final feature presentation finished and we went our separate ways to our homes.

As I entered our dining room, I heard the bickering of voices. Pa was yelling once again. When my sister Paula saw me she raised her voice to Pa and told him to go to bed before she told Frankie how bad he was getting on tonight. Pa went directly to his bed. In a few minutes, all was quiet in the house and I too went to bed.

The next day was a regular school day. The bell had rung and the students were seated quietly in their desks. I asked the students to take out their homework so that I could examine it. I walked slowly up and down the rows without incident until I came to row number five. That was Harry's row. I stopped at his desk, and, seeing no work being offered up for inspection, I asked, "Mr. Narine, where is your assignment?"

Harry's face revealed bewilderment and confusion.

Again, I probed, "Mr. Narine, I am waiting to examine your assignment."

At that moment I was not Frank, the friend; I was Mr. Boodram, the teacher.

I continued in my role as teacher and inquired in a very earnest but matter of fact manner, "Mr. Narine, what could you have possibly been doing last evening that would have prevented you from completing your studies?"

Harry's expression was one of complete incredulity. He could not believe what he was hearing. He did not expect this from me, his friend; especially when it was I who had encouraged him to go to the movies.

I could not help myself; the teacher in me took over.

"Mr. Narine, I can see that you are well; your family too, is well, I hope?"

Harry nodded.

"Well, then, Mr. Narine, I can only conclude that since you are well and all the members of your family are well, you are irresponsible. Your homework, Mr. Narine, takes precedence over everything else. Mr. Narine, you will finish your homework in detention."

Harry was beside himself. He could say nothing. He finished his assignments and served his detention dutifully.

Some days later I asked Harry to accompany me to a movie. I offered to treat. Harry flatly refused my offer and, sparing no detail, let me know why.

"Frankie, how could you ask me about my homework in front all the students like you did not know me?" He inquired solemnly. "Man yo embarrass me big time. We suppose to be friends. Ah know yo is me teacher in school. Ah respect that, but yo treat me like a nobody."

At that moment I realized that I had really hurt Harry. I had to do something to redeem myself.

"Harry, I am sorry. I made a mistake. I did not mean to put you down in front of everyone. All I can say in my defence is that I guess I was trying to be a responsible teacher."

I thought that I was getting through to him so I continued, "Now Harry, let's go to the movies. It's a double feature: a western. I have money for both of us. Now, come on, let's go," I urged.

"No way, Frank. Today yo is my friend, but tomorrow you become Mr. Boodram, and I don't know you! No chance. I have homework to finish—your assignment too. I learn me lesson. "

I ended up going to the show alone. I was truly annoyed that Harry wouldn't come with me but I knew that I should not blame him.

It was a difficult adjustment for both of us but in time we came to understand each other's new role. Our friendship survived this rough period.

———+———

At the end of one school day, Father Fennessey brought a visitor to my classroom. It was a Mr. Georgeson from the U.S. Embassy in Trinidad and he was conducting a follow-up investigation on Harry Narine's application to join the U.S. Military. Father Fennessey, acknowledging my years of involvement with Harry, first as a friend and later as his teacher, felt that I was better equipped to answer questions regarding Harry.

Mr. Georgeson was professional and polite in making his inquiries. His first set of questions was factual and I answered them in a direct and honest manner. His next question, while equally direct, was however, more personally invasive.

"Mr. Boodram, with respect to Mr. Narine's character, do you have any personal knowledge of any serious infractions committed by him?"

I found it difficult to respond with my former candour. I hesitated, knowing that Harry's future could easily depend on the way in which I framed my answer. I further knew that my personal integrity was also at stake. I knew that Harry's personal conduct was not without blemish. He was not perfect. I needed to find a way to reveal the truth about Harry but I needed to do it in such a way that when Mr. Georgeson looked at this truth he would regard it through a lens that would allow him to see honour beyond the indiscretions.

I chose my words carefully. "Mr. Georgeson, before I answer your question, may I ask you to come with me to see the neighbourhood where Mr. Narine grew up? I believe a more complete perspective can be drawn by witnessing his surroundings first hand."

Mr. Georgeson hesitated for only the briefest of moments before he consented. My admiration for this white man grew; he was willing to step out of his rule oriented world to see life from another point of view.

We drove to Harry's neighbourhood and showed him his modest home. There were cows grazing in the back yard not too far removed from the house.

Harry's father just happened to arrive with a cartload of feed for the animals. When he saw me, he approached.

"Chacha," I began, I want you to meet this gentleman. He is from the U.S. Embassy and he has come to check up on Harry's application."

"But, Frankie," he protested, "Ah not presentable. Ah have to change me clothes."

I tried to tell him that he was quite decent just as he was but Chacha's pride would not accept my words as true. Then, Mr. Georgeson came forward, and, stretching out a receptive hand to Mr. Narine, introduced himself. The two men chatted briefly and it appeared as if Mr. Georgeson was genuinely interested in Mr. Narine. After a few minutes had elapsed, Chacha asked to be excused so that he might tend to his pressing duties. As he left our company, Mr. Georgeson, commented, "That is quite a father. He appears most dedicated and wise."

I hastened to agree and added, "There is something else that you should know about this family. Something that Harry's application would not reveal. Mr. Narine lost his wife many years ago when his children were very young. In order to provide for his children he had to work long hours away from home and in the fields. As a result, the children practically raised themselves."

"I understand," said Mr. Georgeson. "Life has been particularly difficult for this family."

"Absolutely," I agreed. "Now, the reason that I brought you here is that I wanted you to see the reality of Harry's life before you judge his conduct. Harry has had his share of troubles; he may have been mischievous; he may have stolen petty things; he may have skipped school occasionally. All these things are true. But, given Harry's special circumstances, is it not remarkable that he has never participated in any behaviour that would be deemed criminal? In a neighbourhood like this, under circumstances like Harry's, it is easy to be led astray. Would you not agree therefore, Mr. Georgeson, that Harry is an exceptional person deserving of special consideration?"

Mr. Georgeson turned to me and reflected thoughtfully, "Thank you, Mr. Boodram. I see the picture you have framed for me. I now understand your concerns and I will keep everything in mind while I reflect on his file."

Mr. Georgeson turned to leave when once more I engaged his attention. "Mr. Georgeson, my home is situated right over there." I pointed to a most modest and almost inconspicuous home across the street and down a few houses. We both began to walk in that direction.

The understanding that not only was I Harry's teacher, but also his neighbour dawned. "Mr. Boodram, it would appear that you and the young Mr. Narine share some things in common," noted a reflective Mr. Georgeson. As we walked, he added, "I noticed that you addressed Mr. Narine as Chacha; are you related?"

"No, we are not related. The term "Chacha" is used as to indicate respect and affection. Mr. Narine is my neighbour and as we were growing up we needed to show respect but to call a neighbour "mister" would be too formal, so we call the adults that are close to us Chacha (for the males) or Chachee (for the females)."

We were now standing at the entrance to my yard and I motioned for him to enter. The day was terribly hot and I asked, "May I offer you a cool refreshment?"

"Certainly," was his accommodating response. "Perhaps a glass of water?"

As we approached the steps of the house, I invited him to come inside.

Upon seeing an inviting bench under the shade of our sprawling mango tree, Mr. Georgeson simply walked toward that bench, removed his jacket, and sat down comfortably. "It is so hot," he remarked, "and if you don't mind, I'll just sit here." Just then a refreshingly cool breeze drifted in to the yard confirming his good choice to remain outside.

I soon returned with a glass of ice cold water which he downed in no time. When I offered to replenish his glass, he declined but thoughtfully commented, "I believe I am beginning to understand the bigger picture. I will be able to render a decision soon." Then he took his leave.

I could not help but admire the unassuming manner of this quiet gentleman. Because of his openness I was able to intervene on Harry's behalf and I was somewhat hopeful that the result would be positive.

As things turned out, Harry was successful in his bid to join the American military. We lost touch over the years and I have not seen him since he left for the States. I assumed that my association with Mr. Georgeson had also ended with the conclusion of Harry's business, but I was mistaken. Mr. Georgeson and I were to meet one more time.

42

DOLLY AND THE EMBASSY

SOME YEARS after dealing with the situation regarding Harry Narine and Mr. Georgeson, a new concern arose; this one involved my eldest sister, Dolly.

Dolly's husband, Bob, had left Trinidad to find work in the United States. Dolly remained behind with their three small children, Merlin, Sharmin and Baby. Several months had already passed and both Bob and Dolly were suffering from the long absence. They were desperate to see one another and Dolly had already taken the initial steps to apply for a U.S. visa. She filed the necessary documentation and began the long process of waiting for a response.

Some weeks later, Dolly was informed that she was scheduled for an interview. The weeks of waiting had taken their toll on her and she was anxious to begin the process. On the day of the interview, Dolly traveled to Port of Spain and joined the dozens of other people waiting in long lines outside the embassy. By the time she was called in for her interview, she was tired, hungry, anxious and confused; this made her easily intimidated by the officiousness of the interrogation. Unable to articulate with precise clarity her reasons for wanting to visit the United States, her request for a visa was dismissed. The word REJECTED, emblazoned in bold red capital letters on her passport, announced her failure to the world.

Dolly returned from her interview bereft of hope. She then faced the difficult task of informing Bob. Telling him that she had been unsuccessful in obtaining a visa produced even more anguish for them; Dolly, an extremely private person no matter what the circumstance, wept openly. Bob was heart-broken. Their dual sadness permeated our home; we became a family consumed in sorrow.

Everything in me wanted to help; wanted to somehow make the situation better. I was at a loss to know what to do. I felt powerless.

Dolly's tears moved me to take action. The next morning I decided to visit the embassy myself. To what end I did not yet know.

I arrived at the embassy sometime before 9:00. Already there were long lines of people queued up outside. I have no rational explanation for what happened next. I only know that I walked past that whole line of people and entered the embassy office directly.

No sooner had I accomplished this feat then I was spotted by Mr. Ragoonath, a well dressed man in his mid thirties who had the unenviable job of enforcing the rules and ensuring that proper protocol was observed. He carried a distinct air of authority about him and wasted no time in challenging the legitimacy of my presence.

"You there, do you have an appointment?"

"No, but may I ..." I began.

"No!" was his emphatic response, not showing the least interest in my rationale. "Make an appointment before you come to the embassy," he chastised.

"May I book an appointment now?" I queried.

"No. Go home and phone for an appointment."

"But, I ..."

"Go!" he ordered. This final command was punctuated by the flexing of muscles in an obvious attempt at intimidation. I knew that Mr. Ragoonath was perfectly within his rights to detain me and deny me, but I questioned the manner in which he conducted his business. The open flaunting of his authority caused me to leave the building feeling discouraged and defeated. I found little comfort in the knowledge that I had at least tried to help Dolly. I wandered aimlessly around the outside of the building and ended up in the staff parking lot. Mindless, my eyes drifted around the names assigned to the various parking spots. One name jumped out at me: Georgeson. My heart skipped a beat. Could this be the same Mr. Georgeson that I dealt with regarding Harry Narine? I dared to hope that it was. But, how was I to find out for certain? There was no car parked in that spot and I certainly couldn't re-enter the building; Mr. Ragoondath was still on patrol. My eyes were transfixed on the nameplate. I turned to leave the area when a car pulled in to Georgeson's parking spot. I walked ever so slowly away hoping to catch a glimpse of the driver. A man stepped out of the vehicle; I thought that he looked familiar but I wasn't absolutely certain. Suddenly shy and embarrassed, I began to turn away. For ever so brief an instant our eyes met. A hint of recognition registered in Mr. Georgeson's eyes and he offered, "Do I know you?"

"Yes, Mr. Georgeson. We met recently. You came to see me a St. Charles School in Tunapuna."

"Yes, I recall; it was about a student of yours."

"Harry Narine," I added.

"Yes, of course. And you are his teacher."

"Yes, Mr. Georgeson. Frankie Boodram."

"Mr. Boodram, I remember you now. How are you? Tell me what are you doing here? Can I be of any assistance?"

Was I hearing correctly? Did this man who held an important position with the American Embassy just offer to help me? I must be very careful not to appear forward or presumptuous. But, I do need his help for my sister, Dolly. Maybe he is the answer to our prayers. How do I talk of Dolly's predicament without compromising myself or Mr. Georgeson's position? Some inner voice urged me to trust this man with the complete and simple truth. I heeded that voice.

"Mr. Georgeson, I have my sister's passport with me. Her application for a visit to the U.S. was denied. I want to help her but I don't know how to help her. I just don't know what to do or where to turn." These statements came bursting from my mouth in quick succession. I was almost embarrassed. Had her mental state not appeared so fragile and her emotions so desperate, I might not have had the courage to say anything at all. It was done. The words were out there to be judged. I waited.

Mr. Georgeson may have been surprised but he did not show it. He did not dismiss me or my concern. He spoke gently and reassuringly.

"Mr. Boodram, if you don't mind, please come with me to my office where we can speak more privately and without interruption."

I followed him back inside the building and together we made our way toward the front office. Mr. Georgeson asked me to wait at the door to his office for a moment. While I was waiting outside the door, Mr. Ragoonath passed by and immediately recognized me as the unwelcome intruder. The closer he got to me, the more flushed his face became. His eyes were glued on me penetrating me with the full force of his disdain. Mr. Georgeson came out of his office and spoke quietly to Mr. Ragoonath for a moment. Mr. Ragoonath quickly left and then returned carrying a large file which he dutifully handed over to Mr. Georgeson.

After handing over the documents, Mr. Ragoonath passed by ever so closely to me and stared coldly at me. The disgust he felt for me was plainly carved in his look and manner; I felt both judged and condemned. Mr. Georgeson, however, was completely oblivious to the exchange between us. With documents in hand, Mr. Georgeson now invited me into his office.

"Mr. Boodram, your sister's name is ...?"

"Dolly," I blurted out and then quickly corrected, "I'm sorry; her married name is Dolly Maharaj."

His fingers quickly flew through the files searching for Dolly's documentation. Upon finding the correct file he opened it and thoughtfully perused it. After a moment of silence, he spoke. He chose his words carefully; it was apparent that his intention was not to accuse but rather to inform.

"Mr. Boodram, I see that your sister, Dolly, was rejected. The comments that were made in her file would seem to indicate a certain illogic in her statements at her interview." I was certain that that was Mr. Georgeson's polite way of saying that Dolly had been lying to the officers conducting the interview. I had to find a way to show him that even though it appeared that she was not telling the truth, she was not intending to lie.

"Mr. Georgeson," I began, "my sister, Dolly, is unaccustomed to the ways the world. She is shy and innocent. She could be easily intimidated by anything or anyone who appeared the least bit officious. It is my feeling that she felt intimidated by the investigating officers. That is not to say that the officers were intimidating. I am merely suggesting that the officers, just by being officers, were naturally intimidating to her. This, coupled with the exceedingly long wait in line, caused her to become tongue-tied and inarticulate when it came her turn to testify on her own behalf as to her reasons for wanting to visit in the U.S. This could easily have given the officers the impression that she was not telling the truth. I can assure you, Mr. Georgeson that it was never her intention to deceive anyone. That would be the last thing in her mind."

Mr. Georgeson listened thoughtfully to my comments. He wanted to know more about the relationship between Dolly and her husband, Bob. I responded with as much insight as I could. His concern was that she might not return to Trinidad once given the opportunity to enter the U.S. In my heart I knew that Dolly would never abandon her children no matter how much she missed her husband. I knew that she just wanted to be able to visit Bob; she had every intention of returning to her children in Trinidad.

So, with a clear conscience, I was able to appeal to this gentleman, Mr. Georgeson. "Dolly and her husband are apart. They miss each other terribly and it is very hard on both of them. Once they have a visit, Dolly will return home to Trinidad."

"And her children, Mr. Boodram, what will happen to them while she is away?"

"Why, our family, my mother and all of the rest of us, would gladly take care of them. Our nieces are no problem. Not only are they delightful, we absolutely adore having them around."

Mr. Georgeson seemed surprised. "You mean you would *adopt* them while the parents are away?"

"Absolutely. We are family. We would be happy to do it."

Mr. Georgeson was quiet as he reflected on all I had just revealed. Suddenly, he became animated and declared, "Mr. Boodram, it is not right."

My spirits sank. I began to feel uneasy. Had I presumed too much?

He continued in a tone that suggested that something was amiss in this situation and I became alarmed. "It is not right," he repeated. Then he continued, "One should not separate children from their parents."

What a relief!

Mr. Georgeson then opened up Dolly's passport, stamped it and held it out to me.

"Here," he said.

He handed me her passport. It contained Dolly's visa approving her for a *six month* visit to the United States. Furthermore, the approval was granted not just for Dolly, but for her three children as well!

Needless to say, I was overwhelmed.

"Mr. Georgeson, we are indebted to you Sir."

"Mr. Boodram, I remember how well you advocated for your friend, Harry Narine. And, here you are once more trying to assist someone else, your sister. I appreciate your sincerity and your openness. Good luck Mr. Boodram." He opened the door; we shook hands and I left. Outside the door, I stood, quietly dazed by all that had just transpired. Was this real? Did I finally have some good news to bring home to the family? Everything felt very ethereal and dreamlike; the difference between this and my regular dreams, however, was that this one had no nightmarish quality about it.

Mr. Georgeson completely dispelled the Trinidadian myth which branded so many Americans as loud and arrogant and greatly deluded by the misconception of their own sense of superiority.

Here I remained to discredit that assertion for I had just borne witness to a completely magnanimous act of an American official. By the simple stroke of a pen he had completely reversed Dolly's fortunes. Whereas her initial request for a three week visa had been summarily rejected by others in his department, Mr. Georgeson saw fit to grant far more than had originally been sought.

I stood in the hallway bewildered by all that had just transpired. *What had just happened? Was this really real?* I felt that I had just witnessed a miracle. While I was thus engaged in those blissful musings, my spirit was uplifted and I was absolutely certain that nothing could destroy my optimism.

Then I saw Mr. Ragoonath.

He was watching me.

There was an obvious air of disapproval and contempt in his look.

"Please," I prayed silently, "don't come to me; just this once, leave me alone."

I was having a most rare and beautiful experience and I wanted so much to preserve the perfection of the moment. In a flash, Mr. Ragoonath descended on me: replete with belligerent attitude and authoritarian manner. Even his eyes were on fire.

"So yo think yo some smart Indian?"

I said nothing.

I tried desperately to cling to the positive encounter I had just had with Mr. Georgeson; I reflected on his most gracious disposition hoping to stave off any confrontation that might develop between Mr. Ragoonath and me.

Mr. Ragoonath would not accept my silence. Entrenched in his own negativity, provocation now became his weapon of choice.

"Well, Indian, yo think you can fool the white man. Yo fool no one. Yo think yo intelligent." He then closed in on me, blocking the hallway so that I could not easily walk away.

I tried to reason with him. "Please, I apologize for not taking my place in line. You are right. I did not intend to jump ahead. May I now leave?"

I was humbling myself, trying to make up for my indiscretion. Mr. Ragoonath would not be appeased; he was a huge pit-bull, unwilling to relinquish his bone. Once more, he began to debase me.

"Well yo think you can just walk in here and have your own way. Yo think yo special or something? Yo not! Yo is common like a stray dog!

In fact, yo a low life Indian. Indians like you always trying low dodges. You went crying and crawling to the white man; you are nothing but a low life snake." He had exhausted his arsenal of insults and his words, like bullets, seared my soul.

He took such great satisfaction in humiliating me. In that very moment, I saw clearly into the heart of that man and witnessed his naked truth. He was a brute: a bully to the core. No amount of fine apparel could disguise this reality.

While he might have been justified for chastising me for appearing to circumvent proper procedure, he had no cause to berate me with such vileness. That I could not, indeed, I *would* not tolerate. I sought to defend myself. Accordingly, I took a step towards him and declared rather emphatically, "You can take a coolie out of the gutter, but you cannot take the gutter out of the coolie!" (Note: the term coolie is a derogatory slur meaning a low class Indian.)

Mr. Ragoonath was shocked by my boldness. He was speechless, but only for a moment.

"You called me a coolie!" he sputtered.

"Yes, I did. You are a full-grown coolie!"

"But I am not a coolie," he protested.

Obviously, my words had affected him. I knew that to use such a derogatory and inflammatory term would serve to get his attention. Having achieved that goal, I therefore avoided any further remarks that might appear to be disparaging.

I changed my approach.

"Now, Mr. Ragoonath, may I ask you a question?"

"Yes, what is it?"

"Are you an educated man?"

"Of course I am an educated man!"

"Then act like an educated man. Be civil."

Again, Mr. Ragoonath was rendered speechless.

His soul had been wounded and his body bore the evidence. Gone was the look of superiority. Gone was the haughty, self-righteous attitude. His body buckled noticeably from the verbal blow. He hastened to escape to a less threatening environment.

When I felt my anger subside, I left the building. I quickened my pace in order to focus my attention on anything but that most recent unpleasantness.

I hastened home to meet Dolly. I did not greet her immediately with the good news as I had decided to make a little game of it.

"Well, Dolly, how're you doing today?"

"Ah trying to hold up, but it not easy these days. Yo know how it is, Frankie." Her eyes began to tear up.

When I saw the tears, I could not keep the good news to myself any longer. I handed Dolly her passport. She had no idea that I had taken it. I did not consult her for fear of falsely raising her hopes and I did not want her to suffer any further.

Dolly looked at her passport but did not open it.

"Go ahead open it," I urged.

She opened it.

Her eyes grew wide doubting what she saw.

"But, Frankie, it says I have a Visa for six months."

"Yes!"

She smiled and then managed a quiet but sincere, "Thank you, Frank."

The good news spread rapidly through the family and everyone shared in Dolly's happiness. Then the questions began. Everyone wanted to know how I was able to secure clearance for Dolly and for her three children. I played down my role in the matter stating only that I had been extremely lucky.

The family wanted to celebrate. When Dolly suggested that we order Chinese food, Boysie and Sylvan and I reached for our wallets. Dolly declined our offers of help and insisted that this was to be her treat. It was heartwarming and encouraging to see our family this happy, this close; we were united in happiness.

Because everyone thought that I had played a significant role in Dolly's success in obtaining a Visa, I was accorded a measure of respect. I basked in the sunshine of that recognition.

As time went on, it appeared that I was gaining the confidence of the family. That I was able to secure a Visa for Dolly after she had been rejected by the American Embassy made me a bit of a celebrity. Friends and neighbours consulted me about their plans to apply for a Visa. I chose to downplay this incident; I did not wish to be perceived by the embassy as some kind of an upstart. I was grateful that I was able to help Dolly. Now when anyone sought my assistance in this regard, I limited myself to the task of ensuring that the application forms were filled out properly. In time I was asked to help less and less. Life soon returned to normal.

For the most part, life became routine; routine that is until something happened to cause a ripple in the quiet waters of my world.

43

HG 4117

MY BROTHER-IN-LAW, Sylvan, Pinky's husband, had an established reputation working as a supervisor of the electrical department of well respected company that assembled busses in Trinidad. Sylvan was interested in boosting his income by operating his own taxi service during his off hours. His plan was to purchase a reasonably priced used vehicle, fix it up, and thus transform it into an attractive and wholesome taxi. When he was ready to actively pursue his dream, Sylvan consulted me. He did not need my help in any way regarding the mechanics of the car; (not that I *could* ever be of any help in that area; my ineptitude in that area was well publicized.) Sylvan, on the other hand, was an extremely skilled craftsman in this area himself. No, my expertise (if one could call it that) lay in the realm of the visionary. Sylvan seemed to feel that I had a special knack for seeing the extraordinary in the ordinary. My love for cars was well known and Sylvan trusted that I could help him select just the right vehicle to begin to transform his dream into reality. Our first mission therefore, was to find the ideal fixer-upper.

Our initial search yielded no results. We checked out cars in the immediate vicinity of Tunapuna and then widened our search to include towns in the surrounding areas. Any vehicle that was remotely interesting was priced well beyond Sylvan's budget. Sylvan became discouraged. I, however, remained hopeful and insisted that we not abandon his dream prematurely.

It was with some reluctance that Sylvan accompanied me to see yet another used vehicle. This one was located right in our own neighbourhood. His eyes sparked with interest when he first saw the car and he began his initial inspection with a measure of eager hopefulness. The spark soon faded from his eyes however, and Sylvan was not hesitant about pointing out the cars many flaws and hastened to conclude that this was not the right vehicle.

"First off, Frank," he began, "the price is too much. I can't pay that much money. Now, Frank, take a look over here. See, the hood is tied down with rope; that's not a good sign. Look inside at the upholstery; it's all ripped up. Somebody abused this car too much. Look at all the dents!"

It was obvious that he was not impressed. He motioned to me that he intended to go. I told him that I wanted to hear how the car ran hoping that a strong, smooth engine would reignite his interest in the vehicle. What a mistake that was!

The owner came over, put the key in the ignition and turned: nothing. The second attempt produced a very different result. Never before had I heard such a clangor and clatter; the car positively erupted with noise. We covered our ears. Sylvan prepared to leave.

"Come on, Frank. This is a piece of junk. Pinky will not be impressed. If she sees this car, she will quarrel with me, big time. Let's go."

I, however, wasn't prepared to give up just yet.

"Sylvan," I urged. "Let's try to see this car, not as it is, but what it could be."

"But, Frank," he protested, "this car is no good. Ah telling you so myself. We wasting precious time. Now, let's go."

Still not ready to give up, I encouraged, "Sylvan, I know we can transform this car. You can do a lot of the work yourself. And, you know the right people to call to help you with the rest. We can do this."

To humour me, Sylvan said, "Okay, Frank. Tell me three good things about this car and maybe I'll consider it."

I responded to his challenge with enthusiasm. "I'll gladly tell you. Number one; it is a Zephyr. You know how much you like this type of a car. That car is in demand on the island and it is a very popular car for a taxi. Number two; you know how to repair this kind of a car easily. And number three is that this car is not ancient; it is a recent model. Moreover, the body may look beaten up, but it is sound. Even the engine is sound despite all the noise. The rest can be fixed, and it won't cost a fortune. There, that's more than three reasons."

"Okay," responded Sylvan, "but I still don't like the price; it cost too much."

The dealer was standing at the counter watching our animated conversation. Sylvan's hands were flying in every direction as he spoke. He sensed Sylvan's displeasure.

I left Sylvan and began to walk towards the dealer; he left his counter to meet me.

"Frank, it looks like Sylvan is not happy. He doesn't want the car?"

"He says it needs too many repairs."

"But, he is a mechanic. He could do so much for himself."

"True, but he has a problem."

"What problem?"

"He can't afford to pay the asking price and then finance all the repairs that the car needs. Together it is just too much."

The dealer paused.

"I am not sure; it cost me a bundle. But, I suppose..."

Just then Sylvan turned to leave.

"Where he going?" the dealer asked.

"Look," I interjected, avoiding the question. "Reduce your price a bit and I'll see about getting him back. But, before I do that, there is something else you should know."

"And what's that?"

"This car needs to be off your lot."

"What? Why?"

"Well, it looks bad; as though you are selling a piece of ..."

"Okay, okay, I got the picture. Call Sylvan."

I motioned to Sylvan to come back.

He and the dealer talked. The dealer came up with what I thought was an attractive compromise. At my urging, Sylvan agreed to the deal. But, he was decidedly not happy with the transaction. He muttered unintelligibly as we towed the vehicle all the way home.

We parked the car directly in front of our house. There it sat: dented and unsightly; held together only with rope, it looked exceedingly ugly.

Gradually, the neighbours began to gather around the car. They stared and shook their heads in disbelief as if to say, *Sylvan, you bought this piece of junk!*

I feared that Sylvan's reputation was suffering under the strain of my decision and I felt sad for him. I too began to question if buying this particular car was the right decision.

At that very moment my brother, Boysie appeared. He took one look at the car, shook his head and walked away. Sylvan did not even try to explain anything to Boysie. He knew by Boysie's silence that Boysie too was questioning Sylvan's rationale.

When Pinky appeared and saw the purchase, she was anything but subtle in her condemnation.

"This is a piece of junk, Sylvan. You gone *loco*?"

"But Pinky," Sylvan protested, "Frank says it ..."

"Frank don't know better. You do, I can't believe a smart man like you bought this piece of ugliness." Then she walked away in utter disgust.

I felt so sorry for Sylvan. Pinky really let him have it. She wasn't afraid of hurting my feelings. Everyone knew that I know next to nothing about cars. Sylvan is the one who shone in that area. He usually commanded such respect. To see him so diminished; first by our neighbours, then by Boysie, and finally by Pinky, caused me to feel guilt. Finally, he turned and looked in my direction and said, "Frank, I hope you know what we are doing."

"Sylvan, trust me, this car is going to be a Number 1."

"Yo sure, Frank? So far you are the only one who is for this deal. I am definitely having second thoughts. Everyone is against it. Ah just want you to know what's on my mind."

"Well I am glad you got that off your chest. You feel better now?"

"As a matter of fact, I do."

Hearing him say those words was a distinct relief. I too felt much better.

The very next day Sylvan and I towed the car to an upholstery shop in El Dorado Village. Sylvan knew the owner very well; in fact, they were great friends.

Sylvan seemed to have recovered his confidence and was soon in command barking out the orders. His instructions were very precise; the original upholstery had to be completely stripped. It would be replaced by a striking two-tone green material that I, myself had selected.

When this was accomplished, we next took the car to the body shop. Everyone there knew and liked Sylvan and had no problem accommodating his wishes. Sylvan was like a little king in his element. He boldly gave orders as to what he expected. No one in the repair shop said no to Mr. Sylvan Ramcharran! Each person had his own individual duty and was responsible for meeting certain deadlines set by Sylvan. Over the next few days we visited the various workers to ensure that his instructions were being carried out—his way. The days passed, and soon it was time to view the finished product. We headed directly for the body shop and beheld a green vision of sparkling chrome. Every dent had been repaired and every scratch erased. The automobile was truly magnificent. Sylvan stared in disbelief at the new creation. His eyes shone with obvious pleasure as he approached his prize.

What was that that he just saw? Did a fly attempt to nestle on this hunk of gleaming metal? Flies had to be taught a lesson not to deface Sylvan's baby. Immediately upon seeing the fly, Sylvan reached out for a clean cloth. He snapped that fly in mid air before it could besmirch his treasure. The unsuspecting creature expired instantly.

The owner of the garage could not contain his laughter; he knew at once that Sylvan had fallen in love with his creation. Once matters were concluded at the body shop, we headed for the upholstery store. We found that owner eagerly awaiting our arrival. He was ahead of schedule and was most anxious to begin transforming the car's interior look. We were barely out of the car when the seats were completely removed. It wasn't long before the dramatic two-tone green material magically converted the once unworthy "heap of junk" into a credible taxi worthy of carrying the most distinguished of passengers. The dashboard and the side panels were replaced with newer versions of themselves. Not only were all these changes attractive, they also appeared authentic: it was as if the car had never had another look. All of these alterations had been accomplished according to Sylvan's master plan which contained the highest of standards.

Finally, the metamorphosis was complete and Sylvan moved in for his final official inspection. We held our collective breath. Would he be satisfied? Sylvan opened the driver's door. He said nothing. We waited. His eyes consumed every morsel of that car. Finally, he whispered, "Is this my car? Is this the same car I brought in?"

Only one task remained. He had to start the engine. It purred beautifully. Exploding with pleasure and excitement, Sylvan gushed, "I don't believe it; this can't be the same car. Frank, ah real happy." He need not have made any comment; his happiness was beyond obvious.

It was now late afternoon that same Saturday and we headed home. We wanted to arrive before darkness fell for we hoped to enjoy the sweet taste of vindication. Almost everyone had written off this car as a piece of junk and accused Sylvan of losing his mind. Redemption was near.

Gliding through town, we could not help but notice the looks of awe and envy that were cast in our direction. A former "unbeliever" met up with us when we were stopped at an intersection and queried, "Sylvan, that can't be the same car, can it?" We received many similar endorsements along the way. After each such comment, I noticed a positive difference in Sylvan; gradually he was regaining all the confidence and esteem that had been lost because of this most questionable purchase.

Soon we arrived at home: 26 Back Street, Tunapuna, Trinidad. We were about to face the biggest challenge of all—Pinky.

We need not have worried however. Just as she had shown no restraint in condemning the car when it was initially purchased, she was equally forthright delivering her praise.

"Frankie boy, is this what I called junk? I take it all back. This car is gorgeous."

Another critic, Boysie, emerged from the house and added his apology. "I was wrong, Sylvan. Yo is still the man!"

Sylvan beamed at the compliment.

I still remember the licence plate we had put on it: HG 4117. That's how we came to refer to it.

Every time Pinky and Sylvan ventured out in that vehicle, they attracted crowds of appreciative onlookers. Later, Sylvan confessed, "Frankie, I did not see this car the way you did. You saw beyond the rope and dents. You were right about it. I know that now."

Sylvan would never know how much weight those words carried with me. I too felt vindicated. Thank you, HG 4117. I have never forgotten.

The ripple of discontent that had threatened earlier was now calm, and once more I smiled, never suspecting the real storm that was just around the corner.

44

MANMOHAN: THE REBEL

THE RELATIVE calm that I was experiencing at home, helped to strengthen my resolve to maintain a disciplined but meaningful atmosphere within the classroom.

Because my students came from very diverse backgrounds, the possibility of conflict was an ever present reality. Many students were deprived in some respect: socially, economically or culturally (or various combinations of the three), and the classroom was an obvious arena for the oftentimes inevitable clashes. It was not uncommon for a student to explode violently. When this happened, we, as teachers, were within our rights to choose to administer corporal punishment. Because this was often the expectation and custom, we required no special sanction from the principal for certain types of infractions.

Some of the students deeply resented teachers who chose to exercise this form of punishment and banded together. They created a counter code of their own in which they promised to punish any teacher who exercised corporal punishment, vowing that *they would pay for it one way or another.*

I did not know that such a code existed; what's more, I did not know that I was about to be tested by a student named Manmohan.

Manmohan was in his third year of high school. Far from being a model student, he was well-known for his laziness and had been dubbed *Lazy bone* by the teachers. In fact, nearly every teacher had a favourite story to tell about him.

One day, when all seemed quiet in my room, when each student seemed absorbed in independent work and when I, myself, was occupied with marking assignments, Manmohan leaped out of his seat and violently struck another student across his face.

Immediately the class was plunged into chaos. I had to act.

Knowing that the confusion began with Manmohan, he became my target. I hoped that by gaining control of him, I could reclaim the rest of the class.

"Manmohan," I declared, "go to the room!"

The *room* was a small area, about six feet square, that was reserved for private consultation or private discipline. Much to his credit, Manmohan complied with my order. I was able to restore a sense of calm within the classroom and attend to the student who had been assaulted. Outwardly, he appeared fine but I felt that he too needed a moment to compose himself; I therefore assigned a trusted student to accompany him to a tap where he could get a drink and at the same time calm his emotions. He seemed relieved when I indicated that I would be attending to Manmohan directly and that I would return and receive his side of the story a little later.

This was my first year of teaching and nothing that I had encountered thus far prepared me to address this type of situation. I searched for answers as I headed for that room.

In the far corner slouched an angry and defiant Manmohan. I sensed that he was not willing to accept without complaint, the natural consequences of his actions. I do not know what compelled me to talk to him before administering his punishment but I did.

"Mr. Manmohan, I do not know the details of what happened but I do believe that you were provoked in some way. You, however, went too far. Hold out your hand!"

He did not comply.

"Mr. Manmohan, let me help you." With that, I reached for his hand and placed it outstretched before me.

I administered four lashes: two on each hand. When I was done, I furiously flung the strap in utter disgust. I hated having to resort to that type of punishment for I remembered how degrading it felt to be on the receiving end.

We remained in that room in absolute stillness. Neither one of us knew quite what to expect from the other after such a display. Eventually, I grabbed two chairs and placed them directly opposite one another. I sat down on one and motioned for Manmohan to do the same. He flatly refused. That refusal constituted open defiance and if not handled properly could make the situation much worse. Instinctively, I knew that I needed to create a legitimate distraction for myself.

Choosing to overlook his defiance for the moment, I asked for an excuse. "Mr. Manmohan, would you excuse me please for a moment? I need to check on the class." This was designed to buy us both a bit of time. I could now catch my breath while I took up a lesson with the class. All the while, my thoughts were with Manmohan. Once satisfied that the class was contained, I returned to him.

Upon entering the room I made the following statements: "I'm sorry I had to strap you. That was necessary. It is done. Now, would you tell me what got you so angry that you backhanded a friend?"

At first, he said nothing. He paced the floor seething with anger. Then he declared, "Yo strap me first. Yo suppose to *talk* to me first and *then* strap me. Now you want me to talk. How come you strap me first? Why yo do that? Tell me."

Although he was angry, he was still talking. That was significant. If only I could keep him talking, I was hopeful that his anger might diminish.

"Sit down, and I will tell you," I directed.

Again he remained standing.

"I thought that you really wanted an explanation," I countered.

"I do," he affirmed.

"Then oblige me by sitting down and I can begin to explain."

He hesitated; moving around the room as if staking out his territory. Finally, he sat. I was grateful for that was a significant concession.

"Manmohan," I began, "you must have had a very good reason for what you did. I too had a very good reason for what I did. If I did not strap you right away, I don't know that I would have had the heart to strap you after hearing your story. And, as much as I would feel for you, I would be required to do what was appropriate. I felt that four lashes were in order. Now it is done. I am sorry that I had to strap you. I don't enjoy strapping. Now, tell me why you struck your friend so violently."

Manmohan was quiet. I could tell that he was carefully weighing his options. I knew that I had to be patient.

Silence.

I waited.

Finally, he broke his silence.

"My father threw me out of the house this morning. He beat me good. He slapped and kicked me. That is private; yo can't tell anyone."

"I am sorry that happened, Manmohan," I sympathized. "Now, tell me about you and your friend."

"He was my best friend. But he no friend any more."

Manmohan became very quiet.

"Did you talk to him?"

"Yes, and ah found out that he is making a move on my girl. He told me she said I was out of the picture. Ah so mad, ah want to kill him. And my friend advised me to get another girl. Man, I lost it."

"Manmohan, you got caught with life dealing you too many bad cards. You need a break. Tell you what. Take the rest of the class off. Get yourself ready for the next class."

"Yo not sending me to the principal? Yo not expelling me from school?"

"No. You are going through some tough times. One thing I realize is this. You must not strike out on your friend anymore. I need you to be at school. You have had too much on your plate already. Manmohan, I have to get back to class. Before I do, I would appreciate very much if you would promise me that you will try to go to your next class, please? And, you could *solve* one problem for me."

"What's that?"

"You and your friend need to talk. That problem between you two needs to be settled. Will you think on it please?"

He made me no promises and I was pensive as I returned to class. And, at the end of the day, I found out that my troubled student *had* attended his classes. In fact, I was elated to see both Manmohan and his friend coming toward me.

"Mr. Boodram, my friend and I talked. We are going to be okay. Thank you for helping. You okay too, Mr. Boodram."

"Thanks Mr. Manmohan. I am happy to see that you are solving your problem. I am proud of you both."

They left together: friends once again. Manmohan's words came back to me. He had said that I was okay too. I couldn't help but think that perhaps I had done something right in the midst of all the turmoil. His remark was encouraging and it went to the very heart of me.

There was no *script* for good teachers to follow as far as I knew. I did recognize however some of the pitfalls that teachers could fall into and tried to avoid them. In the absence of any professional training, I relied heavily on common sense and compassion to guide my decisions. In light of this, I felt extremely fortunate that the incident regarding Manmohan concluded on a positive note.

It was not until later that evening through a conversation with Harry that I discovered just how disastrous this situation could have been. He explained that I was lucky to be "all in one piece" for Manmohan carried a concealed weapon which he vowed to use on anyone who threatened to hurt him. Having witnessed Manmohan hide a knife in his pants, after I ordered him into the *room*, Harry was most apprehensive about my safety.

Harry continued, "Frankie, ah glad you are all right; ah worried about you."

I grew anxious after Harry revealed this information and began to question my actions. Had I placed myself unnecessarily in harm's way?

Harry's next remarks however, removed all doubt.

"Frankie, yo looking worried. Don't. Manmohan said you are a good teacher and a good person too. He hates most teachers most of the time. Whatever you did for him, worked. So don't change. He is impressed. And in my books, I give you full marks. Just don't tell anyone I said so."

I allowed myself to bask in the warmth of his remarks. At that moment he made me want to be a teacher forever and ever. And yet, teaching was not the profession that I had originally chosen for myself.

45

THE OTHER DREAM

FROM AS far back as I can remember I had always wanted to be a lawyer. From as far back as I can remember my father had always wanted me to become a lawyer also. His reasons were different from mine. He wanted me to become a lawyer so that I could straighten out my brother, Boysie. I wanted to become a lawyer because I held on to the idealistic notion that lawyers served an important function in the world: they could help others; they could especially help those who were poor. This notion grew from the special circumstances within my own community. Most of the people there could not afford to hire a lawyer and it had been my dream to become a lawyer so that I might help those less fortunate. That was my secret dream.

I soon concluded that if I wanted to realize my dream I would have to leave Trinidad and study law in England. Becoming a lawyer necessarily entailed spending a great deal of money. Money, however, was one commodity that I always seemed to have to little of. As a first year teacher I was earning $15.00 a month. At that time, that sum of money would buy perhaps ten average-sized, locally grown, chickens. Indeed, my salary was a modest one, even by Trinidadian standards. It was, however, a reliable one. Duty and honour demanded that I offer this money to my parents to help with the family finances. Accordingly, I took my very first pay and offered it to my mother. Ma directed me to Pa.

"Pa, here is my salary. It is fifteen dollars and it is yours."

"Frankie, thanks. But yo keep yo money. You have ambition and you will need this money. I will manage."

Our conversation was short but direct. I did not fail to understand the magnitude of my father's generosity. God alone knows the huge sacrifice my parents were making. In addition, by allowing me to keep my own money, my father was indicating his approval of my choices in life. I felt as if I had just been blessed by both of my parents.

My salary, however, in and of itself, was hardly enough to satisfy the financial demands that a law degree required. I needed to boost my income. To accomplish this, I decided to offer private lessons to students who required extra tuition. I ran in to one small problem, however: many of the students who needed extra help could not afford it, and I could not afford to offer the tuition for free. Eventually, I came up with a solution. I offered free tuition to students at school during the day to students who could not afford to pay. On evenings and weekends and gave private tutorials to the students whose parents could afford to pay for them.

It seemed that every minute of my life was fully occupied and I had little time for any social activities; my vision totally consumed me. The year virtually flew by and soon it was time to initiate preparations for my move to England. The decision to go to England took on an urgency that I had not anticipated.

On the island, rumours abounded that England was about to introduce a new immigration policy that would put strict limits on the number of people entering the country. If this new policy were to go into effect, it would make it extremely difficult for me to go abroad at a later date. I therefore made a decision to go quickly in order to take advantage of the present policy.

I was bringing affairs both at school and at home to a conclusion. I secured passage on a ship and in one month's time, I was due to sail. I was anticipating finding day time employment in London; this would leave my evenings free to pursue the type of schooling that would eventually lead to a law degree. Since I did not have any real contacts in England, I would be on my own virtually. Lately, however, I had developed a friendship with the Ojah-Maharaj family from Las Lomas. I had taught two boys from that family and over the year, I had become friends with the entire family. On countless occasions I had been a guest in their home and the recipient of their generosity. Their friendship was a gift that I treasured deeply. The eldest son was living in England. The father, upon hearing of my plans to travel to England communicated with his son on my behalf. As I had no other contact in England, this young man was able to secure lodging for me in London. I entertained the faint hope that he might also venture to "show me the ropes" once I arrived in London.

For whatever reason, I had not yet discussed my plans with my parents. It was now time to face them.

My father was not well; he was convalescing at home, recovering from a bout of pneumonia. I cannot recall a single day, before this, when my father had ever been sick. In anticipation of my travel abroad, I had commissioned the services of a local tailor to make me a blue suit. I thought that I would use the suit as a means of initiating the conversation.

"Pa, I want to show you my suit. I hope you like it." I was swelling with pride as I showed him my brand new blue suit: my first suit ever. He looked at it for the longest time but said nothing.

Eventually, I ventured to break the silence. My statement was simple but solemn, "Pa I am making plans to go to England. I want to be a lawyer."

"A lawyer," he repeated. "That's good for you. Ah happy and proud. Ah wish ah could help yo. Sorry, Son."

There was a sincerity in his tone and in his words that surprised me. Seldom had I heard such care and genuine concern. Pa rarely spoke to me in this caring manner. I became slightly alarmed and began think that he really must be sick. It was only later that I began to appreciate the irony of his next remarks.

I held up my blue suit in front of him for closer inspection. Again he stared at it as if transfixed. Then he responded; his voice was quiet and deep.

"Well, Frankie, it is the right colour."

There was a distinct but distant sadness in his voice as he spoke and I was at a loss to understand why. He said nothing more.

Over these last years, Pa had said very little to me. He allowed me a freedom at home; a freedom to work hard to pursue a career.

During this time, I maintained the ritual of shaving Pa once or twice a week. Even though we did not talk, there was a communication in our mutual silence; our understanding of one another grew right amidst our silence.

I remember his strong work ethic; he always worked hard to provide for his family. I often wondered what he thought; what went on in his mind; he never shared.

In these later years, I do not remember him cursing and misbehaving as blatantly as he once did. I am told that this was due in part because of my presence at home. I often wondered at the strangeness of my expanded role within our home; it hardly seemed reasonable that I should be given such power and such responsibility.

Pa would often direct Ma to consult with me on important family matters. In fact, when an offer of marriage was proposed to my eldest sister, Dolly, my parents sought my counsel. Being accorded this kind of status at home meant that my personal conduct had to be above reproach. This expectation threatened to suffocate me. For this reason I kept my life private.

I recognized that for all the demands that seemed to be placed on my life, I enjoyed a certain luxury of freedom that my sisters were denied. Tradition. Tradition.

As was the custom in my home, my sisters were not allowed to date. To be seen in the company of a young man would be regarded as indiscrete; to be seen holding hands with one would be regarded as criminal. For this reason, if I were ever to have an interest in a young lady, it behooved me to act with discretion for I carried the weight of responsibility for the family. The supreme irony of life in my neighbourhood was that unless I was seen actually courting a young lady, I was not considered to be a man. This was how the average male's manhood was esteemed. Whenever a boy from our neighbourhood was seen holding hands with his girlfriend, his action was celebrated and he became the toast of the town. And me, Frankie Boodram, how was I regarded? I was the neighborhood disappointment. Because I was never observed keeping company with a girl, I was a laughing stock. Rumours about me abounded. In fact, one fiery suggestion spread like wildfire.

Someone announced, "Frankie wants to be a priest!" Although untrue, this idea somehow grew wings as it spread throughout the neighbourhood. And, later, when it received confirmation from both my elder brothers, it rocketed into orbit.

I became an easy target. I was both disrespected and rejected not only by my peers but also by my brothers. I bore the sting of their rejection in silence. The pain was locked deep within me, threatening to engulf me in despair.

Had I been seen openly courting a young woman, I would have been admired; I might even have been considered a "hero". And yet, had any one of my sisters been found in a similar circumstance, she would have been heavily chastised. Such was the state of affairs that plagued our Indian society. It seemed to me that we were the champions of the double standard. Indian men were not held accountable for their questionable indulgences; Indian women, however, were not only held accountable but also considered responsible for *any* indiscretion perpetrated *by* them or *upon* them. Further, she would be cast aside as "damaged goods" by all who knew her. Her "shame" would spread and infect the reputation of the entire family.

The very men who so eagerly practised and perfected *sin* were often the first to condemn any woman caught in an apparent indiscretion; as if she had invented the very sin in which they themselves indulged. Such was the prevailing thought amongst some of my countrymen in the late 50s, early 60s, and into the 70s. Undoubtedly, vestiges of this thinking remain today to plague the lives of innocent women everywhere.

I wanted to discover another world; I needed to experience a different way of life. I hoped that my anticipated journey abroad would yield some new insights. At the present time, however, all eyes were on Pa, who was still recuperating at home.

School was some short blocks away from home so I usually went home for lunch. This one day in particular, the sun was so unbearably hot that I decided not to venture out in the heat. Then, a feeling of urgency stole over me insisting that I go home. I am eternally grateful that I followed my instincts.

I was just finishing up my lunch and preparing to leave when I heard Pa ask Ma, "B [that was Pa's pet name for Ma whose name was *Bissondaye*], I need a shilling for the bus. I go to the hospital today. Ah don't have no money."

"Okay," Ma replied as she turned away to privately search out her *orni* for the required change. (Ma often kept a bit of pocket change tied in the corner of her *orni*.) She whispered something to herself and I caught a glimpse of a glistening tear overflowing on to her face. Instinctively I sensed her hopeless desperation. She had nothing left to give him; not one single penny.

Such a situation, viewed from today's perspective, hardly seems significant. Pa needed twenty-four cents—only one shilling, but Ma did not have it to give.

Despite our differences and our lack of communication over these past few years, I could not bear to see Pa suffer, especially since I had the means to prevent it. I went into my bedroom. When I returned I quietly called to Ma.

"Ma, give this to Pa. Do not tell him it is from me."

I handed her a dollar.

"Frankie, thank you, Son."

I could sense that she was overwhelmed by this offering and I whispered, "It's okay, Ma."

I began to leave. I made it out into the yard when I heard a voice call my name from the open dining room. I turned to look back. There was Pa, leaning over the half wall, "Frankie, thank you, Son, for the dollar."

I smiled and waved happily to my father.

He returned my smile.

As I headed for school, I felt a peace that had eluded me for many years. My spirit was renewed. Perhaps there was still a chance that Pa and I could rekindle our relationship.

Two days later, that hope—that dream was dashed.

46

PA'S DEATH

I WAS IN the middle of class when Father Fennessey came in and stated simply, "Mr. Boodram, you are needed at home. You go. We will take care of your classes."

I cannot describe adequately the feelings that consumed me. It was more than sadness, more than despair. It must have found its expression in my face for I met a neighbour on the way home who stopped me to ask if I was okay. Not wanting to talk, not able to talk, I simply nodded and continued on my way.

I did not know for certain what had happened at home, but my heart told me that Pa had died. I did not want to believe my heart. I needed proof. Scores of people gathered on the street in front of my home would be the first sign of proof. There was no one gathered outside. Furthermore, there was no public wailing, no screams of sorrow.

The tenseness lifted from my body. My heart began to relax. Perhaps my instincts were wrong. *Perhaps Pa is still alive. He may be critically ill, but still alive. There is still a chance for us.* I was now driven by the urge to see him. Indeed, I was optimistic.

All was eerily quiet as I opened the front door. The two front rooms were crammed with bodies. Each face stared blankly at me as I entered the room and asked, "What's happening?"

My words signaled the unleashing of the storm. My mother erupted with grief. She convulsed towards me and, clinging to me in desperate agony, cried out.

"Frankie, oh God! Yo Pa is dead. What go happen to we now?"

She screamed and screamed until there was no life left in her. I was shattered. The enormity of life's new challenges consumed me. Ma sat motionless, completely drained of emotion, incapable of shedding one more tear.

I reached out to her and drew her close. We remained like that until she broke the silence with her sorrowful whisper, "Frankie, how we go bury your fader? He use up de *su-su* money." (The su-su money was money collected by the neighbours. Each month each neighbour contributed a few dollars to the su-su. The amount is allowed to build over a period of about six months after which time a new round begins. Each contributor is allowed to borrow the entire amount of the su-su to take care of any personal emergency. Pa had already received his turn earlier in the month in order to repair his truck. Furthermore, additional money was owing on the repairs and the outstanding balance was due.) Pa's death had left our family financially compromised. I could not burden Ma with this additional worry. I had to find a way to ease her devastation.

I consoled Ma and reassured her that all would be well. When things seemed relatively calm, I withdrew from the house and sought a quiet place in back of the yard. There I was overcome with grief. The tears that I had restrained just a moment earlier now flowed freely. Ma's abject grief was consuming; I felt her pain. I then realized that I was due to sail to England in a couple of weeks. I was not sure what I was going to do. I felt that life had thrown a curve my way and I was having a difficult time holding this particular curve in stride. I was so confused.

Soon Boysie came looking for me. Because he witnessed me at the depth of my grief, he thought that I had taken complete leave of my senses. He began to upbraid me for my lack of strength. Just then, as I was beginning to regain some of my composure, a group of concerned neighbours began to gather around me in the back yard. It was in front of all these witnesses that Boysie chose to show his annoyance and begin to castigate me publicly.

"Frankie, Pa dead and yo carrying on? It is time to act like a man. Ma need yo, we have to figure out things. So stop being stupid and be a man."

From those comments, it was quite obvious to me that Boysie had once again assumed the role of the big brother. Had he stopped there with his criticism I might have been inspired to "snap out of my moodiness." Boysie, however, was just getting started. He seized that opportunity to denounce me further for my apparent lack of manliness. In his eyes, I did not measure up.

I endured his criticism in front of all my neighbours and at the height of my own personal grief. I still had enough sense to compose myself and appear respectful of my elder brother's advice. This action met with the approval of all those gathered outside and soon we all returned to the house.

The question of how we were to manage the expenses involved with Pa's funeral was uppermost in my mind as we reentered the house. How were we going to cover the cost of the burial? Clive had just started working full time; Boysie was not yet working, and I had just given notice to my school of my intention to leave for England to pursue my studies abroad.

Once inside the house these thoughts evapourated. Ma's cries of agonized grief completely filled the room. Her slight frame was being supported on either side by Paula and Pinky. Despite their very best efforts to remain strong for Ma, each had given vent to her own sorrow as evidenced by their tears. Whether they fully comprehended the nature of the events surrounding them, the three youngest children, Basdaye, Kalie, and Suresh, wrapped in Kay's protective arms, each took on the face of sorrow and played out in miniature the scene that was before them. The scene overwhelmed me and once again I had to turn my face aside and direct my attention to other details. My mind drifted to my eldest sister, Dolly who lived several miles away in the country. Since there were no telephones where she lived, there was no easy way to get word to her. Yet, I knew that she would hear of the tragic news very soon by word of mouth. Bad news always seemed to travel quickly. I knew that Clive, too, would soon hear the news and be on his way. I was certain that he would take Pa's death very hard. Lately, Pa and he had been on very good terms. After a dismal start in the world of work, Clive was finally on the right path. Pa had managed to secure employment for Clive at the same company for which he worked. Clive now owned his own truck; Pa was proud of his eldest son.

My eyes wandered over to where Boysie was standing in the far corner of the room. His face looked pensive. I wondered what was on his mind. Was he remembering that not too long ago Pa was desperate to have him join him in his business? Was he feeling any guilt for turning him down? Did he know how much it hurt Pa both financially and emotionally, to have to hire a driver to drive his truck because he, himself did not have a licence?

The financial benefit was but one of the reasons that Pa had wanted Boysie to come to work with him. Perhaps more pressing was Pa's desire to see Boysie assume his share of responsibility as behooves a young man. Thus far, Boysie had given no indication that he cared to pursue any type of career path. He much preferred the easy road and cared nothing about sharing the road with Pa. I must say that I understood Boysie's rationale and had some sympathy for his situation. For years Boysie had been brutalized by Pa, both physically and verbally. Is it any real wonder then, that Boysie wanted to steer clear of any association with Pa that promised to give him no reprieve from the harsh criticisms that plagued him in his youth. (The ultimate irony in all this is that immediately following Pa's death, Boysie took up the reins where Pa left off. Not only did Boysie assume Pa's job, he took on more responsibility at home as well. He plied Pa's trade tirelessly for the benefit of the entire family. Indeed, it seemed that out of Pa's ashes was born a new Boysie. Truly, before Pa died he had planted the seeds for success in his two oldest sons who followed closely in his footsteps.) Such were my musings as I looked around at my family. The question of the cost of the funeral again surfaced in my thoughts and it was time to address that issue. I realized that I had some money set aside for my trip to England and I decided that I would dedicate that money to help secure the burial of my father. Accordingly, I now directed my attention to the details that preceded the burial.

That evening we set up a tent at the side of our home to house the many visitors who were to pay their respects. Among the many friends who came was my very dear friend, Kamal Ojah. I was so happy to see his familiar face. After greeting me and expressing his condolences, Kamal placed in my hands a gift. I opened my hands to reveal a considerable sum of money. Before I could voice any protestation, Kamal insisted that I take it. Kamal wanted to help. My pride wanted to decline his offer but Kamal's perseverance prevailed and eventually I was persuaded to accept his offer. Indeed, I am indebted to Kamal; he offered me a way out of our financial despair. I do not know if Kamal knew just how much I appreciated his gift. It came at a time when it was most needed.

I was most thankful too to the many friends who visited our family that evening. Although our grief was overwhelming, their thoughtful presence was heartwarming and we did not feel so alone—at least not at that moment.

Soon it was past midnight and most of our visitors had left. The immediacy of the tragedy had passed and intensity of the day's drama was replaced by the routine of preparing for the burial. Those who were spending the night soon settled down. Some played cards while others chatted quietly in small groups. Several others found a small nook where they managed to steal a few hours of sleep. It was during this time that I chose to sit down in the tent and think about all the things that had been done to prepare for the funeral. Arrangements had been made for the grave to be dug; a Hindu priest had been contacted to perform the ceremony; a coffin had been purchased; and finally, the death certificate had been secured. This last activity had been accomplished with a great deal of difficulty and was accompanied by a disturbing reality.

It had been my responsibility to secure the death certificate from Dr. D, the attending doctor. Late in the day on the afternoon of Pa's death, I contacted Dr. D and made arrangements to visit him at his office. Once at his office, I was allowed in to see him rather quickly. Dr. D then began addressing me in a most curious manner.

When he began to speak to me, I became very nervous. "Your father's death could have been prevented. He should not have died the way he did. I hold *you all* responsible. I've already told your mother this..."

"What did you tell my mother...?" I began but then caught myself. I had to contain myself for I felt that I must not disrespect the good doctor.

"Sorry doctor," I apologized.

The doctor then addressed another issue that equally disturbed me. "I suppose you came to collect the death certificate." Then he announced, "There is an outstanding bill and it is huge. Your parents were not able to pay the bill in full."

"Doctor what is the bill?"

His response stunned me. The amount we owed was more than twice my monthly salary.

I then asked the good doctor, "Doctor, will you accept what I have in my possession now? And allow me to pay the balance later on at an agreed time?"

"I can not do that," he snapped. "The bill has to be paid in full and you have to pay it before you receive the death certificate. The bank is still open. Go, and come back with the money, and I will have the certificate ready."

I left his office in shock. Dutifully, I went to the bank and obtained the money—every cent of it. I returned to Dr. D's office and observed that there were no other patients waiting to see him. I was subsequently ushered into his office with some urgency.

The good doctor made no attempt to hide his preoccupation. "Do you have the money? Do you have *all* of it?"

I took out the envelope containing all the money, and just as I was about to give it to him, a voice from deep within me urged, *This is not right!* Just as I was about to hand over the envelope, I pulled back my hand and declared, "Doctor I have changed my mind. I have decided to obtain that death certificate from another doctor at a *reasonable* price."

I paused.

The doctor was obviously stunned. "You cannot do this. I am the doctor. You will pay me, or else..."

"Or else what?" I interjected. "We do not owe you that kind of money. I have been in contact with my mother every step of the way ensuring that your fees were paid. And now you have the nerve to manufacture such a ridiculous sum of money owed to you. Do you think that you can hijack our family? Your reputation is on the line doctor." I stopped for a moment to let it all sink in. Then I continued, "Now, Doctor, I am prepared to *pay* you a fair price. Are you willing to *receive* a fair price?"

Obviously perplexed, the doctor paced the floor. Then he asked angrily, "Where on earth did you learn to speak English in that manner?" I ignored him. The true picture of this *good* doctor was being revealed. Obviously, after visiting our family several times and discovering that we were uneducated and poor, he concluded that he had found another gullible *Indian* family ripe for the picking. He never expected anyone to question him. After all, *he* was a *doctor*, indeed a *god* amongst gods. And, what poor simpleton was likely to question his judgment. He knew that poor families like ours were only too willing to listen to the doctor. The fact that he accused us of being negligent regarding Pa's death was a ploy; he was trying to establish a climate of guilt in our minds. Past practice had probably confirmed that family members who felt guilt over the death of a loved one would willingly pay any amount of money to erase their guilt. Furthermore, the family was likely to pay the doctor to avoid having a reputation as the family who could not honour their debts.

I truly marveled at the level of deceit in this doctor. Clearly, he had become very proficient and adept in this aspect of his *work*. I considered us a fortunate family indeed not to have encountered him sooner in our lives. Up until that time, we had been blessed by doctors who were truly moral and ethical when it came to treating the very poor. I remembered a time when Ma had to see a doctor but had no money to pay his fees. He treated her fully aware of her circumstances. She offered him payment in the only currency she had at her disposal: fresh eggs and vegetables. The doctor accepted her payment with humble graciousness trusting that if Ma could honour that debt some time in the future, she would. There were no veiled threats or open accusations. Ma was allowed her dignity and we were spared humiliation.

The memory of countless stories like that while I was growing up led me to believe that doctors were the true guardians of the sick. Never before had I encountered the likes of this Dr. D. A love of money rather than a love of healing appeared to be his true motivation for becoming a doctor. I fully acknowledged that doctors were entitled to a fair wage for their services; what I strongly objected to was the blackmailing of families, especially poor families, in order to extract more money than would be warranted under normal circumstances. Such acts are morally shameful.

Standing before me was the *good* doctor. His attitude seemed to be changing. He now appeared somewhat anxious. He looked at me with some degree of curiosity and asked pointedly, "What work do you do?"

I hesitated for a moment before answering him. I truly did not wish to engage in any further conversation with him for I found his character to be deeply offensive. I answered simply, "Doctor, I am a teacher."

"Well, that is splendid. I congratulate you," commended the *distinguished* doctor.

"Perhaps I have made a mistake," allowed the doctor. "I do see hundreds of patients and as a result I might have retrieved the wrong account inadvertently."

He then attempted to adjust his fee by proposing an amount only marginally less than the original. Again I voiced my objection. Finally he made a proposal which, although still high, was more acceptable.

I paid him.

"Well, young man, it was certainly a pleasure meeting you. Good luck," oozed Dr. D.

I could not believe my ears. Here was the good doctor still pretending to walk the high moral ground; still clinging desperately to the belief that he was a good man. I found that truly objectionable. I could not let it stand.

Just before I left the office I asked, "Tell me doctor, I am curious, how is it that you never *once* asked how my mother is doing seeing that she has just *lost* her husband, *your patient*? Let me answer. You are neither a liar nor a hypocrite. You don't even *pretend* to be compassionate because it doesn't even *occur* to you. It is not part of your creed. And what is your creed? Oh, I have it. Indeed, your *creed* is *GREED!*"

The good doctor was in a state of shock; incapable of formulating any kind of response. Feeling completely vindicated, I walked out.

——————

With the death certificate now secure in my possession, I felt relieved. I knew however, that I could not tell anyone what had just transpired between Dr. D and me. To do so would run the risk of arousing further anger within the family.

Upon returning home, I sought refuge in a quiet corner of the tent. Ma appeared as if from nowhere, and sat quietly beside me. Her sad eyes betrayed the intense agony within; I had great difficulty maintaining a calm and strong spirit.

"Frankie, ah know yo going to England soon. Wha go happen now son? Wha yo going to do?" Her quiet manner did little to disguise her real fear. I knew that she was consumed with worry over my upcoming trip to England. Her mother had just died six months ago. Her husband had died just hours ago. And now, her son was thinking of going away also. The burden of all those losses weighed heavily on her mind.

I knew what I had to do. Without any hesitation I resolved, "Ma, I am not going anywhere." She looked at me and once more began to cry; soft tears began flowing from a grateful heart. I realized that she knew I was sacrificing my trip on her account and, not wanting her to feel any further pain brought on by guilt, I added, "Yo know, Ma, I don't have enough money for the trip. If I stay back, I can work longer and save up some more."

She saw right through my words and placed a hand on my shoulder. She whispered, "Yo fader gone, but ah still have yo."

I may have thought that I understood her. The full impact however, was yet to come.

Then she was gone. I remained in the tent completely engrossed in my own thoughts. My mind drifted freely and my soul ached and ached. The full reality of my situation struck me and I felt completely helpless. Nearby in the open yard, there was a sacred spot upon ceremonial flowers and incense were offered up to God according to the Hindu tradition. A flag had been placed on a large bamboo and was planted in that consecrated ground. Looking up at that flag reaching up to the heavens, I could not help but wish that I, too, could reach to the heavens and see into the mind of God. I began to wonder about Bhagawan, our Hindu God. I had a great deal on my mind and I needed some answers. "So, Bhagawan," I asked, "how come Pa had to die *now*? How come you are throwing all these obstacles my way *now*?

"First you brought me into this world—poor.

Okay.

"Next you made me provide *for* myself *by* myself?

Okay.

"Now my future is unsure; I have to make it on my own two feet.

Okay.

"Now tell me, *how am I going to go to England now? Can I leave my mother? She has no resources. What am I to do?"*

I felt somewhat relieved by having asked the question. I had had a moment to discharge my mind to the Almighty. *Was He listening?* There was no answer; He did not let me know—at least, not then.

The next day, the day of the funeral, dawned bright and sunny. A busy day was ahead for all of us and by late afternoon, the funeral procession was scheduled to make its way to the burial ground a short distance away. Just minutes before the procession was about to begin, the weather changed. It would appear that Pa had awakened the Gods against their will and the heavens opened up and our community was deluged with rain. It rained as I had never seen it rain before. *What had Pa done to provoke the wrath of the gods?* The ravine beside our house that collected the waters from the mountain overflowed its banks. The waters gushed through our yard and literally threatened to engulf the floor of our home! As if this weren't enough, another problem threatened when some of the mourners began rushing inside our house seeking shelter. Soon, many bodies were crowded our modest living room. The floor was built with boards which could not accommodate the collective weight of the ever expanding crowd. I was worried the floor would collapse from under them. The heavy downpour blasted our home again and again and the waters rose alarmingly.

Pa's open coffin was in the center of our living room. Until now, I had avoided looking at Pa. An unseen force compelled me forward and I was drawn to him. Someone urged, "Say your goodbye, Frankie. Yo fader is going: never to come back."

I looked at Pa and he seemed utterly at peace in that coffin. In my heart and in silence I managed these sentiments, "It is all right Pa. Go in peace. This life of yours was too hard Pa. God take you now. Goodbye."

Just then the rain ceased as easily as it had started. The floodwaters began to subside quickly. The priest signaled for the procession to begin and another torrent of tears poured from the family. My sisters held Ma as she cried out in grief. It appeared that Ma wanted to hold on to the coffin and accompany it to the gravesite. Alas, that wish was not to be realized as it was not customary for women to accompany the funeral procession to the gravesite.

Against these conditions, the funeral procession commenced. Soon we were at the gravesite and I stared at the rudimentary hole dug in the bare earth. It seemed unnatural that Pa should placed in that hole. Then the Pundit began singing an Indian hymn–a most sorrowful refrain. Others joined in with the singing. I did not understand the words, for I did not know Hindi. But, I understood the sentiment of that plaintive hymn. My soul understood that the lyrics described Pa's journey from this earth to the Great Beyond. There, hopefully Pa will have found the peace that had proven so elusive here on earth.

I too had found my peace with my father. I contented myself with the knowledge that we had torn down the barrier that had divided us over these last years together. The single act of his acceptance of the dollar that I had offered just a few days ago, symbolized the acceptance he was extending to me. Had he not accepted it, that memory would have haunted me as his final act of rejection; now, however, that memory has become my spiritual redemption and allows me even now to honour my father.

Thus was my father finally laid to rest.

47

PHILOSOPHICAL MUSINGS: HINDUISM AND CHRISTIANITY

OUR HEARTS were heavy as we returned home. The condolences offered by some of the veterans and elders of our town were very much appreciated. But, three comments in particular proved a challenge to my understanding. One man remarked: *Your father's time had come*, while another explained: *It was his time; he had to go*, and finally someone pointed out: *God sent for him.*

I did not fully comprehend these remarks. They all supported one point of view: a person dies when another power deems it necessary. I had troubles accepting such beliefs because they did not make sense to me. Throughout my life I remember times when I would ponder over questions surrounding life and death. *Why was I born if only to die? What, then, was the purpose of life? It seems that death followed birth, but birth precipitated death. What awaited the spirit, the soul after death? Is death the final state? Is there any kind of life after death?* These questions absorbed much of my thoughts when I had occasion to be alone.

Somehow the notion that we live beyond death always made sense to me. If that were true, then our life on this earth must mean something; it must count! *What then was our responsibility here on earth? Was there a spiritual code to govern our earthly conduct?* If this were true also, if there was a spiritual code that governed our lives here on earth, then it simply did not make sense that a Power higher than ourselves controls our death; why would such a Power get to decide who dies and when? Consider this, if that power is God, and as such dictates the moment of our death, then wherein lies our freedom? If God is the arbiter of our accomplishments, then where is free choice? If man has no freedom, but is subject to the will of God, how then can there be sin? If there is no sin, then how do we define virtue? These were the types of questions I wrestled with in my spirit; I wanted to know more.

Two philosophies brought with them two disparate points of view to challenge my understanding: Hinduism and Christianity.

According to Hinduism, while a man lives his life on earth, every act and every thought is recorded by the Great Almighty. At the time of death, the Book of Judgment is opened. The man's life is examined and the sum total of all his actions and thoughts are judged. The decision to either promote him on to the next stage of life where he takes one step closer on the path to his ultimate unity with god, or return him to earth to live once again as a form of life on earth. While sincere prayers and divine thoughts help to balance the scale, they can not obliterate the sins recorded on the other side of the scale. At the hour of death, there is no quick redemption or miracle.

Christianity on the other hand offers complete forgiveness as a fundamental gift of faith. Even at the hour of death, if one repented of one's sins, still one could be forgiven. According to Christianity, it is possible for the most evil of sinners to attain salvation and find a place with God regardless of his past. This one Christian precept puzzled me.

So much of what Jesus advocated in the Sermon on the Mount and in the Parables offered hope and promise. Yet I found it difficult to embrace completely the Christian vision.

There was a reason for my deliberation. First and foremost, I was born and raised a Hindu. And, inherent in Hindu teachings, was the understanding that one must govern one's own conduct; indeed, one was totally responsible for one's own conduct. I accepted easily the idea that each of us is responsible for our own actions. Yet, the idea that there could be redemption as understood by Christianity was not without merit. These two teachings of Christianity and Hinduism formed a spiritual coin that I have pocketed all my life.

There are times when it may have appeared that I may have misplaced my spiritual coin. The truth is I would eventually return to my former stance and claim the best from each world. Then there were times when I felt that I had to choose one side of the coin over the other; this thought always brought with it great anguish. And then, some time later the thought occurred to me that I did not have to make a choice. *Could it be that the teachings of Christianity and Hinduism rather than contradict one other, reinforced the best in each other?* I arrived at a resolution to allow Hinduism and Christianity to rest side by side in my spirit; I did not have to play one off against the other. I came to a kind of understanding: *There has to be a God, and this God created all the peoples of the world. Did he offer the monopoly of the Ultimate light to one people condemning the rest of His other people to eternal damnation through no fault of their own? How could that be? There must be a measure of God's Divinity in all the peoples of the world; such a Divinity must be that gift that Almighty God gives each person freely. Therefore He gives us the choice of how to live our lives. We decide whether we choose virtue or sin.* But as for the question of whether or not we have a choice regarding our death, I still have no real resolution. Perhaps those men who suggested that my father's death was ordained might know something that I in my youth was not yet privileged to know. I set all these musings aside to once again return to the demands of a family in mourning. What I did not realize then was that I was about to enter into a different *kind* of mourning.

48

CIVIL SERVICES

SHORTLY AFTER my father's unexpected death, a Mr. P had a discussion concerning me with both my neighbors and my two elder brothers—Clive and Boysie. Because Mr. P held a prominent position in government, his opinion was highly regarded in our community. Following their discussion, it was their collective opinion that I should resign my position as a teacher and apply for a government job. My esteemed neighbour pointed out that I would earn twice the salary at the civil service that I was currently making as a high school teacher. Furthermore, he suggested that since Pa had died, it only made sense for me to resign my job at St. Charles Boys' High School, as a more substantial salary would be needed to support the family.

I had such great reservations about leaving my teaching position. I felt a passion surge within me when I was teaching. I had grown accustomed to my students and over time I was accorded a level of respect and cordiality from both the parents and the students. I had been accepted. I felt that I had indeed found my niche in life. Teaching had enriched my life as nothing before had done and I did not wish to resign; however, the collective wisdom dictated that I resign. Accordingly, against every instinct in me, I resigned from my teaching position and applied to the civil service.

Because of the recommendation given by my esteemed neighbor on my behalf, I was granted an interview. During the interview I was praised for my accomplishments. In particular, I was praised for having obtained *Second Class Certification* during my first year of teaching. That I had been teaching while carrying a full load of courses, proved to be of special interest to my supervisor. Immediately following the interview, I was hired.

I was hired but was I ready for the life of civil servant? It was a strange destiny that led me away from teaching and plunged me into the Civil Service. My experiences at the Civil Service became memorable indeed, but not for any normal reasons.

So, here I was—a member of the Civil Service—a government employee. On my first day at the job, I was directed to a large table; on the back side of the table was a chair; it was now *my* chair. The table itself was littered with many files; the disorganization was obvious. At the front of the table sat another employee; he was instructed to let me know what my duties were. Following the requisite introductions, I was given my responsibilities: I was to *check* and *recheck* the files given to me. This I did. But there was a slight problem; I did the checking much too quickly. When I turned to the employee sitting across from me asking for more files, he signaled to me to wait. Several minutes later he handed me some more files. I checked and double checked them and soon I requested more work. It was not forthcoming however, so I was left to my own resources. Tom, the worker who sat across from me at the table, would get up and leave periodically. At those times, I would be left with virtually nothing to do since I received my work from him.

Once, when a supervisor visited me, he pointed out that I should *pace* myself better. He even hinted that I should not ask for more work and made it plain that I was 'creating a problem for everyone else' when I did that. I was uncomfortable with his remarks and felt awkward in his presence.

I soon discovered that life at this office lacked any meaningful human interaction. I did not seem to fit in and I began to miss my teaching career. I yearned for the type of human contact that it provided in abundance. Teaching was not easy; at times it was emotionally challenging, at other times it was thrilling. Teaching completely absorbed my time and my energy. Boredom was a stranger as time passed by quickly. In my job as a civil servant however, oh, how the time dragged. I was literally and physically facing the clock. Soon I became its prisoner as I watched as every minute of every day tick slowly by. The sheer tediousness of my job caused me to suffer excruciating pain and I became an unwilling captive of time. The system boasted a hierarchy; and I was at the lowest level. I really did not know how I was going to survive.

One day not long after I began my job at the civil service, on a day when I had caught up on all my *checking and rechecking,* I left the department and went for a walk. The tedious repetition of the job left me feeling bored and listless.

When I returned from my short walk, I headed immediately to the table and completed the new assignments that awaited me there. Later on that day, the department head summoned me to his office. He explained that I needed a change: it was his opinion that this particular office assignment was not suited to me. He notified me that I was to be transferred elsewhere almost immediately. I was surprised by the urgency of the transfer and no one ever told me the specifics of the rationale behind it. I was left to think that without my knowing it, somehow I was a problem. These difficulties at work filtered into my life at home and created even greater problems for me in my own community.

My neighbourhood contained a small grocery store which devoted a part of its footage to housing a modest liquor store. It was customary for the men to gather there after work to enjoy a cool beverage and talk. It was not unusual for the store to become a type of court house where the men would hold *town hall* type meetings and engage in heated discussions and debates over one issue or another. Shortly after my *transfer,* my name was brought up and I became the topic of conversation. Mr. P announced to all who were present that I had turned out to be a huge disappointment. He intimated that he had gone to great lengths to secure a government job for me and that I appeared to be both extremely ungrateful and insensitive regarding his efforts on my behalf. He explained to everyone that I had to be transferred out of the department for insubordination when I offended my superior (who just happened to be a personal friend of his). Mr. P related that he felt extremely embarrassed by my actions and he felt personally compromised for his role in getting me hired.

To the men gathered in that shop on that day, it was an open and shut case. No further evidence other than that provided by Mr. P was required. There was no need for cross-examination or deliberation; an immediate consensus regarding my guilt was rendered:

That Frankie is no good. He should be ashamed. He bring disgrace to Mr. P. He is not appreciative of the good fortune. He bad.

News that I was an ungrateful rebel spread quickly. The elders of our town scolded and chastised me; many shunned me. Both of my elder brothers, Clive and Boysie, avoided me. Their silence screamed their denunciation of me for having brought shame upon the family. They said that *they* had to suffer for the shame that I brought to the family for having been *transferred*.

Neither Clive nor Boysie ever came to me to hear my side of the story. Did they not have a heart for me, their younger brother?

Once, shortly after the transfer, I saw my brothers and a group of their friends socializing at a gas station near our home. I did not yet know of their feelings toward me as I approached them in complete innocence. I was so happy to see them all; I'm sure my face was smiling. I had not quite reached them when I heard the humiliating denouncements from their friends. My brothers said nothing in my defence; they even showed pleasure by chuckling at a smear they thought was particularly funny. Hearing their laughter wounded me to the core. It seemed that everyone had joined the club whose sole motivation was to *get Frankie*. There could be no doubt about my brothers' loyalty. Their actions gave tacit consent to the findings of the town council who were out for blood: my blood. I tried not to show how deeply I had been wounded but the pain of their scorn translated into a lifetime of hurt.

Why was I being persecuted? I did not understand. I tried so hard to do the correct thing. Sometimes it simply was not good enough. I expected my esteemed and respected neighbor, Mr. P, to offer me counsel and help me along. This was not to be. His popularity grew at my expense. He seemed very comfortable riding the swelling wave of adoration. In fact, he became like a god in the community and sometimes I felt that I ought to kneel in his presence. I had been advised on various fronts to humble myself and seek the wise counsel of Mr. P.

Still grieving the loss of my father, whom we had buried but a few short days ago, I found myself now buried in a grave of scorn. I determined that I would not seek the *sage counsel* of Mr. P; I preferred rather to take my chances at the office.

It was not long before I knew my fate. I had been *demoted* (they called it *transferred*) to another branch of the service, the Licensing Office. This office, located outside the limits of the town, posed certain challenges. It was not near the convenient and familiar downtown environment and in addition, I was now required to pay extra transportation fees for a longer commute. I wondered whether my *beloved guru* had a hand in my *transfer*.

Another office, another administration to get accustomed to; how would I fare under these new circumstances?

49

MR. M. SINGH

THE NEW office to which I was transferred was responsible for the issuing of driver's licences and vehicle registrations and also for the transfer of licences. It was a busy place and soon I became comfortable. I had little time to relax. I was pleased to have an area to call my own even though the booth to which I was assigned was small. My chief duty was to attend to the members of the public who came and stood in long lines to wait for their licences. I settled down very quickly into my new routine. Unlike my previous placement, I felt that I was now occupied with meaningful work in attending to the affairs of the general public; this engaging experience had me looking forward to each new day with eager anticipation. My coworkers seemed very accommodating; at long last a sense of that elusive peace was once again within my grasp. (That is, until I encountered the second in command, Mr. Mongol Singh.)

Mr. Sevenson, an Englishman, was the man in charge of the licensing office. Next in the chain of command was his right hand, Mr. Mongol Singh. It appeared that Mr. Mongol Singh certainly enjoyed the sound of his own voice for, according to all staff accounts, he was constantly barking out orders—even when they were unnecessary. It would seem that Mr. Singh thought that the operations in the office would come to a halt if he was not around to direct our every move. From time to time, he would come down exceedingly hard on one worker trusting that in this manner, each employee would be too intimidated to step out of line. I am certain that Mr. Singh felt that it was his presence and his presence alone that afforded the office its stability.

One day Mr. Mongol Singh approached me and loudly ordered,

"Get these licences done. I want them done by the end of the day!"

"Okay, sure thing," I responded compliantly.

I knew that Mr. Singh was using me to do favours for his friends and relatives. By having me prepare their licences in the office they did not have to be present. This would save them both valuable time and money. Ordinarily it would take someone hours of standing in line while dutifully waiting a turn to complete the licensing process. That extended wait often cost the average person the loss of a day's wages.

I never questioned Mr. Singh whenever he brought these *suspect* forms to me; I always obliged his requests. In fact, oftentimes I would work through my own lunch hour to ensure that his request was met. Never once did he thank me.

Mr. Singh assumed an air of command that was both unmistakable and unattractive. The office workers huddled together in private to give voice to their negative feelings about him. I purposefully avoided those situations for two reasons: firstly, because I was relatively new on staff, I did not want to get caught up in office politics; and secondly but perhaps more importantly, Mr. Singh was my supervisor and I was determined to accord to him the respect that his position warranted. This respect however, was soon to be challenged.

A neighbor of mine asked if I would do him a favour by preparing his license for him. He indicated that he could not afford to go without pay for the day that it would take for him to stand in line and personally attend to the task. I had great sympathy for his cause and consented to his request. This idea snowballed and soon many of my neighbours were seeking my assistance for similar reasons. As a result, I spent a great deal of my lunch time devoted to securing licences for my absentee neighbours. I was more than willing to this small task for members of the community. It was my hope that performing this type of service for them would help restore some of the dignity that I had surrendered earlier.

I made no attempt to hide my action because I was doing it on my own time. Mr. Singh however took serious objection to my activities and protested vehemently. He ordered me to stop any further proceedings immediately and then commanded that I not help anyone again. Then, with his very next breath, he ordered me to complete the licenses that *he* had submitted. In spite of the duplicity inherent in his request, I complied. I did not wish to give the impression that I was uncooperative in any manner. I therefore completed all the licences that he handed to me. But, I still had a dilemma. *What was I to do with the re-*

maining unfinished licences that I still had from my neighbours? I decided that I would complete those licences but would no longer accept any new ones. Satisfied with my solution, I went back to my work.

Mr. Singh, unaware of the nature of my personal resolution, witnessed that I was continuing to provide licences for my neighbours. Without consulting me or communicating with me in any way, he concluded that I was uncooperative and noncompliant. Subsequently, he reported me to Mr. Sevenson, our superior, and charged that I was insubordinate; this charge in itself would be serious enough to see me once again demoted.

I shuddered at the realization that I was in deep trouble for a second time in my short stint in the civil service. I made an attempt to communicate with Mr. Singh in order to explain my conduct. He would not afford me a proper hearing. I sought his understanding; he dismissed me with disrespect. Eventually, M. Singh came to my office and escorted me to Mr. Sevenson's. Fearing the worst, I felt sick to my stomach.

No sooner had we entered Mr. Sevenson's office than I was besieged by a volley of verbal attacks from the mouth of Mr. Singh. There he stood, superior in rank but small in height; and, as I was about discover, even smaller in stature.

I really was surprised that Mr. Singh had reported me to Mr. Sevenson. I said nothing. This was Mr. Singh's moment to seize the spotlight; this was his moment to glorify himself by vilifying me.

In spite of Mr. Singh's caustic allegations, Mr. Sevenson greeted me politely and asked me to be seated. I expected Mr. Sevenson to conduct the interview, but the diatribe of invectives that exploded from Mr. Singh's mouth prevented him from saying a single word.

"This Mr. Boodram is uncooperative and disobedient. What is worse is he is contravening government policy. I am certain that Mr. Boodram is charging his friends for doing their licenses. That action is wrong. He should be dismissed immediately or, barring that, at least severely punished!"

My God, what have I actually done to cause Mr. Singh to denounce me with such venom? I felt like a criminal and looked to Mr. Sevenson in complete bewilderment. He motioned for me to sit opposite him, and indicated for Mr. Singh to take a place at side of the desk. Mr. Singh declined; he chose to pace the floor and assumed an air of self-importance.

"Mr. Boodram," Mr. Sevenson began, "you are reported to be doing favours for your friends. Is this true?"

"Yes, Sir."

"But, Mr. Boodram, this is against policy. Do you accept money or other favors from your friends for performing such a service?"

"No, Sir, I do not...."

"Liar!" screamed M. Singh. "I know his kind. He makes money. It is like a business for him. He doesn't do it for nothing. Do not let him fool you."

"Thank you, Mr. Singh," Mr. Sevenson interjected politely.

I could not help but note how composed Mr. Sevenson remained throughout the undignified ranting of Mr. Singh. In addition, Mr. Singh was completely oblivious to the fact that he was now unwittingly attesting to his own disdainful conduct.

"Now, Mr. Boodram, tell me why are you continuing this practice despite Mr. Singh's suggestions to stop?"

I noted Mr. Sevenson's choice of the word *suggestions* instead of *orders*. I felt safe with him. He was a man of sensitivity and dignity. "Sir, I made a mistake when I accepted the first request. I live in a neighborhood where most people are very poor but very hard working. When they asked for my help I did not want to say no. They would be disappointed if I turned down their requests, and I genuinely wanted to help them. Because they are my neighbours, I consented. I am terribly sorry for the troubles I have caused, Mr. Sevenson."

"Thank you, Mr. Boodram. But I must ask if you are accepting any kind of favors for providing this service to your neighbours?"

"No, Sir."

"He is lying," interrupted Mr. M. Singh. "People like him, they lie all the time! And worse yet, when they get caught they pretend to be innocent. That makes him the worst kind of a liar."

"Thank you, Mr. Singh," interjected a most patient Mr. Sevenson.

Obviously disappointed that he was not able to completely execute his missile of condemnation, Mr. Singh withdrew a few paces. I sensed that Mr. Sevenson was not about to nail me to the cross of denunciation that had been so hurriedly constructed by Mr. Singh and I could not help but think that this same cross might very well be used for his own ultimate condemnation.

Mr. Sevenson continued, "Mr. Boodram I must ask you to discontinue this practice of doing favors from now on. May I count on your cooperation?"

I said nothing as I contemplated my response. Mr. Sevenson, sensing my hesitation, asked, "Mr. Boodram, is there a problem with what I have asked you to do?"

I paused for I did not know how to explain my situation.

"Mr. Boodram, just tell me what is troubling you."

"I'll try Mr. Sevenson. Are you asking me to stop completely? Does that mean that I must no longer help anyone who asks me for a favor?" I paused, and glanced hesitantly in the direction of M. Singh. His face assumed a look of discomfort and his body slumped to reflect a stance that was less than imperial.

"Mr. Boodram what exactly are you trying to say?" questioned Mr. Sevenson.

Mr. Singh's face contorted. He no longer looked intimidating. He knew that I was in a position to disclose his duplicitous behaviour and to reveal that it was *he* who set the standard for *my* actions.

Mr. Sevenson awaited my response.

It would be so easy to incriminate Mr. Singh! Some primal force within me took delight in the thought of implicating him. I felt a sense of empowerment. One word from me and he could be discredited. The question remained, *would I act on that impulse?*

Mr. Sevenson awaited my response.

"Mr. Sevenson, in response to your question, allow me to explain the situation that I am experiencing."

Mr. Sevenson glanced at Mr. Singh whose face was now virtually tilted up against the wall in utter frustration. He had no idea what I was going to say. It must have been so hard for him to contain himself.

"Sir, the neighborhood I come from is a poor one. People who come to the licensing office give up as much as a day's pay. That is quite a sacrifice for a poor man. They come to me with such expectation. It is as though they see me in a position of advantage. They would be terribly disappointed and hurt if I did not help them.

"I see, Mr. Boodram," an understanding and cordial Mr. Sevenson acknowledged.

"Sir," I began.

"Yes, Mr. Boodram."

"I still have some of these licenses in my possession to complete. May I finish these please? Of course I would do the work on my own time I assure you, Sir."

Before Mr. Sevenson could respond to my request, Mr. Singh suddenly came to life. He could not contain his agitation. The fact that Mr. Sevenson seemed to understand my predicament and might accommodate me seemed to cause him extreme agitation.

"No way," an exasperated Singh declared.

"Mr. Singh, let us allow Mr. Boodram to complete the remaining licences. It will be all right."

Then Mr. Sevenson turned to me and spoke pointedly. "Mr. Boodram, finish what you have. Then you are to refrain from doing any future favors from now on. Do you understand?"

"Absolutely Sir, and thank you for your understanding Mr. Sevenson. It is appreciated."

As I exited the office, I could not help but admire this Englishman, Mr. Sevenson. His understanding and forbearance of my plight translated into a civility of manner that I truly appreciated. At the same time, I wondered what Mr. Sevenson thought of Mr. Singh . . . He must have recognized the shallow and aggressive arrogance of this man who was ready to slam me without so much as a second thought. By acquiescing to my request to complete the few remaining licences, Mr. Sevenson effectively denied Mr. Singh any kind of victory. Mr. Singh must have been terribly crushed. I then began to wonder about the nature of the conversation between Mr. Sevenson and Mr. Singh after I left. *Might Mr. Sevenson take this opportunity speak to Mr. Singh regarding his objectionable conduct towards me?* I did not have to wait long for my answer; a furious Mr. Singh soon approached me at my booth and taunted, "So, yo think yo smart Boodram. Look out. Make a wrong move and you are history; that I promise you!"

I often wondered why people in authority lauded their authority over those in lesser circumstances. What was it that possessed some people to take pleasure in trampling their subordinates? I found myself thinking Mr. Singh was not only unwise but also imprudent. A part of me wanted to tell Mr. Singh how reprehensible his shallow threats were to me. Another part of me, the rational side, realized that such a confrontation would accomplish nothing aside from escalating Mr. Singh's obvious distaste for me. I needed to keep my job so I said nothing. Thereafter, M. Singh targeted me with extra attention, inspecting everything I touched, trying to find some fault with my work. I became the horse that he intended to whip into compliance or ride into the ground. It was obvious to everyone that he bore no love for this animal; it was his sole preoccupation to extract every inch of service from this subordinate with the hope that the animal would give up. But, Mr. Singh was in for a rough ride. My determination to survive far outweighed his efforts to break me.

One fateful day a situation arose that I could not tolerate. Mr. Singh whisked by my station and commanded in his most dismissing manner, "Boodram you will go for lunch at 1:00 today."

He then disappeared. I was given no opportunity to express any concern that I may have had regarding this sudden time change.

My lunch hour was usually scheduled from 12:00 o'clock to 1:00 o'clock. At 12:00 o'clock sharp, I shut down my booth and went for my break. When I returned shortly before one to resume my duties, I was somewhat surprised to find Mr. Singh firmly rooted at my station. My colleagues looked alarmed.

As soon as he saw me, he bolted for Mr. Sevenson's office. From his animated behaviour and his frequent glances in my direction, it appeared that I was in trouble.

Mr. Singh soon returned to my booth, ordering me to accompany him to Mr. Sevenson's office once again. Even before I could take a seat in the office, Mr. Singh fired off his mouth.

"Didn't I tell you Boodram to take your lunch hour at 1:00? Well, didn't I?"

I found it difficult to respond to this accusing tone. I could not respond.

Mr. Sevenson intervened, "Mr. Boodram, did you not understand Mr. Singh?"

Still, I could not respond. I felt so uncomfortable. Mr. Singh had poisoned the environment with his hostile manner. I bowed my head.

"This is pure insolence," declared Mr. Singh.

Sensing by my posture that there was something more than insolence at play here, Mr. Sevenson interjected, "Mr. Boodram, is there a problem? Can you explain your action to me? Why did you ignore Mr. Singh's request?"

Encouraged by Mr. Sevenson's calm tone and measured manner, I ventured an explanation. I felt safe with Mr. Sevenson and reasonably assured that I would receive a fair hearing.

"Yes, Mr. Sevenson," I began. "I believe I can explain my actions. First of all, Mr. Singh did not *request* that I take lunch at 1:00 o'clock, he *ordered* me to take lunch at 1:00 o'clock. He then left before I had an opportunity to explain to him that I had a dilemma. I had already committed myself to an important engagement during that time and I could not miss it. I tried to find him to explain but was unsuccessful. And you, yourself, Mr. Sevenson, were not in your office either, so I was unable to consult with you on this matter. If only Mr. Singh had *talked with* me, we might have been able to work things out. I am so terribly sorry Sir, to have caused you distress. I apologize."

Mr. Stevenson thoughtfully pondered my words. Finally, he spoke.

"Mr. Boodram, I understand. You may return to your station now, thank you."

As I returned to my station, I heard the song, *Sad Movies Make Me Cry,* playing softly on the radio. I had heard that song played several times before but this time the song took on a new meaning for me. The lyrics of the song recount a story of betrayal when, quite by accident, a girl discovers that her boyfriend is cheating on her with her best friend.

The betrayal that I felt at that moment, while different in nature from the one revealed in the song, was, nevertheless, still betrayal. This theme of betrayal that pulsed through the song lyrics resonated in my spirit. I too, began hurting at the betrayal I felt at the hands of Mr. M. Singh.

M. Singh had devoted large stores of energy to trying to discredit me in front of Mr. Sevenson. His efforts were unsuccessful not because he did not try hard enough, but because he failed to realize that Mr. Sevenson, an Englishman and a gentleman, was committed to the concept of fairness and civility. I trusted my instincts about Mr. Sevenson's character. Further, I felt that I could rely on him to recognize that M. Singh could be a bit of a bully and that I was something of a victim in all this.

The fact that Mr. Sevenson did not see fit to reprimand me did not sit well with M. Singh. He could not contain his disdain for me and again felt that he had to put me in my place once he returned from Mr. Sevenson's office. That, I simply would not allow. Even I had a limit to the amount of bullying I would tolerate. So, when M. Singh began to threaten me,

"Boodram I am telling you this, I will see to it that you ..."

I decided to defend myself, fully aware that to do so might very well cost me my job.

"Mr. Mongol Singh, stop your barking!" I began.

M. Singh, momentarily shocked by my rebellion, appeared to be at a loss for words. This effect lasted only for the briefest of moments however and once again he resumed his threatening manner.

"Boodram I am going to see to it if it is the last thing I do..."

"Mr. Singh, stop your howling. For heaven's sake, do you not understand? You cannot threaten me or anyone else any more."

"What? Let me tell you, Boodram, I'm going to ..."

"What are you going to do? Get me fired? You are not in a position to get me fired. You have revealed yourself to be a bully. You put Mr. Sevenson in an awkward and embarrassing situation. How can he, a reasonable man, defend your unreasonable actions? You display such antagonism such disdain for your workers..."

"What! You dare lecture me!"

"Yes, I am telling you. Mr. Sevenson saw through your shallowness, your assumed air of self-importance. He felt compromised by your lack of good basic common sense. Moreover, I am certain that he is stressing over your obvious lack of competence as a manager."

"Boodram, let me remind you that I am your superior."

"No, Mr. Singh. You are not my superior. You are merely one of my bosses. At every turn your arrogance and stupidity betray your lack of integrity. You are an Indian, just like me. We come from similar roots. You, however, are now in a position of privilege; your station in life gives you an opportunity to be gracious and accommodating; it does not give you permission to be cruel and overbearing. You have been given an advantage in life; you could choose to lead by example. Tell me, Mr. Singh, please tell me, why is it that when an Indian is put into a position of advantage, he abuses his power by exploiting those whom he should be leading? Why, Mr. Singh, why?"

This outpouring left me drained.

A somewhat deflated and more subdued M. Singh reached for a nearby chair and sat down. He gave momentary vent to some incoherent mumblings under his breath.

I continued, "Mr. Singh, please, I beg of you, give us our due respect. Mr. Sevenson is going to be observing you. You are going to need us to support you. Get off our backs. Stop riding us so hard. Let us do our jobs. And, when you can, help us. We would really appreciate your support; you are supposed to be our leader, try leading for a change. "

Some of the workers resumed singing the chorus from the song, *Sad Movies*. Now that I had stood up to Mr. Singh, I no longer felt the extreme sense of betrayal as before. I stood up to him, not just for myself, but for all the other workers who had endured his abuse without complaint. They protested in secret and only to one another. They valued their jobs almost as much as they valued their lives and did not want to make their complaints public. I understood this. Knowing that my future career was headed in a direction that did not include the civil service, I took a chance and challenged Mr. Singh. I did it for them as much as I did it for myself.

Outside of my booth, a long line of customers, awaited. I resumed my duties. From that moment on it seemed that Mr. Singh and I had developed a new understanding and he no longer pushed me around. As time passed he seemed even less overbearing and arrogant. To be sure, he did retain a measure of his old self. I did not wish him to so completely transform himself lest he lose his colourful and vibrant personality. He managed to find a balance between authority and superiority with which we all could live.

A few days later, Mr. Sevenson called me into his office. He wanted to know how things were going generally. I explained that Mr. Mongol Singh and I had achieved a better sense of communication; and that on the whole there seemed to be a better spirit all around. Mr. Sevenson then asked, "Tell me about your plans for the future." I was both flattered and surprised. It was then that I informed Mr. Sevenson that I would be traveling to the U.K. shortly. To that, he responded, "Mr. Boodram, I am delighted to hear that. What do you hope to accomplish in England?"

"I wish to study Law, Sir."

Mr. Sevenson then smiled, pondered a brief moment, and then uttered this sentiment, "There is no doubt in my mind that you will be successful in any undertaking you choose. Good luck to you."

I honestly felt truly appreciated by this gentle man. My spirits were lifted and remained so throughout the balance of my work life at the licensing department. Perhaps some good resulted from the airing of my differences with Mr. Singh. The real silver lining behind this cloud called Mr. M. Singh was yet to be revealed.

50

PREPARATION FOR ENGLAND

IT WAS now six months since my father's death and once again I was making preparations to travel to England to study law. My short sojourn at the licensing department came to a meaningful end. Mr. Singh showed graciousness at my departure that I had not expected. Not only did he wish me well in my future endeavours, he took time to chat sincerely with me. That was truly appreciated. The rest of the staff was equally engaging and wished me well as they handed me a small gift wrapped in colourful paper.

When all the well-wishing ended, I felt the absence of one personality: Mr. Sevenson. I looked around, hoping to find him when I again encountered Mr. Singh. As he approached me he repeated the words that had become so familiar to both of us. "Mr. Boodram, Mr. Sevenson wants to see you in his office now. I, personally, am going to escort you."

The words were familiar but the speaker was much changed. A smile accompanied the words and the former hostility had long since been replaced by cordiality. M. Singh ushered me into the office with such a genuine pleasantness I again marveled at his transformation. He then left me alone to have a few final moments with Mr. Sevenson.

Upon seeing me, Mr. Sevenson got up out of his chair and came to greet me at the door. "Mr. Boodram, I am happy to see you. Please be seated."

I felt honoured with the attention that this man whom I so admired was showering on me. I did not know what I had done to deserve it.

"Mr. Boodram," he began, "I wanted to thank you so very much."

What was I hearing? This was all wrong. "Sir, it is I who should be thanking you; you have done me such an invaluable service. You have shown me such courtesy, such respect, at a most vulnerable time in my life."

"It may be so, and I thank you young man for the sentiment, but it is I who is indebted to you. You have done a remarkable service for me. I can not go into details. What I may disclose however, and I am happy to say this to you, is this: you possess integrity and character in full measure. Such qualities are scarcely present these days at a time when they are desperately needed. But, Mr. Boodram here I go babbling, and you must be so busy. Best of luck to you."

With that he opened the door and again shook my hand most respectfully. I was most reluctant to take my leave. I wanted to bask in the sunshine of those words for they had elevated my spirit and I craved more. Even though I did not fully comprehend what Mr. Sevenson was intimating, I knew instinctively that his words were more than mere words. Having come from the mouth of a man whom I greatly admired, they were imbued with the kindness, civility and humanity that so characterized Mr. Sevenson himself. Because of these expressions, my life was personally enriched. I could hardly believe the good fortune that was presently being visited upon me. Only a short time ago I was overwhelmed by the swelling tides of contempt, humiliation and ridicule; I was close to drowning. The only thing that had kept me afloat was the little raft of courage that I managed to keep under me.

Comments like these coming from a man like Mr. Sevenson, contributed greatly to boosting my self-esteem. They would certainly be needed when the tides of my life inevitably changed once again.

———

A healthy spirit also prevailed on the home front. My family was filled with pride in anticipation of my successful studies overseas. I was to be the first from our family to venture abroad to attend school; that, in itself, was huge.

I however, had some reservations about leaving. All of them had to do with how it would change life for those left behind at home—especially for Boysie and for Ma. My leaving meant that Boysie alone would be left to provide financially for the rest of the family. Boysie and I spoke at length about the situation and he convinced me that he was more than willing to take up the challenge. He explained it to me this way: "Frankie, before Pa died I had no interest in nothing. I wanted no part of Pa. Today, I have a job that my fader give to me. I have responsibility big time. I will look after Ma and the children. Don't worry." I knew that I had his blessing.

The situation with Ma, however, was a little different. Her words indicated a willingness to let me go in an effort to keep me focused on my goal. (Only later, when it was too late to do anything about it, I discovered her truest feelings.)

The last few days before my departure were spent bolstering one another for what lay ahead for each of us.

On one of our last nights as a family, Pinky, along with my other sisters, announced that they wanted to buy me a gift to remember them by. (I do not recall the actual gift discussed, just the sentiment surrounding it. The suggested gift could have been anything, but I am going to say that it was a tie, for I absolutely loved ties.)

So, Pinky came up to me and asked simply, "Frankie, what can we get yo for a present? We know yo like ties. Kay has picked one. We want you to choose the colour. Okay?"

When I discovered that Kay was the one who would be purchasing the gift, I gently discouraged their plans. I knew that Kay would stop at nothing but the very best, even though the cost might be prohibitive. I could not allow such extravagance on my behalf even though the gesture moved me.

Then I proclaimed what would really make me happy: Chinese food followed by Pinky's homemade coconut ice cream for dessert. The mere mention of this request had me drooling in anticipation.

While they may have been disappointed that I turned down their offer of a gift, neither my sisters' actions nor their words betrayed any disappointment. Kay's comment, "Frankie, is that all you want," seemed to set everyone on a new path.

So it was decided. A day was set aside during the upcoming weekend to honour my request. No expense was spared and we indulged in an eating extravaganza like nothing I had ever before seen. One or two dishes may have been prepared at home, but the bulk of food was purchased from our favourite restaurant above the Hi Lo grocery.

No apologies accompanied our healthy appetites, as dish after dish was devoured. The feasting seemed to go on forever. Our chatter was loud and animated; I don't know if any one of us truly listened to what any other one of us had to say. It did not matter however as we all were happy in the moment. Tales were being told; memories were being shared. No one was silent.

But, I was missing something. My craving for that coveted homemade ice cream had not yet been satisfied.

"Pinky, I don't see the ice cream; where is it?"

"Oh, shims, we forgot the ice cream, Frankie. We plain forgot. Sorry."

"It's okay," I managed to say. But it was not okay and I was sorely disappointed. I started to get up from the table so that I could indulge my brooding away from their eyes. *How could they forget my ice cream?* I pouted to myself. They could have forgotten anything else but the ice cream and I would not have been disappointed. Ice cream, especially homemade coconut ice cream was my favourite decadent indulgence. I did not know how to feign contentment if I were to be denied my ice cream.

"Surprise!" yelled a mischievous Pinky. "Hold your horses, Brother; everything is under control." Then she ordered, "Kay, go get the ice-cream."

An obedient Kay went outside mumbling under her breath, "That Pinky, all she like to do is give orders."

As Kay headed for the shower stall outside I was dumbfounded and silently protested her sudden desire to take a shower when I needed my ice cream.

To my delight, Kay brought out the ice cream making machine from the shower stall where it had been cleverly hidden. The girls had pulled off their masterful plan and I was truly surprised. "So yo think we forget yo Frankie; how could yo?" chastised my sister, Paula. The three conspirators Pinky, Paula, and Kay devised this scheme to tease me. It worked like a charm.

And now only one task remained before the ice cream would be ready to be served; the pail had to be hand churned to transform the liquid milk into solid ice cream.

I remember Kay starting the process, but she soon became exhausted and cried out for help. When she saw her brother, Boysie, idly standing by, merely watching the proceedings, she insisted that it was his turn. Boysie gave his typical response.

"Well, me ain't doing that."

To which Pinky responded disdainfully, "Men."

In an effort to salvage the wounded reputation of all men, I felt that I should volunteer my services.

"This we have to see!" shouted an animated Paula as she and Kay gathered everyone around. (It was most unusual for me to engage in any activity remotely classified as domestic, but my appetite for ice cream was proving to be a most seductive incentive.) I began turning the handle on the machine. Apparently I was less than accomplished at this simple task; Pinky complained that I was jerky and unskilled; I guess I lacked the smoothness and rhythm of a talented ice cream churner. Delighting in my awkwardness, she further declared, "Ma, look at Frankie; he acting *pohar* (an expression meaning incompetent). Everyone laughed at that comment, including me, for it was not often that my sisters had a chance to poke fun at me. I was always so serious. They indulged themselves fully in the laughter. It was good to see everyone so happy.

Once more Pinky attempted to give orders to Kay. She told Kay to take another turn at the churning. Kay would have none of it and both Paula and she ganged up on Pinky and insisted that she take her turn at the handle. Without comment, Pinky attacked that machine with a vengeance and in no time at all the ice cream was ready.

Mr. Boysie stood at the very head of the line for the ice cream and proceeded to line everyone else up behind him. The three youngest children, Bas, Kalie, and Suresh, felt that because they were the youngest, they should be served first. Imagine their shock when Pinky filled the first dish and handed it to me for testing, stating simply: "Frankie, taste it and tell me what you think."

Amidst a chorus of protests everyone else waited while I took my first mouthful of that homemade coconut ice cream. No one had to wait long for the verdict. My smile and contented sigh confirmed that I was indeed in heaven. I wished for nothing more. Watching the delight as everyone had a share of the ice cream has certainly been recorded in my mind as one of my life's sweeter moments.

It was the night before my departure and once again there was a gathering at our home as everyone came to wish me well on my journey.

A quiet sense of elation pervaded our home; it provided the perfect screen to cover the disquiet in my soul. That night after everyone had left, and all were asleep, I alone lay awake, pondering; I was thinking of nothing in particular and then I was thinking of everything. I had so many questions. *Was I a fool? Was it right that I should leave my family? What was it like to be in England? How was I going to live?*

Right now my life was fairly comfortable. Since beginning work at the Civil Service, I was able to help provide a few amenities for the family: a stove, a fridge, and the addition of a new room. I had become accustomed to a certain lifestyle. Every Sunday, Ma and the girls would go out of their way to prepare an extravagant meal for the family for we could now afford a few extras as Boysie and I had combined our resources. Boysie and I had formed a team; he provided the groceries, I provided the amenities. I loved this life.

Yet one area of responsibility still fell on my shoulders: decisions and discipline; Ma had completely deferred these areas to me since Pa's death. The family responded to my directions and all were respectful. It seemed that I had grown into this role step by step and gradually accepted more and more responsibility. At times the sheer weight of this added responsibility proved a very heavy burden and I missed the simple life afforded to one without such adult preoccupations.

One thing however, became increasing clear. I understood that whatever it was that I wanted out of life, I alone had to work for it. This message was crystal clear: if I want it, then I must go and get it. There was no aunt or uncle, no mother or father able to assist me. I was on my own. This venture to England was part of the plan I had carved out for myself.

That night I steadied my mind as I called on courage to be at my side. Yes, the dream of going to England was a colossal one; the ever closer reality of that dream was proving a challenge to my spirit.

At some point during the night I must have fallen asleep. Soon I was awakened by the crowing of the cocks and rays of sunlight pierced through the open crevices of my bedroom. A new day had dawned and a new adventure awaited me. What would it be like?

51

DEPARTURE AND THE S.S. ANTILLES

THE *S. S. Antilles* was due to depart from Port of Spain in the early afternoon; its destination was Southampton, England. When we arrived at the docks, it seemed that a million people were gathered to see us off. We made casual talk as we gathered outside. After completing a tour of the ship, a great deal of conversation ensued regarding the wonders of this fabulous vessel.

The blasting of a horn signaled that it was time for all visitors to disembark. I decided to leave my berth (in tourist/economy class) and came up to the deck to wave a final farewell to my family. I soon wished that I had not done so. The ship had now pulled away from the dock but I could still bear clear witness to what was happening on shore. From the deck of the ship I saw my mother desperately reaching past the restraining arms of Boysie and Clive in a last futile effort to reclaim me. The scene was a haunting reenactment of the day Pa died only this time the supporting cast had different players.

Pa had died a mere six months ago. Shortly before that, Ma's mother had passed away. The suddenness of these two deaths, left Ma in a very fragile state. In a few short months, Ma had suffered the deaths of the two people that she depended on the most: her husband and her mother. And now she was watching me leave her. My departure must have seemed, to her at least, as a third death. *How could I have so miscalculated what my leaving would mean to her?*

The image of my mother being restrained tore at my insides. I returned to my berth in utter despair. To further compound my distress, the swaying of the ship brought on motion sickness that kept me confined to my quarters. My new adventure certainly had a most inauspicious beginning.

Locked away in my cabin I had only my guilt for a companion. *Perhaps I had made a mistake; perhaps my departure was premature. Ma needed me. She was far too fragile and vulnerable. How could I have lived with her these past few months and not noticed her diminished condition? Was I that impervious to her pain? Had I been that self-absorbed?* Then her words came back to me. The full impact of their meaning swept my breath away: *Yo fader gone, but ah still have yo.*

There was, however, no turning back. I would have to find a way to live with the knowledge that I had been a further contributor, albeit an unwitting one, to her suffering. Her burden was far too great for her to bear alone; I should have been there to deflect some of the pain.

Despair seized me as the *S.S. Antilles* entered the open sea.

PART IV

England

52

ADVENTURES ON THE
S.S. ANTILLES AND THE OPEN SEAS

A S THE *S.S. Antilles* headed for the island of Grenada there was widespread joy onboard. I however, chose to remain in my modest cabin. Neither my spirit nor my body felt the least bit celebratory. The seasickness that seized me as we left Trinidad seemed to take over all my emotions. Invariably my thoughts led me to reflect on my mother's despair.

Jeff, a young man who also was travelling in tourist class, noticed that I was ill and offered me a pill to ease my physical distress. It seemed to give me relief (at least from the physical symptoms) and towards the evening of that first day, I was able to join the others for supper.

Supper was served in an enormous common room that housed several large dining tables. Each table could accommodate about ten people. I was happy to see Jeff as I walked into the dining room and he and I sat together at a table comprised mainly of other young singles like ourselves. We introduced ourselves to everyone and were soon at home engaging in the usual small talk. Everyone seemed to feel very comfortable very quickly. Our preliminary conversation revealed that we were all approximately the same age. One man, Ravi, was the sole exception; he appeared to be in his forties. Soon we were served our first meal onboard ship. It was quite different from our regular Trinidadian fare; we made every effort to enjoy it even though it was in desperate need of spices. We were confident that we would soon become accustomed to this new cuisine. After supper Jeff motioned for all of us to join him on deck.

Once on deck we could see the lights of the island of Grenada. The mountain range seemed to dance in their brightness. The ship, now on the open seas was an island unto itself with its whole host of activities. We went up to the very top deck to get the best view of the festivities. Upon further investigation on the second deck we discovered another dining room. This dining room dwarfed our simple dining quarters and was richly adorned with what seemed to us a rich extravagance and we thought *surely such an ornate room must be reserved for royalty.* The dining room possessed such finery that I felt relieved that I did not have to sit amidst such ornamentation. The next day while anchored off the shore of Grenada, we picked up a small contingent of soldiers. Since these soldiers were going to occupy the tourist class quarters, twenty passengers from that section had to be removed and accommodated elsewhere. The entire ten people from our table were among the twenty selected. As a result, we were immediately upgraded to second class. In an instant we had become passengers of the upper decks B the so called high class. At first this seemed to be a welcome improvement in our humble accommodations in tourist class; but while the accommodations were of a higher quality, second class came with higher expectations. A certain level of etiquette and dress was expected of persons travelling first or second class. These tourists paid a much higher price for their fare and were afforded a much different treatment than those of us in tourist class. Since there was no dining room devoted exclusively to first class, the passengers from first class and second class dined together in the same dining room. The passengers from these two decks mingled freely together. There were no obvious barriers to their interaction.

Because we were patrons of the third class or tourist class, there were no dress codes; we dressed casually—even in the dining room. The tourists accommodated in first and second class however, were expected to dress more formally—especially in the dining room. While suits and jackets may have been optional in first class, the wearing of a tie was not. In this dining room, the passengers were seated in the midst of great finery. A full array of silverware adorned each of the dining room tables. This presented some degree of discomfort at our table. Not everyone knew how to use the various pieces of silverware. (*Ahem! Frankie to the rescue.*) Those lessons from the waitress in the restaurant in Port-of-Spain were about to yield huge dividends. Because of those lessons, I felt somewhat confident that I knew a thing or two about dining and I took the lead at the table. To my great delight, I soon discovered that I was not the only one who knew a little. Each of us knew something and when we combined all of our skills we were soon dining quite comfortably. Struggling together to overcome our common discomfort unified us in a way that might not have been possible otherwise. A mutual friendship grew from this initial bonding as the eight of us (four males and four females) became comfortable with one another.

Each island stop along our way offered us an opportunity to increase our sense of trust and acceptance. Far removed from the normal cares of our previous lives, we developed bonds quickly with one another.

Sailing on the *S.S. Antilles* with a group of comrades was proving to be a tremendous experience for me for as luck would have it, I was quickly becoming a centre of attention. You might wonder why I, of all people could claim such attention. I wondered too. This is what I was able to figure out. The *S.S. Antilles* was a French liner and the crew spoke very little English. I was the only one in our entire group who, in high school, had taken some French courses. My French, although rudimentary in form and crude in application gave the appearance that I knew the French language. In the dining room, my rendition of *voulez-vous*, *pardonnez-moi*, and m*erci beaucoup* won the appreciation of my tablemates. Since the others in the group knew no French whatsoever, it may have seemed to them (impossible as the thought may seem now) as though I were a professor of the French Language—Caribbean Style! This made for a delightful *tete a tete* with the waiters and waitresses.

And, to my utter surprise, my new friends, my seven travelling companions, greeted me daily with affection. I went back many times to draw from this well of friendship. My spirit was thriving and my confidence was boosted. I received an additional surge in both these areas when we docked in Jamaica, our final stop before crossing the Atlantic.

Since we had a few hours layover in Kingston, Jamaica, our group decided to go to a bank to exchange some currency. When we got to the bank, we took our places at the end of the long lines of people waiting for service. One of the cashiers, upon seeing our group join the long line, motioned in our direction for someone to come forward. I looked back to see who it was that was being so singled out for special treatment. As I looked back, the person in front of me touched me on the shoulder, and said, "She's calling *you*."

I looked at the cashier; she smiled and *seemed* to be signaling at me to come forward but I would not allow myself to believe it. So, still unsure, I pointed to myself awkwardly. Then the cashier stood up and loudly whispered, "Yes, you."

Immediately I became self-conscious. All eyes were on me. *Why I was extended this courtesy*, I wondered. The fact that the cashier was so radiantly beautiful made it all the more puzzling. I was unaccustomed to being beckoned by anyone let alone an attractive young lady. I advanced toward her window. Once there, she chatted cordially with me, completed my currency exchange, and wished me well. *She was so friendly*. She said that she hoped that I was enjoying Jamaica. (Well, she certainly helped me to enjoy Jamaica that much more.) I went outside to await the others. I was still mystified by this young lady's obvious but puzzling attention to me. It seemed curiously enchanting.

Eventually the group came back together again and Pearl, one of the girls, inquired, "Frankie, you know why she called you up to her till?"

"No."

"Well, how you feeling? I know why. Do yo want to know why?"

I did not ask why. I was too embarrassed.

The others, however, make it very obvious that they wanted to know so Pearl explained,

"Guys, there is a world cricket match presently being played here in Kingston:—India versus the West Indies. The cashier thought that Frank was a famous Indian cricketer: a cricketer who is very good looking. She thought Frank was that famous person."

My newly acquired friends laughed heartily at that information. Pearl remarked that I "was not that bad looking". Thankfully, no other comment was made regarding my looks. The fact that the attractive cashier found me somewhat good looking was a foreign idea to me. Yet here I was taking great delight in this rare moment. *Life is good*, I mused as we headed back to the dock.

Thereafter I noticed that my friends, both male and female, were seeking my company. Such experiences made me feel that not only had I been accepted by the entire group but that I held their confidence as well. Things were looking up in my world. The despair surrounding my departure had begun to diminish and I began looking forward to the rest of the journey. From time to time my mind recalled that beautiful young lady at the bank in Jamaica; it was a sweet moment and made a beautiful memory. For once Life had dealt me not a blow, but a promise—a promise of good things to come. I smiled that smile of hopeful anticipation and wished that feeling would never go away.

The *S.S. Antilles* departed Kingston, Jamaica for France. We would spend five long days on the open seas before we would see land once more. We prepared as best we could for this unbroken voyage. While we all loved our times together, a small problem emerged which threatened the general health of the group.

Everything began innocently.

As we began our voyage across the Atlantic, Pearl began paying attention to Pierre, our waiter. Pierre was very handsome and bore a strong resemblance to Tony Curtis, the movie star. Because Pearl was English speaking and Pierre was French speaking, they were not able to communicate very well. They needed a translator; the translator turned out to be me.

Whenever Pearl would ask for something, I would faithfully translate her request, but I was almost always a bit playful. Once, Pierre asked me to tell Pearl that she was beautiful. I took it one step further however, and, after telling her that he thought she was so beautiful, I told her that he wanted to ask her out.

She consented.

Then I went to Pierre and suggested that perhaps he should ask her for a date. He became very excited at the prospect. Needless to say, I was at the centre of their budding romance and I was enjoying every moment of my matchmaking.

At another time, Pearl and Sandra came to see me about a personal matter. In confidence they explained that a couple of the young men from our group were making advances to them and they were uncomfortable. They wondered whether they might have given certain signals to warrant such attention. They loved life the way it was with our group and did not want to spoil it with any romantic complications. The girls expected me to correct the situation.

I approached the young men and explained the situation regarding the girls. They listened dutifully, then informed me of a problem that they were having. They suggested that *I* was partly to blame for their problems. *Dear me, what have I done* I wondered.

The young men made their concerns abundantly clear; they felt that they were being ignored by the girls. Furthermore they charged that the girls were favouring me over them. They noted that the girls were always seeking my company over theirs and they wanted to know why, (especially since I was not actively pursuing them).

Needless to say, I did not see things the way they saw them; but, since I was at the centre of this mass of confusion, I felt that I needed to find a resolution.

I asked Pierre to bring coffee for the eight of us in a quiet corner of the dining room. Then I invited (perhaps required) the group for coffee. I assumed the role as mediator and requested that each member speak openly and truthfully. I began by explaining that our friendship together was valuable not just to me, but to all of us. I urged, "Whatever we choose to divulge at this meeting should not challenge our friendships. If anything, it should serve to strengthen our regard for one another and should be respected as a first step to finding a solution that works for everyone."

Each person in turn, spoke; it was refreshing to see that even though each was airing what was perceived to be a problem, each also demonstrated a caring regard for the others. Some general recommendations resulted. The boys were no longer to pursue the girls; the girls were to seek the camaraderie of *all* the boys. Thus it was resolved. We all were in agreement. My relief was immense. What could have turned into a fiasco, ended well; I was regarded as a hero of sorts for my part in the resolution. How my life was changing! I was becoming *the man*. That realization made me smile.

In a couple of days, life would once more prove challenging. We were two days away from Lisbon, Spain.

53

LISBON, A PLACE OF SURPRISES

No sooner had we disembarked the ship in Lisbon, Spain for our layover when our eyes beheld an utterly shocking sight. Nothing I had experienced in Trinidad could have begun to prepare me for what I witnessed on those Spanish streets: a young child perhaps eight years old and of *fair* complexion was *begging* on the streets.

Her thin arms thrust two live chickens up in the air begging any passers-by to buy them from her. The desperation on her face was as real as any I had seen on the faces of beggars in Trinidad. We all had seen children beg before, but not one of us had ever seen a *white* child beg. We grew up believing that if a person was white, he/she was privileged. A person's white skin was equated with elevated social status and wealth. That a white person could be so poor that he had to beg was inconceivable.

This scene contradicted every belief that I held about white people and their white world. My understanding of the universe had just capsized and I did not understand *the why*. The world was completely inverted.

In my small sphere (and from the perspective of my narrow experiences only) the whites comprised the advantaged class. The two terms, disadvantaged and white, could not coexist on the same page. Everything that was fine, beautiful, cultured and elevated defined what it was to be white. The whites stood on the highest rung on the ladder of class hierarchy. Never in my wildest imagination could I have ever conceived that a white person could be as poor as this child who now stood before us begging.

The longer we looked at this small child, the less her colour mattered. Truly her colour was immaterial; her need was paramount. We could understand real need, true desperation. Her need was evident as she pleaded for the sale of her chickens. While we could not buy the chickens, we did give her some money, and for the next little while we continued our journey in a silence.

The hills at Lisbon, Spain stretched ahead of us in regal splendor. Ravi, the oldest in our troupe, took the lead in our expedition. We approached a cemetery that enticed us with its statues and stone edifices. The beauty of the stone structures was so alluring that we could not resist taking a closer look. We had no idea that the dead could be accorded such luxury. Each building competed for our attention; we were in awe of our surroundings. With our imaginations stirred, we left this site. The girls headed to the shopping area whilst the boys followed Ravi downtown.

We soon came to a large and most curious building in the centre of town. A modest sign, written in Spanish, announced the name of the establishment. Not one of us thought to ask Ravi what the sign meant; we followed him in complete faith. Where Ravi went, we trustingly followed.

Ravi climbed the flight of concrete stairs that led the way into the building. At the top of the stairs near the entrance he paused and rang a bell. Moments later, a woman from inside the establishment opened the door. They spoke in hushed tones in Spanish. We did not understand what he was saying. The woman held the door open wide and we all followed Ravi inside to an exquisite room. The walls were richly adorned in shades of red and gold velvet; the plush red carpet delivered us into a large area replete with inviting chesterfields and oversized chairs. Before we had time to begin to digest this scene and begin to process what all this meant, beautiful, young women, dressed in what I could only describe as immodest dresses, entered the room and draped themselves over the furniture.

Ravi turned to us.

"Well, boys, take your pick. Are they not beautiful?"

He himself was smiling broadly as he examined the ladies appreciatively. He motioned to one of the women dressed in a flaming red. His smile widened as she approached.

Jeff and I exchanged quick glances. It was obvious that he too was uncomfortable with the situation. In the beginning I wasn't certain what type of establishment we had entered. I was however seriously concerned. I could see that Jeff shared my concern. Then one of the girls approached me. Her tone was inviting and her manner most provocative; I was immediately uncomfortable. Jeff and I seemed to be coming to the same conclusion at the same time. I began an awkward retreat. Jeff joined me. Together we tried to motion to Ravi to indicate that we were leaving, but he had disappeared.

Once outside Jeff and I did not speak for what seemed like hours. Silence reigned as we made our way back to the dock. As I reflected on what had just happened, tried to understand what Ravi was thinking by bringing us to such a place. I could only guess that he had anticipated that we would be pleased by this excursion. It probably never occurred to him that we would be uncomfortable. The whole experience seemed surreal. My world had not contained such realities. My closest frame of reference came from the movies. This reality was all so confusing.

By now Jeff and I were close to the wharf where our ship was docked. Just ahead of us was a bus stop where a group of high school students dressed in blue and white uniforms had gathered. As we neared these students, we slowed our pace. One young lady approached Jeff and asked him a question.

Since he did not understand her question he turned to me. I had a very limited understanding of Spanish and could not sustain any type of prolonged conversation. I did however, understand her question. It was simple; she just wanted to know the time. I managed to communicate a satisfactory answer to her and as a result a conversation of sorts ensued.

The other girls joined in as we exchanged ideas about our countries. What seemed to fascinate these girls was the idea that we lived in a tropical island with no snow and no cold. The girls were fascinated by the idea of palm trees, beaches, and shorts being a year round reality. We found their company and their questions delightful.

Just then Pearl and the other girls returned to the dock. They joined in the conversation until it was time to exchange goodbyes. As we slowly took our leave, one of the girls ran towards me shouting,

"Frankie, my picture, please take, please." I looked at the picture and I looked at her; I appreciated her gesture of friendship. With a smile, I placed the picture carefully in my wallet. Then she hugged me, whispered something in Spanish, and left. That moment brimmed with an innocent enchantment. My friends gazed at me but said nothing as we headed to the ship. I pondered the events of that day. Ravi had planned an encounter with *chosen* damsels. That plan went awry. Then, quite innocently, Jeff and I chanced on a different meeting with another group of young ladies. There simply was no comparison. Is it not strange how life unfolds at times?

Ravi was already on board the ship when we arrived. He was obviously impatient. He quickly took me aside and got right to the point. There was more than a hint of agitation in his voice as he scolded, "Frankie, you think you better than the rest of us? How come you didn't show any appreciation for what I did? Man, I paid for you. I wasted my money on you man. You are not a friend. You shame me." Clearly Ravi was angry and hurt. He had no way of knowing that I was a complete stranger to such experiences. It was now apparent that such events were a familiar part of his life. While I could quarrel with his choice of life, I had no quarrel with him. I searched for the right words.

"Ravi, I am so sorry."

"Frankie, why didn't you stay? Tell me that."

I was quiet. How was I to answer Ravi? Did I really know why I didn't stay at that house with those girls?

"Ravi, it happened so soon, so unexpected. I was not prepared. I now realize how generous you were. Can you forgive me?" While Ravi remained quiet perplexed, he no longer appeared as angry.

"Rav," I continued. "I have a favour to ask you."

"What favour?"

"I would like to do something for you at the next port. Perhaps you would let me take you to a show or a restaurant. Would you?"

He looked at me for a moment. The beginning of an understanding seemed to flow through him. Then he responded.

"Frankie you are different. I bet you don't drink. Come to think of it, I've never heard you swear. You don't indulge in a whole lot of things either. Do you?"

I said nothing. I couldn't. I did not know how to respond.

"Look," Ravi continued, "I said some things to you at the beginning. Pay no attention. You want to take me out. That's okay. You are different and a bit strange. But you are okay."

"Thanks, Ravi. I appreciate that." I was grateful that Ravi allowed us to continue in friendship. Alienation was avoided and I was relieved. Despite our differences, we could still be friends.

As we were about to join the others Ravi surprised me as he continued. "Frankie, you are going to England. It's easy to become corrupt. You hear me. Don't change man, I wished..."

His voice trailed off and he never finished his thought. I understood. I did not need the thought to be voiced.

"I hear you Ravi. Thanks for everything especially your understanding." He smiled. All was well again. I had left Trinidad hoping to expand my horizons and gain an education. Already an education was unfolding.

54

A GALA EVENING

A GALA EVENING awaited us on board the *S. S. Antilles*. We were on the open seas approaching the Azores. We all dressed for supper and assembled at the lounge awaiting the official announcement. Our friendly chatter revealed our good spirits. Then, quite out of the blue, Pearl asked, "Frankie what that girl, that Spanish girl give you at the bus stop?"

"She gave me a picture," I stated simply.

My response spawned a chorus of questions and comments. Everything that was said was said in good taste. I was teased, yet no one sought to offend. I could not help but reflect how unlike this teasing was from the teasing of my past when everything that was said to me under the guise of teasing was really designed to hurt me and diminish me.

Again, here among these new friends, I was once more *the man* of the moment. I was unaccustomed to this positive energy and secretly savored every moment. My spirits were elevated; I was grateful to be part of this group of friends.

Soon the announcement came that supper was served and we proceeded to the dining room without delay. Everyone else seemed to be of a similar mindset. It appeared that all were famished. I for one felt that I could not have waited a moment longer. We took our places and awaited our servers.

The ship, by this time, had entered the open seas once again and was rocking dangerously from side to side. The novice passengers (of which I was one) showed their alarm. Looking out the porthole on one side of the dining room, I clearly saw the sky. Looking out the portholes on the other side, all I could see was water. Indeed this giant ship was tilting precariously from one side to the other. I tried especially hard to conceal my fear.

Sensing that the passengers were anxious about the weather, the captain addressed us. He explained that we were in the Azores, where the warm water and the cold water met. This sometimes resulted in violent eruptions. He continued, "It may appear dangerous to you passengers who are unfamiliar with this area, but let me assure you that it really is quite routine." He punctuated that statement with the flash of his huge smile. His words had a calming effect and we relaxed our fears somewhat. We took our seats, eager for the diversion that eating would provide.

We were simply amazed with what happened next when the food was brought in to the tables. Our cutlery and plates were securely clamped in place with silver clamps. Even the tables and chairs were anchored securely by clamps to the floor. I could not have imagined that dining could be made so secure. What was truly amazing was that these ingenious clamps did not detract from the overall look of the room; in fact, they had a unique attraction of their own.

While the ship continued to tilt from one side to the other, we tried not to show our fear. Now that all the clamps were in place supper was about to be served and we all were virtually starving. A server brought in a huge silver platter and placed it on the table; an embroidered cloth covered the contents of the platter. It seemed that the main entrée was to remain a mystery for a little while longer. *What was it?* We all waited in anticipation as our server, with an air of bravado, removed the cloth, to reveal a fish; the head was intact and the eyes were open wide and stared directly at me. The body of the fish was drenched in a pale creamy sauce. Those eyes—they kept staring. My body began to revolt; a foul sensation entered my mouth as my stomach churned violently; I tried to escape to the bathroom; I did not make it! So much for attempting to maintain an air of sophistication when the body is in distress! Some things just cannot coexist.

The *S.S. Antilles* was now headed for our final stop—Southampton, England.

55

SOUTHAMPTON

WE DOCKED at Southampton three hours ahead of schedule. As we disembarked, our group was struggling with mixed emotions. On the one hand we were relieved that we had at long last arrived safely. On the other hand was the realization that we were now about to head our separate ways. It was truly a bitter-sweet moment as goodbyes and addresses were exchanged.

"Frankie, give us your address and phone number," Pearl insisted playfully.

"I will, when I know. I don't have one as yet," I responded. I had their addresses and I promised to stay in touch. I surveyed the scene. Hundreds of people were milling about. There was excitement and joy and tears as relatives and friends reunited.

I watched as my friends left one by one; soon they all were gone. I alone was left and no one was there to greet me. Bissondath Ojah-Maharaj, the son of a friend from Trinidad was supposed to meet me. I looked around, scanning the departing crowds looking for one friendly face; looking for some indication that I had not been forgotten. There was no body lingering, hidden by the shadows, shyly waiting to greet me. Then a strange sensation gripped me. *I did not know what this man looked like; how will I recognize him?*

While I did not have a photograph of him, he did have one of me. Such knowledge did little to dispel my feeling of unease. And my unfamiliar surroundings served to heighten this feeling as each minute passed and no one came to be at my side.

The weather was changing quickly. Soon, even though I was still inside the building, I was so cold that I felt frozen! It was March in

England and the light Trinidadian clothing I was wearing was insufficient for this brisk climate. I wondered how anyone survived this freezing weather. I kept looking around. *Where is Mr. Ojah-Maharaj? Why is he not here?*

I noticed that there was a gate at the side of the building. It was open giving a panoramic view of the surroundings. I ventured outside and approached the gate with curiosity. I wanted to get a better look at this country. Suddenly a great gust of wind assaulted me and I buckled under its force. "Who lives in a climate like this?" I asked again and again. I could not begin to imagine that anyone could survive let alone want to live in such a harsh climate. My bones were shaking from the intense cold and I hastened my return to the relative warmth inside.

As I awaited my deliverance, melancholy found its way into my body. My eyes welled up without my bidding. Unsolicited thoughts found a home in my mind. *What am I doing here? I want to go back home.* Such were my very first moments in England.

About that time a security guard approached me and explained, "Sir, I have to lock up the building, would you be leaving soon?" The guard's tone and attitude were most polite and respectful as he spoke. After I explained my situation to him we chatted and he advised me to phone my party and let him know my predicament. He then took me to the phone booth where I dialed the number of Mr. Ojah-Maharaj.

I could hear the phone ringing on the other end.

"Hello," a voice answered.

"Mr. Ojah-Maharaj, please."

"One moment please." Then silence, that eternal silence.

"So sorry, Sir. He is not here. He left."

I took that as a good sign. He must be on his way here. He will be here soon. I was about to say a thank you and hang up when the voice continued.

"Oh, Sir, my mistake. He is still here. Hold the line please."

"Thank you."

"Hello." The voice was reserved but dignified.

"Hello, Mr. Ojah-Maharaj, this is Frankie Boodram."

"Oh, you are very early. As you see I am still in London. I was just about to leave to come greet you," he explained.

"What am I to do?"

"Tell you what. You travel to London. It would be much easier for both of us."

"How do I get to London?"

"Simple, my friend. Find the train station, and take the next available train to London. I will find you. It will take some time. Don't worry old chap I will be here at the station, waiting for you."

"How shall we recognize each other?"

"That's easy, I have a picture of you. Better get going. You don't want to miss your train."

"I will do that right away. Thank you"

"See you soon." Then he hung up.

My spirits were slightly raised. We had made contact. He would be waiting for me. For a moment I had felt lost and defeated. Now I had purpose. The security guard was obliging as he helped me secure a cab to take me to the train station. Even that seemingly small action on the part of the security guard had great significance for me. Through his willing nature and polite manner, he had lifted my spirits. I felt fortified.

The cab soon arrived and the cab-driver stepped out to greet me, "Hello."

"Hello," I responded.

"And where are you headed, Sir?"

Sir? Had I heard correctly? Had this white gentleman just called me "Sir."

Needless to say I was shocked. I had so much to learn. I was not *culturally* prepared for persons of white colour to address me thus. The driver awaited my response and I directed him to take me to the nearest train station. I was about to lift my suitcase when he politely objected, "I will get that, Sir." Again I was stunned as this white Englishman carried my suitcase to his car.

This was my second major culture shock in less than a week. Again, I was left thinking that nothing about my life in Trinidad had remotely hinted at the existence of such a reality. The driver, sensing that something was not quite right with me inquired, "Is everything all right, Sir? You do seem a bit out of sorts?"

He would never know just how much "out of sorts," I was. After asking him to take me to the train station I explained that I was a little overwhelmed at the moment, but that I would be all right soon. He accepted my explanation without further comment.

The cab gave a welcome reprieve from the cold wind swirling outside. It did not however, seem to be generating much heat. I prayed that the station was not too far away for soon I was freezing just sitting in the back of the cab.

Then I heard these most welcomed words: "Here we are, Sir. Train station to London. And if you hurry, Sir, you might just get a train to London any minute."

Heartened by my apparent good fortune I thanked the driver and paid the cab fare. I even included a little something extra I was so impressed by this accommodating English driver.

After leaving the cab, I hurriedly entered the station to purchase my train ticket. The cashier pointed me in the direction of the train. Oh, my Lord! To catch the train to London I would have to cross over three sets of tracks. *How do I get across? Surely I was not expected to risk my life by crossing all those tracks. There had to be another way.* I looked up and down the tracks and noticed a set of stairs on the far end of the station. The stairs led up and over the platform. From there, there were stairs leading down to the other side. With ticket in hand, I grabbed my suitcase and sprinted for the stairs. My body had not had such a workout since I was a child and I was panting heavily as I rounded the final set of stairs. I could see the train. I raced across to the platform only to witness the door close on my face. The train gods seemed to be conspiring against me. My extra efforts were ignored by an uncaring train that was already headed away from me.

I felt reduced. Once again I was a child, and like a child, I wanted to call out, "Train, please stop. Don't you see me? I am still here. Please stop."

My unspoken pleas were unanswered. I watched the train move away slowly. Not wanting to concede defeat just yet, I ran along the platform after the train hoping against hope that somehow the train would miraculously stop for me. For a brief moment the train actually appeared to slow down. My heart skipped a beat. In that moment I imagined that the train had heard my plea. In reality, the train was gathering momentum and was speeding away from me. When I realized this, my hopes were dashed. I was despondent. Nothing was working out; there were barricades at every turn. I felt defeated. I clutched my only friend, my suitcase, ever closer to my body and huddled near a post.

For nearly an hour I was an invisible observer on that platform. Many trains came and left; not one was my train. Train passengers moved to their own rhythm; my presence made no difference to their world. The occasional one would nod or smile; no one spoke to me directly.

When my train arrived I boarded it quickly, thankful to be on my way finally. The only thought now occupying my mind was *would Mr. Ojah-Maharaj be there to meet me.*

56

LIFE IN LONDON

W E PULLED in to the London station. As I disembarked the
train, a tall distinguished man approached me.
"You would be Frankie Boodram."

"Yes."

"Follow me." His immense frame towered over me. Everything
about him, except his complexion, seemed English: his conservative
tone, his reserved manner, and, most noticeably, his accent. As the evening progressed it became increasingly obvious that Mr. Ojah-Maharaj
was completely at home with every nuance of British culture.

After securing a taxi for us, he commented, "I suppose you need
dinner?"

"Yes, I'm starved."

"All right, I will see what can be done." He directed the taxi to an
East Indian restaurant. I found this somewhat unusual for I had anticipated that we would be going to his place and I was really looking
forward to his hospitality. I had not particularly enjoyed the last meals
aboard ship and I had been secretly relishing the thought of some
good Trinidadian home cooking. Nonetheless, I counseled my spirit
to be content at his chosen restaurant. While the cuisine was different from that found in Trinidadian restaurants, the meal was delicious
nonetheless.

Over dinner, Ojah-Maharaj explained that he had booked me a room
in a home for men. To say that I was surprised by this revelation would
be an understatement. I was sorely disappointed. Since separating from
my new friends on board the S.S. Antilles, I was suffering the pangs of
loneliness. Now new feelings of estrangement flooded my soul in this

country that was not my home. With Ojah-Maharaj, I had hoped for a reprieve from these feelings. I had anticipated that I would be a guest in his home for at least my first night since I was a fellow Trinidadian.

Disappointment was quickly becoming my only reliable companion since arriving in London. I sensed that I had better start getting used to the feeling. In all innocence, I believed that it would not be presumptuous of me to hope that I might have been invited to his home; courtesy customarily dictated such action in Trinidad. Perhaps this was yet more evidence of a cultural difference.

Yet, the idea that I was to have a room all to myself became somewhat appealing when I had time to ponder its benefits. After supper, we hailed another taxi and headed for this "home for men."

Over dinner, Ojah-Maharaj gave me some items of clothing that he had purchased on my behalf. The warm coat was especially welcomed and I donned it immediately.

The journey from the restaurant to the boarding house revealed interesting aspects of London.

The surroundings were so different from Trinidad. Even in the dim light of the evening I could see that the houses were attached to each other and that there was a noticeable absence of space between homes and buildings in general. The street lamps were tall and stately and gave off a dim but gentle light. I was particularly impressed with the road construction. The roads were made of cobblestone rather than our customary asphalt or concrete and the stones were woven patiently into interesting and somewhat intricate patterns.

Upon arriving at the boarding house, we paid the taxi driver. This clean-shaven uniformed driver had proven to be a man of impeccable politeness. I was impressed.

As the taxi sped away, we turned to face the front of the three-storey building that was to be my home at least temporarily. It held no appeal for me. It seemed that all the houses on this street and the next resembled each other and had no real character or charm. A hedge about two feet high separated the property from the street. A small yard with some flower beds brightened the otherwise uninviting house. I was not impressed.

Bissondath Ojah-Maharaj, now perhaps feeling slightly uncomfortable, expressed, "Now Frankie, it is rather late."

I was shocked for it was not even 11 pm. The night was still young. He continued, "Everyone has retired now. We shan't wake up anyone. As we go up the stairs, we must be very quiet. Your room is on the third floor. It is small, but I dare say it looks rather comfortable. You will make do until the morning at which time I shall contact you. You understand?"

No, I did not understand. I was quite bewildered. My bewilderment was compounded by the speed with which he was about to make his exit. *What kind of an introduction to England is this?* I asked myself. *Where was the family gathering? Where were the friends? Who was to greet me the following morning?* Despair placed its now familiar grip around my heart. I fought hard to rid myself of my expectations; I truly tried to be more accepting of my situation.

Fighting back feelings of rejection, I turned to Mr. Ojah-Maharaj, and told him that I would look forward to seeing him the next day.

With that, he opened the door and we entered the building in silence. The hall light although dim, allowed us to note that everything on the first floor was clean and orderly. As we headed up the stairs they creaked. Bissondath again cautioned me to be careful and we proceeded to the third floor. Once there he opened up a door to reveal a room that was barely large enough to hold a small bed and a dresser.

"This is your room," he informed. "Now look here at the wall." There was some sort of contraption on the wall. He informed me that it was a heater and then placed a coin in it. Soon heat started to filter into the room and the frigid cold gradually disappeared.

Then he uttered this cautionary footnote "When you change to get into bed, do not fall asleep without first turning the knob on the heater to the off position. The fumes can be extremely dangerous if the heater is left on. So, turn it to the off position."

I nodded to indicate my understanding.

With that final warning, he left.

There I remained in that undersized room with an unfriendly and potentially deadly heating apparatus. Loneliness and despair threatened to engulf me once again. Fatigue proved to be a stronger force than either of those feelings. I changed and climbed into bed to escape the day's harshness. Just as I was about to doze off, I remembered the warning about the heater. I forced myself to stay awake until the money in the unit expired; I then turned the heater to the off position. I quickly climbed back into bed and pulled up the covers, for a chill had already descended on my small space. I could not help but wonder, *What on earth am I doing here?*

It was then that the full intensity of my loneliness and isolation took hold. I allowed myself a few moments of indulgence. Then, as I reflected on the day's events I had an insight. I had no right to be upset with Bissondath. I had no right to expect anything more from him than he had given. Yes, he was a fellow Trinidadian but his life in England was far removed from the Trinidadian expectations. I had innocently imposed my Trinidadian expectations on this young man. I had no right to do so. He was expected to secure me a room; this he did. If anything I should be grateful. From here on in I must stand on my own two feet. With that realization my heavy spirit lifted; thoughts drifted to home and I began to wonder about Ma. *Was she alright? How could I have left her in her condition?* I allowed myself to mourn for her. Some time later I drifted off to sleep.

The next morning I woke up around 10:00 a.m. I looked around the room. Everything felt strange. It wasn't just that I was in an unfamiliar space; even the air felt strange. It was so cold. I had pulled the covers right up to my neck. Somehow, the toe of my right foot had found its way out of the covers and it was exposed. That toe somehow stretched itself out and made the mistake of touching the bed's metal frame. What a brutal shock! The frame was ice cold. Immediately my toe sought refuge under the covers. I feared venturing out of the warmth. I knew that the idea of hibernating under the covers was out of the question so I forced myself out of bed. I was ready to embrace my first morning in London.

After getting dressed, I headed to the first floor. The landlady saw me and greeted me in what I thought was a most unusual and decidedly *unBritish* manner.

"So you're the late one. Breakfast is already served but I suppose you need some breakfast; I could prepare you something. Come with me."

I followed her to the basement where there were several tables with matching chairs set up in restaurant fashion. Each table was covered with a red and white checkered tablecloth and topped off with a vase of flowers. By the time I arrived, most of the tables were vacant. Only a couple of people remained, each at their own individual table. They were having tea and reading newspapers. Each seemed consumed in solitude. There was no conversation. Each seemed perfectly content with his isolation. I however craved conversation. It was my key to sanity. There was only the occasional glace in my direction; each kept his own counsel.

"I could get you a cup of tea," the landlady offered.

"May I have a cup of coffee?"

"Did you say coffee? I could get you *tea* right away?" I was quiet. "Oh well, I will get you coffee. And to eat, Sir?"

"What may I have?"

"Will you have cereal, Sir?"

"Yes, Maam?"

"Coming up, Sir."

Soon I was being served cereal with my coffee. The landlady explained that breakfast was served until 9:00 a.m. only. I made a mental note of that information and then began to look around hoping to engage someone in conversation; no eyes met mine.

It would have been so easy to become melancholy; I made an effort to be positive however and reminded myself that I had a clean room in a respectable home. *Enjoy it.*

With my newly minted positive attitude, I decided to step out and explore my new surroundings. Excitement filled my veins as I dressed and headed outdoors. This time I donned a heavy pullover that Bissondath had brought for me. Although it was somewhat bulky it was warm.

It was March 21st as I stepped outside to the glorious sunshine. There was something decidedly uplifting about that bright sunshine. I walked slowly to ensure that I did not miss a single sight. This lasted for about a block before an icy wind blew through the bulk of my sweater chilling me to the bone. This was followed in quick succession by another gust of wind; I folded; it was that cold. The cold winds just would not stop; soon I began to feel as if a sheet of pure ice had engulfed me completely. By now, I was on all fours crawling back to the house, trying to avoid the icy wind.

After returning to the boarding house, I spoke to the landlady about my difficulties with the weather. She explained, "You certainly are not dressed appropriately. You need proper gloves, a scarf, some unders, and a coat."

I knew what gloves, scarves and coats were but I had never heard of *unders*. I was too shy to ask.

I returned to my room to don more appropriate clothing and then headed outside once more. I stood up to the icy wind but somehow I was still exceedingly chilled. I made a brave attempt to explore my near surroundings but soon abandoned the effort and returned to my room to await Bissondath.

I cannot describe how happy I was to see him. Seeing him again was like having a little taste of home. I was hoping to be invited to visit him and the rest of his family. He must have anticipated my request for he soon explained that his wife worked evenings. Because she left for work before he arrived home, they had to hire a babysitter for a couple of hours each day. He further explained that because of this difficulty, it would not be easy for him to meet me on a regular basis. While disappointed, I understood.

The next day I was both surprised and excited when Bissondath invited me to accompany him to his flat. I was about to have my first look at a real apartment in the city of London.

It was most comfortable. I was most comfortable. Finally I was in the home of my fellow countryman and some of my loneliness evaporated. He introduced me to his two little boys who were both under the age of five. Although they were a bit active, they were still loveable children.

Bissondath had gone to the trouble of preparing some supper and we sat down to share a meal together. It felt so good to be with him in his home at last. Suddenly an idea came to me and I shared it with him. I suggested that I could come each day and look after his children during that period of time that he had been hiring a babysitter. Bissondath accepted my offer without hesitation.

Soon we developed a well-established routine; each day when I arrived at the flat the table was set, the children were playing, and supper was already prepared. Bissondath did not talk about his wife and, while I found that both curious and unusual, I did not seek to intrude on his privacy.

Meanwhile however, I had more serious concerns. I needed to find employment. Bissondath purchased a newspaper, and together we inspected the want ads in search of available positions. I followed this up by sending applications to the various employers that we had selected.

As well as looking for work, each day I would seek to get to know better the area in which I lived. This task was not as easy as it sounded. Not only did each street look the same but they all appeared to run in the same direction. On many occasions I actually became lost. When I thought I was on one street, I had actually wandered off a couple of miles onto another street without realizing it.

One day when I lost my bearings, I approached a policeman and I told him of my predicament. Upon hearing my concerns, he immediately stopped a local bus and gave the driver precise instructions regarding where he was to let me off.

I was pleasantly surprised by the courteous attitude of the police officer and by his willingness to help me out of my difficulty. As the bus arrived at my destination I reached into my pocket for the required bus fare when the bus driver spoke up, "No charge, Sir. You have a good day." Not only were the British people polite, they were also generous. I found this to be a most charming quality.

And charmed I was once again when Bissondath passed on an invitation for supper from Mrs. Bissondath; I could hardly wait.

The day finally arrived and I made my way to their flat. As I rang the doorbell, Bissondath invited me in and led me into the living room where the boys were playing quietly. I still did not see any evidence of Mrs. Bissondath and I was a little uneasy. *Where was she? I thought she had invited me. Was I wrong?* I was too shy to voice my questions. Then, while Bissondath and I were making small talk, a woman's voice called politely, "Frankie, I am sorry I have not been able to meet you before. Welcome."

Those were among the most beautiful words I had ever heard. I was both relieved and happy to finally meet Bissondath's wife. I had begun to think that perhaps I had somehow done or said something offensive and that she was deliberately avoiding me. Soon all five of us were seated at the table. Mrs. B, while exceedingly polite and gracious, remained somewhat distant. I sensed a reservation in her; something intangible was preventing her from receiving me fully. I felt this instinctively but I did not dwell on it for I rationalized that such an attitude may not be without just cause.

I therefore resolved to make no overt attempts to befriend her. I was however, cordial and responsive in my conversation. I sensed that this was the right approach for I felt a measured and modest acceptance. It was a positive beginning.

Gradually I was becoming more and more comfortable. Soon, another event emerged that had a significant impact on my life.

57

THE INTERVIEW

I RECEIVED A letter inviting me to interview for a position in a tax office in the Neasden area of London. I made an appointment for the interview; I was exceedingly anxious and excited for, unknown to anyone, I was almost completely out of money.

Finally the appointed day arrived. I took the bus and headed for the interview. I arrived early so I thought that I would go and explore the area to get a better sense of the environment. I was extremely delighted at the Neasden area. I fell in love with the district and was excited to see that the building where the interview was being conducted was a most "acceptable" four storey building. I felt somewhat relieved for I had heard horror stories from fellow Trinidadians who had been employed in places that could easily be called "dumps."

I made my way to the reception area where I was subsequently escorted to a nearby office. My immediate observation was that all the workers were white. Such an observation deserves some explanation. In Trinidad it was easy to develop a bit of a complex regarding the white class. It was easy to think that the whites were superior to all other races. Hence I was feeling a little bit inferior and slightly insecure as my eyes took in an all white work force. I feared that I was not yet ready for such a change. I was intimidated at the thought of being in the midst of an office that was "white." I began to wonder whether this was where I belonged: an understandable reaction, considering my circumstances. And now, to be interviewed by a white person and to be surrounded by an almost all white work force… My thoughts raced. I needed courage to help me stay calm and composed.

The time for the interview arrived. As I entered the office, I was greeted by two men: Mr. Campbell and Mr. Charles. Both men appeared stately and distinguished. Mr. Campbell seated me while Mr. Charles thanked me for coming. I was struck by this simple courtesy and my feelings of anxiety began to subside. The interview began, first with a series of matter-of-fact questions which I was able to answer in a straight forward manner.

Then, Mr. Campbell queried, "Mr. Boodram, if you would, please tell us why you applied for this position."

I responded simply and truthfully.

"Since arriving in London, I have sent out many applications. Your company, Sir, was the first to invite me for an interview. Here I am, Mr. Campbell."

"Have you formed an impression about our establishment?" Mr. Charles asked.

"Yes, I have. As I walked through this floor, I noticed that everyone without exception was focused on their work. I also noticed that everyone was very polite. I am impressed by not only what I see here, but also what I have observed in this neighbourhood as a whole; I like it very much."

The gentlemen looked at one another and whispered. Under other circumstances, I might have been uneasy as these two men whispered; yet I remained calm and took no exception to their conduct.

"Mr. Boodram, you mentioned that you liked this area, yes?"

"Absolutely, Sir; I came on the bus a couple hours ahead of our scheduled interview and took some time and checked out the surroundings. The area has a certain charm that I find appealing. I would like to work here, Sir."

"Well let us have a go at your credentials; we have examined your resume and it is excellent. You have been teaching?"

"Yes."

"And what caused you to leave teaching in Trinidad to come to London, if we may ask?"

"Certainly. I wanted to participate in another experience other than Trinidad. We are a terribly small island and I wanted to expand my horizons. England, I believe, has a great deal to offer and I would welcome a chance to be part of the team here, Sir..."

"Mr. Boodram, we have one concern. We would like to have a little talk about it. May we?"

"Of course."

"Mr. Boodram, can you be comfortable here with us? After all, there are only three other persons like yourself. We..."

"Sirs, let that concern be. I will be comfortable here and furthermore, I *want* to be here."

"In that case," Mr. Campbell interjected, "congratulations."

Mr. Charles got up and walked with outstretched hands to greet me.

"Mr. Boodram, it is our pleasure to offer you the position."

I was bursting with so much joy that I could hardly contained my excitement and responded, "Thank you, Sir. I accept your offer."

"Can you begin this Monday?" Mr. Campbell asked. I deduced from his interest that he was to be my direct supervisor. I was inwardly delighted for I just had a very good feeling about him.

"Yes, Sir, I can."

"Well, Mr. Boodram, allow us to welcome you aboard," a pleased Mr. Charles congratulated.

Imagine those words "allow us to welcome you" being said to me. In all my life I never expected to hear such expressions, let alone by two such distinguished British supervisors. For so long in my own beloved island of Trinidad, I had been made to feel less than worthy. I had developed such a limited opinion of myself. Now, I was being offered a position in this worthy white establishment! Joy flooded my soul. No it was more than just joy, it was also the joyful peace that comes from acceptance and the joyful anticipation of working in an establishment that valued you as an actual person—a normal person—a smart person.

I was elated. That day, a modest transformation took place; I allowed myself to indulge in that feast wherein the food of intelligence was consumed by an unaccustomed but nonetheless hearty appetite. Mind you such a transformation was merely born. Would such a transformation take root, grow and blossom?

I was at ease at my job. People at the office were polite and extremely helpful. I performed my duties to the best of my abilities. Life assumed a routine: a good routine. I would get up, go to work, and then return directly to Bissondath's apartment. Occasionally Mrs. B would be there, and on her day off, she would engage me in conversation. Gradually I came to understand her initial hesitation to meet me. I learned that Bissondath had invited other guests and friends, particularly West Indians, to their flat from time to time. Such encounters did not go very well because some of these guests overstepped their bounds. Not only did they lack basic manners, some were outright crude. Further, Mrs. B revealed that a couple of these Trinidad boys were most inappropriate in their conduct toward her. She felt terribly uncomfortable and awkward in their company. Quite naturally, she sought to distance herself from such meetings. She had informed her husband that she never wanted to extend her friendship to another boy from Trinidad. For some reason, she had set aside that attitude with respect to me and I felt her acceptance not just as a friend of the family but as her friend too.

The fact that Mrs. B now welcomed me without reservation gave rise to a quiet feeling of accomplishment.

Life was progressing joyfully both at work and at my new *home;* at long last life had promise.

58

STAN

A T THE office, there was a remarkable young man named Stan. At six feet ten inches tall and one hundred and fifty pounds, Stan was a slim giant. His unbalanced gait inevitably drew attention to his feet. It was the area between the top of his shoes and the bottom of his pants that was truly mesmerizing. Because his trousers stopped a good four inches short of his shoes, as he walked, several inches of his white socks were always visible. Although this aspect of his attire was the cause of much gentle ribbing, Stan was loved dearly. Stan and his associates were the strength at the core of the office. They represented office life at its very best. This *inner circle* was much admired and often envied. As a newcomer, I greatly admired their style and camaraderie and wondered in silence what it would take to be accepted into this auspicious group. Their ability to instantly transform the mood in the office from serious and all business to light and fun loving was legendary. This transformation happened twice a day over tea—British style. Two times a day someone would take orders for tea and crumpets. Although I was not accustomed to this practice it is one I adapted to quite readily. During this time, the whole staff was transformed. An air of light hearted freedom invaded the room punctuated occasionally by bouts of craziness. I loved every minute of it even though I was not yet a direct part of it. It was enough to simply witness it vicariously.

Although not yet an insider, I did not feel like an outsider. The group did not have an exclusive air about it. I knew that I had to be patient. In time I hoped to be part of the staff. At this point in my life, I was content to let life unfold in its own natural rhythm. I was one of the few fortunate immigrants who had succeeded in finding a job (suited to my level of education). I considered it a privilege to be working in the tax office.

Immigrants flocked to England from all over the world. Many came from the West Indies and Asia. Employment was extremely difficult to obtain and many accepted jobs as unskilled labourers and domestics. Nonetheless, each immigrant was extremely grateful for any job no matter how menial the work or how menial the pay. They were looking far into the future hoping that their children would be afforded better opportunities in their lives.

This large influx of immigrants however, brought with it a multitude of problems; some of which were proving to be a blight on the British landscape and on the British reputation. Overcrowded conditions and massive unemployment often led to disturbing unrest and racial tension. This was especially true in the city of London.

One evening, not long after I arrived in London I saw a hint of this tension. A group of West Indian men was walking along one side of the street; it was obvious that they had been drinking as they were exceedingly happy and boisterous. If this same group of men were in the West Indies, behaving in the same manner, their behaviour might be considered merely colourful or vibrant but still within acceptable norms. By conservative British standards however, their behaviour would appear to be loud and outlandish. A group of London residents was walking on the same side of the street towards the West Indians. The closer the Londoners got to the partiers, the more uncomfortable they became. The Londoners decided to cross the street rather than face the rowdy crowd of men.

They whispered amongst themselves as they crossed over. They glanced back at the loud theatrics of the immigrants and their disdain of the group although subtle still resonated. Even though nothing concrete was advanced by either side it was apparent that Londoners felt that they were being invaded. I too recognized in moments like this that the invasion was not always welcomed.

In that moment I recognized that to be fully accepted in this new land, we, the immigrants, had to cork the bottle on our undesirable habits. Behaviours that might be easily accepted as normal in our native land were often regarded as uncouth and uncivilized here. Ignorance of this fact did not help further the cause of our acceptance by the British. It was sad to note that too often we fostered an image that lacked the courtesy and civility that was a cornerstone of British society. Because we were often insensitive to this fact, we may have falsely accused the British of being racist. While many a British citizen may have demonstrated an occasional air of superiority, a measure of good sense on our part would suggest that we needed to infuse our behaviours with a modicum of simple manners and courtesy to disarm the general body of mistrust felt by the British public.

I suspect that any indiscretion committed by any immigrant served to further harden the British perspective against us. It would then appear only natural that they would seek to avoid crossing paths with us. Being an immigrant in England in those times was not always easy; one truly had to struggle to make it. Yet, by some strange twist of fate and the protection of the gods, I seemed to have a charmed life in England. Stan proved to be the catalyst that initiated this life at the tax office.

Fortune began to smile on me the day Stan paid for my tea and crumpets. He left his usual group of friends and came to my desk.

"Hey Frankie, I wonder if you might consider joining us for a drink at the pub. Would be jolly fun! What do you say, old chap?"

I thought for a moment. So far I still did not drink, not even socially. My decision to wait until I turned twenty one had remained firm up until now.

Stan urged, "I am sure that you will enjoy the experience old chap, what say you?"

"Stan, I want to come but I have a situation." I confided.

"Out with it chap, I am positive your situation can be solved. What's the problem?"

"Stan, I don't drink..."

"Oh, sorry old chap. "

"But I do want to go; do you suppose I could be there and just have a non-alcoholic drink? That would be great."

"Of course you can, absolutely! Well, see you after work, old chap."

That evening after work Stan and his other friends from the office came for me and soon we all were comfortably seated at the local pub. The scene was truly remarkable. Stan ordered a beer for himself and a non-alcoholic beverage for me. Soon everyone was chatting. Then our group joined forces with another group. Politics, religion, sportsBno topic was taboo. No one person or group dominated the conversation; it seemed that everyone was on an equal footing. I learned later that all who gathered at the pub came from different backgrounds. Here the butcher and the doctor, the ditch digger and the dentist, all stood on even ground. I enjoyed the hearty (and often pointed) exchange of views advanced by so many individuals. In Trinidad, we tended to stereotype people and identified them according to the jobs they held.

Those who had "elevated" positions like doctors or lawyers, claimed recognition and respect. This tendency to stereotype was noticeably absent at the pub; that, for me, was truly remarkable. For a moment, I believed that I was at an institution for higher learning. Our friend Stan could easily have been mistaken for a distinguished professor, such was his ability to converse and engage his audience. He captivated us all.

Stan was accepted and well known in the pub circuit. Over time I developed a solid respect for him. On one occasion, someone asked Stan a question about capital punishment; he seemed to falter. I was shocked when he turned to me for support. At first, I was self-conscious but I did offer some feeble reply that I felt confirmed my lack of intelligence. To my great surprise, Stan declared, "Here, here, Frankie," and the others joined in acclamation.

I was in a fog and had no idea that others sanctioned my response. Following Stan's lead, others began to include me in their conversations; I realized that my earlier response to Stan's question on capital punishment must not have been as stupid as I had imagined. And, what was the feeble comment that I had made to Stan? First I explained that I had vacillated on that issue for some time and since I was not able to decide I then referred the matter to some higher authority; except—I had not yet discovered what that higher authority was. I honestly felt that my answer was less than intelligent for it could be interpreted as an excuse to avoid giving an opinion, but Stan assigned some wisdom to my response and I was able to stave off those familiar feelings of inadequacy. What a tremendous experience that was! I was ecstatic to be part of this group—no longer an outsider looking in. I belonged. I was accepted.

The practice of coming to the pub on a regular basis was exhilarating. I made sure that nothing would detract from that activity; I was growing increasingly accustomed to that way of life.

Yet, I needed to re-examine my original purpose for coming to England. *Why did I leave Trinidad to come to London?* I now had to address this question and, depending on the answer, another decision may have to be made.

59

A REMINDER

BECAUSE I had left Trinidad with the express purpose of studying law in England, I now had to again set my sights on that goal. I therefore applied to and was accepted at a Polytechnic College in London. I made certain that the classes I signed up for were classes that would allow me to pursue studies in law at a later date. I still wanted to become a lawyer. In my mind, lawyers stood for justice; they upheld and nurtured the ideals of justice and honour. How much my decision was based on my intense dislike of the practice of *some* Trinidadian lawyers who moved only to the drum of bribery I can not rightfully say. These lawyers exacted a heavy toll on the poor—the very clients who could least afford to pay a legitimate fee let alone finance additional sums for the purpose of bribery.

At times, these practices seemed rampant in Trinidad. Bribery was not solely restricted to lawyers; it was very much alive in other occupations—doctors, teachers, civil servants, police, and politicians to mention a few.

Looking back, I now see the many reasons that compelled me to study law abroad. Perhaps a part of me wanted to fulfill my father's dream—to be the first "professional" in our family. I also I envisioned myself championing the case of a poor client, adopting his cause as my own and defending him passionately. I suppose I romanticized the nature of a lawyer as a champion—a knight righting a wrong on behalf of someone less fortunate and less able. Perhaps my ideas were unrealistic. Nevertheless, I knew that I wanted to be a lawyer. The idea was firmly rooted and I began attending evening classes to this end.

My life now was full; I worked during the day and attended classes in the evening.

60

FRANKIE AND SOHAN

AROUND THIS time, Bissondath's brother, Sohan Ojah-Maharaj, had arrived in London. I was exceedingly happy. I had first met Sohan as a student at St. Charles High School and soon we became friends. It was a pleasure to have Sohan in London and when Bissondath suggested we share a flat together, we readily agreed. We lived like brothers. Sohan soon secured employment in a respectable hotel; he was content to be gainfully employed, except for this one fact—his job involved shift work. Once our routines were established, both Sohan and I were quite comfortable. Although Sohan and I strove to be fair and generous to each other, we were not always successful. I recall one occasion where I was less than fair to Sohan.

It happened on a Saturday when Sohan was at work. On this day I planned to visit the famous Oxford Street shopping area in downtown London. I had never been in the heart of the city before and was excited as I had heard so much about it. Thus far I had traveled by bus everywhere in London, and now I was about to take the tube. As I descended a series of steps I was struck by the number of people milling about in the underground. Truly I was in awe. That an actual train traveled through such a tunnel seemed inconceivable, yet I could understand how very practical such a concept was! After asking directions I boarded the train. I was at once both overwhelmed and delighted at its incredible speed and smoothness. I was so lost in thought that I missed my exit. Thankfully, I was able to get off at the next stop, and with the assistance of a very helpful attendant, I managed to catch a train going in the opposite direction. Soon I was at the Oxford Street exit. Excitement gripped me as I excitedly descended from the train to begin my exploration of this world famous street.

I began walking, taking in the scenery. I was utterly fascinated by the candy and chocolate outlet shops. When I had thought I had seen it all in one shop, another shop popped up which seemed even more attractive than the previous one. Of course I visited many of the shops on that street, and I simply could not comprehend the existence of so many stores, each vying to outdo the other in an unending street of a thousand shops, each with its own special charm. The vast array of the shops of London was bewildering and as I walked in sheer amazement, I came to a corner where I noticed a greeter dressed in a tuxedo summoning the passers-by. As I approached, he motioned for me to enter. A wonderful movie was about to start. To give my tired legs a rest, I decided to stay for the movie. From the sidewalk I walked down an ornately decorated staircase. This led to a vast basement which boasted a fine cinema. The feature film that day was one by the Bowery Boys. I became excited as I was a great admirer of their films. This particular film had been a huge hit in Trinidad so I gladly purchased a ticket. As I entered the lobby I was immediately struck by the rich and luxurious décor of the cinema. Beautiful, deep, red carpet blanketed the floor. Right away I noticed that the cinema was not divided up into sections as it was in Trinidad—Pit, House, and Balcony. Here you were allowed to sit where you pleased. I also noticed that the patrons of the cinema were well dressed; some even wore suits. A sense of decorum prevailed.

I took my seat. As the movie progressed, the audience responded with quiet laughter B it might even be characterized as somewhat subdued. This behaviour was so far removed from the hearty laughter and generous displays of enjoyment that characterized the patrons of the cinema in my home town in Trinidad that I felt obliged to constrain my own laughter. Even when I felt that such laughter was warranted, I felt restricted. It was as if I had to follow cues from the audience to know when to laugh and when not to laugh. At one point, I was so engrossed in the film that I forgot myself and laughed out loud at a scene that struck me as particularly funny. My laughter seemed to strike a chord in the cinema and for a moment, the atmosphere seemed free and uninhibited with other patrons joining in with hearty laughter as well. Soon, there was a slight cough from one viewer. It was not the sound of an actual cough, rather it was the sound of an 'a-hem'; I took it as a reprimand from an individual who judged that such unrestrained laughter should be contained. I got the message. I stopped laughing at once.

The effect of this quiet reprimand on me was so strong that thereafter even when the audience laughed, I constrained myself. It was awkward but I was afraid to let myself go—afraid of making a mistake—afraid of offending. For the rest of the show I did not laugh. My first movie in London became a memorable experience as I came to understand a hint of the cultural differences between Trinidad and England. That was my first barometer.

As I left the theatre I mused about movie going in England. Movie goers in England naturally assumed a restrained and refined attitude: an attitude that I did not possess, nor did I want to possess. I still much preferred to respond to films with my emotions for I loved the natural display of enjoyment. Because of this experience I did not attend as many movies as I would have liked while I was in England. (Anyone who knows how much I love my movies will understand what a sacrifice this was.)

I continued to stroll the streets of London fascinated by the sights.

One sight in particular was simply incredible. In the window of a restaurant there was a display of chickens being roasted on a rotisserie. This was new to me. In Trinidad our vendors sold chicken in small pieces. I remember them making the most irresistible fried chicken during the fifties and the sixties. One chicken at that time seemed to yield a thousand small pieces while lines and lines of impatient buyers awaited their turn to sample this mouth-watering dish. Here in London I saw several whole chickens in a glass case being roasted. But, what truly baffled me was the price. It was only two and a half shillings! That was downright cheap; I could not believe my eyes. I wanted to ask if the price advertised was indeed the price, but I refrained since I did not wish to appear ignorant. Reluctantly, I moved on. As I proceeded down the street, again I saw yet another store displaying the same type of rotisserie chicken at a similar price.

"Well," I mused, "there can be no mistaking the price. That has to be the bargain of the century," I concluded.

That chicken was irresistible at that price. I did not need any further incentive. Without any hesitation I entered the store and purchased my first whole chicken in London. I was certain that Sohan would appreciate my find. I decided to walk and calculated the distance between where I was and where I lived to be about a two hour walk. That was not a problem for at the end of the road I was going to surprise my friend Sohan with my special purchase.

It was about an hour later that my journey led me across a beautiful park with a rich display of trees and flowers. Ducks were plentiful in the man-made lake, and many visitors congregated there as well. I walked until I came upon an attractive flower garden. There I observed a young couple locked in an embrace completely oblivious of the rest of the world. While their public display of affection surprised me somewhat, I was more startled by the fact that they had divested themselves of their outer attire and it was bitterly cold out (at least by my standards). *Was this an example of English freedom?* I certainly had a great deal to learn.

I continued my journey through the park. By now, I was exhausted and hungry and the park seemed endless. I made my way to a convenient bench which provided just the right setting for a nibble. I reached into the bag and grabbed a leg. I didn't get just the leg. The entire section of that roasted bird dislodged easily and the leg, thigh, and wing appeared as one unified piece. It just did not seem right that any one part should be separated, or returned to the bag. I quickly devoured it all: leg, thigh, and wing. As I continued my journey towards home, hunger pangs gripped me again. At first I tried to talk myself out of any further indulgence. I tried to tell myself that I had already consumed enough chicken. But then, as the pangs persisted, I reasoned that just one more nibble would not hurt. I would still have an ample amount to share with Sohan. I was by now more than halfway home and after a quick nibble, I still had half the chicken left. I enjoyed my snack as I strolled through the park.

I am ashamed to admit that after walking a little distance, I again felt somewhat fatigued and hungry. Again I considered my options, again I decided to indulge my appetite. But, I did not feel particularly guilty for my indulgences for I reasoned that the English climate combined with the exhausting walk, required above average nutrition. I continued walking and exploring this vast park with its myriad of pathways. I must have retraced my steps a thousand times or so it seemed, yet never did I rail against myself for my mistakes as every single section of this London park was a thing of beauty. Then suddenly I was out of the park. I calculated that I was a mere fifteen minutes from home. I checked the bag and discovered that only a thigh and a small wing remained. As I neared the apartment, common courtesy suggested that I should not offer such a *tiny* amount to Sohan for it might appear to be an insult. I certainly did not wish to offend my friend. I reasoned that I would make amends to him at another time. For now, I would do the right thing and not insult him with such a meager offering. Thus I finished the remaining portion. I had now consumed the entire chicken. As I entered the apartment, I could honestly say that I was not the least bit hungry. My appetite was perfectly satiated.

Unknown to me, however, Sohan had come home from work early that day to prepare dinner for us. Sohan was an accomplished chef and had prepared a spicy and aromatic dish. Normally such aromas would stimulate my appetite, but today, for some reason, they made me slightly nauseated.

The table was set for two. With a sheepish smile, Sohan explained why he was giving himself a smaller portion.

"Frankie, I waited for you. I got really hungry. I had a snack. You must be starved. Go ahead, eat and I have more for you."

The gods certainly had a sense of humour. There was no getting out of it. I had to partake; Sohan was excited and anticipated my joy at his culinary creation. I had to feign enjoyment. I knew that I was being punished for my earlier indiscretion. I ate. At Sohan's insistence, I ate even more. (Shortly after that I did get sick but I managed to hide it from Sohan.)

Days later I confessed. Sohan was a little upset. To make amends, he let me treat him to supper. All was well again. Thus life again became agreeable. I was working at a place I liked, studying to improve my future prospects, and living amongst friends. I had to admit that I was off to a remarkable start in London. I would often wonder if my life in London was real. *Was I dreaming?*

Soon life became even better when I joined the cricket team.

61

HEROISM SHORT-LIVED

B Y TRINIDADIAN standards, I was never considered to be an athlete of any real measure. At best, I might be considered a "good enough" cricket player. I had no illusions about my limited abilities. That I could be a "first class" player even for one moment in time was merely a distant dream. Sohan, Bissondath, and I, along with two other Trinidadians, joined a London cricket team. The sport of cricket was a big event in England. Team members, who had families, usually brought them to the games—especially to games held on weekends. These days became important family days. Each of us became a part of each other's family. Indeed we became one extended family. A picnic atmosphere always surrounded our weekend games with tea, sandwiches, and dainties playing a major role. The actual playgrounds were clean and up to date—everything was first class. It was always a pleasure to play. One day in particular, I had the rare pleasure of a once in a lifetime experience.

The team we were playing although predominantly English, like ours boasted a few West Indians players. One of their West Indian players was a highly skilled and greatly feared Jamaican player; his abilities as a bowler were well-known. As luck would have it we were the first to bat. We followed the normal tradition of placing the very best batters first; the least accomplished batters were placed last. As each of our prominent players took his turn at bat, each was decimated by this towering Jamaican bowler. Our best batters proved not to be good enough; as each batter was sidelined, the young Jamaican grew in confidence. As the inning came to an end the opposition seemed to command an insurmountable lead. Victory was theirs and they knew it. Already congratulatory gestures were being exchanged by their beaming team. It was just a matter of time; soon the final two batters (of which I was one) had to take their places. The game had to be concluded; I was on deck.

The Jamaican made his delivery; a fast ball was directed to the wicket. I stepped forward on bended knees. I swung the bat and made perfect contact with that fastball; the ball shot upwards like a rocket then plummeted in the far stand—a perfect six. There was silence on both sides. Our team's silence was the result of the glorious surprise that such a hit meant for us. The silence that enveloped the opposition was the result of sheer shock. I, too, was shocked by my own good fortune. The ball, now retrieved, was handed to the Jamaican once again. He took a longer run intending in part to strengthen his delivery but also to strike fear in the heart of his opponent. His strategy was intimidation. He began his pitch.

His delivery had significantly changed. This time the pitch fell short of the wicket and bounced back and forth towards the wicket—a tricky situation indeed. I leaned back and struck the ball squarely along the ground; that ball eluded the players for a perfect four. Again expressions of shock filled the park. A cheering section formed; my name was being chanted; new energy infused itself into our team.

I cannot explain how or why I played that well that day.

Every thing I did was incredibly executed; I batted perfectly defying the odds and baffling our worthy opponents. We won the game. Our loyal fans cheered hysterically. I was carried around the field on the shoulders of my teammates in true hero fashion. That day was the culmination of every childhood dream I ever dared to dream. I was showered with praise from every quarter. Even our worthy opponents reached out a congratulatory handshake. I felt my pores open so that I could better absorb every ounce of ecstasy that that moment provided. The celebrations continued at our captain's home where I continued to enjoy being the centre of attention. I was on a high. No drug could be more powerful than the natural drug of adoration. I was in cricket heaven. As a result of my outstanding play that day, I was promoted to the higher rank in the batting order. My life there was short.

There was no repeat performance—nothing I did even remotely resembled my former play. Soon I was demoted to my original place in the batting order. Actually it was a relief. I was happy. The pressure was off and I was still part of the team. Together we formed a supportive family of friends.

Life in London was good. I had a good job where I was now accepted as part of the social fabric at the office (due in large part to our loveable Stan). In addition, I was part of a cricket team and was also able to attend evening classes to further my career. England had embraced me; England had offered me her promise. Here I was free to follow my dream. I grabbed tightly to this promise and clutched it close to my soul. I wanted for nothing. It would seem that I was the picture of contentment.

Although at times my life seemed challenging and exhausting, I had no reason to complain. I was fully aware that there were many disadvantaged souls in every third world country that would gladly trade places with me. I was not prepared to surrender my good fortune.

Often Sohan and I were invited to share in the lives of our new friends: some were Trinidadians, others were English. These encounters added a completely new dimension to our lives. Our eyes and our spirits were constantly being opened to the British way of doing things. Politeness was at the heart of British family life. While the families I knew disagreed, they were not disagreeable. I never witnessed the kind of cursing and beatings that were all too common a reality in my life in Trinidad. This gave me a new perspective on life; it allowed me to see how some people from another culture interacted. I was quietly grateful for every such opportunity as it afforded me a rich and varied life.

Now, summer was close at hand, and with it came the further promise of stability and hope. Sohan and I began planning trips to other countries; Ireland, Spain, Italy and France were slated for the near future. It was exhilarating to look forward; the future looked so bright. Yet darkness threatened from the shadows.

62

THE LETTER

LETTERS BEGAN arriving from my sisters. These letters never once hinted at my mother's true condition. My sisters wrote that things were all right at home; but, my instincts expressed another truth. They told me that Ma was having troubles. What they did not tell me however was just how troubled she truly was.

Then, I received *the letter*. It was from a close neighbour who wrote, "Frankie, if you don't come now, you mother go die. Then you will come for her funeral." Those two lines from a trusted friend pierced my soul. I could not get them out of my mind. I was confronted with the reality that I was responsible for Ma's declining health. Again I questioned the wisdom of my decision to come to England. Again I felt that I should have deferred my plans to a much later date. I should have been at Ma's side. My joy fled; guilt riddled my soul.

All that England had offered, all that she promised, now became a fading illusion. The knowledge that I must soon return to Trinidad became a pressing reality. My spirit was divided and I could no longer function properly in England.

I shared with Sohan and Bissondath my decision to return home. They understood my situation and offered me a glimmer of hope. Bissondath counselled, "Frankie, we understand. Your mother is most important to you. We know that. If she is ill, and declining in health, your place is at home with her. So go. But it is not the end. You will want to come back. When the time is right and you will know it, then come back. We will be here. You will have a place, a home with us, always."

I looked at Bissondath and Sohan—these two brothers—treating me like a brother. I was so moved I could not speak. Sohan put his hand on my shoulder as a symbol of his support. I knew then without a doubt that were I to experience difficulties of any kind, Sohan and Bissondath, without hesitation, would have been my anchors. They fully understood the responsibility I bore towards my widowed mother.

They, of all people, understood that as sons, our place during times of difficulty was at home, helping to shoulder the burdensome responsibilities. This expectation, while unwritten, was etched in our hearts from the day we first acquired knowledge. A son was expected to do his duty. It was a sign of respect. Even though I knew what I had to do, I sought Bissondath's counsel regarding my next step. By sharing the responsibility of decision making with him I may have been hoping to share some of the sadness that accompanied such decisions. Perhaps I was naïve enough to think that by reaching out to him I could keep the certainty of my impending sadness somewhat at bay. Bissondath explained that I must report my predicament to my supervisor Mr. Campbell. This I did the very next day.

I knocked on Mr. Campbell's door.

"Come in."

"Frankie, good to see you, may I help you."

"I hope so, Sir."

"Is there a problem?"

"Yes, there is."

I did not know how to tell Mr. Campbell my problem. I did not wish to appear unappreciative of all his efforts on my behalf. Further, I did not really know how much I should disclose regarding my mother.

I looked at him and allowed my instincts to guide me.

"Mr. Campbell, my mother is ill. I need to be at home."

"Frank, may I ask the nature of her illness? Is it a particular illness?"

Of course, Mr. Campbell was thinking that some physical illness had befallen Ma.

I explained, "Ma's mother and my father both passed away within a year of each other. She is having grave troubles coping. She has been left with a large number of children and the situation has become overwhelming for her."

"Frankie, I am sorry, truly sorry to learn about your mother. And you must be awfully troubled. What are you proposing to do?"

"Sir, it seems that I have to resign from my job. I don't want to. I love it here."

"Then don't resign. Write us a letter explaining that you wish some time to visit an ailing mother. The letter can be brief. We will give this matter due consideration and contact you thereafter. How does this sound?"

"Mr. Campbell that is an excellent idea. Thank you ever so much for your understanding, Sir."

"Understanding? Frank, we too have our mothers. Hopefully we would do no less than you are doing. Now I wish you well. We will talk soon again."

I left Mr. Campbell's office very much relieved. He gave me a way out of my troubles for the short term. I felt encouraged; I did not expect such consideration. Within a day or two I had written the letter requesting leave to return to Trinidad. I submitted it directly to Mr. Campbell. Upon reading my letter, Mr. Campbell handed me a letter that he had written, granting me a leave of absence for one full year. He smiled as he continued, "Go home. Take care of your mother. And return to us. We will certainly do what we can to offer you a position here on your return. Your performance and conduct with us is exemplary. We are happy to have you here Mr. Boodram."

In truth I was humbled by Mr. Campbell's words. I could not help but recall some of my Trinidadian acquaintances insulting the British with callous remarks that the English were racist and insensitive. While this statement may have held some truth, it was not true of British society in general and definitely not true for Mr. Campbell in particular. Mr. Campbell's actions brought honour and esteem to the English. He did not have to be as accommodating as he was. Indeed here was the embodiment of all that it meant to be an English gentleman.

That day when I left work, I went for a walk. I walked aimlessly from one street to another. When I saw a park rising in the distance I made my way there for it seemed strangely familiar. On one side of the park was a bench situated beneath a sprawling tree. A tiny pond in which some ducks were swimming was close by. I sat down on the bench and took in my surroundings. The sky was a soft blue, and only an occasional cloud appeared. If there were other people in the park I did not notice, for it seemed that I alone was in the park. In fact, at that moment, I owned that park.

After leaving Mr. Campbell's office I felt most uneasy. While it is true I was relieved by Mr. Campbell's counsel, something else was plaguing my mind. *Why was I not at peace? Was it because I did not wish to return to Trinidad as yet? Why was my spirit in turmoil?* Again I looked ahead of me, my eyes searching the skies for answers. The soft blue skies were reminiscent of something else. What was it? I looked at the tree that seemed to want to embrace the heavens. Then it came to me. I had seen blue skies that were not these blue skies; I had seen a sprawling tree that was not this sprawling tree; I had taken repose and contemplated life in another place that was not this place. Everything here reminded me of the secret place that I had claimed for myself in Trinidad. It was as if I were being transported back in time.

Not too far from where I lived in Back Street, Tunapuna, the Northern Range Mountains could be seen rising up in the distance. There were times when I would take the road that led past the hospital to the mountain. From there a tiny trail snaked its way up the mountain and on this trail I discovered a ledge—just the perfect spot for quiet meditation.

The ledge was hidden by several trees and remained largely undetected. At one corner of this ledge grew a giant tree. What a magnificent view this ledge commanded! One could see clearly across the top of the towns to the far end to the shores of Port of Spain. I claimed this haven as my own; since it was I who discovered this treasure, it was I who owned it. It was there beneath that tree on that ledge that I sought solace from life's harsh realities. It was there too that I railed against God when He hurled such daunting obstacles to block my path. This little park in London was but a tiny replica of that very haven that I had claimed for myself in Trinidad. I found myself brooding. I was much overdue with my "talk" with the Almighty.

So I turned to the Heavens and railed once more.

"So Dear God, it is not enough that I am in England to take care of myself—okay. Help me to understand Your way. It does not make sense. Why are you sending me home to Trinidad? How come I am feeling so guilty? I am despondent. Is this Your doing? Am I paying for a sin? Whose sin? Mine?"

I discharged all these questions and all my misgivings and left my troubles with the Divine One. Once having done this however, another concern suddenly dawned on me. *How do I return home 'empty-handed'?* The term 'empty-handed' was synonymous with failure. In my world, any Trinidadian who ventured abroad to study and returned home without achieving that goal was indeed considered to be a failure. In my neighborhood failure of this type invited contempt and condemnation. There was no doubt about what awaited me in Trinidad—sheer ridicule. Undoubtedly I would be the butt of many jokes—the desecrated chalice of soured wine. This pestilence of derision was a critical reason that explained why many islanders who went abroad and did not achieve their desired and professed goals chose to stay abroad rather than return home to Trinidad to be victimized. The fact that I was no failure, the fact that I was returning home to fulfill a time-honoured tradition of taking care of my family, would offer little shelter from the scorn and condemnation that would be hurled my way. I resolved that since I was no failure, I needed to be brave and resolute. My destiny seemed clear; I must return to Trinidad, yes, but I must be invincible in spirit. Such a mandate became my mantra. It simply had to be thus...

As I came away from the park, I felt less anxious. I boarded a bus and headed to the apartment. I made myself memorize every detail along the way as though it was the first time I was seeing it for I did not know when next I would behold those sights.

63

FINAL DAYS

S OON SOHAN would be home. We all gathered at Bissondath's and chatted away throughout the evening. We smiled smiles that looked like the smiles of happiness but underneath all was a heavy melancholy. No one would voice the words but we each knew that I might not return to England as hoped. The bitter-sweet evening came to an end and emptiness invaded my soul. I had to be brave and make believe that I was somewhat optimistic about my return to Trinidad; I owed that much to my friends. I needed to move on with my life so shortly thereafter I booked my passage on a large luxury liner headed to South America. In only two short weeks I would be making my way back to Trinidad.

I was concerned about the hardship I would cause Sohan by leaving for he alone would be responsible for the rent. He assured me that that was not going to be a problem. In fact he joked that it would be a welcome change to live alone and not have to take care of anyone. He covered up well.

Soon Sohan and Bissondath organized a get together to celebrate 'not my going away' event but 'my coming back'. I had to promise that I would *try* to return. That appeased my friends. Their little get together turned out to be quite a gathering. Bissondath's flat was overrun with people; they came, not so much to honour me as to party. And party they did. It was very late when the last guests left.

I felt very fortunate to receive such an outpouring of good will. And, if I was surprised by that gathering, a further surprise awaited me at work.

One day about two days before my last day at work, Stan came to see me. It was about half an hour before closing time and I was at my desk working.

"Frankie, I need to see you for a moment. I have something to show you. Would you come?"

I followed Stan. (I can still see that Stan walking ahead of me, his pant legs about four inches short of his shoes. What a sight.) He headed for the stairs. I could not recall ever having taken that stairway to the storey above but I continued to follow. As I did, Stan led me to the executive lounge. Mr. Campbell and almost all of the workers from my floor were there.

"Surprise!" they all yelled. I was flabbergasted.

"Let the party begin," a beaming Stan proclaimed.

I could not have been happier with the response. Praise came my way from all quarters. One would think that I was a movie star, I was accorded such generous attention. Then Stan signaled everyone by clinking his glass.

"First let me thank Mr. Campbell for allowing us this moment to wish Frank a bit of a *bon voyage.*"

"Here, here," was the common response and a generous applause accompanied Stan's recognition of Mr. Campbell.

Stan then turned to me and expressed, "Frank Boodram, sorry to see you leave. We do hope you return to us."

Everyone became quiet as Stan was poised to resume. He seemed serious and intent.

"Frank I want you to know that you are a principled young man. You possess vision and you show purpose. We salute you my friend, our friend."

"Here, here," an eager audience burst into applause.

Can this tribute be real? How can I, a simple West Indian boy, be hearing such words from such a man—and a British man at that? I was ecstatic but at a loss for words.

I was grateful when Stan took the emphasis off me and declared, "The cake—we must cut the cake—and who will cut the cake with Frank?"

This too, however, proved embarrassing. Stan actually expected that someone would volunteer to cut the cake with me. I was surprised by the generous response of volunteers. Stan pointed to Elizabeth who was standing at the back, to come forward. (Stan used to try to encourage me to engage the attention of some of the young ladies on staff. I always declined to act on his suggestions for I was very shy and I sincerely felt that such advances on my part would be less than appropriate. After all, I was West Indian—a brown West Indian and should know my place in white British society.) But, nevertheless, here I was with Elizabeth at my side. We cut the cake and as we did she whispered that I would be missed. She then made her way back to her friends.

Nonetheless I was flattered beyond measure. The party came to an end but how I wished it had not. I felt appreciated and valued; I was somebody here. These feelings strengthened my spirits and, as I suspected, I was to need this strength in Trinidad.

64

SURPRISE ON SURPRISE

Soon I was on board a ship headed for Trinidad; my departure was now a painful reality. My melancholy at leaving England prevented me from taking any pleasure in exploring the extravagance of this luxurious ocean liner. I was content to remain a recluse in my cabin; content to brood over the loss of my newly minted life in London. I was surprised by how much England had grown on me over the past ten months. I was surprised by the extent of my attachments in all areas of my life. I feared that I would not easily or quickly return.

One day I was walking on deck just looking around. Suddenly I fell; perhaps I tripped. My face was scratched a little and my body ached. While attempting to get up, I heard a concerned voice shout. "So sorry, so sorry, it is my fault. I was careless. Are you okay?"

I looked up. There was this figure looking down on me. I could not see his face for the sun blinded my vision but I felt the sincerity in his voice. He held out his hands to help me up.

"I am Carlos. This is my wife Maria. My children were playing. I play too. I trip you. We are sorry. You hurt badly?"

"No, just a little surprised. I am alright."

Carlos, Maria and the children proved to be just the distraction I needed. Their friendship became a tonic that restored my emotional equilibrium. We developed a friendship and met frequently. I learned that Carlos and Maria were from South America. They were returning to South America from a brief and unhappy time in England. Maria confessed that they felt like they were second class citizens in England. Maria further confided that she felt that the English "did not like us because we speak badly." While both of them understood English quite well, they were not completely conversant in the language. Imagine my shock to hear Maria declare, "The English do not see us as white. They look down on us."

I really was taken back by this confession for Carlos and Maria and their children were indeed white. What an irony of life that they who *were* white did not feel accepted because they did not *speak* white. While I, on the other hand, an obviously brown boy in England, felt acceptance there as I spoke no other language but English.

I understood their discomfort and while I wanted to allay their pain, I knew that they were not yet ready to receive any words in defence of the British. While they longed for home, I longed for England. I tried to get them to focus on the joy they would feel upon returning home to their families and to the familiar tastes and smells of their own country. They complained continually about the tasteless food of the ship. It was not so much that they were denouncing the food on board the ship as they were longing for the familiar spices of their homeland. They were starving for a spicy homemade meal. When I understood that I knew how I could help them. I proposed a plan.

"Carlos, Maria, come with me to my family in Tunapuna. This ship will be docked for quite a few hours when we land at Trinidad. You will visit with my family."

"We give you much trouble Frankie. We have kids," apologized Maria.

"No trouble. My family loves children. They will welcome you as family. Besides they will cook; they love friends. They will prepare a meal you will like. Please say yes."

Carlos looked at Maria who excitedly blurted out, "We come, we come. Yes."

Up until this point I had kept my plans to return home to Trinidad private. Not one single soul in Trinidad knew that I was coming home. That was the way I wanted it.

My friend Sohan, on the other hand wanted to inform his family in Trinidad about my plans to return. He thought that he should inform his parents, especially his dad for we had become quite close before I left for England and would willingly come to meet me at the ship.

I asked Sohan to let me have my way on this matter this once, and while he protested, he finally agreed. Now I had two surprises for my family—my own unannounced return and the unexpected bonus of my four new friends. My surprise however, took on a life of its own and I was the one to be shocked.

After disembarking the ship in Port of Spain, I secured a taxi to take us all to my home in Tunapuna. Maria and Carlos were excited at the prospect of meeting a real Trinidadian family. I was excited for them to meet my family and enjoy some real Trinidadian hospitality. My family was always most generous in that regard. They loved meeting new friends. Soon the taxi was in front of my home. Carlos insisted that he be the one to pay the driver and remained inside the taxi to accomplish this task. Maria and I were the first to step from the taxi. I held the nine month old baby while Maria escorted the three year old.

Some curious neighbours had already congregated on the street to see who was arriving in the taxi.

This is how the scene played out from their perspective: Frankie was with a woman and two children. Then the whispers began along with some raised eyebrows.

"Oh my gosh! Frankie have a ready made family. He gone for less than a year and already he have a wife and two children."

That sentiment spread like wildfire; although false, I had to deal with its painful and embarrassing ramifications for years to come.

By now Maria and I and the children were in the yard. Ma was also in the yard doing the laundry. When she heard footsteps and voices, she turned around. Then she saw me; she dropped her laundry and ran to me.

"Frankie, it *is* you."

These were the only words she uttered as she clung to me. Her tears streamed unrestrained. Then she pulled back, smiled, and said, "Ah so happy you here."

Then she saw Maria and the kids; by now Carlos was also in the yard.

Ma gazed at everyone a bit perplexed.

"Ma, these are friends from the ship. They did not enjoy the meals on board and they are starving for a taste of something spicy."

Brightness lit up Ma's face. "Welcome, come inside."

We followed Ma's lead. Introductions were made to the rest of the family and soon Carlos and Maria were totally embraced as one of our own. Ma created a feast in no time at all. My sisters were especially thrilled for they had not seen Ma move with such agility and happiness for months. They swore it was a new Ma in their midst.

As the festivities drew to a close, my friends took their leave. Their spirits were elevated and I do believe that they were able to approach that last leg of their journey with some fond memories. I accompanied them back to the ship where we faithfully exchanged addresses. We had every intention of staying in touch but for whatever reason we have failed to do so. But, I do have the memory of those special few days tucked away.

I returned home subdued and melancholy. Everyone awaited my return eagerly. We had not yet had a chance to share any words regarding my unexpected return to Trinidad. But, just as I entered the house, Boysie stole me away and wasted no time in telling me just how he felt about the situation.

Once we were alone he made no attempt to mask his disappointment in me. This was evidenced by his barrage of blunt statements.

"Frankie, why come back man? Now I have to face the music. I have to defend you to everyone. Yo bring shame to the family. Everybody will think you failed. You went to England. You did nothing. You should have stayed there, Frank."

Boysie was hurt and annoyed. He had no idea why I came back, nor would he accept that Ma needed help. To attempt to speak to Boysie, to explain my reason or decision to return would simply have ended in frustration for me. Nothing I could say would have changed his mind. If anything, any comment from me would serve only to strengthen his belief that I was a loser. Thus I chose what I considered to be the wiser course of action and received his reproof without challenge. Perhaps at some later date he might be able to receive my words. But, that time was not now. By the time Boysie had finished with me, I was very despondent. Not wishing to reveal my saddened state to the family, I decided to go for a walk. I mentioned to Ma and the others that I was just going for a short walk and that I would be back in a few minutes.

I left home and started walking. At first, I had no idea where exactly I was going. I knew only that I needed to compose my wounded soul before I returned home.

If my mind did not know where I was headed, my feet did for they headed instinctively to the home of my friend, Boy. Once I realized where I was going, I began to hurry. Already I was feeling better just anticipating a warm reception.

In order to get to Boy's I had to pass by a gas station. The workers at this station were all friends of my brother Boysie. From somewhere in the darkness, a snickering voice brought me out of my reverie.

"Hey Frankie, where the kids? Ah hear yo hav two kids and yo was away for less than a year."

A second voice derided, " Frankie, what yo learn man, to be a magician? Yo will have to teach us." Waves of laughter followed as they enjoyed their own easy humour.

I did not respond. My hope that I would be granted a period of grace from the inevitable derision was dashed. My spirits fell and I left the gas station disheartened. Even the knowledge that Boy and his family were totally supportive and devoted could not heal me from this fresh wound.

Boy and I met during the last years of high school; immediately we became friends. Boy introduced me to his close friend, Roderick, and eventually all three of us became friends.

Soon after meeting me, Boy brought me to his home to meet his dad, (Uncle Roop) his mother, (Tantie Darling) and his two sisters, Savi and Indra. Quickly we all became friends.

Tantie Darling was very open in her display of affection and I felt very much welcomed at their home. Inviting me to dinner, arranging visits to the beach or river, and taking me along on family drives, are some of the many things Tantie did that me feel appreciated. Uncle Roop was a bit more difficult to read. He appeared quite reserved, and, not wanting to appear intrusive, I kept my distance. One night all this changed and I truly felt like family.

Boy's family owned a modest house that doubled as a business. At the front of the house and facing the Eastern Main Road was the business end; a thriving grocery/rum shop.

One Sunday evening during one of my regular "dinner and a visit" with the family, some "friends" came by. These friends who did not have a television set, wanted to watch the popular show *Bonanza*. Knowing that Boy's family had a television, they decided to visit. True, Boy's family did have a television but it was kept in a bedroom. Soon, this modest bedroom housing the nineteen inch TV, became a living room that was fairly busting at the seams trying to accommodate the various bodies. Eventually everyone squeezed into place.

It did not matter that the TV was in black and white; it did not matter even that at times the picture was obscure and the sound intermittent. Everyone was more than willing to volunteer an interpretation. We were happy just being entertained.

Throughout the show, Uncle Roop was very accommodating and obliging to all his visitors. But, by the time the show was over, he needed his privacy. Accordingly, while the ending credits were yet playing he turned off the television and executed a couple of massive yawns. Much to his dismay, these yawns were ignored. No one took the hint. Everyone was so spirited about just being together, that the idea of leaving never crossed anyone's mind. Uncle Roop employed a more obvious strategy; he grabbed a large pillow and held it tightly in his arms. I caught on and immediately announced that I was leaving. Uncle Roop smiled appreciatively and announced rather loudly, "Good night, Frankie. So good to have you. Ah glad to go to bed now, ah tired."

Boy was shocked by his father's apparent boldness in ushering me out, but the strategy worked. Everyone followed my lead and began to say their goodbyes also. As the others followed me out of the house, I was surprised to see Uncle Roop running out trying to catch up with me before I reached the street. When he caught up with me he confided, "Frankie I didn't mean you. You is family. I wanted them to go. Now come back."

What greater compliment could I have received! From that moment on, I had no doubt about how Uncle Roop felt about me. I was truly honoured. Never again did I feel separated from Uncle Roop.

Some time later, Tantie received a new shipment of shirts for the business. She asked Boy to try one on in front of me. Then she asked me how I liked it. It was a magnificent shirt and I told her so. It was then that she handed me a bag containing an identical shirt. Such was her generosity to me. If there had been any doubt about my place in this family, that single act erased it. I definitely felt that I was part of this family.

Boy's sister, Savi also took a special interest in me as she attempted to bolster my confidence. She felt that I was far too shy. She wanted me to adopt some of her brother's confidence. She did confide in me however, that she thought that Boy might have been a bit too confident for his own good. (Why wouldn't he be confident, given his good-looks and charm?) I knew that my sisters certainly adored Boy and he became a favourite when he defended them to me. In time, I too became a favoured friend to Boy's family. It was natural then that I reached out to this second family for support in my distress.

As I reached Boy's home, I opened the gate and literally walked in to Tantie Darling herself. She was ever so shocked to see me. "Frankie, man you could give me a heart attack! What happened? You ok?"

Before I could answer, she had yelled out to everyone that I was there. Uncle Roop, Savi and Indra all ran out and greeted me excitedly. (I believe that Boy had already left for Canada to pursue his studies.)

There was such commotion, such joy to see me; this was exactly the remedy I needed to counter my former dejection.

Everyone started asking questions at once. They all wanted to know why I had come back. I did my best to explain. I told them that I was not ill, nor was I on holidays. But, I could not quite bring myself to explain the exact reason why I left England to return to Trinidad.

While I was searching for what to say next, Tantie took me aside and spoke, "Frankie, I know you. You came home because of your mother. She is not doing well. Right?"

I nodded. "Boy, you doing something good for your family. Anybody with any sense can see that. So don't hang down yo head. And anybody say anything ignorant or stupid to you, will answer to me. Frankie, ah happy to see yo. Man, yo looking good!" Tantie was just the right tonic, I left for home in much better spirits.

When I returned home, everyone was preparing for bed. There was no time for conversation. It would have to wait for another day.

In spite of Boysie's strong condemnations, I was not unhappy. I could still see Ma with that smile that lit up her face. And, I could still hear Kay's comment to her, "Madame B, yo favourite son is back. And now yo happy." Everyone had silently acknowledged that salutation. That was a most telling moment for I now had tangible confirmation that returning home was the right decision. I was at peace.

Tomorrow was Monday and everyone would be off to school or work except for me; I had no plan for tomorrow. That was such a strange concept for me. I trusted however that someone greater than I had a plan for me. For now, I was content to prepare for bed. I found myself in my room—my familiar surroundings. I heard a tap on my door. It was Ma. She asked, "You want to shower, Frankie?"

"Yes, Ma."

"Here, I have your towel, Son. And here is soap. And Frankie, Son, God bless you." She was gone.

I headed outside for the shower. As the cold water poured over my body, I looked up at the night sky from the open shower stall. It was then that I affirmed that a power greater than I had dictated that I be here with my mother. She had already embraced my homecoming and her happiness was evident. I knew that she understood my present mission at home.

Soon I was in bed reflecting; I saw England once more. She seemed so far away, so very far away. My spirit was longing to return and I promised, "Some day, perhaps not soon, but someday, I shall return."

Then I was asleep.

Day dawned. The cocks crowed and the birds chirped in the early morning light. The sun streamed through my window. I felt its warm presence; indeed I was in Trinidad.

Everyone was busily preparing for school or work. Outside people were rushing, or not rushing for their trains; others were simply poised on the street exchanging conversation.

Life seemed to be standing still. There was no haste. I felt that I too had time. I headed for our capital, Port of Spain. Once there, I felt as though I was rediscovering Trinidad. But, by the time the second day came around, I felt something was not quite right. Everyone had purpose; each went about the day with a reason, a plan. I was without a plan or a purpose. I did not feel complete; something was amiss.

I was without a job. That was a harsh reality. I knew I needed to find a job right away. I resolved to check the job market the very next day. That evening however, my friend Dickie Ali came home to see me. He carried a simple message.

"Sister Dorothy wants to see you."

What a surprise.

I wondered…

PART V

Return to Trinidad

65

SISTER DOROTHY

I COULD HARDLY contain my excitement. Sister Dorothy wanted to see me. I had tremendous respect for this nun and I was curious to find out why she had sent for me. I went to her office the very next day. After greeting me, Sister came right to the point.

"Frankie, I sent for you for a reason. A teacher on staff has left suddenly. Now, I know you are very shy. And you probably would not want to teach in a high school for girls. I don't blame you."

What? Had Sister Dorothy just offered me a teaching position in her school? For a moment I was incapable of movement or sound. Sister Dorothy continued.

"Frankie, could you help me out? Just until I get a replacement. Would you accept this position temporarily? As soon as you get a job of your choosing, you can be free to accept. But could you help me for the time being?"

I was reluctant to accept, and Sister seemed to know why. She had first come to know me when she became my French teacher in my final year as a student at St. Charles Boys' School. She understood that while I may have grown up with six sisters, I really was quite withdrawn in the company of girls. The prospect of teaching in an all girl school terrified me! I was silent.

Then Sister Dorothy changed her tone and adopted a very serious and formal manner.

"Mr. Boodram, in your stay at the boys' school you were well respected. You are a teacher and a good one at that. Now be that teacher once more. You will be fine. "

And the words that proceeded from my mouth were, "Yes, Sister."

Did those words mean that I was accepting the job? I really do not know for sure, but Sister Dorothy seemed to have no doubt.

Immediately my future was sealed with these words: "Mr. Boodram, congratulations. I will see you on Thursday."

When I looked up at her she had a huge smile on her face. Then she was gone. What had just happened?

When I said, "Yes, Sister," I was merely acknowledging her as my former teacher. I was showing her the respect and esteem due her. I did not for one minute think that I was accepting a job.

Had Sister posed this question to me directly, and asked, "Mr. Boodram, will you accept the job?" I honestly do not know what my response would have been. As it was, I now seemed to have accepted a job at this all girls' high school without any conscious effort on my part. Is it not curious how life steps in and shapes our destiny?

Thus, for the second time in my life, I was offered a teaching position in a Catholic school. The fact that I was born a Hindu did not seem to have any bearing on the matter. Sister Dorothy knew that I was a product of the Catholic boys' school. Perhaps that is what weighed most heavily in my favour. In any event, this job offer testified to the confidence that Sister Dorothy had in me.

This girls' school was highly regarded on the island. Sister Dorothy's leadership and teaching style commanded respect and admiration and set her apart from her peers. I considered it an honour to be part of her school.

I had been home but three days following my return from England. Destiny determined that I was not to be idle for long; I submitted to her decree.

The girls' school was located on the Eastern Main Road. It was annexed to the Catholic Church. The entire building was extremely old and a plan for a new high school was being drawn up.

A great deal of public funding was required in order to build the new school and Sister Dorothy headed up the fundraising committee. She was skilled in the art of fundraising and always managed to convince distinguished members of the public to grace the coffers of the Catholic purse. Even people who did not regard themselves as distinguished felt almost saintly after falling under Sister Dorothy's spell and contributed time and again to each of her worthy causes.

Sister Dorothy sought me out and came by the staff room before the start of class. I was sitting in a corner under the guise of being buried in work.

66

FIRST DAYS

IT WAS my first day at St. Charles Girls' High School. To say that I was nervous would be an understatement; I was a wreck. The truth is I was consumed with an awkward consciousness that the students were not just students; they were girls—every single one of them was a girl. I was at the very most, only four years older than the youngest of them. I was most conscious of my youth and my vulnerability in front of them and was hesitant to enter the classroom. I dreaded the moment. Then I heard the voice of Sister Dorothy as she whispered, "Mr. Boodram, it is time for you to begin class." Then, sensing my discomfort, she added, "You'll be fine," she smiled. She then placed her hand on my shoulder and whispered, "Have a nice day." With that she was gone.

I summoned every bit of courage I could muster and I walked into that classroom filled with girls. Never before had I seen so many females in any one place at any one time; never before had so many pairs of female eyes been focused on me alone. I was embarrassed and terribly conscious of my every movement. I worried about faltering or making a misstep. I worried about my voice; would it crack; would it even be audible.

As I took my place before them at the front of the room, all thirty-five uniformed bodies rose in unison and greeted me.

"Good morning, Mr. Boodram," they chanted. They were respectful and serious as they stood awaiting my signal inviting them to sit. I could not respond. I did not yet trust my voice. If my voice failed me it could destroy the respectful attitude in the classroom. I could not risk it. I had to buy myself some time. Instead of attempting to speak, I decided to walk up and down the aisles under the pretext of examining the class. I assumed an air of command as I walked. No one laughed. No one snickered. No one spoke. My silence commanded their complete attention in that moment. Before attempting to speak, I paused for a moment, allowing my instincts to guide me. I did not wish to do anything that might undermine the courtesy that had thus far been extended to me. I stood before the class and motioned with my hand for the students to be seated. Their response was immediate.

Then I spoke. "Good morning students, thank you." I did not trust myself to look directly at them. I chose a point on the wall at the back of the room that was just slightly above their heads. When I looked there it appeared that I was looking directly at them. I was however addressing that point on the wall. This strategy allowed me sufficient space to grow accustomed to addressing this new gender.

I decided it was best to keep a professional distance from them; I did not seek to be their friend and avoided the temptation of engaging in small talk. As the first few days passed, I became more and more comfortable; yet never was I really relaxed. My good sense dictated that I remain detached from their casual banter and everyday concerns. I did not want the students to regard me as being too familiar with them. I was concerned with their mental development and academic success. It was for those reasons that I chose the path of detachment. I was serious about my role as a teacher and did not want to appear compromised by any measure. Thus the days gave way to weeks and once again Mr. Boodram the teacher emerged. His goal was to take charge of the students and gain their respect.

So far it seemed that I was enjoying some success as a teacher at this girls' high school. The question, 'Was Sister Dorothy satisfied?' constantly plagued me. At the beginning of my term, she intimated that the assignment was only temporary. *Was she still thinking of replacing me?* She never approached me regarding this matter and I never applied anywhere else. Because she never made any effort to secure a replacement for me, I assumed that this meant that I was doing relatively well.

Over the next few weeks, my comfort and confidence grew as the staff offered advice and suggestions with respect to dealing with a class of girls. I took full advantage of any advice that was shared in this regard for I felt that I was in dire need of such counsel. In time, I began to develop a measure of stability and confidence.

Not long after I began teaching at this girls' school I made a discovery. A student is a student regardless of gender. When I began teaching these girls, I was overly conscious of the fact that the students were girls. Because of my upbringing, I was taught to treat girls differently because of their gender. I questioned my ability to be fully effective as a teacher for I wondered if I could reprimand a female student if it ever became necessary to do so.

One day one of the students did not complete her assignment. This same student had neglected her responsibilities twice before and each time I had given her an opportunity to correct her mistake. On both occasions she failed to take advantage of my leniency.

Without thinking, I immediately reprimanded her in front of the entire class. She was shocked. The whole class was stunned. I too was amazed at my own reaction. I did not know that I was capable of administering such a reprimand to a young lady. That is when I knew that in this classroom, I was not Frankie Boodram the person I was Mr. Boodram the teacher. And at that moment Mr. Boodram was fully in charge. He was not reprimanding a female student; he was reprimanding a student. Gender was irrelevant. And that recognition, that a student was a student regardless of gender meant that I was capable of handling any student, male or female. This insight helped to shape my growth as a teacher.

As time progressed I became more comfortable with my role as teacher and became less conscious of the fact that my students were female. I was growing more accustomed to the idea that these young ladies were students. Yet I cautioned myself not lose sight that these students were also young ladies. This was an important consideration because I had to be ever mindful that my conduct as a young male teacher in this all girl high school was exemplary and above reproach. This unwritten law was honoured by all the male teachers on staff.

As the weeks passed, I soon felt that I was a full member of the staff and accordingly I set my sights on staying at this school. Neither Sister Dorothy nor I ever broached the subject of my replacement. And, truthfully, I was quite surprised at how quickly I became attached to this school in spite of the fact that it was full of girls.

67

THE NEW SCHOOL

SOME TIME later, Sister Dorothy concluded her very successful fundraising campaign for the new girls' school and a new residence for the nuns. It was largely through Sister Dorothy's tireless efforts and superior leadership that her vision became a reality. The two buildings were constructed on a piece of property located on the very street where I lived, Back Street. For me it was a most fortuitous move.

An air of excitement invaded the school body as we gladly prepared to surrender the old for the new. The new school did not boast any state of the art achievement, nor did it hint at luxury or extravagance. If anything, it would be described as simple. Yet, in spite of its simplicity, it was exquisite. The grounds were spacious. A huge gate located on Back Street prevented unauthorized access to the grounds. This gate remained closed until school was in session. From there the road led to the far end of the grounds where the residence for the nuns was constructed. Close to the gate and along the left side of the road was the school: a two storey building. The staff room was located on ground level close to the street; the principal's office was on the opposite end. The cafeteria was somewhat hidden behind the principal's office.

Opposite the school, on the other side of the road, was the playground. A display of religious statues was anchored at the centre of an attractive bed of flowers. The area bordering the street at the far end of the playground featured concrete walls. Barbed wire and broken glass was embedded in the top of the concrete blocks. It would seem that the existence of the broken glass and barbed wire may have been incongruous with the concept of Catholicism and Christ. The mere presence of such crass symbolism seemed totally inconsistent with the concepts of charity and love promoted by the church. Yet it must be understood that the church had to protect itself from a certain faction of the population that might seek to take advantage of its charitable reputation.

Because mischief and crime sometimes seemed the only way to counter the ill effects of widespread poverty and unemployment in Trinidad, the island was often steeped in violent crime including murder. Thus, the church, when considering its new constructions, had to factor in some safety options; this naturally led to the adoption of a barbed wire and broken glass solution. All in all, these new structures stood out prominently from the modest homes in the area.

It was during my first period class in the new school that a curious incident occurred. The classroom was located on the second floor facing the street. The windows were open as gentle breeze blew through the room. The formalities marking the beginning of the period were concluded and I was about to start class. Across the street a radio was playing. The soft breeze carried the enchanting voices of a new singing duo up into the classroom. The group was called Paul and Paula and the tune they were singing was their new hit aptly titled *Hey Paula*. Something about this song distracted me momentarily. The students noted that I was uncharacteristically distracted and one of them felt bold enough to ask, "Mr. Boodram, do you like my song?"

"Yes, I like the song very much."

"Thank you, Mr. Boodram for liking my song," she beamed.

"You're welcome, Paula," I responded.

The rest of the class seemed to take this as some kind of cue that I was open for questioning and before I could return the day's lesson, I was bombarded with questions from all quarters.

One question in particular stayed with me. One girl asked, "Mr. Boodram, how come you are so strict? You hardly smile and you don't make jokes."

I was silent for a moment, taking some time to genuinely reflect on her question. Before I could formulate an answer, another student interjected hoping to soften the harshness of the previous comment. "Mr. Boodram, don't get us wrong. We appreciate you and we like the way you teach. We do learn."

"Well thank you, young lady."

I rested my notebook on the desk and began walking up and down the aisles saying nothing. I was not inspecting their work; I was simply reflecting. Then I stood in front of the class, leaned back on the chalkboard, and remarked, "Well, students. Shall we just have a little talk amongst ourselves for a few minutes?"

You would think that I had just offered these students some precious gift. They were very happy and excited. I could tell by the way that they looked to me that they expected that I would be a central part of the proposed dialogue.

Unaccustomed to this new role, I played my part tentatively at first. "Tell me, students. How are you enjoying your new school?"

A flood of responses returned to me simultaneously. It was sheer pandemonium. But, it felt good. The atmosphere was relaxed and the smiles were universal. Then above the din came the voice of one student asking me a very pointed question, "Mr. Boodram, how do you like this school? You tell us."

The class became remarkably quiet as all eyes focused on me awaiting my response. The quiet was so markedly intense that I felt compelled to say something—anything.

Then I began. "Well, I do miss something of the old school. I miss the long, winding hallways, the creaky floors, and the faded colours of the wood. I do miss the mystique and charm that belonged to the old high school. But, there *is* something that I definitely do not miss." Then I paused. Their eyes brightened with expectation. They whispered to each other and still I said nothing. It was obvious that they were expecting more. One impatient student asked rather pointedly, but respectfully still, "Sir, what did you not like about the school?"

And another called out, "You have to tell us. We want to know."

"All right, I will. I did not like the incident regarding the snake."

"What snake?"

"Did you say a snake?"

There was an insistence in the faces of the students that I could not ignore. I had ignited a spark which they fanned into a flame. I felt that I must now control this flame before it became an uncontrollable fire. To accomplish this, I decided to tell them the story.

"Some time ago in the old school I was teaching a morning class. Everyone was busy and focused. Suddenly, one of the students put up her hand and pointed to the open ceiling. No words came from her mouth. A look of terror was frozen on her face."

I paused.

"What happened?" begged an impatient class.

"There, in one of the rafters of the ceiling, a huge snake was lodged.

Its body was slowly unravelling as its head began to descend from the rafters. Panic seized the girls as each one recognized that this snake was about to join their ranks. One by one they bolted from the classroom."

(What I did not tell my students was that I too was about to run away when I realized that I was the teacher and I had an obligation to stay behind.)

"I found a large broom in another part of the school and immediately returned to the classroom where I successfully managed to guide the snake outside."

One student asked, "Where did the snake come from? How did it get into the school?"

"This was a classroom was close to the back yard of the school. The snake had made its way from the bushes, scaled a four foot high wooden wall and slithered up the wire mesh attached to the ceiling. Obviously from there the snake had easy access to the rafters."

The girls seemed to have loved the story for soon they were clapping and cheering. They thought that I was brave to confront the snake and were not shy about expressing their sentiments.

"So students, now you might understand why I like this school better. For if anything, there will be no snakes making their homes here."

Once again they clapped.

"Now students," I challenged, "we must return to our work. Thank you so much for listening so respectfully and attentively to the story about the snake. We took a few minutes from the regular class to have a little chat. Now, we must get back to today's lesson."

I gave them the instructions for their new assignment and asked if there were any questions. One student asked, "Sir, do you mean the *entire* assignment that you gave has to be finished for *tomorrow*?"

"Yes."

They all settled down to their work. I marvelled at how they were able to listen to the story and still do their work. I was also heartened at how respectfully and quickly and uncomplainingly they began their assignments. This was a turning point in my teaching career. It marked the beginning of my story telling days in school. I realized that there was great currency in relating such small anecdotes to the class. The students were happy because they felt that they were getting away from doing work, and I was happy knowing that sometimes I could get even more work accomplished with them when they were offered these little *treats*.

68

A HARD ADMISSION

THE LOCATION of the new school was both a blessing and a curse. It was a blessing in that I now had a very short walk to work as I lived only a couple of blocks away. It was a curse in that it served to reveal a major failing in my own personal character. It saddens me to recall my behaviour.

At that time in our lives, we tended three cows at home. The milk from these three cows served to supplement our family's meager income. Each morning, my mother would walk the cows down Back Street over to the savannah to graze. When I was at the old school, her activities had no impact on my life as we were located several streets away. Now that the school was located on the same street where I lived, I was embarrassed daily by her morning activities and the commotion that often resulted by her ushering these animals down the now busy street. With the new school came increased traffic so, now when Ma engaged in this morning ritual, it sometimes tied up traffic when she ushered the cows across the road. Occasionally, the students themselves were delayed because of the traffic jams. More than once I would overhear the girls complain about this woman and her cows. I was very embarrassed when some of the students found out that this woman was my mother. At first, I was embarrassed because her activity revealed that I had come from a very poor family. I was also embarrassed because I did not have the emotional courage to tell the students myself that the woman steering the cows was indeed my mother. I lacked the emotional maturity to be proud of her and to defend her honourable work. By failing to defend my mother I also failed myself. I had the perfect opportunity to recognize and elevate her and all mothers like her.

Was I ashamed of my mother? Why did I remain silent? My mother, more than any other, did not deserve my silence. How I regret my lack of action. *Was I a coward?* I truly regret that as a young man I did not seize that opportunity to declare to the world that that woman was my Ma and that I was proud of her. I wish that I had had the maturity and the conviction to stand before my students and publicly declare, "Yes, that lady is my Ma. And there is no other Ma like her in this whole world." It would have been the right thing to do. I am ashamed to admit that I remained silent. Ma, you did not deserve my silence.

69

PARENT/TEACHER MEETING

I DO NOT recall ever having a Teacher/Parent meeting at our former girls' high school. Yet at some time in the early years of the school, a Parents-meet-the-Teachers event was scheduled in the upstairs area of the new school. At the far end of the floor was a stage. The principal asked all staff members to take their places up on the stage. It was from the stage that the teachers would be introduced one by one to the parents and visitors gathered below. Following those introductions, the event would take on a less formal attitude allowing the staff members to mingle with the parents meeting with any and all who wished for such an engagement.

Sister Dorothy began the introductions. She had barely started when a loud voice from the parent body boldly inquired, "I want to know who Mr. Boodram is!" I noted that this very large voice belonged to an equally large woman. Her manner was compelling although her tone suggested annoyance. Her comment created an awkward calm in the room.

Sister Dorothy, unwilling to surrender me to the whim of this woman, was uncertain as to what course of action to take. Was she to continue with the introductions and defer these comments to a time when they could be addressed privately or tackle the issue right away? I determined that I should identify myself publicly at that moment and face up to any criticism that she may throw in my direction no matter how embarrassing they should prove to be. My heart was pounding as I stepped forward and declared, "I am Mr. Boodram."

All were silent.

The woman bent her head for a moment. She was in complete command. I felt my palms begin to sweat; I prepared for the assault. It took every ounce of strength in me to hold up my head just a little. Her hesitation was wearing on me. I prayed for the attack to begin so that it could be over.

"Mr. Boodram," she began. She looked me squarely in the face. I could not hide from her piercing eyes. Her next words shocked me. "Yo is a good teacher."

What? I could not believe it. I shook my head as if to clear my ears. Then she continued, "My daughter Patricia comes home and tells me about how hard you work for the students. They respect you."

Now I really was embarrassed. I felt even more awkward because I had stepped forward one pace and so I stood as if set apart from the rest of the staff. I wanted to move back to my original place. Before I could take that step, this mother redoubled her praises for me. Now, totally embarrassed I could only stare completely dumbfounded. At the conclusion of her remarks she raised her hands over her head and began clapping. Others joined in and I wanted nothing but to return to my former anonymity. Quickly I stepped back to my former place stunned by this recognition.

What was truly remarkable was that the parent who made these remarks, was the parent of a girl who was not the typically cooperative and agreeable student. It was not that the girl was rude; rather she was unresponsive, and at times, moody. Often her assignments were incomplete and untidy. Because I was genuinely concerned about her achievement, I gave her several in class detentions so that I could assist her with her work. I remember asking her to see me for help at lunch time. In spite of all these extra offers of assistance the girl never gave any indication whatsoever that she appreciated my help. Her response to my offers was less than enthusiastic. I never would have guessed that she had anything good to say about me. If I could have expected anything it would be that she might report to her mother that I had been picking on her. Such was the nature of the denouncement that I was bracing myself for from this mother.

I did not expect this type of recognition especially from that mother. I had been singled out so publicly with such rich praise that again I was embarrassed. Yet in its own way this praise was deliciously sweet. Thereafter it seemed that I was to be the target of much good hearted teasing and commendation. I took it all in and smiled at my momentary good fortune.

70

AN EVENT—OR NOT

THERE WERE several other male teachers on staff at the all girls' school. One in particular displayed extreme talent in the area of fashion design. He had such promise in this area that he was able to stage his own fashion show at the Holiday Inn in Port of Spain. That hotel was the most elegant and sought after place in Port of Spain to stage an event. My friend and fellow co-worker, Dickie Ali, and I each received personal invitations to attend this gala event by the designer himself. It promised to showcase some of Trinidad's most beautiful models. Being invited to such a prestigious affair made us the envy of the neighbourhood. I was really looking forward to the event.

The much anticipated day arrived. Dickie and I had to go to Port of Spain early in the day for some reason and by mid-afternoon we were on our way home. I was driving when Dickie suggested that we stop off at a bar in San Juan to meet up with some of his friends.

San Juan was about half way between Port of Spain and Tunapuna. The bar was a favorite of the locals and already boasted quite a few patrons. Most were downing either the local Carib beer or a rum and coke. Not being familiar with bars in general and drinking in particular, I was at a loss as to what I should order. Dickie, however, appeared very much at home in the surroundings. He looked as if he was really enjoying himself among these friends. I, on the other hand, was intensely self-conscious. I was rebuked and often derided for not joining others in a drink. I had been accused of considering myself superior to those who did choose to drink. Wanting to avoid any hint of controversy, wanting to have nothing spoil our perfect day, I turned down a beer and agreed to have a stout instead.

I was under the erroneous belief that a stout was non-alcoholic.

Someone declared, "Bottoms up," and everyone, including me, downed his drink. I began feeling strange. I did not understand the new sensation. Another round was poured for everyone and I had a second bottle of stout.

In no time at all, I was on my third bottle and things were happening to me that I did not understand. I did not know that I was intoxicated. I did not know that the alcoholic content in certain brands of stout drinks exceeded the alcoholic content of a regular beer. I had chosen a stout because I thought that it was healthy drink; it was widely heralded for its strength giving properties. I can testify first hand to its strength, for after consuming three of them I felt invincible. Suddenly I was without reservation; I felt totally free. My body was floating; no, it was flying. I had entered another realm.

(I don't recall being anywhere close to intoxicated before in my life. The only other time I even remember having had a drink was one Christmas when I was a child of eleven. Pa poured me a glass of wine. At first I was delighted. I felt so grown up. Here I was sitting with my dad and his friends having wine. The first moments were glorious; I was in heaven. What followed however was less than glorious and while I may not have been in hell, the time I spent in the outdoor latrine was a far cry from heaven. That experience was sheer disaster for me.)

Back at the bar I was experiencing no pain or discomfort. On the contrary, I was simply too happy. After bidding farewell to our companions, Dickie and I headed for my car. It was a good forty feet from the door of the bar to my car but the road seemed much longer. For some reason I could not hold a steady path. And, the car itself appeared further and further away with every step. Finally we reached the car. I climbed into the driver's seat and started the car. I did not know that I was in no condition to drive. I just thought that I was very happy. Normally I was a very cautious driver and was careful to observe the laws of the road. Not that day. I felt completely free, totally uninhibited. I became quite daring and careless. Upon reflection, I realize that I was lucky to have survived that day without hurting myself or anyone else. It was just a four mile drive from the bar to home and I made it in record time. I drove through numerous lights not knowing if they were red or green. I was dangerously dumb! I am grateful that I did not hurt anyone!

While I did not hurt anyone by having an accident, I did hurt my family. It hurt them to see me in such a state. They were shocked and disappointed. Someone confided in me later that no one in the family would have ever conceived that I could ever be intoxicated. Such a thought was totally unfathomable. My family held me to such a high standard that no mistakes would be allowed. In their minds, I could not and would not do any wrong. Increasingly I was looked to as the tower of strength. There were to be no loose bricks in that tower.

As soon as we arrived home, Dickie directed me to the outside shower. I stepped in not realizing that I was still fully clothed. The water was cold. Someone placed a towel over the top of the shower. I peeled off my clothes and dried myself off. Eventually I made it to my room and soon I was asleep!

Some time later Dickie came by all dressed up for the evening's festivities in Port of Spain. I was still asleep. Dickie woke me up and I too prepared for the evening.

I can still see the eyes of my sisters and feel their intense scrutiny as they watched me struggle with my tie. I managed to complete the task satisfactorily. Ma looked me over and then winked at my sisters. They smiled. For now all seemed well. Dickie and I headed for the Holiday Inn. Again I drove. I had not progressed very far when I pulled off the road.

"Dickie, I think that you had better drive," I suggested. Dickie took over the wheel for he too knew that I was not yet free of all the effects from our earlier activity.

Soon we arrived at the hotel. Style and elegance commanded the ballroom and the decor boasted an upscale extravagance. It was soon time for the fashion show. The models came in one by one displaying the newest artistic creations. A thoroughly enchanted audience thundered its approval with generous applause. If I had forgotten for one minute that Trinidad was the birthplace of some of the world's most stunningly beautiful girls, I was fully reminded that night. The fashion show was followed by a most decadent supper which in turn gave way to an evening of dancing.

The band began playing. The music was most inviting. Indeed, if I knew how to dance I would have been the first on the floor.

(Once following my graduation from high school, I had an opportunity to go to a dance. The boys' school and girls' school got together under the leadership of one of the nuns and organized a graduation dance of sorts to celebrate our achievements. I was much too shy and self-conscious to allow myself to even entertain the idea of attending such an event. I told everyone that I had to work that day so I could not attend. I still found being in the company of young women quite a challenge. If my brother Boysie had known of my decision he would have taken exception to my conduct. He quite naturally would have preferred me to be seen in the company of girls. This would somehow prove to him and to his friends that I was a real man. In fact, a rumour started when I first started teaching in the Catholic school. It was noted that I did not drink or date. Because of this, some people jumped to the conclusion that I was headed for the priesthood. In my circles at that time this comment was not considered complimentary. My brothers, Clive and Boysie felt terribly let down. They never sought to defend me when I was castigated in their very presence. Had they not been present, the ridicule would have been easier to bear.

Soon I was dubbed with a new name. I was called Monsieur Fennessey—an offshoot of the name Father Fennessey—the principal of Boys' Catholic School. It would seem that my peers favoured the convenient put down over understanding. Every day I was tormented and derided for walking the straight path. My road had little time to devote to the pursuits of women and dancing.)

Back at the ballroom, I truly envied those who could dance. My friend, Dickie was one such person. I watched him as he danced and he looked ever so comfortable accompanying his beautiful young partner.

I sat alone at the table surveying the room. My eyes were drawn immediately to one of the beautiful young models. She was sitting at a table simply chatting. I found myself heading straight to her table. Remarkably, I was neither conscious nor hesitant! Once I reached the table, I stood up very straight, extended my left hand with my fingers tilted upright, awaiting her response.

I said nothing; not even, "Excuse me. May I?"

For this one moment in life, I felt grand. I smiled. She rose, excused herself from her friends, and joined me on the dance floor! I reached out for her hand, she reached out for mine. The orchestra was softly playing a waltz and we began to dance. I was not me any more; I became the music. When my lovely partner accidentally stepped on my toes she apologized to me! My confidence soared. The moment was miraculously transformed and I was on top of the world. When that dance ended neither one of us made a move to return to our tables. The next dance began. Then gradually feelings of consciousness crept in! I lost my feeling of bravado. The lingering effects of the afternoon indulgence had vanished completely. I was again myself—sober and conscious. The mood changed instantly. My companion returned to her table and I returned to mine. And there I remained, self-conscious and alone, for the rest of the evening!

71

THE ERRAND

IT WAS the morning of a regular school day and Sister Dorothy sent me to Port of Spain on an errand. My fellow teacher and friend, Dickie, joined me. Dickie wanted to visit one of his relatives and asked if we could sidetrack a bit to accommodate his request. Dickie further assured me that this venture would not be a problem for Sister Dorothy. I knew that he and Sister Dorothy had a very close relationship so reluctantly I gave in to his request trusting fully in his insights. Our sidetrack took more time than either of us anticipated but soon we attended to Sister Dorothy's errand and returned to the school. I headed for class immediately. I was late.

Later in the day, Sister Dorothy sent for me. When I entered her office I was greeted with her serious business voice. She was cold and pointed in her address.

"Mr. Boodram, not only did you take too long to run my simple errand, you were late for class." Clearly she was agitated. I was embarrassed.

"Sorry, Sister," I managed.

"Thank you." Then she continued, "What I would like to know is why you were late?"

I found this question rather startling. I knew that Dickie had gone in to see her earlier and I assumed that he would have explained to her why we were late.

"Sister, did Mr. Ali not explain why we were late?" I asked.

"This is not about Mr. Ali," she countered. "I gave you a responsibility. You did not fulfill it. Therefore my issue is with you. You were in charge!"

I felt compromised. It was not my place to put the blame on Dickie. He should have assumed the blame for himself. I said nothing about Dickie. I simply apologized.

"Sister, sorry. It won't happen again!"

Needless to say, this encounter left me feeling chastised! My admiration for Sister Dorothy was challenged.

My relationship with Sister Dorothy seemed somewhat threatened. Yet, I did learn a valuable life lesson from this situation that I still carry with me today; if you are in charge, you are responsible for what happens under your command.

Up to this day I do not know what transpired between Dickie and Sister Dorothy. Dickie and I never spoke of it again but our personal relationship, while mutually cordial, was never the same after that incident. I am still puzzled by the situation.

In time the incident was forgotten by the rest of the staff and teaching once again became my complete joy. Until one day, when the Vice-Principal, Sister Benito, decided to challenge my behaviour.

72

SISTER CLAIRE BENITO

THAT DAY I was on outside supervision. When the bell rang, students lined up outside the classrooms. Because these lines sometimes crossed the entrance road through the school ground, the entrance gate had to be closed to prevent vehicles from using the road. This ensured the safety of the students standing in line. Within the entrance gate was another door that late students used. After the second bell sounded, this door was closed and locked. I was about to perform this operation when a beggar appeared at the gate seeking alms. I allowed him to enter and watched him as he headed for the principal's office. I never gave my action another thought. I regarded it as a simple fact of life that this man would ask for help, receive some help and then be gone.

During the interval of time between the ringing of the bell and the actual commencement of classes, teachers gathered in the staffroom making last minute changes for the day's lessons. While many of the teachers were still in the staffroom, the vice-principal, Sister Benito entered.

"Mr. Boodram, you should know better!" Her words were clear and defined and her voice commanded attention. She continued, and her voice heightened, proclaiming her authority. "Yes, Mr. Boodram. You flaunted our school policy. I saw you. You deliberately let the beggar in. No beggar is allowed in when the gate is closed. Now, what do you have to say for yourself?"

I was startled and embarrassed by these charges and could find no words of response. I bowed my head to think how I might respond. Then she stepped closer and threatened.

"Sister Dorothy has to hear about this. She will be awfully disappointed in you Mr. Boodram and you are one of her favourite people. She is not going to like what I have to say to her especially since you are one of her favourites."

I was about to say sorry, but, after hearing her threats, I simply could not do it. Sister Benito's attitude of superiority prevented me from apologizing. I felt that if I were to apologize at that moment, it would further encourage her self-righteous attitude—an attitude not in keeping with Christian traditions.

"Now Mr. Boodram, do you wish to say something in your defence before I see Sister Dorothy?"

"Yes, Sister, I do!"

"Come on, let's have it," she demanded impatiently. If she was expecting an apology she would be sorely disappointed.

I looked her squarely in the eye, and said simply, "Sister, I felt it was the Christ- like thing to do. Do you think Jesus would mind that I let the beggar in?"

Her eyes blazed with fury. She tilted her head and raised her hands in disgust. Clearly Sister Benito was dethroned. I did not feel sorry for what I had said to her. My only regret was that I had spoken these words in front of the staff. To them I offered my apologies.

With a wave of his hand, one teacher dismissed the incident and urged, "Frankie, forget her. Go to class."

Another consoled, "She had it coming good!"

In spite of this support I was troubled by Sister Benito's accusation and by my own response to her. I wondered silently what Sister Dorothy would think of my conduct. After all, I did disrespect Sister Benito, did I not? Then, as I was about to go to class, a hand rested on my shoulder. It was Sister Paul.

"Mr. Boodram, may I speak with you?"

"Yes, Sister."

"Sister Benito means well. She tends to see everything in black and white. She meant well."

"Sister Paul, I did not mean any harm by letting in the beggar. I could not help it. The beggar seemed so needy, so desperate."

"Mr. Boodram, I know that. I realise that it must have been extremely difficult for you to keep him out. I believe that if Sister Benito were in your place, she too might have done the same. Her bark is worse than her bite and as vice-principal she has much on her plate. See what I mean?"

I listened respectfully to the words of this white nun, Sister Paul Xavier, who had only recently come from America to join our staff. She was tall and stately. Both staff and students alike loved her. There was a precious quality about her and I felt safe in her presence.

Then she looked me straight in the eye and spoke directly to my soul. "Mr. Boodram, your soul is precious and God loves you as you."

Then she was gone. A lightning bolt of compassion had just struck me down. Her face, so serene, so concerned, so divine, offered a glimpse of the soul that walked in the path of Jesus himself. My heart was transformed. (Was it any wonder then, that on November 22, 1963, when we heard Sister Paul scream, " Oh, no! Oh, no!" we ran to her classroom. We found her collapsed on the floor. She had just heard the news of the assassination of President John F. Kennedy. Through her agony we all learned of the tragedy of his death. Through her also, we learned what President Kennedy had meant to America.)

On my way to class, I could not help but marvel at how unlike one another these two nuns were. I was impressed by the manner in which Sister Paul defended Sister Benito and I knew that I had been in the presence of a near saint.

After class, rather than wait to be summoned by Sister Dorothy, I went to her office. When I entered her room, she did not acknowledge me immediately. She appeared to be deep in thought. I thought that I was in deep trouble. When she spoke she was calm and she chose her words with careful deliberation.

"Mr. Boodram, I am confident that our Lord understands your kindness to the beggar. But, I am equally confident that He also recognizes the cautious nature of Sister Benito. She has been charged with the awesome responsibility of looking out for the welfare of all of us. Do you take my point?"

"Yes, Sister, and I am terribly sorry for my conduct." It was so easy to make my apologies to her.

"Thank you, Frankie Boodram. I knew I could count on you. I am proud of you and the way you are progressing. Now, let's say you made a mistake with Sister Benito. Now share your apology with her also."

"Yes, Sister."

And, so it was decided. I was to apologize to Sister Benito. I left Sister Dorothy's office wondering how best to approach Sister Benito. There seemed to be such a divide between us, not just personally, but also religiously.

Sister Benito had spoken to me on several occasions about converting from Hinduism to Catholicism. She pointed out that all staff members were Catholic and ended by concluding that I should become a Catholic too because I was teaching at a Catholic school. Despite her best efforts, she was never able to sway me. She did not alter my position.

All our lives, we Hindus who attended Catholic schools, were told that we worshipped idols and that we were bound for hell. I lived with that criticism as a student in a Catholic school. I had studied the New Testament and the Acts of the Apostles and tried to understand the teaching and values of Christ. I felt that the Sermon on the Mount was a blueprint for the very best human conduct. In my mind it was a moral charter by which an individual could navigate life. That biblical passage seemed familiar and I was at home embracing its precepts. To me, at least, it seemed that Jesus was advocating precepts that had been taught to me all my life through Hinduism. I felt honour bound to advocate for Christianity by example. I was at peace with these two schools of thought—Christianity and Hinduism.

They have become two towering trees anchoring my soul firmly in the spiritual soil of the universe. And when the religions of the world have gone mad trying to conquer one other in the name of God, I wonder if God Himself would not seek the shade of two trees whose roots, though separate, are enjoined in harmony.

With such a vision planted firmly in my mind, it would have been a difficult task for anyone to remove me from the rooted soil of Hinduism. Thus I did not see the need for conversion for I had already embraced the essence of Christ and his teachings. I wondered if my vice-principal had become frustrated with my stubbornness. She must have found me a bit ungrateful. She must have regarded me as a sheep astray for far too long. I owed it to her to make amends. I did the right thing and apologized to Sister Benito.

Since that incident, Sister Benito and I have kept a respectful distance from one another but I was always mindful that she would be closely scrutinizing my behaviour for any hint of Hinduism. I welcomed her scrutiny for I knew that I was indeed faithful to the tenets of Christianity with my students. If sister only knew how hard I tried to be faithful...

73

LIFE OUTSIDE THE
CLASSROOM—PRIVATE LESSONS

I AM GRATEFUL to the students of St. Charles High Schools—boys and girls- for the opportunity to grow and explore the world of teaching! Through them, I tasted the fruits of satisfaction and fulfillment. Now, I wanted more of it.

Several months had passed since I returned from England and it was becoming increasingly apparent that I would not be leaving Trinidad to go abroad in the near future.

Tutoring after school and on week-ends allowed me to undertake the purchase of a small vehicle. The parents of some students who required tutoring could ill afford the expense. For those parents I offered to tutor their children at school during regular breaks and at the lunch hour. Both the parents and the students appreciated my efforts on their behalf and would often insist on paying me. Knowing that this would cause financial hardship for the family I allowed them to offer me gifts of fruit in exchange for my services. Both parties could feel good about this type of transaction. Their looks of appreciation always elevated my spirits and left me wanting to do more for the children.

On the other hand there were parents who could afford to engage me to tutor their children privately at home. To do this, I needed a vehicle. Just having a car of my own, seemed somehow to elevate my station in life.

One student lived in on the Eastern Main Road of St. Augustine, near the University. The home was the size of a mansion. Homes in this area were regarded as belonging to the high class. In the minds of the poor, these extravagant homes could only be seen in their dreams. Imagine my sense of awe then when I was engaged to tutor a child from such a home. The circular driveway was lined with alluring beds of flowers. A variety of fruit trees adorned the well-manicured grounds. I parked my car on the driveway and approached the home. Some dogs barked to announce my arrival and a servant approached. Just as I was about to identify myself, the lady of the house appeared and invited me in. She showed me several rooms where I could conduct the tutoring sessions. I chose the room with the most picturesque view of the lush gardens. The mother then introduced me to her young daughter, a shy girl just entering her first year of high school. Just as we began our tutoring session, the servant again entered, this time bearing a glass of juice.

"Please, Sir. Madam send this for you. Please take."

I very nearly died of shock, this humble man calling me, "Sir." He could very well have been my father. It was a distinct honour to be addressed in that manner. I was unaccustomed to such ceremony. It was a wonderful experience. Such little considerations (along with my generous pay) took the pain out of my extended work week.

Tutoring afforded me an inside look at the fascinating lifestyle of the rich. This was a double edged sword. On the one side I became saddened because we had so little. But, on the other side, it made me just that much more determined to work hard to acquire a few of life's little luxuries for those of us still at home.

74

THE NEEDS OF THE FAMILY

As a family we were now doing better economically. More of us were working and contributing. Boysie had the responsibility of providing money to cover our day to day grocery expenses. He worked extremely hard to meet his obligations. (It was through Boysie's efforts too that our home was equipped with indoor plumbing; but that did not happen until long after I left home to study in Canada.) Before Pa died, we did not have hydro, a gas stove or a fridge. In the years following my return from England, my salary went towards the purchase and upkeep of those items. I managed to save a portion of my salary for my next venture abroad. To pay for household improvements, I combined the monies earned from private tutoring with a part of my teaching salary. My sisters, Pinky and Kay, also had jobs. Their modest salaries also helped to provide additional improvements to our home.

As a teacher, my starting wage was $15.00 a month. Just before I left Trinidad, in 1967, my monthly wage was $140.00. A fridge cost $1300.00 while a stove ran about $1000.00. To purchase these two items alone was no easy task.

Our expenses again mounted when I employed a carpenter to build a bedroom complete with a small closet for me. This was a new addition to our small home and, although quite costly, was nonetheless, essential. (I occupied this room until I left for Canada some years later.)

While the carpenter worked on this project, I examined him and his craft closely. It was through this means that I acquired some very basic carpentry skills. Thereafter I attempted to repair and replace some of the rudimentary cupboards in our modest kitchen. Ma was most appreciative of my efforts in this regard. Thereafter, she often joked that I was born with a hammer in my hand for it was quite common for me to be fixing or repairing things around the home.

Thus the picture at home was now very clear. Boysie worked to provide for all our meals while I, in one way or another, provided for the little extras. Our needs were so great that at times it was difficult to put money aside for my studies abroad. Most of what I earned had to be channeled to the general upkeep of the home. It was an unwritten expectation that the boys of the family provide the means to maintain the family.

There were other expectations. One of them concerned marriage.

75

MARRIAGE PROPOSAL

AFTER PA died I received a proposal of marriage.

While I was yet a student at St. Charles Boys' High School I had become close friends with a young man named Jagdis Mallaram. We grew to like each other's families very much. We visited one another's homes regularly and his family became my family and mine became his. We were the closest of friends.

Sometime after Pa's death, Jagdis' father sent for me. He set up a specific time for me to come for dinner. I found this most unusual for we were not accustomed to such formality in our relationship. I was curious and a bit excited as I went to dinner. The dinner went on as usual. Nothing out of the ordinary transpired. Conversation was light and abundant. Everyone was present as usual sitting around the table in their regular places. It was after dinner that Mr. Mallaram beckoned me to join him in the living room. He motioned for me to sit. We two were alone in the room. That was most unusual. Jagdis would normally have been there right beside me adding his voice to the conversation. I noticed that Jagdis and his sisters were some distance away in another room.

Once I was seated, Mr. Mallaram pulled up a chair close to me and began to speak.

"Frankie, you know you father and me good friends."

"Yes."

"And I know you a good boy. You obey your father's wish..."

I was quiet and now a bit uncomfortable. *Where was he going with this?*

I didn't have to wait long to find out. He came straight to the point.

"Well, your father and I agreed together, that you will marry my daughter."

I was in a state of shock.

"I see how well you get along with the family—so, we set the date? And don't worry about the expenses of a wedding. Don't you worry. All that will be taken care of. Besides, we have a surprise gift for you! Ok?"

Without waiting to find out what the surprise gift was, I got up. I did not know what to say to this caring father. I managed only a curt, "Thank you, but I am sorry. I cannot marry your daughter." I left the house awkward and embarrassed. I did not even look for Jagdis to say my goodbyes.

I was caught totally off guard. I loved and adored the Mallaram family. The girls were like my sisters. Therefore when the proposal of marriage came I could not entertain it any more than I could entertain marrying one of my own sisters. Yet, I knew at once that a great honour had been bestowed on me by this honourable father.

When Jagdis and I next met, I sensed that he too had been caught off guard with his father's proposal. He was perhaps even more embarrassed than I over the experience. This incident served to highlight the extent to which our fathers would go to ensure a secure marriage for their children. Recognizing the love that was at the root of the proposal, we managed to put aside the awkwardness and resumed our friendship.

The idea of marriage, while somewhat appealing, was not yet foremost in my thinking. I still had the responsibility of unmarried sisters at home and my as yet unrealized aspiration to resume studies abroad. I could ill afford to entertain the possibility of my own marriage either financially or emotionally. All my extra energies were devoted to saving for university. Jagdis was well aware of my intentions and was able to explain to his family that I had a prior commitment in my life. Such an explanation would be well received and it would not appear that I had willfully or cheaply rejected the proposal or the sister. We remained friends with each other's families but in time, we each moved on in our separate ways. Jagdis is another friend whom I have not seen for decades. Yet, still, he remains my friend in my memory.

Two other incidents dealing with the subject of marriage come to mind. The first occurred while my father was still living, while the second occurred some time after his death.

A young man named Bob had seen my eldest sister, Dolly, at a wedding and became interested in her. (I think it was a wedding because that is how most of us West Indian boys and girls would first have occasion to meet one another.) Custom dictated that Bob not approach Dolly to express his interest (at least not in too overt a fashion); he had to go to Dolly's parents (my parents) and share his intentions with them. He told them that he wanted to marry her and that he wanted their permission to ask for her hand. For whatever reason, my parents did not give their approval right away. They came to me and sought my counsel regarding the suitability of Bob as a partner for Dolly. I told them that I admired Bob. He possessed a great deal of personal integrity. With that assurance from me, they gave Bob their blessing. Bob and Dolly were married shortly thereafter. I have often wondered why my parents consulted *me* regarding Dolly's marriage. I sensed that they were beginning to recognize the responsible adult within me. This was to be the first of many times when I was handed such responsibility regarding family matters. Over time, especially after my father's death, more and more of the family decisions were concentrated in my hands.

After Pa's death, my sister, Pinky was the next one to be offered a marriage proposal. Sylvan, the intended bride-groom, expressed his intentions to Ma. Again, Ma consulted me. There was something about Sylvan that I took to immediately and I gave my consent. Shortly thereafter, Pinky and Sylvan were married in a modest ceremony at our home.

After Pa died, my brother Boysie was the first to recognize the stark reality of the responsibility placed on each of us as elder brothers in a home that lacked a father. He was the one who informed me that it was our duty as Hindus to ensure that our sisters were securely married before we considered that path for ourselves. He reminded me that it was "the Hindu way" and cautioned me not to forget it.

In our own way each of us devoted our energies to this cause. It was not easy. There were times when I felt that the demands placed on our shoulders were too challenging and frustrating.

Because it was *the custom*, our sisters were not allowed to date. This created a dilemma. If the girls were not allowed to date, did that mean that the boys could not date either? It should have, but it did not.

I knew from personal experience that some Hindu boys "dated." I felt that I should not date if my sisters were not allowed to do so. I did not want to appear to be blatantly courting a double standard in front of the family; if my sisters were not allowed to date, neither must I. I cultivated friendships with girls but that is what they remained—friend-ships. I longed for the freedom that other young men possessed—the freedom to pursue girls. I felt terribly constrained. At times life was painfully solitary. Yet, even during these times of difficulty I experienced moments of joy. This joy resulted as a consequence of the special attention that was afforded to me by my family—by my mother and my sisters in particular.

At this particular juncture in my life, I was working long hours. After completing a full day of teaching, I would go straight to some students' homes where I offered private tutoring. I tutored most evenings and week-ends. My mother saw how busy my life was and recognized that I had very little time for anything else but work. She, along with my sisters, began to extend little courtesies to me that made me feel very much appreciated.

No matter what time I got home from my tutoring sessions, a hot meal always awaited me. My mother took the time to sit me down and bring me my meal.

My laundry was always taken care of by my youngest sister, Kalie. She laboured without ceasing in her care of both Boysie and me. God bless her. Thanks to her, our shirts and trousers were always meticulous and our beds were always made. Before breakfast Kalie was sure to have my shoes polished and my shirt and pants selected. The shoes would be placed at the foot of the bed while the shirt and pants were neatly lain out on the bed.

(Does this snapshot of life at home not seem princely? Indeed, we as males have been accused of demanding to be treated like young royalty by the female members of our family. To the casual observer perhaps that may hold a measure of truth. In my heart I know that this is not my truth. I know that perhaps no one but me will ever truly understand my life. At times even I do not understand my life. Perhaps we are not meant to fully understand ourselves in this life. Perhaps that will come in time.)

My brother Boysie also claimed his share of attention. His approach and his disposition however were very different from my very serious attitude. Boysie was more playful with our sisters, especially with the youngest one, Kalie. He seemed to require her attention all the time. He could not (or *would* not) dress without her help. He always sought out her opinion regarding how he dressed, and more importantly, about how he looked.

Boysie valued his looks and sought the approval of all of his sisters. He craved their attention and approval. To see him in action brought a light hearted deliciousness into all our lives. He wanted them, each one of them, to tell him that he looked good and that he was handsome. My sisters were eager to indulge this whim and always accommodated him. I am left to wonder if at anytime any one of them might have exaggerated the truth just a little in order to humour him.

Truly these were special and innocent times in our lives. But, there was a darker side to our innocence. Sometimes this innocence caused pain.

I now realize that Boysie and I must have created havoc in our home. As hard as it is, I must face up to our *innocent ignorance.*

Boysie was expecting company one Sunday afternoon after lunch. He had given strict orders that he wanted a certain special dish to be prepared. When he discovered that the dish had not been prepared he went looking for the reason why. He was less than pleased. Then he found one of our sisters resting on a bed. That is all that he saw. A sister. Lying down. Not working. Not doing as he had asked. When he became enraged all hell broke loose. Boysie unleashed his belt and began to strike her with it. He must have felt truly justified in his rage. To him, she appeared to be disobedient, disrespectful, and lazy. From his violent reaction, one would think that she had committed a most heinous crime.

I am sad to have to admit that I stood by and watched him as he beat her; I did not go to her aid. *Why did I not intercede on her behalf? Did I think that he had just cause for his action?*

This sister, this young girl, struggled to get out of bed and headed to the kitchen. As she walked she raised her hands to shield her body from any further blows.

Ma shouted, "Stop! You don't know! Stop, please stop!"

And what was it that Boysie and I did not know? We did not know that it was *her time of the month* and she was ill. That helpless young child endured that attack without a word of retaliation. The difficult truth is that it very well could have been me disciplining any one of our sisters for the same offence. Boysie and I did not know this condition regarding girls. Even though we had six sisters we were never taught about such matters. In reflection I wonder how many times my sisters endured a bit of hell because of our ignorant innocence.

I do remember that I too was subject to bouts of anger which now seem totally inexplicable. I remember being particularly agitated one day. While I do not recall the reason for my agitation, I do recollect only too vividly my reaction. I threw a glass bottle on the floor in the direction of my sisters (the supposed offenders). The bottle broke into splinters and spread in every direction. My youngest sister, Kalie, was struck by the shards of glass and they became lodged in her ankle. I recall the blood that gushed from her foot; I recall that she needed medical attention; I recall too the scar that she still bears today testifying to my misguided anger. I am appalled by my own reaction and I apologize for my stupid and reckless conduct. I am further humbled by the fact that that sister has continued to be loving and caring towards me and has never once challenged me on my behaviour that day.

I have no reason to doubt my family's accounting of my behaviour when things were not done to my satisfaction. I am told that if for some reason, my shirt was not ironed perfectly, if there was a single crease somewhere, I would role up the offending article and demand that it be ironed all over again. While I have no real memory of this, I am told that if a single button was missing from a shirt, I would cut off all the buttons and demand that they all be sewn on right away. It is only in my adult years that my sisters confided that my behaviour was far too critical and demanding.

Kalie was not the only one wronged by my hands. Indeed, in my efforts to be a good disciplinarian, I have hurt other members of my family.

I recall an event that involved my sister Kay. The situation was simple. Kay had been invited to a party after work one Saturday night. She had done the right thing and had asked Ma permission to attend. Ma gave her permission.

I returned home from a tutoring session later that afternoon. Kay was all dressed up and very excited. She smiled broadly when she saw me and asked innocently, "Frankie, how do I look?"

Ignoring her smile, I declared, "You are not going anywhere."

Her smile faded and was replaced with a look of incredulity. She could hardly believe her ears. But, much to her credit, she was obedient. She withdrew to the bedroom.

Kay had cause to resent me. *Had she not shown generosity in her spirit a thousand times more to each one of us in so many different ways? Why did I react the way I did? Why did I not just say, "Kay, you look beautiful"? Why did I feel that I needed to be so stern? Was it simply because she had not received my permission also? Was not my mother's permission sufficient? What was the source of my angry reaction? Was I so intent with my responsibilities for raising the girls properly and wanting them to remain innocent that I forgot that they were now becoming young ladies and needed a little freedom? Had I felt that my freedoms had been so restricted that I was unable or unwilling to grant any?* At this moment, I do not recall the exact reason for my decision. I only know that I have regrets.

Kay, however, was not about to let that situation remain unchallenged for long. But she herself would not be the one to launch the challenge. She had too much respect for me to do that. Besides, she knew that I was stubborn and when confronted, rightly or wrongly, I became even more unyielding and resolute. Kay may have withdrawn to the bedroom but the matter was far from concluded.

One Saturday afternoon I returned home to find two of my closest friends sitting at the table. Their every need was being catered by my all too eager sisters. These two boys, Boy and Roderick, were like brothers to my sisters and in turn, my sisters treated them like princes. They loved coming to our home because they always received a lot of appreciative attention from the girls. The boys never overstepped their bounds by showing anything more than a brotherly interest in my sisters. If they ever would have, they would never again be invited home. My responsibility to protect my sisters extended into my friendships with my male friends. If I could not completely trust them around my sisters, they would be friends outside the home only. Boy and Roderick had my complete trust.

My sisters trusted them also for they confided in them the details of my "bad behaviour." They prevailed on their friendship with my two friends by having them "reprimand" me regarding my behaviour towards the girls in general and Kay in particular.

I did not get even the most perfunctory of greetings before Boy laced into me. Boy commanded the moment. Roderick acted as co-counsel. The girls were the plaintiffs. As soon as Boy spotted me coming up the stairs, he began citing the charges against me. I had no trial. Everyone, including my two good friends, assumed that I was guilty. I could make no defence. I was silent as the litany of offences was listed. Boy concluded his remarks with, "Frankie, you too strict with your sisters. They don't deserve the kind of punishment you give."

I was shocked by this attack from my friend. I did not respond. I could not. I turned to leave when Boy charged, "What's the matter Frankie? You like to dish it out, but you can't take it?"

Without saying a word, I went outside. Roderick followed. Still reeling from the attack I could not focus on Roderick's words when he tried to engage me in conversation.

Roderick returned to the house and brought Boy outside to me. Boy flashed a smile hoping to indicate that we were still friends and then he too tried to talk to me.

I could not receive anything that either of them said for I was still seething with anger. I did not trust myself to speak.

Roderick wisely directed both of us to his car. He drove to an ice cream shop to help us cool down. It worked. Soon I was able to speak and explain my reactions. I was able to tell Boy that I really did not mind his criticisms regarding the way I was handling my sisters. I objected to him delivering his remarks in front my sisters. Roderick agreed that Boy's remarks should have been directed to me privately.

Boy seemed focused on the ice cream and did not respond. I knew that our friendship was still intact when he got up, walked over to me, and said, "Hey, Frankie, let's all go to the movies. My treat."

He flashed a smile and all the hurt evaporated—on both sides. I knew that that was Boy's way of apologizing. I accepted. In that moment our friendship was solidified. Boy knew that he could talk to me about concerns; he *now* knew how to offer his criticisms. I knew that Boy and Roderick would continue to "advise" me when they felt that I needed advising. I did make an effort to be more understanding in my dealings with my sisters. I was not always successful, but I did try.

There is a kind of explanation—not justification—for my conduct. Even before Pa died, the responsibility for making many of the family decisions had fallen to me. After Pa's death, these responsibilities mounted as Ma would not or could not make the decisions herself. I had no real life experiences and no real role model other than Pa. My soul felt the burden of those responsibilities. Carrying the load as family disciplinarian so early in life tore at my insides. I think I felt robbed of my own youth. The actions that I took troubled me then and still haunt me today. It is a sad reality that the male members of our family (Clive, Boysie, and I) were prone to explosive bouts of anger. In today's climate, these actions would be regarded as abusive and violent. Back then, such reactions were considered normal; that is all I knew; that is all our father knew. We may not have liked it but it was familiar. Just as our father before us disciplined with the belt, so too did Clive, Boysie and I. We all succumbed to the uncivilized practices of our elders. Earlier accounts detailed Pa's efforts at discipline.

76

LIKE FATHER LIKE SON

OUR ELDEST brother, Clive, was quickly becoming a second Pa. In fact, in this one area at least, he was Pa's clone. While Boysie and I were still in elementary school, we took turns cleaning out the cow pen and sweeping the yard. On this one particular day, it was my turn to clean out the pen. My duties included shoveling up the cow droppings and transferring them to the dung heap just outside the pen. (These droppings were a valuable by-product of the cows and when sold as fertilizer it added a good penny to our modest income.)

When Clive came round to examine my efforts, I had already finished cleaning up the dung (or so I thought) and was busy at my next task: collecting the urine that the animals had released the previous night. (The concrete flooring in the cow pen was sloped so that any urine passed by the animal naturally flowed away from the centre and pooled in a collection area at the edges. This urine was diluted and eventually used to fertilize plants.) I had to be extremely careful not to spill any on me. The odour from the urine was very strong and defied even the most diligent washing. If I went to school carrying that most unpleasant scent, it was a virtual certainty that I would be vilified at every turn by those parasites who were my classmates.

I was so focused on carefully collecting the urine that I did not notice the fresh deposit of droppings from the cow. Clive, however, did notice. After accusing me of carelessness he ordered me to clean up the mess.

As I began the cleaning task I must have muttered something under my breath. To Clive, it appeared that I was being rude and for this offence he grabbed me and hurled me into the air. It was a rather sensational feeling—this flying in the air. That is, until I landed at the top of the dung heap and became immersed in the fresh manure!

"Yo want more—just open your mouth!" Clive railed. I knew better than to respond for that would invite further indignities. I remained silent and Clive left me alone.

I cleaned myself up as quickly as I could and joined my friends in a game of marbles that was already underway. If Clive only knew that I was muttering to myself about missing the game perhaps he would have understood that I was not being rude to him; but, perhaps not. Sometimes there was just no telling what could set him off. I was careful and never dared to openly challenge Clive. He was too strong a force. But, Boysie possessed just the right amount of daring to test him when an opportunity presented itself.

One day, Boysie was sweeping the yard dutifully but, according to Clive, carelessly. In his haste to complete his chores, Boysie failed to use the customary *cochea* broom (a broom made out of dried branches from the coconut tree). If used properly, this broom left very pleasing sweeping patterns on the dirt yard. Boysie's rushed efforts did not produce those special patterns on the yard. When Mr. Clive inspected Boysie's work, he was not satisfied with the results and ordered that Boysie do it all over again with the proper broom.

Clive found the cochea broom for Boysie and handed it to him but not before generously smacking him several times with his weighty hands. As Clive left, Boysie complained because he had to start the job all over. This time he had to follow procedure which meant that he had to start from the part of the yard closest to the pen and work his way directly across to the other side using a broad sweeping motion with the cochea broom. Boysie's fury, punctuated by expletives, could be heard for miles. Eventually Boysie calmed down and began to attend to his task. This time he did it correctly for a distinct and lovely pattern began to emerge on the dirt yard.

Soon, Boysie was fully recovered from his earlier frustration and actually became enamoured with his own accomplishment. When Clive returned for the next inspection, he found Boysie giving admiring looks at his handiwork. Mr. Clive was not yet a fan for a few leaves from our nearby mango tree had blown onto the carefully swept work despoiling the creation. For some unknown reason, Mr. Clive blamed Boysie for this and yelled at him and called him a few choice names.

Boysie, totally frustrated that all his efforts were not being appreciated, reacted without thinking. He flung the broom away. He did not intentionally give it any direction but the broom landed ever so close to Clive. This in turn, set Clive off in a fury of rage and the two ended up in a scuffle. There was no real contest, for Clive was twice the size of Boysie and he quickly locked Boysie in his mighty arms. Then he headed towards the dung-heap. Moments later all that we could discern was a pair of arms and the top of Boysie's wee head helplessly flailing amidst the fresh manure. Poor Boysie.

Clive must have inherited his brute strength from Pa; indeed the adage "like father like son" seems a definite fit here. Clive routinely threw us into the dung- heap! While I never harboured any ill-will towards him for that, what he did on another occasion, disturbed me for a long, long time.

One day, just as I was heading off to school, Pa asked me to run an errand for him. He wanted me to deliver a package to the grocery shop that was about a mile away. Even thought I was being asked to do this I knew that I had no choice in the matter. Pa's children were not allowed to voice dissent. So, off I went running at full speed to the shop. I gave the shopkeeper the package and turned to leave. School was about to start and I would just have time to make it if I left immediately. But the shopkeeper would not let me leave despite my pleas that I would be late. He seized that moment to defame my Pa. He called him a drunkard and proclaimed that Pa was always short on money and never seemed to have enough to pay his debts. We were not alone in the shop. The presence of others seemed to fuel his fury. His insults and abuse continued to captivate as well as entertain his audience. This shopkeeper and his oversized ego enjoyed being the centre of attention at the expense of my father and me. I made a conscious decision to endure this indignity in silence. I feared that I would only add to his anger if I said anything. Finally I was allowed to leave and I ran as quickly as I could to school.

Even though I ran all the way, I discovered that classes had already started. Standing on the pavement just outside the school I debated what to do. A wind blew some mango leaves in circles at my feet.

I looked up at the school. Through the wire mesh I saw my teacher brandishing a whip in front of the class. I was absolutely mortified. "Oh, God," I prayed, "how am I to go in his classroom, now? I am late and I am sure to be beaten. I just can't face that teacher's licks and humiliation."

The sight of that belt, the idea of walking into the classroom late, and the anticipation of the teasing that necessarily would follow, suffocated my brain. I was unable to think straight. My legs seized unable to carry me forward. They moved into reverse.

"Come on legs, help me to school!" They refused to obey. Suddenly I found my legs carrying me further and further away from the school.

It was never my intention to skip school. The punishment for such an action was too severe to warrant contemplation. Students who deliberately skipped were flogged on their bare bottoms in full view of their classmates; the entire school would know of the disgrace. Such a flogging and the humiliation that accompanied it were not easily survived.

Soon I found myself crossing a set of railroad tracks and approaching a local cemetery. With reverence and timidity I entered the hallowed grounds.

I sat down on the grass and contemplated the day's events. I wondered about my action. *How would it be perceived?* Since I did not *mean* to skip school, I reasoned that I did *not* skip school. I soon had myself convinced that, although I missed school, I did not deliberately skip school. I resolved to tell Ma the truth later, when I returned home. She would understand.

With my conscience somewhat eased, I began to explore my surroundings. There were such beautiful structures in the cemetery. *How come people buried the dead in such richness?* I moved on. In front of me was a fresh grave. As I approached the gravesite, I saw the hole first hand.

"So that is where the dead is placed, in that lonely hole," I thought as I wandered away. Time passed and soon I felt that I should be heading home for I needed to tell Ma what had happened regarding school.

When I got home I entered the yard from the rear hoping not to be noticed. Clive appeared as if from nowhere.

"Frankie, did you go to school?" he shouted.

The word 'yeah' came cascading out of my mouth before I actually realized it. Why I uttered that word I do not know. I should not have uttered that word. Clive immediately pounced.

"LIAR!" he screamed. Then he grabbed me by the arm and threw me in front of Ma. Ma stood silent, too shocked by his action to speak. "Ma, Frankie skipped school. I saw him in the cemetery with my own two eyes. He is a liar."

"Clivey, maybe we could..." pleaded my mother.

"No, Ma," Clivey interjected. "The teacher has to know that Frankie skipped school. I'm taking him to his teacher right now."

I wanted to yell out to Ma to save me but there was to be no saving that day. Clive had a firm grip on my waist and I could not get away. The more I attempted to resist, the more firm became his grip. Thus he dragged me all the way to school. I tried to reason with Clive. I begged *him* to discipline me. Clive was resolved. He would entertain none of my pleas. Thus he dragged me all the way to school and deposited me in my classroom at the feet of my teacher. Everyone gathered around to hear Clive's public denouncement.

"Frankie is a liar. He skipped school and lied about it. He spent the morning in the cemetery. Teacher, I brought him to you. Teach him a lesson he will not forget."

I had no leg to stand on, in more ways than one. There was Clivey, the brother I most admired, throwing me to this pack of wolves. I was so confused by his action. Why did he feel it necessary to humiliate me so publicly? What had I done to deserve such a fate? In my mind, what Clive did amounted to ordering my public execution.

I stood silently and stoically in front of my accuser. What could I offer in my own defence? I had no words left in me. I felt that I was already dead and all that remained was my burial. This I expected momentarily. The teacher escorted me to his desk at the front of the room.

"Wait here, Frankie Boodram," he commanded as he went to the door to attend to his afternoon students.

I stood there in front of his desk motionless but without tears. A spectacle I became as eyes peered and mouths gaped. The bell had now signalled the start of afternoon classes. More than the usual number of students passed by offering curious stares and glaring at the latest miscreant. Their snickering came in waves bashing the shores of an already weakened soul.

Then my teacher spoke. "All right everyone settle down and be quiet." The class became suddenly quiet. All eyes seemed to be focused on me as he spoke.

"Frankie has been reported by his brother Clive. Clive has called him a liar. Frankie skipped school. That's a serious offence."

As the teacher escorted my brother from the room, I was left in a world of my own. My mind was racing wildly. My heart was beating rapidly. The usual punishment for my offence was a definite flogging... at the very least. Any moment now and the teacher would return and require me to take my pants down. My behind would be open to the scrutiny of all those who were present in the classroom. The news would soon be everywhere and I would have no place to hide.

Even the bravest of the brave broke down in tears at some point during the ritual. Being a Hindu in this all Catholic school and to be so broken, would constitute the ultimate humiliation. It was a humiliation that I was about to experience.

My teacher returned. Already an eager class of spirited students awaited the spectacle! Undoubtedly, the chant, "Down with his pants," was silently thundering in their heads.

The teacher approached, stood beside me and asked, "Frankie, why? Why did you skip school?"

At that moment, I was beyond speech. *What could I say? Would anyone believe me? I was not at class. Who would believe that I did not skip class?*

He reached into his desk drawer and pulled out the strap. I recoiled at the sight of it! I braced for the impending flogging.

I knew that I could not take my pants down! Nor would I allow anyone else to take them down for me. I would have to die first. As helpless and as vulnerable as I was, I was adamant about that one thing. So inspired by my own resolve, I felt for a moment that I had died and I was being transported elsewhere to another time and place. I found myself reaching out to the Great Unknown.

"Oh, God," I cried in my mind, "save me from this please." I remained calm and submitted myself to the overwhelming silence that surrounded my spirit. Then a voice—my teacher's voice—broke the silence.

"Frankie Boodram."

I heard but I did not want to hear that voice. To acknowledge the voice would mean leaving the protected world that I had just created for myself. I did not want to leave. I did not want to hear. Then the voice called again.

"Frankie Boodram, look at me."

I felt compelled to respond. I brought myself to face my teacher. He commanded, "Put your hand out!"

What? What did he just say? Did I hear correctly? Did he say for me to put out my hand? Not, *remove your pants and bend over*? His command shocked me. Gladly I extended my hand to accommodate the request. Never did a hand more happily receive its lashes than mine did on that day. I felt no pain. I do not even remember the number of lashes I received.

I was so thankful to my teacher for strapping me! I felt that I had received a gift for I had not been asked to 'de-pants' myself in front of the class. The tears I wanted to shed were tears of joy. They, however, had to be restrained for such tears would be misunderstood as tears of weakness and would ultimately be used against me by my fellow students. I wonder if my teacher knew how indebted I felt to him for his sensitivity and his kindness.

I was impervious to the sarcastic remarks and the disapproving looks that followed the strapping. I would not give the students at school the satisfaction of knowing that I suffered.

Why Clive chose that course of action to discipline me I will never know nor understand. As a maturing young man perhaps he may have reasoned my case in a way I did not comprehend. Grown-ups often think in ways that young people may not understand. My brother's actions on that day remain a mystery still.

I have now addressed these situations that involved Clive. I too, must have extracted some of that poison of discipline that flowed through the veins of both my father and Clive. For here I was, now a young man, threatening the same type of discipline with my siblings. Inevitably I drew from the well of past tradition, the waters of which were already poisoned.

I remember little about disciplining Suresh our youngest brother and also the youngest of the family. Both Pa and Clive belted Boysie and me indiscriminately. (Truly Boysie received much more than I.) In a similar fashion, Boysie and I now found ourselves disciplining our sisters. My father was capable of belting me mercilessly.

I hope I did not belt my sisters like my father did us. Often I tried to reason with them; something Pa did not practice. Yet I fear that the belt at my hands came down heavily on a few of them, especially Pinky and Kay. I fear that they bore the brunt of my misguided discipline. I know that far too often I succumbed to the recklessness of the day and used the belt unreasonably and excessively.

The power of ignorance teamed with the force of unreasonableness created great harm. I wish I had known better. My past actions grate on my spirit perpetually.

The power of wisdom coupled with the light of reason can do much good. I know that now. I wish that great wisdom had accompanied my onerous responsibilities. Perhaps then I would not have so many regrets. I truly regret any pain that I inflicted in my ignorance.

I shudder to think how my actions are remembered.

I wonder if Pa knew just how reckless and dangerous he was especially when intoxicated. True, Pa worked hard; he worked very hard when he could find work. Each day when he went to the city there was never any guarantee that he would find employment. Pa and his friends drank all the time. Some were out of control with their drinking. While under the influence, some lost their wits and became extremely destructive breaking possessions which, I am sure, took a lifetime to secure.

One case in particular still haunts my mind. It is the story about a father whose rage knew no limits.

77

A FAMILY ... NO MORE

THIS MAN was the father of a large poor family from the neighbouring village of El Dorado. It is said that many lived in that small dirt house; there was the man himself and his wife along with their several children. Adding to this already overflowing house, were the parents of the man's wife. Together this mix of emotions resided, day after long day. The weather was unbearably hot that fateful Saturday and work was hard to find. Skilled at cutting cane and hoping this day to find work, the father visited a nearby cane plantation. Like many others that day, and for many days before, he was not successful.

Willing to do anything, he was getting desperate. The little money he had made previously was quickly absorbed by the many needs at home. After venturing out on this particular Saturday and not finding any work, the man returned home only to find his family arguing.

When his wife asked him for money for groceries he told her that he had no money left. After more intense scrutiny the man revealed that he had spent his very last schilling at the local rum shop. Upon hearing this, the wife immediately began to quarrel with him. Meanwhile, the tempo of the squabbling from the other members of the family noticeably increased. This proved to be too much for the already distraught and much harangued man and he left the house mumbling irritably. Later on, he was spotted drinking at another rum shop. Where he got the money to buy drinks remained a mystery.

Some time later he returned home carrying his machete. His family was still bickering among themselves and his wife blasted him with more criticisms. All he heard was a chorus of complaints against him.

All day he brooded and his anger simmered. Suddenly he was overcome, and an explosive rage took his soul. The actions which followed
were those of a madman. Details of the massacre need not be scribed
here. It is sufficient to note that six people were killed by this man.

The horror of this news spread, shocking everyone who heard it. In
our neighbourhood a quiet air of disbelief pervaded. Never before had
a father committed such an unspeakable act. Worse, the last victim was
a mere infant, the youngest of all the children. Officials recovered the
bodies from the home and the nearby field. There was however, a problem regarding the recovery of the body of the youngest child. A hand
was missing. A passing cyclist found the hand the next day, wrapped it
in newspaper and transported it to the local police station. The cyclist
stopped just outside the police station on the main road to reveal the
missing hand to a police officer who was on duty. I just happened to
be right there when he opened up the newspaper and revealed the tiny
blood-stained hand.

That image is with me still; such tender flesh slashed from one
driven to madness. I remained frozen in the face of this barbarity.

A couple of days later the village again relived the magnitude of
the horror when a flatbed truck transported the six coffins to the cemetery. Fresh tears were shed as the tiny coffin bearing the infant passed
within view. Hundreds of mourners gathered along the railroad tracks
above the street that led to the cemetery. As the death truck slowly
wound its way into the cemetery, a general hush fell over the observ-
ers. We were transfixed by the sight of the six coffins and were wondering why such a tragedy happened. I'm certain that I was not alone
in wondering if a repeat of this horror could happen in another family,
perhaps even in my family.

78

MORBID THOUGHTS

E VER SINCE then I have recoiled in the presence of violence. I was in the junior grade of elementary school when the event described above, occurred. I did not have the sense to understand that all fathers did not use weapons to "silence" their families. I remember asking myself, "Could Pa do to us what the man in El Dorado did to his family?" Each day I lived in fear. Each day that we were alive as a family was a heavenly gift. When Pa would fret, or become agitated I feared that he too might be driven to that unfathomable extremity. Anxiety and trepidation assumed such a great portion of my life that I became a prisoner enclosed in a wall of fear.

Because of what had happened to the family from El Dorado, an innocent situation that occurred when I was a young boy assumed frightening proportions. Pa had planted a vegetable garden in our back yard. One section of the garden appeared to be taken over by weeds. When I saw that I vowed that I would not allow Pa's precious garden to be invaded. I determined that Pa needed some help and that I would be the hero. I was so little that I could barely manage a cutlass or a hoe. Yet, my determination to be helpful was greater than my frailty. Accordingly, I cut down an entire section of weeds and piled them into a lovely heap.

When I completed the job, I awaited Pa, eagerly anticipating his words of commendation. When Pa returned from work, and was unhooking the mule from the cart, I grabbed impatiently at his hands and begged him to come see my work. He obliged. I paraded him to the back yard and exclaimed, "Look, Pa. I'm a good boy. Look what I did!" I was beaming.

Pa uttered some words in Hindi. He sounded angry. This was not at all what I expected. Then Pa grabbed me by the waist and yelled, "You little devil. I'll fix you."

Apparently I had made a huge error for I had chopped down his prized vegetable patch. There were no weeds.

Pa led me to the mango tree. At the side of the tree, resting against the trunk, was a machete.

"I... Oh my God, Pa!" I pleaded.

I saw his hand reach for the cutlass. My small body writhed in fear desperately seeking to free itself from his grip.

Unknown to me, beside the machete was a whip. It was the whip that he grabbed, not the machete. I cannot describe the relief I felt when the whip and not the machete seared my skin. At that moment I did not even feel the pain of the whip. I was happy to still be alive and in possession of all my limbs. I was thrilled because Pa was behaving like his normal self and I received the normal belting. I almost forgot that I was totally innocent and deserved no punishment at all. My motives had been absolutely pure in that all I wanted to do was to help Pa and have him be proud of me. Pa however, saw the situation differently and meted out what he considered a fitting punishment for my devilish prank.

As the weeks passed, I became obsessed with morbid thoughts. Try as I might, I could not help but wonder if Pa could be driven to commit an act of madness as the man in El Dorado had done. I brooded about it constantly.

That all changed one day when I was at the savannah in Tunapuna awaiting the start of a soccer match. Something about the savannah triggered a lost memory. Some time ago, Pa had brought Boysie and me to this very place to see a Hindu religious festival.

Hundreds of people had gathered to take part. As the actors were getting ready, Pa stopped and bought each of us an ice cream cone!

I did not remember ever having had an ice cream cone all to myself. Furthermore, Pa had purchased coconut ice cream, my all-time favourite. Nothing could beat that special treat. Needless to say, I savoured every refreshing mouthful of that sensational, cool dessert. I remembered Pa being so happy, so obliging on that day.

When the show started, neither Boysie nor I were in a position where we could see the actors. Pa, upon realizing our problem, suddenly hoisted both Boysie and me up onto his massive shoulders. We could now see the full range of the show. I was on top of the world. My

Pa was the best. I had it all. Ice cream, entertainment and family. Later on, when those dark thoughts plagued me I called on that memory to sustain me. I realized that we were safe with Pa. The dark fear that was my prison could no longer contain me.

79

QUESTIONABLE TRADITIONS

I FEAR THAT I too inherited a volatile dispositions. I fear also that because of this, I have made grievous mistakes despite my best intentions. I hope that it is not too late for forgiveness.

I tried to delude myself into thinking that all was well in my world. Ma had utmost faith in me and she trusted my decisions. She appeared to be totally at peace with having me at home. I felt supported and respected in my life both at home and at school. Living quite comfortably at home, I, along with my brother, Boysie, was helping to secure the futures of each of my sisters. I began to wonder if the gods had decreed that this was to be the extent of my life.

But, deep inside, I knew a different reality. I felt unsettled. Despite the respect and support I had, I was growing restless. I saw that other young men were free to pursue their dreams. A part of me questioned the tradition that required me to put the needs of the family ahead of my dreams. There was no way to escape the dictates of our Hindu culture. My own dreams had to yield to the dictates of family loyalty and years of tradition. Every day I had to remind myself to accept my life as it was.

Hindu tradition was equally hard on girls. They had to contend daily with the ever present reality of the double standard. Girls had few rights but many responsibilities. Girls were expected to be dutiful, respectful, obedient and hard working. Often they were required to silence their opinions even when the rest of the world was gaining a voice. The decade of the sixties was a very trying time for young women in Trinidad; especially young women who wanted to be seen as open minded and self reliant. Such was the sad case in one Trinidadian family in our neighbourhood.

Just as in our family, the father had died, leaving behind a wife and several unmarried daughters. The two eldest sons who also were not married took over the leadership of the family. They subordinated their needs so that they might better provide for the material needs of the family as a whole. In turn, they demanded total respect from the younger siblings still living at home.

The family tried to be faithful to Hindu tradition in a time when the world around them was changing and evolving. One day, one of their sister's ran away from home. To compound her *sin*, this girl had not just run away, she had run away with a *Muslim* boy. While Muslim children and Hindu children often played together, permanent unions were overtly discouraged. Such a scandal had never before happened in their family nor in the families of any of their relatives. They felt shamed. This shame was expressed in anger.

The brothers especially, were quick to condemn the actions of the sister. They felt betrayed. They felt that the family would be judged by the actions of this one sister. In order to save face in the community, they chose to disown her. She was never spoken of again. So great was the hurt that whenever the brothers were asked how many sisters they had they would not count her among them even as a number. She was no longer considered a member of the family. She was dead. No one was permitted to speak of her in front of the two brothers.

I have often wondered about the foundation upon which such decisions were made. Were they a natural result of Hinduism the religion, or were they the natural consequence of traditional beliefs borne out of practices that once had validity but which now lacked relevance?

What happened to this young girl was tragic—perhaps idiotic! How many times has this same scenario been played out in cultures around the world?

Some years later, decades after the incident, I happened to be visiting with the young girl who had been estranged from her family. I learned that all the sisters had paid lip service only to the verbal decree that ostracized her. One by one each member of the family invited her back into their lives. It did not happen overnight. It was several decades before the last brother let down the wall. On the particular night that I was visiting I bore witness to a conversation between this sister and one of her estranged brothers. We had just finished dinner and were sitting around talking about the old days. The conversation was cordial but, for a time the brother seemed distracted and distant. The sister asked, "Are, you ok? You look lost."

"Sorry. I was lost."

"Where were you?"

"All this talk about the past took me way back to a time that was not very happy. I have wondered about something for a long time but have been afraid to ask. May I ask you now?"

The girl paused. She knew very well the situation to which he was referring. Then she simply said, "Yes."

"Why did you run away with that boy?"

The directness of the question caught her off guard. How she had waited for all these years for someone to ask her that question. Now it was here. Finally, she got to explain herself. Tears formed in her eyes as she spoke. "I was such a young girl. I was foolish and a little rebellious. I was behaving stupid but I did not know it at the time." Then she paused. "I wanted to come back home but I could not. I had no home to come back to. I had no father. My brothers threw me away and my mother could not stand up for me. The question I always asked myself was *why did my brothers not come for me*? I was just a young girl. I did not know my own mind. I looked to you to save me from myself. But, no one came. I had to make my life by myself. No one has ever asked me that question before. Why did you not come for me?"

Upon hearing these words, the brother's pain was evident. He felt such guilt. He had never contemplated the question. Why had he never thought of going for her? The culture to condemn and throw away the condemned seemed so raw and so wrong. At the time it seemed the right thing to do. The safeguarding of the family honour almost demanded it. I understood the mentality only too well for I was such a brother.

Tradition dictated that if a daughter were to stray she was left to perish. She was no longer a daughter. If a son were to commit a similar offence, while he might be chastised he would not be ostracized.

The brother recoiled as he realized the full impact of the family's rejection. He regretted the conditions that made such a decision inevitable; he regretted that such obsolete practices and double standards still existed. He regretted that his decisions were based on such misguided customs. He regretted that his sister had to suffer alone for so long. But now, decades later he had a chance to reclaim his sister and to be a part of her life once again.

Such was my world replete with obsolete customs and double standards. How quickly we young boys picked up the ways of our fathers. Boysie did.

80

BOYSIE'S GENEROSITY

J UST AS his father before him, Boysie loved having friends but most of all he loved to host parties at home. Nothing was too good for his friends. Ma and the girls were always preparing meals and special dainties for Boysie's frequent visitors.

If anyone needed anything at any time, Boysie was the man. Boysie and his truck could be counted on in almost any "emergency."

All the while that Boysie was working, his pockets flowed. His generosity knew no bounds. At times, his generosity even defied common sense. One incident in particular illustrates this point.

In Trinidad, weddings traditionally took place on Sundays. The night before the wedding friends and relatives would gather to celebrate the upcoming event and to prepare for the next day.

The men erected a tent in the yard and everyone came to visit. This type of gathering was especially important for the younger men and women in the community for they had an opportunity to "check each other out" in an environment considered safe by their "protectors" (the fathers and brothers) who were always close by.

And, my brother, *Mr.* Boysie would routinely declare to us that he above all others had to attend those functions as the official family representative since our father had passed away. He considered it his *duty* to attend such functions and never once failed in honouring his obligation. At every opportunity he represented the family. He was often observed "surveying the field," inspecting and prospecting for suitable "pretty girls." At no time could he be accused of neglecting his duty!

One Saturday night Boysie went above and beyond the duty of a friend. The night began like any other Saturday night with Boysie being generous. When it ended, Boysie revealed himself to be not just generous but foolishly generous.

Someone at the Saturday night gathering called out, "Hey, we need a rope!"

Naturally, Boysie was the first to respond.

"No problem. I will go home and get one." Nothing was ever too much of a problem for a friend it seemed, even though it was past midnight.

Everyone at home was asleep. To his credit, Boysie did not attempt to awaken anyone to assist with his search. Boysie looked everywhere for a rope but was unable to find one. He was by now, almost desperate. He had promised a rope and he *had* to bring one; his reputation and his honour were at stake. It was then that he made the foolish decision. Shortly thereafter he returned to the gathering, rope in hand. He had saved the day, my brother Boysie, the hero.

Early the next morning Ma rose and went to the back of the house to the pen where we kept our two cows tied up. On this day, however, Ma could find only one cow. Her wails awakened us all. "A cow is missing! Someone stole a cow!"

Ma had every reason to fear the loss of that cow. That cow represented what little Ma had in the way of independence. By selling the milk from the cows Ma too felt like a contributor to the family income. Since Pa died, she was totally dependent on her working children for support. There was no form of government assistance for widows, no public assistance of any kind in Trinidad. Each family had to make it on its own. Ma kept those two cows, not to earn an *extra* schilling but rather to earn a *necessary* schilling. And at that moment, when she could not find her cow anywhere, her world collapsed.

Soon the neighbours were alerted; a plan was formed and a search party was initiated. Everyone understood the importance of the cow and everyone assisted with the search.

The minutes turned into hours and the heat from the sun affected us all. Ma's sadness increased with the passing of each minute. She urged us to continue with the search in the fields near our neighbourhood. We inspected the area we normally took the animals to feed. There was no sign of the missing cow. Ma felt defeated. Sadly she thanked everyone for their efforts and bid them return home.

But still she did not give up.

She asked her older children to explore a neighbouring field. A large NO TRESPASSING sign loomed. Undeterred by the sign, we began the search anew. In a few minutes we spotted our cow grazing unharmed completely oblivious to the commotion caused by its disappearance. I noticed at once that the rope from around the cow's neck was missing. I wondered aloud where it had gone. That is when a very contrite and sheepish Boysie confessed. "The people at the wedding last night needed a rope. I promised to find one."

And find one he did.

Such was the good nature of my brother, Boysie. Sometimes it defied common sense.

81

THE PERPLEXITY OF
RELIGION AND POLITICS

INDEED LIFE in Trinidad was replete with traditions and customs. My parents observed a certain practice concerning religion and politics which still challenges my understanding today.

My parents, practising Hindus, raised us in the Hindu tradition. Both Pa and Ma were humble people; not given to shows of aggression outside the home. When they taught us about Hinduism, they emphasized certain precepts. We were to obey our parents, honour our elders, be kind to others and, avoid quarrels. All these teachings seemed consistent with the Christian conventions espoused at the Catholic school I attended as a child. Therefore there was harmony between Christianity and Hinduism at this level of life.

Our clothing however, presented a significant problem. I soon came to understand that it mattered very much how one dressed.

It appeared that when most Catholics went to church, they dressed in their finest clothing. Even thought many Catholics were poor everyday working people, they managed to dress well. Both hats and gloves completed the fully dressed look for the women while many of the men wore suits. The casual observer might have thought that the royal family itself was attending the church. A simple Hindu boy like me was easily intimidated by such a fine display of clothes.

Our temple was located on the Eastern Main Road a few blocks from the Catholic Church. I did not attend temple in a regular pants and shirt. My shirt was far too large for me and instead of pants I wore a kind of fitted cloth around my waist. This cloth extended to my feet. In truth I became a spectacle and a target of ridicule as I walked the road to my temple. Monkey! Baboon! Gorilla! Those were but a few of the names the others shouted out at me while they were on their way to Church.

One day while I was again in the midst of this ordeal, I saw another Hindu boy. He was dressed like a prince in regal Hindu attire. I was in awe of him and thought that I had found a true defender in him. To my great dismay, he joined the fray in taunting me chanting the words *ugly ugly*.

He directed their attention to my feet highlighting the fact that I was without shoes. Most of the time, I was without shoes; at times, I might even have noticeable sores on the soles of my feet. Inevitably this made me the perfect target of their taunts.

Some mention should be made here about the innocence of children even in their acts of cruelty. Children are not fully capable of discernment. They did not always fully comprehend the magnitude of their jeers and taunts. Perhaps it is only later on in life that these same children will take a moment to reflect on their behaviours as children. I did not know that then. Back then, those children seemed to take a warped delight in their cruelty. I looked up to the heavens wondering, *Where are the angels of mercy?* It seemed an eternity before I arrived at the temple. Once I arrived, another humiliation awaited. I did not understand the lessons being taught in Hindi; the words, the sounds—everything was foreign. I was scolded severely for my lack of understanding. Sometimes I railed against God, *Where is the joy of religion in religion?* On my way home I avoided the main road, preferring an alternative path. It was not uncommon for me to arrive home late from these religion classes, much to the displeasure of my father. Yes, I had many quarrels with organized religion.

Yet, there was something about Hinduism that was appealing. My father was regarded as a *Brahman*. A Brahman was considered to be a chosen or favoured one and at prayers and special festivities in a Hindu gathering, certain Brahmans were singled out at the end of the prayer to receive certain blessings. The hosts would place a garland around the Brahman's neck and offer symbolic gestures and blessings. A gift of money often accompanied these presentations. As a child I would often accompany Pa to these festivities; it was not uncommon for Pa and his sons to receive monetary gifts. Although these gifts were given to Pa, he would at times allow us a penny or two. This small token was often enough to ease the discomfort of having to sit through these gatherings that could last for hours.

The problem that puzzled me about Hinduism was the fact that my father, a chosen holy man and a Brahman, drank excessively and cursed repeatedly. How could he be both a holy man and a man of such human frailty? Needless to say, I was confused.

Feelings of confusion extended also into the sphere of politics. Politics had its own set of challenges. Roughly 40% of the population was considered Negro; another 40% was East Indian. The remaining 20% was composed of among others, Chinese, English and American. The point to be understood here is that the Negro and Indian peoples were about the same in numbers, generally speaking. Unlike other islands of the Caribbean, there was no clearly dominant group. Trinidad boasted a beautiful mix of several peoples. This gave Trinidad its uniqueness. Yet, such an equal division along the lines of race created an obvious problem politically. At that time the reigning government belonged to the People's National Movement (P.N.M). Since a majority of its members were Negroes, the party was seen as a Negro party— looking out for and promoting mostly its own Negro people. There was dissatisfaction if not open resentment on the part of the Indian People. In fact, the Indian people had an utter dislike for any Indian who seemed an ally of the P.N.M. In fact, this resentment ran so deep that no Indian boy or girl would dare marry a Negro! That was considered the ultimate blasphemy! On the political front, the relationship between Indians and Negroes was strained. Yet socially, on a day to day basis, among the various peoples of Tunapuna, there was a general sense of harmony. Hindus, Muslims and Christians lived peacefully together, except at election time!

At election time, Negroes and Indians fought a quiet war. My Indian parents stopped communicating with their Negro neighbours. Doors and windows were closed. It was as though for a short period of time, discrimination was accepted and if not actually endorsed was openly practiced. This always left me wondering how my ma and pa could shut their doors to our Negro neighbours, especially our Negro friends.

We had such good Negro friends. Nen-Nen, a Negro mother on Back Street, was a matriarch; everyone on our street regarded her as Mother and protector. I remembered a time when Pa wanted to give me a belting. Nen-Nen happened to be visiting so I explained my side of the story to her. She listened to me and understood my perspective. Pa became annoyed with Nen-Nen because she did not take his side. As his annoyance grew, he asked her to leave his property. Truth be told, he did not ask her to leave, he yelled at her and ordered her never to return to his home. Nen-Nen listened to him attentively, yet remained quietly contemplative. Then very clearly and pointedly she explained, "Okay, Budricks. I heard you. Now, I takin' Frankie home with me. He will stay with me. If, by tomorrow, you still feel that I should never return, tell me. Then I will never come back."

By the next day, Pa had settled down and removed the ban he had placed on her. He truly liked and respected Nen-Nen and we children worshipped her all our lives.

Given the kind of regard that we and our parents had for our Negro neighbours, why did we shut them out of our lives at election time? I could not understand such intolerance coming from such religious believers. How could they continue to ignore their friends and neighbours during election time? And, why did Nen-Nen ignore us during elections? Election time was always very confusing. The craziness of this stupidity not only confused me it also infuriated me. Their open discrimination fed this same poison to their children. It was not uncommon for Indian and Negro children to grow up outwardly friendly with one another but inwardly harbour deep-seated hatred. This hidden hatred became the fertile ground of racism which was passed seamlessly from one generation to the next. What a tragedy to rob the innocence of youth of its purity! In this instance I believe that we are truly born into sin, a sin perpetuated by the ignorance of our own parents.

It is against such practices and customs that we grew up as children in Trinidad. I have reflected from time to time about the tragedy that such discrimination can cause. On a personal level I discovered that an attitude of acceptance and understanding was key to effective teaching in Trinidad. Only later did I realize that it was key to effective teaching anytime and anywhere!

82

SWEET TRADITIONS

Pa and the Buns

CLOSE TO six years had elapsed since I returned from England. As a teacher I was treated with respect both at school and in the community. My place at home also was well defined. I was a big brother and father combined, and as such, my authority almost always prevailed.

As a family, we had come a long way and life was most comfortable. We were able to enjoy comfortable meals; Sunday lunch became the event that no one wanted to miss. Sunday feasts boasted two entrees—a combination of shrimp, goat, or chicken, accompanied a variety of Chinese dishes. Regardless of where we might be and what we might be doing on Sunday, we simply had to be home by lunchtime. Ma insisted on this but also we truly wanted to be there for lunch on Sundays. I cannot help but note how different those Sundays were from the Sundays of our early years. When Pa was alive a single boiled egg was shared by several of us. One regular sized chicken would feed our family of ten for several meals. Occasionally Ma needed someone to go to the bakery for a dozen buns fresh from the oven. I always volunteered for this errand. Sometimes the baker would allow a baker's dozen, and put in an extra bun or two or three or four (depending on how much they liked you). Whenever we received extra buns, we got extra excited because we were allowed to have a wee bit more. That little extra piece of bun was a real treat, but nothing compares to the sweet bun I got to keep all to myself; that is a story in itself.

One day Pa and I went to a private cane field, a field belonging to the Caroni Sugar Cane Company, to get some sugarcane tops as feed for our cows. This company sometimes turned a blind eye to those who were trying to help themselves in this manner. At other times the company was very strict and allowed no scavenging of any sort. On this particular day as we approached the fields, we discovered that they were being carefully guarded.

In order to avoid detection, Pa decided that we would take the feed from the rear of the field that bordered the river. To be safe, he parked the mule and cart on the side of the river opposite the cane field. Because of my small size, Pa directed me to collect and push the feed to the river bank where it could easily slide down to the river, well out of sight of the hired guards. Fearing that I had been spotted by the guards, my heart skipped a beat. I worried that Pa and I would be caught and taken to jail. For some reason, I felt that it was up to me to make sure that Pa was not caught. I was so scared. The day seemed endless. My fear was constant. To make matters worse, it was raining. When he felt that we had enough feed, Pa called me down to the river bed where he had bundled all the tops together. The cane tops were made heavy by the drenching rains. We carried these bundles on our heads while attempting to cross the ever rising river. It was dangerous work. The waters were murky and I feared that I might slip and fall and be swept away by the rising waters. I looked over at Pa. He did not appear the least bit alarmed. At long last our cart was loaded and we began our slow trek home.

The hard work, coupled with my very real fears, left me exhausted. I was however, relieved that we had not been caught, and, most importantly, we were not going to jail! On our way home, the mule moved at a very slow pace; he must have been challenged by the heavy load for he stopped several times. That was probably the first and only time Pa showed no impatience at the frequent stops. Pa must have understood the challenge. Suddenly it stopped raining and the sun came out in full force; everything quickly dried up. I could hear the sound of a bell ringing loudly in the distance; it was the bell of the village bun vendor. He sold such sweet delicious buns; the very kind I looked at, longed for, but could never have. *Oh, if Pa only knew that I wanted one so badly this day, if only....*

Then a small miracle happened. On that day, at that moment, Pa stopped along side the vendor and bought some sweet buns. Then, miracle of miracles, he gave me a whole, sweet, hot, fresh bun all to myself. At first, my ravenous appetite directed my indulgence. Then, wishing to savour the moment, I tempered my appetite and managed to extend the delicious moment for a while longer. This went a long way to dispel the pain and discomfort of the day. But, nothing could begin to compare to the bond that I felt with my father as we indulged in our sweet delight. Life was good. Mmmm.

<hr />

I remember one other time when I experienced this same kind of happiness. It was at Christmas time when I was nine or ten years old. As usual, Ma was serving lunch that Christmas Day. Pa was home with us, not out celebrating with his friends as was his custom. Usually, Pa and his friends would visit each others' homes on Christmas Day. These visits began in the morning and at each stop they would have a drink or two. Occasionally they might have a little bit to eat also. It always seemed that the group ended up at our home for lunch. Pa insisted that Ma be generous with her offerings of lunch. When they all left to go to the next home, Ma was left to find lunch for all her children. She would attempt a brave smile as she served what remained of their leftovers for our lunch. Outwardly we never complained. Yet, inwardly we wondered about Pa's *generous* nature; we always hoped he would be generous to us also.

This day was different. It was now time for lunch and Pa and Ma were busy distributing our lunch. We all cherished one dish in particular—curried goat meat. I looked at the display of dishes at the table. I could not believe it! We actually had a full pot of curried goat. I was beaming with anticipation. I did not want anything to go wrong. Pa was happy; we all were happy. As usual, a modest portion of the goat was served to us along with the other dishes. I was a bit disappointed that Pa did not serve a more generous portion since we had an ample amount. Near the end of the meal Pa surprised us all. With a smile that was near mischievous, he administered another offering of the goat meat. Delightfully shocked, everyone made short work of the extra portion. My two extra pieces of meat seemed to be saying, *don't be so quick to eat me now. You may never get so much meat again. Save me for a while.* I lifted these two pieces of meat from my plate and hid them in the right-hand pocket of my short pants. I ate everything else from my plate. No one noticed what I had done. I managed to contain my excitement as I helped out with the dishes. When I was finished, I simply left the house and headed across the railroad tracks to a large field. I was alone. I felt free to just walk and explore. I had no particular thought. I was consumed with a rich feeling; at that moment I had the world's greatest treasure in my pocket—two pieces of goat meat. I found a spot to sit under a large avocado tree. I reached into my pocket for the two pieces of meat. I delighted in their slow consumption. The luxurious feeling of contentment flowed over me.

Christmas time brought other memories also.

Just before Christmas, Pa would visit the shops where he made his deliveries. As a measure of their appreciation, some of the shopkeepers would give Pa an occasional gift at Christmas; perhaps a box of chocolates or a bottle of spirits. I recall one year when Pa did not receive a single gift and he was terribly disappointed. I knew that this year was going to be different as Pa had purchased an entire case of *Solo* sweet drink for the holidays. Coincidentally this was the year that he also received many gifts from his various bosses. Pa was in an exceptionally happy mood as he purchased ice on Christmas day. He placed the full twenty-four bottles of *Solo* in a tub filled with the ice. To this tub, he added sawdust to prevent the ice from melting too quickly. When that was done, Pa gave the nod to Paula to start making the ice cream. (This ice cream subsequently became legendary in our house and synonymous with Christmas.) Paula immediately set about the task. She took over the first round of churning. Next she engaged the services of Pinky who later became the ultimate ice cream maker in our neighbourhood. Together they made several batches of ice cream. Whenever they made the much coveted coconut flavoured ice cream, I was their devoted disciple and would do almost anything to help with the process. (Well, I don't know how true this was in reality, but in my heart I knew I would do anything. Whether I actually came through for them, only my sisters can say.) Our eyes popped in amazement as we gazed upon the tub of chilled *Solo* drinks. Pa poured a small amount of the shiny red liquid for each of us and we were ever so content. Heaven had indeed visited us. Such excitement! Such merriment! Then Pa did a curious thing.

He poured me a small drink of cherry brandy. It did not like me. I did not get to finish what little I had when I felt a need to use the latrine quickly and repeatedly. I never cultivated a taste for Pa's drink. It would be many years before I would have another.

While I may not have had success with the cherry brandy, I did enjoy my affair with guns, toy guns. Playing with toy guns was a favourite occupation in our neighbourhood. Every boy wished he had a cowboy gun and holster. I often made a make shift gun from a piece of wood as did many boys from our neighbourhood.

There were those however, who were able to purchase "real" toy guns; they were more financially blessed. On Christmas Day these boys did not hesitate to show off their shiny new guns; they overran the street while repeatedly firing their cap guns. They made quite a noisy spectacle of themselves and often were resented for their ostentatious and boisterous ways.

I felt that they did not fully value or appreciate their guns, because I often noted that whenever a gun was not functioning properly, the boys would carelessly discard it. After witnessing several episodes of this behaviour, I decided to retrieve these malfunctioning guns without anyone noticing. From these discards I learned the intricate details of the trigger mechanism. Over time I came to understand what the problem was with the firing pin—why it did not work and hence why it was tossed. Most of the time, the spring inside the firing mechanism was either broken or merely dislodged. Then I had an idea. I decided that I would try to make a complete gun using parts from the various discarded guns. I felt that this was a relatively safe option because I would be using parts from many guns. I did not think that any one person would recognize the gun as his own and thus lay claim to it. I quickly enacted my plan and soon I had a refurbished gun that I was so proud of. "Bravo, Frankie. Yo smart; look at the shiny gun you have created. No one has a gun like your gun." After warmly congratulating myself, I brought out my gun and entered into play with the neighbourhood boys. All went smoothly.

You would think that I would know better to leave well enough alone and not do anything to draw attention to myself or my gun. Well, I didn't and my creative imagination went one step too far when I decided to double the power of my refurbished gun and installed two springs to replace the original one spring in the firing pin. When I fired my new update, the caps virtually exploded and smoke billowed from the gun. This commotion aroused the interest of my opponents who looked at me not with admiration, but with curiosity. That should have been my warning that I should stop any further inventiveness. If it was, I failed to heed it. Later, I conceived the idea of doubling the strip of caps in my gun. The end result would be both impressive and explosive; I was correct on both counts. I did indeed commanded attention, but not in the way I expected.

When I fired my powerful gun it exploded with a deafening sound. Thick black smoke accompanied the sound. Now the boys were more than just curious as they angrily grabbed my gun. I was found out. Each boy who had discarded a faulty gun earlier recognized a certain part of my gun as belonging to him. They resented my attempt at ingenuity. I received a collective licking from the whole dissatisfied group. The licking I could handle, but what I could not stomach was the fact that they took my beautiful creation and smashed it to pieces. My poor heart sank. I had to console myself with the memory of that sweet gun. But the lickings were not quite yet over. More were to come. My gun had an equally impressive holster. The story of how it came to be is the subject of yet another story and another licking.

Almost every Christmas my eldest sister, Dolly sewed some fabric to fashion a holster for my gun. But, this Christmas I needed a holster that was an equal match for my newly minted gun. I scoured the neighbourhood looking for ideas. Then I spotted Mr. Morris' garage. I became excited when I saw his collection of discarded cars. I was certain that the solution to my problem was in one of those cars.

As I began to examine each one in turn, I suddenly noticed one that seemed to be a notch above all the others. This particular car was totally intact. Not only were there no noticeable missing parts, it was also sparkling and shining. I reasoned then, that the defect with this car had to be under the hood, for the rest of the car appeared perfectly fine. A closer look inside the car revealed that the upholstery was of a very high quality. In addition, it was my favourite colour—burgundy. For the life of me I could not fathom why Mr. Morris had discarded this car. I could only conclude that he, like some of the boys in our neighbourhood, discarded things that were less than perfect. In this respect, I reasoned that adults were not unlike children. His loss was to be my gain. I'd capitalize on his lack of appreciation. That burgundy upholstery would make quite a beautiful holster for my gun. Such were my thoughts as I sliced off a generous portion of the upholstery behind the driver's seat. I took the material directly to Dolly. She too was struck by its colour and quality. I reassured her that I had retrieved it from an old abandoned car. With that simple reassurance, she then proceeded to sew the holster for me. When she finished, it really was quite stunning. Everyone noticed Dolly's creation and I became an instant star.

A couple of days later, Mr. Morris came across the 'alterations' to the car parked out back of his garage. (Later I found out that it was a classic car and that it belonged to an important customer of his.) Mr. Morris was livid and wanted to know who was responsible for the damage. Well, when word got out it didn't take long to piece together the facts. Frankie was sporting a brand new leather burgundy holster; the car was missing a huge strip of leather burgundy upholstery. Word came back to Mr. Morris almost instantly. "Frankie did it!"

I tried to explain my position to my father. I thought he would be sympathetic. Not so. For the second time that Christmas, I received a licking. Because I was just a child, I simply could not fully appreciate the extent of damage and distress that my action had caused. But, judging from the belting I received, it must have been considerable. My gun toting days were numbered. My one consolation was that for a brief few days, I was not just a cowboy; I was King of all the cowboys! Such memories! Such happiness! What a childhood! What a Christmas!

83

PRESENT TIMES

Ma and the Cows

MA TRIED to help out financially by selling milk from the cows. A noble effort to be sure, but it carried with it unpleasant side effects. Keeping animals in one's backyard signalled low social status. In a hot climate such as ours, animals produced extremely unpleasant odours; these odours were sufficient cause in themselves to make us feel inferior. Members of the upper class never failed to point out when we had any lingering aromas on our clothing.

It would seem that Hindu culture dictated that a man must accept the station into which he was born. (Especially if one is poor.) Subsequently, efforts to climb, even to just the next rung on the ladder, were met with resistance.

I was especially conscious of the fact that my Ma tended cows and that she walked with them in public in plain view of all every day. Here I was: *Frankie Boodram, a teacher.* I dressed as a teacher. I spoke as a teacher. I wanted to be regarded as a teacher. Perhaps, in the eyes of some, I was aspiring beyond my assigned station in life.

When I looked at my mother walking with those cows, I was reminded of our lowly station and I was embarrassed. I know that Ma never meant to embarrass me and that I should not have been embarrassed, but the sad truth was that I *was* embarrassed. In fact, I was so embarrassed that rather than pay tribute to her honesty and diligence, and take pride in her labours, I encouraged her to sell the cows and pledged that I would take care of the family if she did.

I often felt guilty for having aspirations. But, at the same time, I could not live with the shame of witnessing my mother walking with her two cows. I knew that these thoughts were unholy and even that knowledge plagued my spirit. I felt totally conflicted and lost; as if I had fallen into a labyrinth from which there was no escape.

I once made an effort to resolve my conflict. School was over for the day and I was rushing home. As I entered the street, I saw Ma hurrying home with the cows. It was obvious that she was trying to get home quickly; she did not want to embarrass me. Some of my students saw her as did several parents who drove by to pick up their children. I had a choice to make. Would I again ignore her, and pretend I did not know this lady with the cows? I chose to make it right. I rushed up to her and together we walked home, Ma, the cows, and me.

Family Redefined

Traditions and customs were inescapable in Trinidad. Each family may have invented some of their own new traditions just to add flavour to an already colourful existence. But, not all traditions and customs required long term sacrifices and great commitment. Some were very short term.

When I taught at the new girls' school I usually went home for lunch because it was but a short walk. On days when it was too hot to venture out at noon, I stayed at school and had a sandwich in the cafeteria. Although the day was hot, I felt that my body required more than a simple sandwich so I determined to go home where I knew Ma would have a hot feast ready. (Invariably, our main meal, our biggest meal, was at noon.)

On this particular day, Ma had just placed my plate of food before me on the table and I was about to take my first bite, when my brother-in-law, Sylvan, appeared in the yard. Ma expressed visible delight at his presence. As always she was happy to see him.

Without a moment's hesitation, Ma called out to him, "Sylvan, you must be hungry. Come, Son. Sit down. I have lunch for you."

"Sure, Ma," Sylvan replied and he stopped to wash his hands at the outside sink.

Quickly, Ma snatched my plate from under me and went to the kitchen. She returned with two plates in hand, one for Sylvan and one for me. I looked at my plate. Gone was my chicken leg. I looked over at Sylvan's plate. He had my chicken leg! Sylvan flashed a huge appreciative smile at Ma and mumbled his thanks while chomping on the leg, *my* leg. In no time at all Sylvan finished his lunch. I tried to be content with my meatless meal but I must admit that deep inside, I was complaining. I liked my brother-in-law, but I loved my chicken leg! I did not understand why Ma did what she did.

Sylvan left right after he finished so I went to Ma and asked her why she gave my chicken to Sylvan.

Her explanation was so pure and so simple I was ashamed of myself for my negative feelings.

"Frankie, you my son. You is family! We have to treat Sylvan better than family to make him feel like family. He get the best we have. Understand?"

So, that's how it works. When you are the in-law, you get treated special. Not a bad idea, I thought. So I put my conflicted feelings aside. Someday, I too, might be an in-law! And I anticipated that this custom of giving special attention to the in-law was practised by all families. It certainly made good sense. My turn was sure to come at some time in the future.

84

RITUALS OF YOUTH

NOT ALL of life's memorable experiences were negative. While I was yet a teacher at the girls' school, some of my dearest friends contrived together to bring me out of my reserved manner in the presence of girls.

The plot was hatched by my dear friends Kamal, Chanka, and Doc. Earlier, I mentioned that I was able to secure employment at both cinemas in my home town of Tunapuna. Kamal's family owned the Monarch Cinema and Chanka's family owned the Palladium. Through Chanka, I met Doc. Doc was hired by the Palladium theatre to do its advertising. (The manner in which theatre advertising was accomplished then is rather interesting. The top of a car was fitted with a pair of massive speakers. A microphone from inside the car was wired to the outside speakers. When Doc's voice was piped through the microphone and out to those speakers, he could be heard several blocks away in all directions. This was a very successful advertising tool in Trinidad back when I was young. I remember hearing a compelling voice on the loud speakers advertising the movie *Sampson and Delilah*. The star of the show was Victor Mature. I was intrigued by the advertising claims, as were many others from our neighbourhood, and I went to the show. No one was disappointed with the movie as it more than lived to up its billing. It was a memorable epic that captivated our emotions. The scene, where the blind but still mighty Sampson, stationed between two giant columns that supported a colossal structure, was inspiring. As Sampson pushed these columns apart, he brought down the building. He died as a result of his action and we all were tremendously moved by his sacrifice. The advertising of the day was so successful at bringing in audiences that when another movie was advertised as starring Victor "Sampson" Mature, we all begged our parents to let us go. When we finally got to go see the movie, we all were waiting to see our Sampson. He never appeared. There was a Sampson look-alike, but he was dressed in a suit. Never was a group of naïve boys more confused; we felt duped.

Many years have passed since then, and now I was in the car with Chanka and Doc on Saturdays travelling to neighbouring towns advertising upcoming shows. Sometimes Chanka would play music on the loud speakers. He was particularly fond of the music of the Everly Brothers; often he would sing along with the music and carry on as though he were alone in the car. Doc stopped the vehicle in front a restaurant and commanded, "Now, Chanka, we've had enough of your so called singing. You're paying the bill." Chanka paid the bill without protest, and continued to sing. As I recall, whenever we stopped for lunch, Chanka treated us nearly all the time. This made me wonder if Chanka accepted Doc's playful criticism that he could not sing as truth. I wonder.

My friendship with Kamal developed soon after I started working at his family's cinema in Tunapuna. His older brother, Satrohan, was my boss and he was exceedingly good to me and for me on the job. Soon I met his brother, Kamal, and we developed an abiding friendship. Kamal was never crude in speech or aggressive in manner; he was the epitome of compassion.

Occasionally, after I completed my duties in the cinema, Kamal would invite me to take in the rest of the movie. Sometimes we would discuss the movie and exchange ideas about life; on other occasions, we would simply go for bike rides, or for walks along the railroad tracks. As I came to know him better I discovered that he was deeply contemplative and reserved in his private world. Gradually I was permitted to share in his world. He introduced me to his world of literature and music. I too shared his love of music and other common interests cemented our relationship. I admired him immensely and learned a great deal from him.

Sometimes the harshness in my own life directed me to seek the more civilized world of my friend. Not wanting to appear intrusive, I limited my access on those occasions. I remember one singular occasion when Kamal asked me to stay with him at the family home because everyone had to go away for a few days. I gladly consented. Never at any time during those few days was I the least bit disappointed by anything Kamal said or did. If anything, my respect for this gentle soul increased.

Some time later, both Kamal and Chanka left Trinidad to study in Canada. While I was happy for him them, I missed my friends. They made such a difference to my world.

It's time to get back to the plot.

One Sunday, Doc, Kamal, Chanka and I were headed to see a movie in Port of Spain. As we walked, a great deal of the talk centered on the topic of girls; there was no shortage of conversation from Doc, Kamal or Chanka. I was generally quiet when this subject came up.

Suddenly Chanka saw a group of attractive girls walking just ahead of us; they too appeared to be going to the movie theatre. Then, from out of nowhere, came the demand. "Frankie, you have to make a move. You go talk to those girls and persuade them to join us at the movies. It's your turn."

How could they ask me to do that I wondered. *They know how shy I am around girls.*

Suddenly each one of my friends was demanding that I stand up and be counted. *Any man would* was the general consensus. I felt that I had been put on the spot. There appeared to be no way out. I simply had to *step up and be counted*; I was seized with terror for I was totally lacking in confidence when it came to the subject of approaching girls. Yet, at that moment, I knew that it was imperative that I act. Out of our whole group, I was the one who was most hesitatant to initiate conversations with girls. They insisted that it was my turn.

I stepped boldly ahead. I had no idea what I was going to say or do. I knew only that it was important to the group that I show that I had the necessary "smarts" to make a move on these girls.

As I got closer to the group of girls I noticed that they were dressed well and acted quite charmingly. I was reluctant to intrude on their happy conversation. Then I noticed the girl on the far right. She appeared to be the quiet one. I felt that she might be the easiest one to approach; I set my sights on her. I inched my way to her side of the street. *What am I doing? Was I seriously contemplating talking to these goddesses?* I hesitated for I felt like I was being asked to grapple with Death itself.

I still had no idea what I was going to say to this girl and then she turned slightly and I saw her profile. What a relief. Not only was she quiet, she was not the most beautiful of the group. Beautiful girls were extremely intimidating and I would not have dared approach. I assumed that at least I would have a fair chance to make my move on her.

Even the lamest of lines might work with her. The words that I found myself uttering were these, "Miss, have we met before?"

She took a look at me and barked, "HELL NO! NO WAY!"

"Well, well. I am so glad we have never met."

The imperial air with which I had been dismissed, was gone. For a moment she was speechless. Whatever retort she finally came up with never reached my ears for I was long gone.

I was shocked by my own quick response; I did not know that I had the capacity for that type of a comeback. Usually a remark of that nature from any young lady would have driven me to an underground of silent suffering. That did not happen. While I would not say that I was *triumphant*, I do acknowledge that I was relieved that I had not been humiliated. When I returned to Doc, Kamal and Chanka, I smiled. They were curious.

"Frankie, what happened? What they say?"

"Well, they not our type."

"Okay, Frankie. You done good."

I passed their test.

Such are the rituals of youth.

85

TWO "FRIENDS"

FEELINGS OF inadequacy so often plagued me. I wanted so much to enjoy the simple everyday things that everyone else had. I wanted above all a kind of normalcy that everyone else possessed. I so did not want to be set aside—to be rejected. I longed for the everyday goodwill and joy that went hand in hand with neighbourhood teams. People who belonged to such teams seemed to be bonded in a special type of brotherhood.

Because I tutored on Sundays, I was unable to join the regular cricket team and was thus unable to forge a close relationship with the boys from my neighbourhood. I decided to free myself up from my tutoring responsibilities some Sundays hoping that I could be accommodated occasionally as a spare on one of the teams. This thinking worked and I was invited to join one of the teams as a spare. Finally, I felt that I was a part of a group. My involvement although minimal, allowed me an opportunity to make new relationships that had the potential of extending beyond the limited boundary of the cricket grounds.

I cannot describe how happy I was when two friends from the team invited me to join them when they went to visit an ailing relative who lived in a village several miles away. I seized the opportunity and gladly accompanied them. I felt like "one of the boys."

The older of the two boys owned his own car and soon we were off—a happy carefree troupe of three. After we had gone quite some distance from home, one of the boys remembered that he had promised someone that he would do an errand. This errand required us to travel off the regular highway.

Soon we found ourselves coming to an abrupt stop at the end of a gravel road in the middle of nowhere. The area was unfamiliar and seemingly desolate. We piled out of the car to get our bearings. Ahead of us was a small hill. We wondered aloud if one of us should scout it out to see if we could note any familiar landmarks from that vantage point. It was decided that I would be the one to do the scouting.

When I reached the top of the hill, I turned to shout to my two friends. They were climbing into the car. This puzzled me at first until I noticed that they turned the car around and put it into reverse. It was obvious that they were backing up in order to pick me up. *Isn't that great?* I thought to myself. As I reached for the rear door the car suddenly sped up and stopped just a few more feet away. I was confused. I took a few hesitant steps forward only to be met with the all too familiar jeers and taunts that plagued my childhood. My knees buckled under the weight of their insults. My body was further assaulted by the trail of dirt and pebbles that spun out in the wake of their squealing tires as the car sped away.

Feeling mocked and tormented I began the long walk home. The fact that I had to walk several miles did not trouble me. What troubled me deeply was the fact that these two "friends" deliberately planned and executed this humiliation. I could not understand such thinking.

Soon I was back in Tunapuna on my own street. The boys wasted no time in relating the humiliation visited upon me. It seemed that the whole world had gathered on Back Street to witness my mortification. I felt a stranger in my own home town, utterly cast aside. It took a great deal of courage to fight off this last rejection.

Forever I was being taught new life lessons. *When will the humiliation end and life begin?*

86

MAKING PLANS ONCE AGAIN

As I mentioned earlier, some six years had elapsed since I returned from England. It would appear that the urgency I once felt to go abroad to study had diminished. At one time the fire of ambition burned strong in my soul. It now appeared that the fire was contained. In truth, the fire lay dormant.

I did not appear anxious to venture abroad. Was it because I felt guilty to leave Boysie alone to shoulder the responsibility of our family? Was it because I now felt slightly intimidated at the prospect of going abroad all alone? Was it because I was complacent? I am not sure just where the truth resides. But, my brother-in-law, Sylvan, thought that he knew the reason why. One day he approached me and his questions were most direct.

"Frankie, tell me, are you going away to study?"

"Yes."

"When?"

"Well, I still have responsibilities here. I have to take care of ..."

"No! It's time for you to take care of you! Frankie, you are getting so you are scared to go"

"Sylvan, I can't just pick up and leave..."

"Yes, you can. I'll be honest with you. If you don't make a move now, you never will."

I believe that Sylvan was right. He knew that I needed a push. As a result of his questions, my spirit became rejuvenated and I began to make plans to go to Canada.

The year was 1967. I forwarded my applications to several universities in Canada early on in the new year. If all were to go well, I would be at a university in Canada that September.

By June, 1967 I had received favourable replies from four universities. All that remained now was to select the single university that I would attend and visit the bank to secure my finances. I arranged an appointment to see the manager of the Royal Bank of Canada in Port of Spain. I arrived early but did not have to wait long before a polite young lady announced, "Mr. DeCambra will see you now." I followed her through a maze of workers to an office where a secretary motioned for me to sit down. Soon I was ushered into a large, well-appointed office where a well-dressed manager rose and reached out to greet me.

"Mr. Boodram. Glad to meet you. I am Mr. DeCambra. Please, take a seat."

He motioned me in the direction of a most comfortable looking padded chair. He then asked, "Mr. Boodram, how can I be of help?"

"Mr. DeCambra, did I get your name right?"

"Certainly."

"I am thinking of going to Canada to university. I came to straighten out my finances."

"Tell me, Mr. Boodram. What university have you chosen?"

"Well, I have been accepted at four universities. They are in Nova Scotia, British Columbia, Manitoba and Ontario."

"And what university in Ontario?"

"Lakehead University."

"Well, I will tell you one thing. You will not want to go to the Lakehead."

"And why is that, Sir?"

"Well, I am from Sault Saint Marie. It is close to the Lakehead. It is, Mr. Boodram, in the middle of nowhere. There is nothing but lakes and trees and hills. You would be surrounded by wilderness. In the winter it snows and snows. Everything becomes frozen."

I was listening. To me his description was rather romantic (in a poetic sense). I had always been fascinated by the winter landscapes in the movies. His descriptors, rather than repel me, intrigued me. Almost unconsciously, I began liking the Lakehead University option.

"You certainly do not wish to go to the Lakehead. What are your other choices?"

"There are no other choices, Sir. I am going to Lakehead University!"

"But you know nothing of the other universities. You should at least..."

"Thanks, Mr. DeCambra. There is no need. I loved the picture you painted. It'll be fine."

"You sure?"

"Yes, I am."

"All right Frankie Boodram. I respect your choice. Now, shall we examine your account?"

After inspecting my bank account, Mr. DeCambra was concerned. He cautioned me that I did not have adequate finances to embark on such a journey; he strongly advised that I take more time to build up my funds.

I, however, insisted on going to Canada and would not consider putting it off any longer. I bade farewell to the engaging manager, Mr. DeCambra from Ontario, Canada. He was a gracious man and I was pleased that I had met him.

I knew that I did not have sufficient funds to go to Canada and I was very concerned. What I did not completely realize was just how limited my funds were. I had to put aside these concerns for the time being as another matter required my immediate attention. That matter concerned a motor car.

I had just sold my car. I needed the money from the sale of the car for my trip abroad. At about the same time that I sold my car, my brother, Boysie, set his sights on an attractive car that he could not afford. He asked me if I would consider a joint venture; he wanted me to advance him a certain sum of money in order that he might purchase the vehicle. He promised that he would sell the car when I needed my share of the money. He was certain that there would not be any problem in reselling the car since that particular car was always in high demand; he intimated to me that my money was secure as the resale value was assured. His argument seemed reasonable. To entice me further, he sweetened the pot. He suggested that the car would be almost exclusively mine to use. He then took me to see the car. I must admit it was attractive and I could not resist the deal. True to his word, Boysie let me have the car whenever I needed it.

87

"CAR TROUBLES"

S HORTLY BEFORE I was to leave for Canada, I was involved in a car accident. One Saturday night I was headed to Port of Spain when suddenly, it began to rain. The asphalt became quite slippery; I drove very cautiously. Ahead of me the flashing bright lights of an ambulance and a police car signalled that there had been an accident. Looking ahead through the rain, I could barely make out the front of the wrecked car. It was facing me. I continued to slow down. Suddenly, there was a thundering noise behind me and in an instant my face was thrust against the windshield. I had been struck from behind.

The police, who were just finishing their report on the first accident, investigated my situation and determined that there was extensive damage done to the rear of my car. The elderly man who hit me was intoxicated. He was also very agitated. The police took him into their custody and urged me to go to the hospital. I declined. I wanted to find out what charges were being initiated against the other driver. The police were very vague in their responses. The elderly driver was already inside the police cruiser; his wallet was open and sitting in plain view. *Was I witnessing an actually bribe?* Now I really was sick. Not only did I suspect police corruption, but also I was now painfully aware that my brother would be devastated when he learned about the damage to his beautiful car.

The police ordered me remove my car from the scene. I hesitated for no one had yet volunteered any information regarding the status of the accident. I asked the police to tell me whether the driver was being charged for drunk driving. They declined to release any such information. After much urging they gave me the name of his insurance company. Then I made my way home. That night my burden was heavy; I felt guilty about the accident. Moreover, I had only a few weeks to resolve the matter before leaving for Canada. I spent a restless night.

In the morning I arose early and waited for Boysie. When he got up, I told him about the accident. He approached the car, inspected the damage, and walked away. He did not utter a single word. It was awkward; I wanted him to say something. *Yell at me, if you want! Say something!* He said nothing. I was deeply anguished.

I needed to do something. I decided to visit the insurance office in Port of Spain. But, without a scheduled appointment, I was not given access to any official. When I tried to make an appointment, I was informed that the agents were very busy and it would be quite some time before anyone would be free. I explained to the receptionist that I was in a bind, as I had a limited amount of time to straighten out the matter. I asked her to assist me to secure an appointment. She made no promises. I told her that I would return the next day and take my chances.

The next day I was back in the office. The receptionist acknowledged my presence but said nothing and the hours ticked by. Much later that afternoon, when a client did not keep his appointment, the receptionist obliged, "The manager will see you now."

I was ever so grateful as I entered the office of Mr. Wu.

"And you are?" Mr. Wu asked.

"I am Frankie Boodram."

"Mr. Boodram. I am very busy. I have but a few minutes. What can I do for you?"

"Mr. Wu, may I sit down?"

"Well, we don't really have the time to sit down. Why are you here?"

"There was an accident two nights ago. The driver of the vehicle who ran into me is insured by your company and..."

"Well, I know nothing about it. I have to have a report. Then I can deal with you. Sorry."

"Mr. Wu, when might you be able to see me?"

"Perhaps in a couple of months. We are extremely busy."

After a long period of silence I asked, "Mr. Wu, is there a chance, Sir, that I might see you in a few days? Even if you see me for five minutes, I would appreciate it. I realize you are extremely busy."

"And what would be the point of your visit?" Mr. Wu demanded pointedly.

"Sir, if by a miracle you had the report of the accident, you might be able to help me. I am aware that you are extremely tied up."

"I offer no guarantees. I will try and see you on Friday, briefly."

"Thank you, Mr. Wu. I'll be here early." I stood up and reached out to shake his hand. Mr Wu ignored my gesture and headed across the office to his filing cabinet. It would appear that I had been put in my place. I should have known that Mr. Wu would not permit me to shake his hand. That courtesy was reserved for individuals who regard each other as "equals." It was obvious that Mr. Wu considered me "inferior." I was not very optimistic after meeting him.

On the way home, the taxi passed through the town of St. Augustine where several doctors had set up business. I noticed the sign of the doctor who had attended to my father during his illness and deliberately avoided any contact with him. His sign however, gave me an idea. I decided that I should have a doctor examine me just to be on the safe side. I had the taxi stop and headed to one of the other doctor's office. I had no appointment; I knew that I was taking my chances, and the doctor might not be able to see me. I entered and made my inquiry as to whether the doctor might see me. I was lucky. After only a short wait, I was in to see the doctor. I explained to him that I had recently been in an accident and that I had some discomfort in the neck area. He was concerned about the bruises I sustained; he also discovered some swelling on the side of my head. Apparently, I was more seriously injured than I had realized. He gave me a prescription and requested that I schedule a further appointment. I did.

I told my brother about my dealings with the insurance company. He was pessimistic and cautioned me that I was up against *Big Business*. Boysie reminded me that people like us were not important; we did not really count. Boysie's frankness and pessimism was disquieting. The reality was however, that if I didn't get the car fixed within a couple of weeks, I would not be able to sell the vehicle in time to recover the money I had initially invested in it. And, without this money, I would not be able to go to Canada. My situation was developing quickly into a crisis. I had to focus on making careful and thorough preparations for my next visit with Mr. Wu on Friday.

Friday arrived and I went to Mr. Wu's office and sat. I waited. Mr. Wu had not yet arrived at his office. When he did arrive he did not acknowledge my presence. I waited all morning. Soon it was lunch time. Mr. Wu left his office, walked directly past me and again failed to acknowledge my presence. The afternoon found me in what was quickly becoming my usual seat. Mr. Wu returned after an extended time at lunch. Again I was ignored. The day was almost over before I was finally called into Mr. Wu's office. Again I was left standing when Mr. Wu declared, "Listen up. I can't really do anything. I have not examined your file adequately. I will contact you when I am ready. What's your phone number?"

"I don't have a phone. Mr. Wu, may I phone you?"

Silence.

"Okay. I will send you a letter."

"Let me give you my address, please."

"No need. It is in the report."

Suddenly it struck me that Mr. Wu had the accident report in his possession and he furthermore, he had actually read the report. Surely the report indicated the nature of the charges against his client. It slowly dawned on me that Wu was giving me the royal brush off. I was about to be taught a lesson on how Big Business in Trinidad functioned.

The insurance company machine was churning efficiently and running at full speed. Peons like me were taken in only to be chewed up, partially digested and then swiftly eliminated. Wu would deal with me at a time of his own choosing. He could choose to make me wait endlessly. And later, when he was ready to throw a few crumbs my way, he would be counting on me to be exhausted and famished and more than willing to accept his paltry offer. His game plan was obvious.

But, now that I understood what I was dealing with, I gathered my resolve. I determined to contain my emotions, not my will.

Wu now stood up and assumed a condescending air once again. And why should he not treat me with such condescension? After all, he was the one with all the power. *Who was I? What did I bring to the table? I did not even have a telephone.* The picture was all too clear to him. I had no status. I could be easily manipulated and dismissed.

"So you will hear from me sometime. That's all," he said, dismissively. He pointed me towards the door.

But, I refused to be debased by that man. My soul rebelled against being treated like a doormat. "Mr Wu," I declared. "I think that I have something here that might be of interest and advantage to you." I rested a large envelope on his desk. The envelope was open. I made a point of not handing it directly to him. I wanted to control his movement. If he wanted to see what was in the envelope, he would have to return to his desk. He might even realize that he was being manipulated. This action would make him slightly uncomfortable. Just the feeling I was hoping for.

"What's that?" he inquired, not wanting to sound too interested.

My hands pointed to the envelope. "Please," I urged without sounding too eager, "take a look."

Reluctantly, Wu returned to his desk and glance hesitantly at the envelope. A certain irritability accompanied his voice as he declared with great disdain, "You all have tricks. You people always want something for nothing. I am running out of patience with the likes of you, Boodram." He raised his hand in contempt as he pronounced my name. I contained my fury for I wanted to shake him until his head fell off. The reference to "you people" clearly demonstrated the extent of his irritation.

Keep calm. Don't lose your cool, I cautioned myself. "Mr. Wu, please open the envelope."

"All right, I will, and then you be gone."

He tore at the envelope and a number of documents fell out.

Over the last couple of days, I had carefully compiled these important documents. The first was doctor's note outlining my injuries and listing my prescriptions; a second note indicated that I had a plane ticket reservation for Canada, while a third documented my acceptance at a Canadian university. Wu failed to see the relevance of the documentation. He merely scoffed at them. Then he read the final sheet of information; it bore the official letterhead of a law firm and confirmed the date of my visit.

Unknown to anyone, I had gone to see a lawyer. I needed advice about my situation. A kind gentleman offered his services, and upon hearing my case, agreed to be my advocate if I were to require one. I stated the name of the insurance company that I was dealing with; I did not mention the name Mr. Wu. The lawyer then asked, "And if I may, might Mr. Wu be the person in charge of your case?"

I nodded. He was silent for a moment and then consulted with his secretary. She began typing something immediately. Before I left his office, he assured me that he would gladly handle my case. I wondered about my good fortune in finding this man to represent me. I had a strong feeling that he must have had prior dealings with Wu.

Before leaving the office, the secretary handed me a sealed envelope addressed to Mr. Wu. My spirit lightened for I felt that the wind of good fortune was blowing my way.

Now, here I was at Wu's office.

Wu looked at the envelope from the lawyer and sat down. He was at a loss; he was unbalanced.

"Mr. Wu, shall I leave?" I headed to the door.

"Hang on. You have a lawyer? You are going to..."

"I have a limited amount of time and I am rather busy. So in plain language, here is the situation. Three points have to be addressed. *One.* Further examinations by the doctor are required. Such visits could escalate the medical costs. *Two.* Delays regarding my departure for Canada may result in extra costs. *And number three.* My car, which was damaged by your client, needs to be repaired immediately. Can we now settle the issue Mr. Wu?"

"You know, we could let the courts handle this."

"Of course. I admit that is a temptation."

"What do you mean?"

"Well, there is a possibility that if you opted to go the way of the court, it might be to my advantage."

He was contemplative for a minute then agreed, "All right, I will arrange to have the car fixed." He opened a notebook, made a phone call, and ordered, "Take your car to this address. It will be repaired within a few days. I hope you are happy now."

No, I was not happy. In fact, I was decidedly unhappy. I felt that Mr. Wu should have ordered that the repairs be done by the company who sold the car, not by some obscure garage. I had no guarantee as to the quality of the work I would receive. Because I was intent on reselling the car I needed to ensure reliable craftsmanship. Mr. Wong, motivated by his bottom line, needed no such assurances. I could not afford to take any risks.

"Mr. Wu, thank you, Sir. Your offer is noted. But it requires further examination I would ask that the car be repaired by the company that made it, Neil and Massy."

"Neil and Massy! I don't think so..."

"We have to do what is right. I have already visited Neil and Massy. They have agreed to help out; one phone call from your office is all that is needed. The car will be repaired on time."

"You already went to Neil and Massy? They did an estimate?"

"Yes, they obliged me."

"What is the estimate?"

"Oh, there is the person to contact. Please phone."

He hesitated as it was clear that he did not want to make that call. To do so, would be tantamount to admitting defeat.

I interrupted his thoughts, "Mr. Wu. I would be ever so grateful if you would conclude matters. And Mr. Wu, you do understand my concern, do you not?"

Wu could not tolerate someone like me taking the initiative. He was most irritable as he made the phone call. Then he barked, "Do you know that the cost of repairs to your vehicle is very high? All right. I have given the okay. That brings me to the end of this business. Now, I hope you are satisfied."

"Well almost, Mr. Wu."

"What is your point?"

I stood up.

"Earlier in our conversation you made some very disparaging remarks. It is most obvious that you have issues with Indian people. I am sure you feel that you have cause. I however, did not in any way disparage your person, or your people. I believe you have overstepped the bounds of civility. On that score Mr. Wu, I would appreciate a response."

"Mr. Boodram, in our business, we can at times appear to offend. I did not mean to offend. And I feel as though I have been the one who has been taken advantage of; at this moment I am feeling as though it is I who has been manipulated."

"I would not, nor could I manipulate you Mr. Wu. I merely wanted a kind of mutual respect. That you have allowed me this moment to restore my dignity is so reassuring. I am ever truly thankful. Goodbye, Mr. Wu."

I started to leave when he stepped forward, hand outstretched. "Mr. Boodram, I am sorry. Good luck in your studies." Mr. Wu then reached out to me and shook my hands. Sometimes miracles do happen.

Soon the car was ready. Neil and Massy did a masterful job. Boysie in particular, was relieved.

Later on, I just happened to be visiting a car company, when a gentleman took an interest in my car.

"Nice car. Is it for sale?"

"Yes."

"You don't mind, let me look inside?"

I opened all the doors and the trunk.

"It looks new. How old?"

"It will be four years old."

"How much?"

"$3200.00"

"I offer $3000.00. You take it?"

"Yes I will."

"I have a small problem. I don't have the whole $3000.00. I have $2500.00. Cash. I am a policeman from Grenada. I will give up a signed paper for the rest. I really like the car."

I hesitated. *Could I trust this man? That five hundred dollars was equal to almost three and a half months of my salary. I could not afford to lose five hundred dollars.*

"My name is Benjamin Joseph Black. I am a family man. You have my word that I will pay you the rest of the money." His forthrightness was reassuring and I needed a quick sale.

"Benjamin. My name is Frankie Boodram. I am a teacher. I am happy to meet you. Yes, I accept your offer. When will you send the money?"

"As soon as I get home, I will make arrangements. You will have it in a week."

We shook hands. Once the paperwork was completed, I made my way home. Later that day I met both Sylvan and Boysie at home. They saw me arrive without the car.

"Where's the car, Frankie?" Boysie asked.

"I sold it."

"How much?"

"At the agreed price, $3000.00."

"You have the money?"

"Yes, but not all of it." Then I explained what happened.

"Frankie, for an educated man, you sure are stupid. You think that Grenadian is going to send you $500? Think again, Frankie. You do dumb things. And you is a teacher. You supposed to be smart! Where is the money?"

I showed the $2500 cash. Boysie took $1500; that was his share. "Now you have the rest. And if yo don't get the rest of the money, don' com cryin' to me. Sorry. I can't pay for you being so trustin' and so stupid. That Grenadian outsmarted you."

Sylvan agreed with Boise. "Boysie is right this time. Yo never going to get that money."

Both Boysie and Sylvan lived in the kind of world where so many people were liars and cheats. When they criticized me, they felt justified. I did not doubt them. I merely felt that in life, we have to be ready to trust someone, sometime, somewhere. We are not all rotten to the core!

Despite Boysie's reprimand, I continued to trust in Benjamin Joseph Black, the stranger. There was something about his demeanour that made me feel that he was honest. His word was his bond. I was *sure* of it.

A week and some days elapsed. Boysie felt justified in attacking me once again. This time, I had some words for my brother. "Boysie, if I lose, *I* lose, *not you*. You have your money in full. You live your life as you see it. Now let me live my life—even if I made a mistake trusting this man. It is my trust. Say no more, please."

Boysie said no more. Time was running out. It was my last week in Trinidad and still I had not received the money from Benjamin. Furthermore, I had loaned a few hundred dollars to a family member who was in distress. I *needed* the monies owed to me to be repaid. It was now only a couple of days before my departure and neither party came forward. I was in trouble. I was brooding. Then Ma reached out to me.

"You so sad, Frankie. Something wrong?"

No answer.

"Frankie, something troubling you. I know."

"Sorry, Ma."

"I have something for you."

She handed me a letter. I opened it. There was a bank cheque for almost $600. There was also a note. It read:

> *Frank,*
>   *Sorry I did not get back to you. I was in an accident.*
> *I am OK. Two of my children were injured. We are doing*
> *better now. Here is the cheque. A little extra for your*
> *patience. Thank you for your trust.*
>   *Benjamin*

"Ma, look! The man sent the money! And he gave me extra. He was in an accident. All is okay now."

"Frank, you be yourself! You know good people. You can tell. Never mind what anyone say. You know best, Son!"

"Thanks, Ma." I was elated. That man, Benjamin Joseph Black would never know that I wanted to return the cheque were I able to do so. The fact that he sent the money was welcomed. It was a moment of quiet but glorious bliss that I experienced. The world was good, despite all its shortcomings. The human race is worth a small investment, is it not?

That evening as the family gathered at the dinner table, Boysie commented, "Frankie, you lucky this time, and ah happy for you."

Sylvan echoed, "Yes, Frankie. We all happy for you. But I have to admit, you're very lucky. Now let's eat!"

Once again I was blessed.

88

LAST DAYS

THE NIGHT before my departure was now at hand. We dined together as a family and many of our friends and neighbours came to wish me well. These were my final moments at home and I was scared. I was leaving home; I was leaving a way of life that was reasonably assured and promising. I began to question my decision to leave.

The party continued on until it was almost midnight. When everyone finally left and I was in my bedroom gathering my things, Ma came in.

"Frankie, Son,"

I looked at her.

"I know why yo left England and came back home. People gave yo hell. They blame and criticized yo. But Son, I know yo came back to help me."

"Ma, it's okay. I am going to be okay. Don't worry."

"I am going to miss you. But I am stronger now. You go, Son. Make something of yourself. Yo always wanted to be a better person. You go. I will be fine, now. And God bless yo."

I do not recall whether I had ever embraced my mother before, but I did now. She gave me the gift I needed, even though I did not know it. She released me and blessed me. She gave me a moral and spiritual freedom that I did not know I needed. Those few words from her strengthened me and I knew that I was free to pursue my life. I was so heartened, until Boysie entered. He was worried.

"What's wrong, Boysie?"

"Nothing. Ah have to say something to you. Ah have to tell you what's on my mind."

"Well, it's okay Boysie. Go ahead. Tell me."

"Frankie, when you leave, I alone have to take care of Ma and the family."

"I know, Boysie. And I thank you for giving me a chance to go to Canada."

"Then go. But know this, Frank. If yo ever get in trouble and yo need help, don't send home for help."

I was shaken.

"Frank, look around here. Who go help you? Who do we have to help? Nobody. Yo on your own, brother. Remember that."

Boysie withdrew from the room.

His honesty was naked but brutal. His words cut deep. Yet, I wondered what pain Boysie must have felt having to speak to me like that. The merriment of the evening had long since dissipated. Now a million thoughts swarmed my mind. Was I doing the right thing? Should I be thinking of myself? Was I abandoning my family and leaving Boysie to shoulder the responsibilities alone? Anxiety set in. Desperation followed. My head began to spin. Despondency threatened. At that dark moment an arm reached out and rescued me from the waters of despair. That arm belonged to a special relative: Arjoon. I did not know that he had stayed back after everyone else had left.

Arjoon, a relative of Ma's, was like her adopted brother. He became our beloved Uncle. When Pa had passed on, most friends and family stopped visiting us at home; but not Arjoon. His family and he always looked for us and over the years Arjoon and I became friends. He became that wise and older brother I needed in my life.

Earlier that evening Arjoon had come to see me and offered me a generous gift of money. He was a very hardworking man and had a large family to support. I hesitated to accept his gift. He would not have it otherwise and insisted that I accept.

Some months earlier, Arjoon had taken me to a site in Arouca, a short distance from the main route. He had purchased a parcel of land, where he had hoped in the future to build a new home for his family. Then he looked at me and said, "Frankie, there is room here for you, too. Think about it." His invitation was clear. And there was no doubt in my mind that he meant it.

And now, here was Arjoon. Once again providing what I most needed on the eve of my departure: a peaceful, reassuring presence. Because of Arjoon, I was able to set aside the sting of my brother's admonition and allow myself to be comforted. Some time later I fell asleep.

Morning came quickly. A gathering of friends and family accompanied me to the airport. There was little time to think or reflect on what was really happening now. I was on my way to Canada. Before arriving there I first was to have a short layover in Brooklyn, New York. The goodbyes were difficult at the airport. I was particularly sensitive to Ma. Was she really ready for this event? Seven years had elapsed since my last departure. I approached her.

"Well, Ma. I think I will be okay in Canada."

"Frankie, you're worried about me. I know. I will miss you."

I remained silent.

"Well, Son, whatever happens at home, you must promise me to finish what you started."

"But Ma, how could I make you that promise? What if I am needed?"

"Stay. Don't worry. Yo gave me a part of your life. You came back from England for me. I know that. Now you must look out for you too. Promise me that yo will stay, an' finish yo studies."

"Ma, I promise to try."

"That's good, Son."

We embraced. She whispered, "God be with you."

I did not look back.

89

ON MY WAY

THERE WAS something in her voice, in her eyes that gave me the courage to leave. Ma was as ready as she ever could be to release me. Was I really ready to embrace Canada?

I boarded the plane and soon I was headed for my first stop: Kennedy Airport. In a few short hours I landed at Kennedy Airport and soon cleared customs. I could not help but notice how huge the airport was. There seemed to be thousands of travellers.

I now had the task of finding my way to an address in Brooklyn, New York. My sister, Kay, and my brother-in-law, Bob, had given me directions but it was no easy task locating the correct bus, and making the appropriate train connections for Brooklyn. I was overwhelmed by the sheer size of everything—the airport, the traffic and the number of people. In particular, I noticed that all the houses were ever so close to one other. There appeared to be no sense of privacy. But was even more glaring was the sight of Brooklyn itself. The streets were littered with garbage and graffiti. I was unprepared for such an unattractive sight. My first impressions of Brooklyn were far from positive. But, later that day, I was exceedingly happy to meet up with Kay and Bob.

That evening we feasted on lamb. An abundance of food overflowed the table in that very modest apartment. Kay and Bob did everything to secure my comfort. I could not have felt more comfortable.

Later that evening, Bob showed me another apartment for rent in that very building and explained that if I were to consent to stay in New York, and go to school there, Kay and he would gladly rent that larger apartment for all of us. I could even have my own bedroom. What an offer! I was flattered. Moreover, I was tempted. Imagine my sister and brother-in-law prepared to do all that for me. Financially I would not have to worry. They both were prepared to pay for the apartment themselves. Yet, I declined their offer. I had to stand on my own feet. They understood, yet they both were somewhat disappointed. That disappointment did not overshadow our mutual delight in being together.

The next day the spirit of Christmas came early. Bob and Kay took me to the various stores in Brooklyn and purchased several items for me to take to Canada—socks, shirts, shoes, and a coat, among other things. Arm in arm we strolled through the stores happy to be reunited. I had to be careful that I did not indicate that I liked or needed anything. Whenever I gave even an innocent indication, either Kay or Bob ran to purchase it.

Kay was so excited when she asked, "Frankie, what you want? Tell me, your sister is here. Anything, Frank."

Those were Kay's sentiments. She who had little was willing to give so much. That heart remained a generous one even here in Brooklyn, New York. I cannot forget Kay, nor must I forget my brother-in-law, Bob. What an absolute joyous occasion I experienced in Brooklyn. Suddenly all the litter and graffiti that consumed Brooklyn faded into the background.

Time crept away from us. Soon we were at the airport. The plane was already in the process of leaving and had to be stopped to allow me to board. With my suitcase in hand, I boarded the aircraft. Even back then, the fact that I was accommodated was unbelievable. And now the plane began to taxi off the runway. Soon we were in the skies headed for Toronto, Canada. In no time at all the plane landed at the Toronto airport. I cleared customs and was later greeted by a neighbour's relative who had left Trinidad and was living in Toronto. This relative took me to his home.

How clean was the city of Toronto! How beautiful were the streets and neighbourhoods! Everything was so unlike Brooklyn. We arrived in a well-kept neighbourhood. Attractive homes were everywhere. Finally we were at the home of my host. Everywhere I looked I saw luxury. When I was shown the room I was to have for the night I simply could not believe it. I had a bedroom—a large bedroom—fully furnished, all to myself. This neighbourhood, this house, this location, all these were fabulous. I was to learn very soon however that these accoutrements were not part of the life of a struggling student. For now I contented myself with enjoying the generous hospitality of my host and his family.

90

LAKEHEAD BOUND

THE NEXT day I returned to the Toronto airport. I was now headed for Lakehead University in Port Arthur, Ontario. I had not disclosed to anyone at home that I had no one to receive me once I arrived. I indicated to the university however, that I would need student accommodations.

The small plane began its ascent.

Thus far on my journey, I had been in the company of family and friends while in Brooklyn and Toronto. I was excited by this new experience. At no time since I left Trinidad had I been confronted by loneliness; if anything, I felt exhilarated.

Aboard the plane, everything was buzzing. Refreshments were being served and there was much chatter amongst the passengers. I looked out through the window and realized that I could no longer see the earth. Actually I couldn't see much of anything because the aircraft was completely engulfed in clouds. I reclined my seat a little and closed my eyes. Suddenly the chapters of my life unfolded, as memories poured like water from the deep reservoir of my mind.

I recalled vividly a special occasion when I was a young student in the junior grades. To celebrate the great cricket match taking place between England and the West Indies, we were released from school for a half a day every day for almost a week to allow for more attendance at the matches. While we could not afford to go to the games, we did manage to see one. We climbed a tree just outside the fence that surrounded the field. Watching the game from that vantage point was thrilling. When we returned home, we played our own game of cricket. We fashioned our own bat from the stem of a coconut tree branch and employed a hard green fruit for the ball. Our childhood bliss did not require costly equipment or an assortment of gadgets. In our innocence, we were the champions of inventiveness.

My memory bank opened once again to another childhood event. I recalled trying to imitate Johnny Weissmuller in his portrayal of Tarzan. We all loved the Tarzan movies. We especially fantasized about swinging from tree to tree using vines the way he did in the movies. One day I attempted to live out this fantasy.

The day began when my father and a group of his friends took us to the mountains for a load of bamboo. After securing the bamboo, the men gathered at the river to enjoy a refreshment. (No task was ever really finished until it was celebrated by downing one or two drinks.) Most of the time the drinks were generous rendering the men greatly refreshed.

I stood at the bank of the river. The waters were most inviting. What made things even more enticing was the appearance of vines dangling from a tree overlooking the water. Immediately I thought of Tarzan. This was my opportunity to transform myself. In my mind, I was no longer Frankie; I was Tarzan, King of the jungle. I stood just back of the river bank and began my run. As I neared the tree, I stretched out my hands for the vines. I sailed through the air and tried on my Tarzan yell. It ended up being more of a yelp than a yell and served only to elicit mild looks of confusion from Pa and his friends. My searching hands latched on to the vine, and for a moment, I soared. Then the vine broke. I plummeted into the dark waters below.

I sank deeper and deeper. *Good-bye*, I thought. *This is the bitter end.* Then, wonder of wonders, I surfaced. For one split second, I saw my father. He was laughing at me. The others were waving good-bye. Once more I went under. I was now certain that death was imminent. My father did not even care that I was drowning. I did not understand. *Did I not matter? Was I not worth saving?* Then, my feet hit something solid. It was the bed of the river. I stood up. The water was barely up to my waist. *How could that be?* Then I realized what my father had known all along. I was never in any real danger for the current propelled me out of harm's way. Truly I had experienced one of the finest moments of childhood. It was a moment destined to live on in my memory: a child's despair, a father's delight.

Looking back, nestled in the bosom of the plane, a feeling of soft exhilaration gently stirred my soul. Contentment surrounded me. Memories flooded my mind.

One memory was different. It was not so much an event as it was an epiphany. It was the first time as a child that I actually understood what I was reading. For so long I read only words. I did not comprehend the fullness of what the words conveyed. Then, one day I started to read a novel about a boy and his family living in the Andes. Suddenly the story of his struggles to make a living made sense to me. I could even begin to relate to the boy. I understood the words. Words formed images. Suddenly, I was seeing what the words were saying, and I was bursting with joy. I could read! I grabbed the novel and held it close to my heart. I felt as though I had been given the key that opened the door to the Kingdom of Reading. I was rich beyond compare. I read and read. I could not get enough of this reading. I began to think that perhaps I might not be so stupid after all. I could read!

I knew that I should be heading for home; I had been absent for several hours. The standard rule in our house was "Be home before dark." I never knowingly challenged this rule but I often broke it. Oftentimes I would become so consumed in play that I never noticed that it was getting dark. The consequence of such an action even though unintentional, was the same as a deliberate challenge. I suffered each beating without complaint. Sometimes I felt that it was a fair exchange for my temporary freedom. Otherwise, I was always an obedient son. But, today was different. I had just discovered the joy of reading. So compelling were my emotions that I wanted to consume and be consumed in my new world. The threat of being belted weighed heavily in my considerations, yet, I did not wish to leave the world I had just discovered. I stayed. What a feeling! What a moment to be alive! Life was bursting as a new creation awaited me in the Garden of Bliss and I rushed to its arms, a loving prisoner.

The humming sound of engines pulled me from my reverie. I looked around. Everything and everyone was still. The plane, with all its passengers and cargo seemed like one mass being held and carried by some greater power. *Where was everyone? What was everyone doing?* There seemed to be no life outside my memory. The once sunny skies had been replaced by dark clouds. The lights aboard the carrier dimmed. I reclined my seat a little more and again closed my eyes.

Old memories surfaced. The face of my beloved teacher, Mr. Series, emerged. He was the first one to bring hope into my hopeless world. With the simplest of words, "You have to send Frankie to high school" he brightened my world. He let me dare hope that I was not a dunce. My heart sent out a silent prayer of thanks to this man who had been a guiding star in my life.

Then another voice emerged. It was the unmistakable voice of Mr. B, the man who had so often shattered my spirit. I could still hear his voice so clear and strong and condemning. Once more his proclamation, "Boodram, sit down, shut up and don't waste my time!" sent shivers up my spine. Once more I experienced the same sense of helplessness I felt back then. I remembered struggling desperately to hold back the tears that cried out to soften the humiliation of such a brute command. Now, the floodgates of that river of tears were wide open, and tears long restrained flowed freely.

Mr. B had insisted that I was stupid. Others had insisted that I was ugly. These feelings of being both ugly and stupid existed as twin towers of truth in my brain; the dismantling of these two mighty structures was not merely a preoccupation; it became a complete obsession. Such was the essence of my entire life's struggle up until now. It consumed me.

And here I am, about to start a new life in Canada, being revisited by these snapshots of a life long past. I take solace in the fact that all of those productive years spent as a teacher in Trinidad have helped me to overcome somewhat the wasteland of inferiority that imprisoned me for so long. Once I questioned whether or not I would succeed at high school. I managed. After I returned from England I wondered if I would survive the storm of criticism that lashed out at me from every quarter. I survived. Finally, I had wondered if I would ever again leave Trinidad. Here I was bound for Canada. Suddenly, the lights in the cabin came on and the snapshots of my life were temporarily suspended. A voice announced, "Ladies and gentlemen, we are now about to land at the Lakehead..." I opened my eyes. My spirit was at peace.

Canada, here I come!

ISBN 142518544-4

9 781425 185442